D1453823

From Sun Cities to The Villages

SUNBELT STUDIES

UNIVERSITY PRESS OF FLORIDA

Florida A&M University, Tallahassee
Florida Atlantic University, Boca Raton
Florida Gulf Coast University, Ft. Myers
Florida International University, Miami
Florida State University, Tallahassee
New College of Florida, Sarasota
University of Central Florida, Orlando
University of Florida, Gainesville
University of North Florida, Jacksonville
University of South Florida, Tampa
University of West Florida, Pensacola

University Press of Florida
Gainesville
Tallahassee
Tampa
Boca Raton
Pensacola
Orlando
Miami
Jacksonville
Ft. Myers
Sarasota

Judith Ann Trolander

 FROM SUN CITIES

TO THE VILLAGES

A History of Active Adult, Age-Restricted Communities

16   15   14   13   12   11   6   5   4   3   2   1

Library of Congress Cataloging-in-Publication Data
Trolander, Judith Ann, 1942–
From sun cities to The Villages : a history of active adult, age-restricted
communities / Judith Ann Trolander.
p. cm.—(Sunbelt studies)
Includes bibliographical references and index.
ISBN 978-0-8130-3604-5 (alk. paper)
1. Retirement communities—United States—History. 2. Cities and towns—
United States—History. I. Title.
HQ1063.2.U6T76   2011
307.76'208460975—dc22   2010054036

The University Press of Florida is the scholarly publishing agency for the State
University System of Florida, comprising Florida A&M University, Florida
Atlantic University, Florida Gulf Coast University, Florida International Uni-
versity, Florida State University, New College of Florida, University of Central
Florida, University of Florida, University of North Florida, University of South
Florida, and University of West Florida.

University Press of Florida
15 Northwest 15th Street
Gainesville, FL 32611-2079
http://www.upf.com

This book is dedicated to the memory of my father,
Everett William Trolander,
whose life taught me to follow my dreams.

Contents

Illustrations

Preface

Having taught urban history since the 1970s, I eventually came to wonder why no book-length, academic history of active adult, age-restricted communities existed. They comprised a distinctive type of community, so they should be well defined for research purposes. The popularity of these communities was continuing to expand. Some of them had actually established their own historical societies and had produced their own histories. Why academic historians had largely ignored them I can only speculate. Perhaps it was because of a general lack of interest in elderly people who were retired, in some cases living behind walls and gates, and who were not thought of as being very significant. However, I myself began to fit the "demographic" of someone old enough to move into these communities and saw a number of my friends, relatives, and acquaintances do that. These communities were significant to me. When I became eligible for a sabbatical in 2005 and no book-length history existed, active adult, age-restricted communities became my research project.

My historical methods included doing a little of just about everything. Some of the historical societies of these communities, particularly the Sun Cities Area Historical Society in Arizona and the Historical Society of Laguna Woods in California, had extensive and fairly well-organized manuscript collections. Several people gave me wonderful tours of their communities and filled me in on their towns' histories in the process. I wish to particularly thank Jane Freeman for showing me Sun City and Sun City West in Arizona; Lucille Retheford, president of the Youngtown (Arizona) Historical Society, who guided me through that community; Bob Ring for his extensive tour of Laguna Woods, originally Leisure World Laguna Hills in California; Ken Walker of the Leisure World Historical Society, Seal Beach, California; and in Florida, John Bowker of the Sun City Center Historical Society and Noreen Stead, administrative assistant at Century Village in West Palm Beach. Other people, such as Jerry Svendsen, who did public relations for Del Webb from the mid-1960s to the early 1980s; David Schreiner, vice president for active adult business development for Pulte Homes, which owns Del Webb and other housing brands in the twenty-first century; and H. Irwin Levy, the developer of Century Village, and his son, Mark, were among those who either granted me interviews by telephone or in person. In all cases, I took handwritten notes rather than use a tape recorder. Besides the usual primary and secondary printed sources, the Internet proved particularly useful for newspaper articles published after the mid-1980s.

My goal was to be up-front with my sources as to my research purposes, but because of my age and middle-class status, it was quite easy to fall into doing some research incognito. When I walked into the sales center at Sun City Center, the salesperson just assumed that I was a prospective buyer. At The Villages, I had previously encountered the noncommittal attitude of the head of public relations, Gary Lester, who refused to say much beyond confirming that The Villages was, indeed, an age-restricted community, so I deliberately decided to tour that community posing as a prospective buyer. My advice to anyone else who might be tempted to do this is to leave your checkbook at home. A new, three-bedroom, golf course home with an in-ground pool for $456,000 in June 2009 was definitely a temptation. However, I resisted and stayed at a motel, not the vacation villas with golf carts that The Villages rents to prospective buyers. In fact, the only time I did take advantage of such a "vacation special" was in 2002, prior to my beginning the research. A cousin had just bought a second home in Sun City Texas, and I decided to check out that community from a potential buyer's perspective. However, for this historical research project, keeping focused on the history, being objective, and not getting sidetracked by retirement dreams was very important to me. Someday I may go back, select some communities as a prospective buyer, and tour them from that perspective; but that is in the future.

As to whether I would be a good candidate for taking up residence in one of these communities, I'm not so sure. Another thing I did incognito was to take the Del Webb Advisor survey for prospective buyers designed to determine how interested I personally was in moving to an "adults only" community and whether I wanted a lot of planned activities once there. I came out way above average on interest in "adults only" communities but somewhat below average when it came to the active adult lifestyle. Among other comments, a Del Webb sales manager assured me that I could pick from the large number of activities at the Del Webb communities "or just sit back and relax."[1] Many people will just outright reject the idea of living in a community without children or will not want to pay a resident fee for a lot of facilities that they don't use. What is important is to recognize that elderly people differ from one another. Companies like Pulte, with its Del Webb brand, recognize that their communities do not appeal to elderly people in general; rather, their goal is to serve a niche market that is growing. Regardless of one's personal preferences, these communities deserve respect for providing an active adult, age-restricted alternative for those who choose it.

While I was working on this history, numerous people helped me out in a variety of ways. I wish to thank my editor at the University Press of Florida, John Byram, and Michele Fiyak-Burkley and the rest of the staff there. I also owe a lot to the anonymous reviewers of this book-length manuscript, plus a leading urban historian Jon Teaford. Cindy Aron, Edward Linenthal, David Goldfield, and additional anonymous reviewers offered useful comments on an article, which is an overview of this manuscript. This article, with the working title "Age 55 or Better: Active Adult Communities and City Planning," is tentatively scheduled to appear in a 2012 issue of the *Journal of Urban History*, but it will be posted at least four months in advance on that journal's Web site under its publish-ahead-of-print feature. My employer, the University of Minnesota Duluth, provided a sabbatical. The academic vice chancellor, interim dean of the College of Liberal Arts, that college's research fund, and the Faculty Research Fund in the History Department all helped to defray research and/or book promotion expenses. I am very grateful to Peter Angelos, technology director for the College of Liberal Arts, and the many other university employees, including student workers, who repeatedly helped me negotiate the technological hurdles in producing this book. With a topic like this one, so many people I encountered shared their insights and experiences with me that they are just too numerous to list. Finally, I wish to thank Sister Joyce Fornier, who looked after my house on some of my longer research trips and whose support and encouragement remained steadfast throughout the long process from research to publication. I didn't take every piece of advice, but I did my best to look at all the issues that people raised; and I take responsibility for any errors or omissions that may have occurred.

Introduction

Ignoring the Obvious

Jerry Svendsen was exasperated. He had done public relations for Del Webb in Sun City, Arizona, from 1961, a year after that pioneering active adult, age-restricted community opened, until 1982. A 2002 article in the *Arizona Republic* credited Del Webb's Sun City, Arizona, with redefining retirement for Americans. Replacing "images of gray-haired ladies in rockers" were "visions of vital people in their golden years, their days booked with golf, dancing and cocktail parties."[1] The problem for Svendsen was that the article jumped from the founding of Sun City in 1960 to labeling as new trends some developments that were decades old. The claim that "lifelong learning is catching on" in twenty-first-century retirement communities had Svendsen retorting, "ASU [Arizona State University] had such a campus in [Sun City] for years." As for another of the *Arizona Republic's* statements, "The new retirees are looking for a different kind of home than their parents. They don't want to be confined to retirement communities or mobile-home and RV parks," Svendsen commented, "Not new." He went on to explain that "a very small percentage of retirees were electing to reside in adult/retirement communities" from their beginning, but those who chose that option were "generally delighted with it." When the authors observed, "A dozen years ago . . . retirement was considered a final phase of life," Svendsen claimed, "Not true." He regarded retirement as having three "phases." They were "go go, slow go, and no go," with some residents of active adult communities continuing "the go go phase deep into their 80's" and "when they get to slow go, they engage less in activities, but retain a fervid interest/involvement in life." If the leading newspaper in the area where age-restricted retirement communities began could be so ignorant of their evolution, certainly an authoritative, book-length history of the evolution of these communities is needed.

Along with a lack of understanding of their evolution is a tendency to take the existence of age-restricted, active adult communities for granted. However, these communities have been significant in two major ways—physical planning and social engineering. With respect to physical planning, they did a lot to popularize both the residential golf course community and the gated community, and they further developed the common-interest community that was rich in amenities for its residents. With respect to social engineering, not only were adults living in these communities required to be of a certain age, but also age-restricted communities banned children under the age of nineteen as permanent residents. Both the physical planning and the social engineering innovations have had a significant impact on the urban landscape of the United States. Thus, it is worth asking how these innovations came about, how they evolved, and what specific impacts they have had.

The early developers like Del Webb of Sun City and Ross Cortese of Leisure World were taking a huge risk in limiting themselves to a niche market, the elderly, that had yet to prove itself. It was a risk that resulted in immediate success. Other developers began building these communities, and they proliferated.

Why was the market there for age-restricted, active adult communities? Part of the answer is because the retirees following World War II were, thanks to medical advances, Social Security, and company pensions, healthier and wealthier than those of preceding generations. The other part of the answer has to do with how the communities were promoted and what motivations disposed a number of retirees to respond by relocating to them. Developers varied somewhat as to the profiles of their target buyers, and successful developers modified those profiles as times changed. Among the individual residents, a fair amount of variation definitely existed. Some residents adamantly did not want to have children around. Others missed seeing young children but chose to live in these communities because they wanted to be around elderly people who were ACTIVE. Still others were attracted to the relatively greater security these communities offered or, depending on the community, a lifestyle free of exterior home maintenance. Whatever the motivations or mix of motivations, those who moved into active adult, age-restricted communities represented a minority among the elderly. However, they were a distinctive and growing segment.

Active adult, age-restricted communities were initially a major experiment in social engineering, but another experiment from the 1960s and early 1970s has so far received more attention from historians. These were the officially designated "new towns" of the 1960s and their predecessors, Columbia, Maryland, and Reston, Virginia. While this is not a comparative study between active adult, age-restricted communities and the new towns, one way of appreciating the significance of the active adult communities is to note their successes in relation to the numerous failures among the new towns and the evolution of those few "new towns" that succeeded. New towns were experiments in mixing people of different social classes, races, and generations. Ideally, each new town was to be a total community that combined housing of different types with industry and commerce. However, in contrast to the active adult, age-restricted communities, the market was generally not there for the new towns with their social engineering goal of mixing different types of people. Columbia, Maryland, did succeed in attracting a fairly high percentage of largely middle-class African Americans as residents, giving it considerable racial diversity but not a lot of social class diversity. Unlike most other "new towns" that failed, Columbia benefited from a variety of funding sources and was in a high-growth area, in its case between Baltimore and Washington, D.C.

The federally sponsored new towns of the late 1960s and early 1970s went so far as to require developers to include a certain amount of government-subsidized housing for low-income people in the communities. However, federal support quickly evaporated. Those few new towns that were a market success, such as The Woodlands, Texas, soon began to downplay their original goal of mixing social classes. Nevertheless, liberals defended the efforts of these communities to educate the public as to the desirability of mixing classes along with the desirability of having total communities for all generations that included homes, industry, commerce, recreation, open space, and greenbelts. If the public did not buy into the new town concept, their advocates tended to blame the developers, the towns' modernistic architecture, government subsidy paperwork, and the public itself for its lack of appreciation of a community based on heterogeneity.[2] On the other hand, developers like Webb and Cortese had enough enthusiastic public support from the start that they did not need government subsidies to launch their projects and keep going. They succeeded because they had good instincts as to what a certain segment of the elderly public wanted, not just in terms of architecture but in terms of an active lifestyle and image plus an extreme kind of community age homogeneity in which no one under nineteen could be a permanent resident.

What was there about their image or situation in a more heterogeneous society that caused a growing segment of the elderly to want to relocate to active adult, age-restricted communities either permanently or seasonally? After World War II, most suburban developers followed the lead of Levitt and Sons, marketing to young families with large tract suburbs. The 1950s was known for its Ozzie-and-Harriet conformity. Society was youth-oriented. Could it be that by moving to active adult, age-restricted communities, the middle-aged and the elderly were rebelling against being marginalized? Historian Jon Teaford has suggested that rather than seeking age homogeneity, residents of these communities "were asserting age-heterogeneity in an oppressively conformity-demanding society."[3] By concentrating the elderly in specific communities, these communities could empower their "active adult" residents, at least in terms of local politics. They could also give an identity to the elderly that could enhance their image and their influence beyond the communities. This study will show how the elderly residents of these age-restricted communities went beyond the developers' images of them and asserted their own values, self-interests, and identity as "active adults."

Both the new town concept and the age-restricted, active adult concept were innovative. As such, they had to be explained to the public in such a way that they would win acceptance. Therefore, the new towns had their educational efforts and visitors' centers. Active adult communities had their advertising campaigns and sales centers. For the age-restricted community, advertising success meant giving the retiree a favorable public image. The public responded to the picture of the "active adult" retiree much more than it responded to the new towns' image of mixed social classes, mixed generations, and total community approach to social engineering. A University of North Carolina study of resident satisfaction in new towns used some retirement communities for comparison purposes and found that the elderly in retirement communities were more satisfied with their environment than were their counterparts in the intergenerational new towns.[4] How and why so many buyers responded favorably to age-restricted, active adult communities is worth exploring, along with how the developers sensed that response would be there and how they elicited it. Also worth exploring is how the residents and potential buyers pressured the developers to make changes as the age-restricted communities evolved plus how these places have changed over time.

Besides social engineering, both the new towns and the age-restricted, active adult communities were innovators in physical planning. However, as with social engineering, the physical planning innovations of the active adult communities were more significant in the sense that they were far more widely copied than those of the new towns. Ross Cortese, who developed the Leisure World communities, was the pioneer in gated communities of relatively modest homes. Del Webb, whose Sun City, Arizona, is the longest surviving of these active adult communities, was one of the early developers of the residential golf course community. He snaked golf courses throughout Sun City to increase the number of house lots backing onto the fairways. Both developers popularized the legal device of common-interest communities to create amenity-rich developments with the ownership and use of the amenities limited to the residents. Other developers picked up on all those innovations, sometimes using them in intergenerational communities, not just active adult ones. In fact, if one follows the history of the few successful new towns up to the 1990s, one sees their developers adopting some of the trends associated with the active adult communities, such as the inclusion of gated neighborhoods.[5] As for at least one of the physical planning innovations of the new towns, a greenbelt (park, agricultural land, open space) around the edge of the community, that practice fell victim to the 1990s "smart growth" charge that it was contributing to sprawl.[6] Much more so than the new towns, the active adult, age-restricted communities influenced the physical planning that other developers subsequently did.

The success of active adult communities and the relative failure of the new towns have other explanations as well that may be rooted in certain aspects of the American character and historical experience. The new town movement originated in the British "garden city" concept and post–World War II European new towns, while the age-restricted, active adult community was a product of the United States from the beginning. What sort of conditions in the United States contributed to the success of active adult communities? Why were the American elderly more likely to relocate to age-restricted communities than seniors elsewhere? The presence of a very substantial number of middle-class retirees in relatively good health was certainly a contributing factor but not all that unique to the United States. In trying to ferret out what it was about the American elderly that contributed to the proliferation of these communities in the United States while they remained extremely rare elsewhere, it is important not to stereotype the residents of these communities.

Historian Frederick Jackson Turner back in 1893 called attention to the frontier as the significant factor in American development. While Turner's thesis has been challenged in a variety of ways, many Americans were captivated by the idea of pioneers moving westward and establishing new communities on vacant land. When Del Webb's Sun City opened outside of Phoenix in 1960, it offered adventurous retirees a kind of pioneering experience. Sun City residents Jane Freeman and Glenn Sanberg captured that sense of pioneering when they published their twenty-fifth-anniversary history of Sun City, Arizona. They dedicated their book in part "To those Sun City Pioneers who dared to leave old ties to establish new homes, new friends and a whole new life of active retirement."[7]

There was also the historian Daniel Boorstin's observation that Americans have a tendency to be transients or move around establishing new communities in the process, which was part of the American character.[8] Certainly, these active adult communities reflected the willingness of a significant number of retirees to migrate a substantial distance to a new kind of settlement. These age-restricted, active adult communities have attracted considerable interest from abroad, but they remain extremely rare outside the United States. Granted, one finds many age-targeted communities in other countries, but specifically age-restricted ones that ban children under adult age as permanent residents are almost entirely limited to the United States.

Given their relative uniqueness to the United States, the communities raise a number of questions about their impact on the nation. For example, how has the continued proliferation of the active adult communities affected the social and political landscape of the United States? What do age-restricted communities say about attitudes toward the presence of young children among some of the elderly? What impact have these communities had on their local school districts, state taxation policies, and other issues? Have they made age along with race and class important monikers of identity? How have they redefined the image of the elderly?

When it comes to historical literature, active adult communities have been largely ignored. Historians have generated a number of books on the new towns, typically lamenting their failures or, in a few cases such as The Woodlands, noting how they have veered away from their original goals of mixing social classes and modified some of their original planning concepts. It is almost as if the commercial success of the active adult, age-restricted communities has made them unremarkable. It is to historian Jon Teaford's credit that in his 2007 survey, *The American Suburb: The Basics,* he did the opposite. Teaford ignored the new towns of the 1960s and 1970s while spending two and a half pages discussing active adult communities as one kind of "lifestyle" suburb.[9] Back then, these communities were unique. Unlike "lifestyle communities" that targeted gays or were built to accommodate equestrians, places like Sun City, Arizona, did not just target the elderly. They deliberately restricted themselves to the elderly.

No academic, book-length history of active adult, age-restricted retirement communities exists. Historian Richard Pells recently mentioned a need for the historical profession to focus more on middle-class history.[10] Likewise, the profession has done very little with the history of the elderly. Some social welfare historians like W. Andrew Achenbaum in *Old Age in the New Land* have called attention to the impoverished and physically dependent image of the elderly, at least until Social Security, company pensions, and greater longevity began having an effect. Historian William Graebner in *A History of Retirement* mentions that after World War II retirement was becoming a commodity to be marketed. However, neither Graebner nor Achenbaum even mentions the emergence of age-restricted, active adult communities. On the other hand, Gary R. Mormino in his recent *Land of Sunshine, State of Dreams: A Social History of Modern Florida* does devote several pages to the subject.

One can also find such items as historian John Findlay's scholarly chapter about Sun City in his book *Magic Lands.* That book chapter is a brief account of Del Webb's Sun City, Arizona, although it does not say a lot about the origins of the community or how active adult, age-restricted communities developed nationally. Findlay repeatedly terms Sun City, Arizona, a "retirement new town." The official new towns were trendy in the 1960s, and other developers at the time sometimes co-opted the rhetoric without fully implementing the concept. Findlay's phrase "retirement new town" would be more accurately expressed as "retirement master-planned community" or "active adult retirement community." The latter is the phrase the Urban Land Institute used when it published a 2001 survey of both age-restricted and age-targeted communities.[11] In any case, Findlay contends that the most distinguishing features of Sun City, Arizona, when it opened in 1960 were the way it superimposed a green landscape on the desert, its pitch to potential buyers from afar to migrate to it, and its theme of a community for the elderly. While social scientists have done a number of studies over the decades on the impact of these communities on their inhabitants, from a historical, scholarly standpoint, surprisingly little is available.

The only other place this researcher has encountered the phrase "retirement new towns" was as a chapter heading in a 1984 book by a group of social scientists, *Retirement Communities: An American Original*.[12] The community profiled was Leisure World Laguna Hills. The authors praise that community's developer, Ross Cortese, for helping Orange County devise a "planned community zone" ordinance that provided a process for developers to do master plans encompassing clustered housing on small lots to allow for more open space plus commercial, recreational, and medical facilities. In other words, their use of the phrase "retirement new town" meant a comprehensively planned, or master-planned, retirement community. They made no attempt to connect retirement communities with the "new town" movement of the 1960s.

A certain amount of popular literature exists. Some of these communities have historical societies that have produced histories of their communities. The best of these are Jane Freeman and Glenn Sanberg, *Silver Anniversary Jubilee: A History of Sun City, Arizona*; Edson Allen, editor, *Sun City West Silver Celebration: The First Twenty-Five Years*; and Tracy E. Strevey, editor, *Fulfilling Retirement Dreams: The First Twenty-Five Years of Leisure World, Laguna Hills*. Margaret Finnerty has published a book-length biography of the founder of Sun City, *Del Webb: A Man, A Company*. In addition, active adult community historical societies have collected community newspapers, created subject files of clippings, pamphlets, and other items, recorded oral histories, and acquired works written by those who have used their resources.

Active adult communities have received attention in the popular literature about retirement destinations. Reporters, along with the advertising and public relations machines of these communities, have added to the literature, as have a few professional writers seeking a mass audience. A recent example of the latter is Andrew Blechman's *Leisure-ville*. However, a book-length, scholarly, historical study looking at the national picture and analyzing the evolution and significance of these communities is so far absent. With this work I hope to fill that gap.

This study focuses specifically on the development of age-restricted, active adult communities, not naturally occurring retirement communi-ties or age-targeted retirement communities. Naturally occurring retire-ment communities are those places, such as college towns, that tend to attract retirees. Age-targeted communities are where developers are marketing primarily to retirees, but they are not age-restricted. Neither type of community bans those under the age of nineteen as permanent residents. Furthermore, neither is likely to have 80 percent or more of its housing units occupied by at least one person who is age fifty-five or older. The age-restricted communities have the highest concentration of the elderly. This history also focuses on communities that have at least five hundred residential units, not single buildings or smaller develop-ments. Furthermore, except for noting the contributions of amenity-rich trailer parks for retirees to the emergence of the concept of the active adult community, this study does not cover trailer courts, recre-ational vehicle (RV) parks, or manufactured-home communities, all of which continue to be tremendously popular with retirees, particularly in Florida but elsewhere in the Sunbelt as well.

In analyzing the history of active adult, age-restricted retirement communities, certain themes emerge. The overriding question is What is the significance of these communities for post–World War II Amer-ica? More specifically, how did these communities develop and win ac-ceptance, then proliferate? In the process, how have they redefined the sense of self-identity of the elderly, changed the popular image of retir-ees, reflected values associated with work, retirement, and migration, called attention to attitudes of the elderly toward children, and made this new, age-restricted lifestyle affordable or accessible to large num-bers of retirees, some of whom may actually continue working? Even among those retirees with no interest in relocating, the marketing of these communities has had an impact on people's perceptions and at-titudes toward the elderly, today usually referred to as "55 and better." In emphasizing age as a component of identity, what effect have these communities had on political issues? Have age-restricted communities been socially and politically divisive? As Hal Rothman points out in his book about tourism in the west,[13] tourists can change places in ways that upset the power of the locals, and that is even truer of the mix of "snowbirds" and permanent residents that characterizes the active adult communities. By concentrating the elderly in specific locations, these communities accentuate the social identity and local political power of a group that tends to be largely overlooked, discounted, or taken for granted in a generally youth-oriented culture. The emergence and proliferation of active adult communities says a lot about the growing affluence, health, and social values of a certain percentage of broadly defined, middle-class retirees in the United States and their impact on social, cultural, and political issues.

I assert that the developers of these communities were not only social innovators but also innovators with respect to certain aspects of city planning in the latter half of the twentieth century. The largest of these communities were built as complete towns with commercial areas, churches, and medical facilities, not just housing developments. Planned from scratch like the new towns of the 1960s and 1970s, they may also be considered among the first "master-planned" communities. While active adult communities did not originate the common-interest development, gated neighborhood, or residential golf course community, they did a tremendous amount to popularize these physical planning concepts. In other words, age-restricted, active adult communities have played a significant but overlooked role in some major planning trends since World War II.

The developers could build the houses, the infrastructure, and the amenities. They could even provide the residents with "activities directors," later renamed "lifestyle directors." However, it was the residents themselves who created a sense of community, even a kind of subculture that reflected their values and circumstances. As such, the influence of these communities on the physical, social, and political landscape of the United States over the past fifty years has gone beyond their physical boundaries. Finally, with the baby boomers hitting retirement, it is worth noting how these age-restricted communities evolved, the trends, values, and contributions associated with them, and their significance. Such knowledge might keep the boomers from "reinventing the wheel."

This book is organized more or less chronologically around the above-mentioned themes. Chapter 1, "Democratizing Wintering in the South," describes how the rich discovered the pleasures of a Florida winter in the late nineteenth century, but people of much more modest means were not far behind them. Chapter 2 focuses on the most important and most famous of the developers of these communities, Del Webb, and how he conceived and implemented the concept of "active retirement" and "a new way of life" for retirees. Webb's best-known and most innovative competitor in active adult communities was Ross Cortese, with his Leisure World communities, the subject of Chapter 3. Chapter 4 tells the story of how the developers "scripted" the active adult lifestyle for their communities and got them functioning socially. By 1980, the first communities were reaching "build-out," giving birth to the second generation of these communities, such as Sun City West. Their expansion brought to a head certain political issues such as familial discrimination for their banning of under adult age children as permanent residents, which is covered in Chapter 5. In Chapter 6 I talk about how the residents modified the developers' script and, in the process, created their own subculture. Not all of this subculture nor all of the residents fit the advertised image. Furthermore, as these communities proliferated and differed in various ways, they appealed to various types among the elderly. And given the expanding size of some of these communities, a wide variety of elderly seeking others like themselves could more frequently find them. Chapter 7 presents the critics and defenders of these communities and notes twenty-first-century trends. The conclusion summarizes the significance of these communities, the values they represent, and how they have affected the social and political landscape of the United States. In it I also note trends and the possibility of projecting those trends into the future boomer years of retirement. While some of the values associated with these communities are controversial, the reader should enjoy the images of warmth and sunshine in the dead of winter, the growing prosperity of retirees, and the improving health and personal energy that has made it possible for increasing numbers of middle-class retirees to participate in what was billed nearly a half-century ago as "active retirement" and "a new way of life" and, in the twenty-first century, is being called "a resort like lifestyle" by one developer,[14] while another promotes his "active adult resort communities."[15]

Democratizing Wintering in the South

"I looked forward to the time when I would be getting on in years and would want to come to Florida every winter," remarked the famed inventor Thomas Edison. He recalled a trip he had made in the 1880s to Jacksonville, Florida, from there taking the train to Fort Myers on the Gulf coast, and deciding "that here was the place for me." Fort Myers at that time had a population of around one hundred. Edison bought ten acres on the river by Fort Myers. The inventor then "had a couple of houses built up in Maine, shipped them to Florida knocked down," and reassembled them on his land.[1] Beginning in 1886, he and his second wife, Mina, wintered regularly at their Florida retreat until he died in 1931. Not completely retired, Edison had a laboratory on his property and experimented with tropical plants in his garden there.[2] He enjoyed fishing in the area and the warm climate. In fact, he attributed his wintering in Florida to adding five years onto his life and remarked, "Florida is a great state for the old folks, when they haven't the vitality they once had. . . . There are a great many more men and women living up North who only have to get in the sunshine for one Winter to become real enthusiastic for the State."[3] Edison was one of the elite of the late nineteenth century who not only began wintering in the South but also urged others to do so.

While wintering in the South, especially Florida, was initially a practice of the wealthy, people of much more modest means soon adopted it. Why were people attracted to the South, especially Florida? What sort of strategies did seasonal migrants of modest means adopt to be able to spend winters in the South? How did Florida and later Arizona contribute to the eventual emergence of active adult, age-restricted retirement communities?

To begin with the elite, Edison had significant company. In his own personal situation, the reason he initially built two identical houses in Fort Myers was his expectation that a business partner would join him there. However, Edison quickly "had a falling out" with that man.[4] Then, in 1916, automaker Henry Ford built a bungalow next to the Edison property so he and his wife "could winter with the Edisons."[5] The Edison story is a good example of one migrant attracting another, but other members of the elite promoted wintering in or at least traveling to, Florida on a more significant, national scale.

A Trend-Setting Elite Practice

Florida in the late nineteenth century was ripe for the development of tourism along with elite winter homes. Henry Flagler first visited Florida in 1878 because he thought its warm climate would help his wife regain her health.[6] He soon became a railroad builder in Florida who also built luxury hotels to generate tourist revenue on his railroad. In 1888, Flagler opened a hotel in St. Augustine and named it the Ponce de Leon after the explorer who landed in that area in 1513 in search of the fabled Fountain of Youth. The name was no accident. Florida boosters identified with the Fountain of Youth legend and promoted the belief "that nature's rejuvenating powers existed in their purest form in Florida."[7] By the end of the nineteenth century, Flagler's Royal Poinciana Hotel and the even more famous Breakers had made Palm Beach the "Queen of Winter Resorts."[8]

Health resorts were a popular kind of tourist destination in the nineteenth century, and Florida's climate was identified as contributing to good health. Medical doctor Daniel Garrison Brinton wrote an 1869 guidebook to Florida in which he noted the advantages to health of a changed climate, especially with respect to those in the early stages of tuberculosis. He claimed they would especially benefit from Florida's moderate temperature, moisture, and wind. Other books about Florida in the 1870s and 1880s asserted that Florida's mild climate encouraged invalids to get some exercise, thus improving their health.[9] In 1885, W. C. Van Bibber gave a paper at the American Medical Association convention recommending that a "Health City" be built in southern Pinellas County, Florida, the St. Petersburg area. Some English doctors hired Van Bibber to find a location for this city. Van Bibber favored the St.

Petersburg area because the average winter temperature was seventy-two degrees, the inhabitants looked healthy, and the area had development potential; but nothing resulted from his efforts.[10]

Another example of a late-nineteenth-century tourism writer who "extolled Florida's recuperative powers" was the poet Sidney Lanier. At one point, he took a job writing a guidebook for a railroad. Lanier described "cadaverous persons" going to Florida and within a few weeks turning into successful hunters and fishermen with ruddy faces and huge appetites. Unfortunately, Lanier soon died of tuberculosis. Another writer, Abbie Brooks, who wrote under the name Silvia Sunshine, warned her readers that they should come to Florida before their health was too far gone.[11]

Tourism historian Cindy Aron has found that nineteenth-century physicians believed that by moving "from an intemperate to a more moderate climate," someone suffering from a disease such as tuberculosis, rheumatism, gout, or asthma could find relief, if not a cure.[12] Aron has also asserted that due to the work ethic, Americans tended to feel guilty taking vacations. However, improving one's health served as a practical justification for vacations and could serve as the major reason for picking a retirement destination.

For James Deering, whose father founded International Harvester, health issues were paramount. In 1910, at the age of fifty-five, Deering retired as a vice president of International Harvester on the advice of his doctors. He suffered from various ailments, the most serious of which was anemia, a condition that medical professionals at the time did not know how to treat. His parents had "a modest winter home" in Coconut Grove next to Miami. James Deering acquired 180 acres on Biscayne Bay, also in Coconut Grove, and in 1916 completed building a palatial, oceanfront mansion in the Italian Renaissance style where he spent his declining years, dying in 1925.[13]

At times, the way Florida promoted its image as a place conducive to good health bordered on charlatanry. The debut issue of *Suniland*, a 1920s Florida promotional magazine, featured an article about a man who claimed to be 109 years old. His advice to would-be centenarians was to live outdoors. He credited the Florida climate, even describing the summers as nice due to the breeze gracing his campsite near Jacksonville. Photos accompanying the article made this man look more like he was around sixty, and even the author of the piece remarked that the man looked about that age. The man's claim to be "the son of James Monroe, fifth president of the U.S." did stretch credulity.[14]

Another practical justification for the elite to vacation in Florida was the investment opportunity that a largely undeveloped state presented in the late nineteenth and early twentieth centuries. An outstanding example was the Potter Palmer family of Chicago. The Palmers built a hunting lodge on a Florida lake. Mrs. Potter Palmer, who visited Tampa when it was a "straggling village" in 1889 and who predicted that one day the street facing Tampa Bay would be lined with "mansions and villas," built a home in that area. Their son, Honore Palmer, built a third Palmer home on the Gulf near Sarasota. Meanwhile, the Palmers were energetically accumulating Florida land on a vast scale. Their holdings, spread over ten counties, amounted to "more than a million acres." Buying in the late nineteenth century before the railroad arrived in Tampa, they paid as little as twenty-five cents per acre for some land. The Palmers purchased from both the state and federal governments, from homesteaders, and from the railroads. Some of their land was used for timber or developed as citrus groves, and some was urban land bought on speculation. By the 1920s, the urban property was worth at least fifty dollars per acre. In the meantime, the Palmers sold off portions of their holdings at mounting prices.[15]

By the 1920s, speculation in Florida real estate was rampant. Some of the famous names in American business of the early 1920s who were not just wintering in Florida but investing in real estate there included the Rockefellers, the DuPonts, John Ringling, Cornelius Vanderbilt Jr., and Barron Collier. By that time, Palm Beach had emerged as the glitziest of Florida resort towns. The wealthy there enjoyed a luxurious lifestyle of private yachts, golf, sunbathing, "blazing flower-gardens and *allees* of palms," and secluded estates.[16] *Suniland* promoted Palm Beach's glamour with a photo of "Countess Mary Millicent Rogers Salm . . . spending the winter at her cottage."[17] Palm Beach's elite reputation lasted throughout the twentieth century and received additional publicity as the famous Kennedy political clan gathered at the family mansion on special occasions during the winter while John F. Kennedy was president and later. The opening of the three original Sun Cities in the early 1960s coincided with this aspect of the well-publicized Kennedy lifestyle.

While Florida was the leading destination of the elite, resort towns and elite developments sprang up in other places in the South. In the late nineteenth century, the railroad expanded tourism to some mineral springs resorts such as White Sulphur Springs, West Virginia.[18] The Georgia coast was another destination of the elite in the late nineteenth and early twentieth centuries. It attracted Thomas Carnegie, brother of steel magnate Andrew Carnegie, and R. J. Reynolds. In 1888, the Jekyll Island Club, a winter resort community off the Georgia coast, opened with such wealthy members as J. P. Morgan, William K. Vanderbilt, and Marshall Field. These men enjoyed a clubhouse and built cottages or occupied apartments during the January to April season when the club was open.[19]

Certain Florida towns specialized in attracting tourists of a different class. Miami Beach emerged during the 1920s as a vacation destination, thanks in part to the development efforts of Indianapolis businessman Carl Fisher, President Warren G. Harding's 1921 visit, the construction of a causeway to the mainland, and the appearance of luxury hotels that appealed to upper-middle-class tourists.[20] The visitors were able to afford these establishments because they typically kept their stays short. As such, they would be classified as tourists as opposed to winter residents.

Some migrants along with the locals were in search of nice homes in quality neighborhoods. In the 1920s, developer George Merrick achieved success with Coral Gables, still a very attractive neighborhood in twenty-first-century Greater Miami. Merrick's father had migrated from Cape Cod to the Miami area in 1899 for health reasons. In 1921, George Merrick decided to develop the family farm, citrus grove, and adjacent acreage into a 3,000-acre planned community. Lot sales began that year.[21] Merrick was the promoter who hired the famous orator William Jennings Bryan to give speeches extolling its virtues to crowds from a platform in the Venetian Pool at his development. The Florida real estate market was red hot, and speculation got out of control.[22] It soon collapsed, with Miami building permits down 40 percent in 1926.[23] To revive sales at Coral Gables, Merrick considered full-page ads in major northern newspapers such as the *New York Times* and the *Chicago Tribune*.[24] However, before he could do that, he personally lost his holdings in Coral Gables.

Merrick then became a real estate salesman, renting or selling permanent homes to well-to-do tourists. When tourism to Miami declined due to the Great Depression, he began direct advertising in the North.

Specifically, in 1936, he mailed a pamphlet listing seasonal rentals and invoking the image of Ponce de Leon's search for the Fountain of Youth while referring to the region's "all healing sunshine."[25] By 1937, Merrick was placing classified ads in northern newspapers urging people to request his pamphlet that had the house listings. In selecting northern newspapers in which to advertise, he looked for those that had Florida real estate columns. Among the newspapers Merrick chose for ads were five in New York and one each in Philadelphia, Baltimore, Boston, Washington, Chicago, Detroit, Kansas City, Indianapolis, and St. Louis.[26] While his emphasis was on the East Coast, he did not neglect the Midwest. His ads for bungalows during the Depression listed seasonal rents from $550 to $15,000.[27] In 1920, Miami's population was 29,000; by 1935, it was 175,000.[28]

Miami was a success story, but excessive speculation in Florida real estate during the 1920s spawned a number of other projects that bordered on charlatanry. Buyers were attracted to numerous town site projects that never were developed, at least not in the ways that their promoters said that they would be. One example of interest, in part because of Del Webb's later use of the town's name, was Sun City, Florida. H. C. Van Swearingen of Ohio established Sun City in 1918 as a 500-acre development bordering the Little Manatee River south of Tampa. Van Swearingen platted 1,700 individual lots in this town that he intended to become a center of movie production. He also constructed a large building to be used for shooting films. Investors bought 1,350 lots there, but by 1927, just one buyer had built a house. Only a couple of short films were made there. As the speculative bubble in Florida real estate began to deflate, Van Swearingen sold his remaining holdings for ten cents on the dollar. Most of the lots ended up in county ownership as a result of tax forfeiture. By 1962, about all that existed on the Sun City site was a post office, some small businesses, and a trailer court.[29] The trailer court has persisted into the twenty-first century. However, the original Sun City by that time had "some very nice homes" as well.[30] With respect to the speculative excesses from the first half of the 1920s, the real estate bubble burst before reformers could propose regulations to curb unethical promoters and unreal hype.

Besides real estate speculation and development, early-twentieth-century highway routes influenced migration patterns. The Dixie Highway system, built between 1915 and 1927, had an eastern route going from Detroit to Savannah on the Georgia coast, then down along the Atlantic coast to Miami. The western route went from Chicago through Atlanta to Tallahassee and Orlando. That early highway system encouraged midwestern motorists to head for Florida's Gulf coast and easterners to gravitate toward Florida's Atlantic coast. Easterners had a preference for railroad travel, which again tended to channel them toward the Atlantic coast.[31]

"Tin Can Tourists"

On the Gulf coast, St. Petersburg targeted lower-middle-class tourists, many of them midwesterners, seasonal, and elderly. Its boarding houses, hotels, rental homes, and relaxed atmosphere made it appealing and more widely affordable.[32] St. Petersburg attracted those upper-middle-class tourists who wanted to come for three- or four-month stays. As early as World War I, St. Petersburg's winter residents increased its population by 50 percent. Many were loyal, returning each winter. To help these winter visitors feel at home along with bringing permanent recent arrivals together, permanent town residents encouraged the formation of state and regional societies. The first was the Illinois Society in 1902, soon followed by the New England Society and others. These societies organized a variety of social activities for their members, such as excursions and picnics. St. Petersburg businessmen used these societies to attract additional seasonal residents. A 1920s Florida tourism writer, Karl H. Grismer, noted that many first-time tourists headed for St. Petersburg because they had "heard so much about the city from the tourist society boosters."[33]

State societies have a long history, going back to the nineteenth century. What the St. Petersburg tourist establishment was doing is reminiscent of those recruiters of foreign immigrants who found a hub of settlers in the United States from a particular country useful in attracting more settlers from the same country to that hub. Midwestern migrants to Los Angeles had begun forming state societies as early as 1882. Eventually, migrants to Los Angeles from all forty-eight states had their own state societies. They formed a Federation of State Societies in 1909. In Los Angeles, the Iowa society began holding an annual picnic in 1887. With attendance swelling to 150,000 people in the 1920s, organizers divided them into county areas. That way attendees could meet other migrants from nearby places. This practice reinforced a sense of midwestern identity as people who, more frequently than those from elsewhere, left their home region and had mixed feelings about being from the Midwest.

Historian Jon Gjerde has called the annual state society picnic "a tribal festival."[34] St. Petersburg's annual Festival of States Parade during the interwar years also qualified as a kind of tribal festival.[35] When St. Petersburg boosters used state societies to recruit migrants, they foreshadowed some of the recruitment techniques of Del Webb and other developers of retirement communities in the mid- and late twentieth century. While state societies largely disappeared in Los Angeles by the 1980s, they have continued to be a feature of the larger age-restricted retirement communities into the twenty-first century.

The rationale behind the state societies was to help migrants connect with others like themselves in their new locations and to encourage more migrants from their home states to come. While her study is not a story of seasonal migration to the South, tourism historian Dona Brown has found that nineteenth-century resorts "carved out their highly specialized social niches, designed to surround the vacationer with congenial company."[36] As such, "extremely fine distinctions of class, religion, family, and ethnicity" separated one resort community from another, making them "far more segregated than most urban neighborhoods."[37]

Since visiting a resort community could lead to a decision to retire there, the history of resort communities as highly segregated places does foreshadow the highly segregated character of many retirement communities. The famous late-nineteenth-century novelist William Dean Howells sampled a number of tourism spots in New England before deciding on Kittery Point along the Maine coast for his retirement home. Brown concludes that along with the scenery and connections to colonial America, Howells chose that place because it "catered to the literary and professional men and women with whom he socialized at home in Boston or New York."[38] In other words, foreign immigrants, tourists, seasonal migrants, and retirees have all long looked for a congenial social environment like the ones they were leaving behind. In fact, they may even have more in common with those they encounter in the new place because they all chose to leave similar social environments, whether temporarily or permanently.

In the winter of 1918–19, the St. Petersburg Chamber of Commerce took seasonal tourist promotion to a new level when it hired a brash, twenty-eight-year-old adman from Cleveland, John Lodwick, as its press agent. Later, the city hired him as publicity director. Lodwick from the start appreciated the value of utilizing home state connections. For example, a couple vacationing in St. Petersburg would stop by the Chamber of Commerce. Lodwick's photographer would snap their picture, perhaps with the couple standing near some palm trees or playing shuffleboard. Lodwick then mailed the photo to the couple's hometown newspaper, where it was often reprinted, free of charge to St. Petersburg.[39] (A half-dozen decades later, Del Webb's staff in Sun City, Arizona, was doing the same thing.)

What was happening in St. Petersburg by the 1920s was also happening in other Florida cities with advocates eager to market them as tourist destinations. Miami's Chamber of Commerce organized state societies, parades, regattas, and festivals. By the mid-1920s, it was advertising extensively in northern magazines and newspapers. Another tourist draw was for a city to become the site of a Major League baseball team's spring training. Tampa began hosting the Chicago Cubs in 1912. St. Petersburg had the St. Louis Browns in 1914 and the Philadelphia Phillies from 1915 to 1919. Among the seven teams training in Florida in the mid-1920s, Lakeland featured the Cleveland Indians and Sarasota had the New York Giants. (Again, sixty years later, Sun City, Arizona, was a home for Major League baseball spring training.) Measured in terms of the number of jobs it generated, Florida's tourist industry came close to doubling during the 1920s.[40]

An activity that some communities have promoted to attract visitors going back to the nineteenth century was adult learning programs. Chautauqua was a way of scheduling an intensive series of lectures over a couple of weeks in a town in part to attract tourists. Historian Cindy Aron notes that Americans caught up in the work ethic may look to justify their vacations not only as ways to improve their health but as cultural self-improvement. (In the twenty-first century, the marketing of Del Webb communities often features adult educational opportunities like the Arizona State University Lifelong Learning Academy at Sun City Festival.)[41] While Chautauqua is usually associated with selected communities in the North during the summer, it did become available beginning in the late 1880s and for more than three decades after that in the Florida Panhandle and other places in the South.[42]

By the 1960s, large numbers of retirees enjoyed company pensions and qualified for Social Security payments, but that was not the case until the 1940s. The Social Security Act passed in 1935, but the first payments to retirees under it did not begin until 1940. Nevertheless, a number of working-class people, many of them elderly, managed to winter in Florida earlier in the twentieth century. For some types of workers, winter was the slow season. For manual laborers, reasons relating to health and aging contributed to the decision not to work, at least in the winter.[43] Obviously, these people had meager incomes, but they still found certain ways to "winter" in Florida if not retire there year-round.

One way was to take advantage of the facilities that certain service organizations, labor unions, and churches constructed. These nonprofits' directors decided that Florida, with its inexpensive land and warm climate, would be the ideal location for a variety of retirement facilities designed to house their older members. An example was Moosehaven, which the Loyal Order of Moose established in 1922 to serve as a retirement development for its elderly members.[44] An example from the mid-1960s was the AFL-CIO's Four Freedoms House in Miami. One did not need to be a union member to move into this 206-unit apartment building, but one did need an income from $3,000 to $4,500 per year and had to be at least sixty-two years old. Four Freedoms House provided some activities and medical services.[45] Yet another example is the Fraternal Order of Eagles, which was renting fifty cottages in the mid-1960s to those who had been members for at least twenty years and were at least sixty years old. That facility included a recreation hall.[46] Since one often had to have been a member of the organization and these facilities were quite small, places like these were an option for only a few.

The way a lot of seasonal residents with quite limited incomes were able to winter in Florida by the decade of World War I was the appearance of municipal campgrounds in cities like St. Petersburg and Tampa. Local governments organized those campgrounds for two reasons. One was for protection against large numbers of roadside auto campers and their accompanying litter by gathering them in a selected spot. The other reason was to benefit from their spending money.[47] Hotels and restaurants were options, but they cost more money than most working-class visitors had, especially for lengthy stays. Also, camping lent itself to social interaction. It was easier to meet strangers. It was also a challenge to live for weeks or months out of a car and an adjacent tent. Campers in Florida made use of "folding chairs, accordion mattresses, knock-down tents, come-apart stoves, and telescopic dishwashers," plus fold-up groups of toilet articles, tin cups, dinnerware, and utensils. Campgrounds typically provided running water and laundry facilities.[48]

One of the first of these municipal campgrounds was Tent City in St. Petersburg. Beginning in 1918, squatters "pitched their tents on a city-owned lot." The mayor regularized the situation in 1920 when he offered free campsites in that location. Two weeks later, around 120 families were camping there. Tent City offered free water, lights, garbage collection, toilets, and showers. Unfortunately for the campers, city councilmen became concerned when a northern visitor described St. Petersburg as "the place where tourists live in two rooms, eat from tin cans, and sit on benches on the street and pick their teeth." In May 1921, the councilmen voted to abolish Tent City. However, several enterprising people quickly opened private campgrounds to fill the breach. Leora Lewis found many takers for her Tent City near Lake Maggiore, where she charged fifty dollars for the 1922–23 season. The next year, campers jammed the new Miller Tent City. Both public and private campgrounds proliferated around Florida during that period.[49]

Across the bay from St. Petersburg, campers were "taking full advantage of Tampa's generosity" at DeSoto Park near Palmetto Beach. In 1919 a group of these campers formally organized as the Tin Can Tourists of the World Inc. As a kind of official insignia, they began placing tin cans over the radiator caps of their vehicles. It became a signal to other members as they traveled that they were part of the same organization, were fearless and friendly, and enjoyed a spirit of camaraderie. The campground with its utilities was initially free. Tampa even allowed children of the campers to attend the local public schools for fifty cents a week. However, as in St. Petersburg, the freeloading campers soon wore out their welcome. Tampa officials decided to eliminate seasonal camping at DeSoto Park around 1926. The Tin Can Tourists simply moved on to other large campgrounds in towns like Sarasota. Jumping ahead to the 1990s, KOA, a leading national chain of commercial campgrounds, had campgrounds near St. Petersburg and Tampa, and the Florida Association of RV Parks and Campgrounds reported very large numbers of seasonal tourists. Camping has continued to be an affordable option for winter visitors.[50]

For those who did not like "roughing it" in the early campgrounds, a number of Florida towns did have apartments available during the winter season for relatively modest rents. A 1924 article in *Suniland* stated that for $1,040, a person could travel to Florida by rail, rent an apartment for the winter season for $400, and enjoy entertainment like free band concerts in public parks and social get-togethers with fellow migrants from his or her own home state. Furthermore, by not heating a house in the North, the winter visitor would save on coal, thus bringing the cost of wintering in Florida down to around $500.[51] Beginning in the late 1920s, Tampa encouraged the renters of modest apartments by running the Riverside Tourist Center. This two-story building "became the social hangout for thousands of old-timers" renting inexpensive apartments nearby. There, the recreation center hosted card competitions and shuffleboard tournaments on its thirty-six courts along with a variety of social events such as picnics, dances, and community sings. Use declined when the Tourist Center was moved to a new location in 1966, and as of 1986, its shuffleboard courts were getting "scant use."[52] This public Tourist Center, with its recreational amenities, was a forerunner first of the post–World War II, amenity-rich trailer courts for retirees and of the clubhouses and recreation centers that in the 1960s dotted Del Webb's Sun Cities and Ross Cortese's Leisure Worlds.

Trailer Parks

For some people, the expression "tin can tourist" meant the metal trailers that began to spring up in the 1930s. In the 1920s, the typical trailer was an improvised, homemade, wooden box perched on a truck or flatbed. Some of the earliest trailer parks, such as Sunny South, established in Miami in 1925, occupied superb oceanfront locations, preempting later, more lucrative development. Manufacturers entered the travel trailer industry in the 1930s.[53] In 1936, the Bradenton chapter of the Kiwanis Club decided to go into the mobile home park business to attract tourists. However, "by the 1950s the Kiwanians were promoting [their trailer park] as an ideal retirement alternative for couples forced to live on monthly pensions that fell below $100." By forbidding residents to work at paid jobs, this park indirectly excluded families with children. This Bradenton Trailer Park featured a variety of recreational and social activities designed to appeal to retirees, such as card parties, dances, plays, and Bible classes. As one trailer park historian notes, "This formula of creating self-contained retirement communities with an active recreational program spread to other trailer parks in Florida and then other warm-weather settings." When retirees dominated a mobile home park, that park largely escaped the stigma associated with living in them. Furthermore, owners of these parks found it easier to secure financing to add more amenities, such as swimming pools, shuffleboard courts, and meeting-room facilities.[54]

Trailers kept getting larger and more elaborate. As late as World War II, the typical trailer lacked a bathroom. That quickly changed after World War II. Trailers expanded from eight feet to ten feet wide, then to twelve feet with "pop-out" sections; their length expanded to forty feet and then sixty. "Double-wides" appeared. Along the way, the mobility of mobile homes fell by the wayside.[55] In 1976, the industry trade association officially changed the name from "mobile home" to "manufactured housing."[56]

Another innovation was to substitute trailer lot ownership for lot rental, which Sidney Adler did with Trailer Estates on Sarasota Bay in 1955. Initially he sold lots for as little as $898; in 1998, a waterfront lot in that park went for $200,000.[57] While mobile home parks for retirees tend to be seen as a working-class alternative, that is not always the case. Adler loaded his park with amenities including a marina and private beach plus organized activities that ranged from bingo to square dancing. Buyers included people fed up with annual lot rental increases in other parks. The enterprising Adler engaged in direct marketing in the North of lots in Trailer Estates. Some people bought lots from a plat map that he displayed in New York City's Grand Central Station. He also sold lots from a booth at Michigan's state fair. To help northerners feel comfortable, he named streets in his trailer park after northern states, such as New York, Michigan, and Indiana. He thought buyers would buy on the street named after their state and would bond with their immediate neighbors, who would also be from that state. Trailer Estates reached build-out in 1960 with nearly 2,000 residents.[58] Adler went on to add similar trailer parks in the "snowbird" states of Arizona, California, and Nevada. He built a park in Michigan, too, with the idea that retirees from his Florida park might want to migrate to his Michigan park in the summer. While lot ownership was popular among retirees, his Michigan park failed. Apparently, few retirees wanted to own two mobile homes.[59] It may also have been that summer was their time to renew their respective ties in their various home communities in the North.

Adler had many imitators for his lot ownership and amenity-rich parks, while others stayed with rental lots or developed subdivisions of manufactured housing. These parks' developers considered social and racial homogeneity a key to their success. In Adler's case, his lot deeds specifically barred future sales to African Americans and those of Asian and Mexican ancestry.[60] Rental parks were just as bad. A flier from Wilder's Park in St. Petersburg dating from 1979 warned residents selling their trailers, "All new Tenants are to be approved by the Office before any sale is consummated."[61] Mobile homes were cheap housing and, thus, accessible financially to a wide spectrum of the population unless certain groups were artificially excluded. As for Wilder's Park, when established back in the early 1950s, it was "out in the middle of nowhere." By 2005, St. Petersburg's black community had engulfed it, but it was still a white enclave.[62]

In being extremely choosy or outright discriminatory in their selection of clientele, retirement trailer court management showed a tendency to take a cue from the resort industry. Late-nineteenth-century resort hotels were well aware of the concerns of potential visitors that the resorts' clientele reflect the sense of identity of those choosing to vacation there.[63] Such concerns about an establishment's social mix may have been even stronger for trailer court residents who were likely to remain for the winter season. One tourism writer has posited that the discrimination in roadside motels in Florida and elsewhere actually worsened in the 1950s because many of them added swimming pools. For example, in 1955, the manager of a hotel in Florida described turning away an African American family. Although he said that he regretted that the family had to spend the night in their car, the white manager expressed concern that if other guests saw the black family staying there and possibly using the pool, it could cost his establishment a thousand dollars in lost revenue from regular visitors who would not return.[64]

Even in the liberal northern state of Minnesota, resorts were highly discriminatory. The Ruttgers family operated resorts on several of Minnesota's most popular lakes. Their brochure emphasized the phrase "CLIENTELE CAREFULLY RESTRICTED." Furthermore, so prospective guests could assure themselves of the kind of social mix they would find, the brochure included a list of major midwestern cities along with the name of a previous guest from each one. The brochure then said, "Ask a Ruttger Guest." Ruttger's was not only excluding African Americans; it was discriminating against Jews as well. The prevalence of resort discrimination gave rise to special resorts for African Americans and for Jews.[65] However, with the decline of discrimination toward the end of the twentieth century, many of these African American and Jewish establishments fell on hard times.[66]

The Minnesota resorts reflected another kind of inequality in the 1950s—the patriarchal family. While they offered a variety of water sports, their primary activity was fishing. More men than women fished. An example was the mother who preferred the educational values of travel for the children. However, she annually deferred to her husband as every year they headed for the same fishing resort.[67] That sense of the patriarchal nature of family decision making in the early 1960s would be reflected as well in the emphasis on golf early in the marketing of retirement communities.

Besides age and race, social homogeneity was to some extent reflected in the home states of the trailer park residents. Probably because snowbirds often recruited others when they returned home, some trailer courts tended to reflect certain states and even communities. In 1969, more of Wilder's Park residents came from New York than elsewhere—thirty-four. Illinois was second with twenty-four. Nine years later, thirty-eight residents were from New York compared to thirteen from Illinois. Thus, Wilder's Park reflected the tendency of more easterners than midwesterners to head for Florida.[68]

While most popular in Florida, mobile home parks proliferated in newer retirement areas. For example, in 2002, Mesa, Arizona, a city of 400,000 near Phoenix, had sixty-three "manufactured home parks," of which forty-five were restricted to those over age fifty-five.[69] At one of the latter, Park Place, residents commonly put their names and their hometowns on the front of their trailers to be seen from the street. As one resident explained, the reason for advertising where they were from was to let others from the area know that they were welcome to knock on the door and introduce themselves. This person remarked that she had met a good friend near her hometown of Red Lake Falls, Minnesota, whom she initially met while out in Mesa. Park Place had so many residents from the area of Red Lake Falls that it had an annual Red Lake County Day so they could all get together and celebrate their home county. This resident had selected that trailer park because she not only already had a relative living there but had other relatives in other senior developments in Mesa, including in Sunland East, a development somewhat imitative of Sun City.[70]

Trailer courts provided inexpensive housing for those on limited incomes, but sometimes the commitment to spending time in the retirement location was more limited than the person's income. Typically, this woman from Red Lake Falls only used her trailer for two or three months in the late winter each year, while her relatives in the Sunland East house with its own pool were year-round residents. Furthermore, she reported that most Park Place residents had left by May, while the majority of residents who owned single-family homes in retirement communities tended to be there as legally permanent residents.

Feminist writer Betty Friedan was quite critical of the ephemeral activities in age-restricted communities, even calling the communities "adult playpens,"[71] but she did have praise for the residents of Adler's Trailer Estates in Florida. Friedan found that most of the residents in that trailer court were from the Midwest and had limited resources, but they also had enough of an "adventurous spirit" to buy mobile homes and winter in Florida. She observed a lot of coming and going among the 1,400 households, something that she attributed to the cramped quarters of the trailers. In addition to enjoying the recreational amenities and social activities, many were volunteers. Some even staffed an ambulance service as volunteers. Friedan quoted one snowbird from Canada as saying that back home they did a lot of gardening, but at Trailer Estates they went to concerts and lectures.[72]

"Retirement" Hotels and Condos

Still another affordable option was the "retirement," or residential, hotel. As the decades passed, once posh, fashionable hotels aged. Several of these in Miami Beach had, by the late 1950s, been converted into "centers for communal living for the elderly."[73] A mid-1960s pamphlet listing retirement facilities in Florida included many hotels.[74] A number of 1960s Miami Beach rental units and condos planned extensive social activities for their tenants in order to guarantee "the older couples . . . a well-rounded social life as well as comfortable accommodations." One of these buildings, The Floridian, included three meals per day in the rent plus "weekly movies, amateur shows put on by the residents, three television amphitheaters . . . shuffleboard, swimming pool, card rooms, bingo, four or five parties a year . . . and private bus service."[75]

St. Petersburg had a number of once-plush resort hotels converted into retirement hotels along with large homes from the 1920s that had been subdivided into small rental units and apartments constructed over garages for added rental income.[76] In at least one case, a new owner of a former motel added more units and a dining room, calling this establishment the El Sol Retirement Club. A Florida businessman, Herman Levin, developed a series of these retirement hotels in various cities. He had one in Lakeland, another in Bradenton, and two in St. Petersburg. In some cases, these retirement hotels developed various connections for health services. For example, several hotels in Miami Beach arranged with nursing homes to take their residents when they could no longer care for themselves. In St. Petersburg, the Huntington had a registered nurse and maintained an infirmary for ill residents. The Aldersgate in Kissimmee offered both "rest home" and apartment facilities with meals and personal services.[77] These retirement hotels foreshadowed the assisted living facilities that would become more widespread within a few decades. In fact, today's independent and assisted living facilities are similar to the old residential or retirement hotels that had proliferated in mid-twentieth-century Florida. Usually cheaper than nursing homes, these "retirement hotels" offered residents more independence as long as they did not need extensive nursing services.

Part of the lure of Florida retirement communities was, and remains, financial. Florida is one of the few states that has no income tax and no inheritance tax. For someone from out of state staying long enough during the year to qualify as a Florida resident, the tax saving can be considerable. Beginning in the 1950s, retirees migrating to Florida skewed the population of the state over age sixty-five above the national average. While one in nine was over age sixty-five nationally by 1980, in Florida the figure was one in six.[78] The elderly wield more political clout at the state level in Florida than they do elsewhere. It is not hard to see a connection between no income or inheritance taxes and the large number of retirees. Also, on the eve of the big influx of retirees, in 1947 Florida instituted a program whereby the state guaranteed minimum funding for school districts. The immediate motivation was to promote economic development through bettering education and to have some sort of answer to the growing concern that underfunded black schools were

unequal to white schools.[79] However, in those school districts where retirees dominated, they could still have a negative effect on local funding
for public education. Since tax policies vary considerably from state to
state, footloose retirees increasingly after World War II discovered that
from a state and local tax perspective, it literally paid to shop around.
Of course, part of the low tax culture of some of the retirement states,
Arizona included, is a low level of public services. Hence, the need for a
volunteer ambulance service in some Florida retirement communities.

Low taxes did add another financial incentive to the relative affordability of the trailer parks for wintering in Florida. While the tax situation is largely the same today, people who rent lots in trailer parks
are facing the increasing prospect of the parks being sold to developers who will put up luxurious condos in their place. That is also true of
some tourist hotels. St. Petersburg is one retirement destination that
has, in the past couple of decades, sought to shed its reputation as an
economical place in favor of a more trendy, fashionable, and expensive
image. Thus, it is more of a challenge to retire to Florida on a budget in
the twenty-first century than it was in the past.[80] Rising land values are
threatening renters in mobile home parks in other states as well.

As waterfront and other choice land skyrocketed in value after
World War II, the cooperative and then the condominium concept was
a strategy whereby retirees of relatively modest means could acquire
ownership of dwellings in certain prime retirement locations. The major difference between cooperatives and condos is that in a cooperative,
the buyer purchases the right to occupy a certain space, while with the
condo, the buyer gets legal title to a specific unit. In practice, that means
the condo owner does not need the approval of the other residents to
sell his or her unit to someone else. Each condo owner pays real estate
taxes directly; in cooperatives, the local tax assessor sends one bill for
the entire complex. Generally, owners of condos have more rights than
owners of cooperatives.

Retirees migrating from New York to Florida were familiar with cooperative apartments back in New York. In 1946, a cooperative apartment building appeared in Pompano Beach, Florida.[81] While co-ops were
popular along Florida's Atlantic coast, in 1958 a developer in the St. Petersburg area along the Florida Gulf coast, Sidney Colen, may have been
the first to develop a condominium in Florida.[82] That same year, Puerto
Rico passed its condominium law, which caught the interest of another

Florida developer, Brown L. Whatley; and his company then became a leader in the promotion of condominiums in Florida.[83] Colen's condominium project, however, came nine years after a condominium in New York and decades after the appearance of condominiums in Europe and Latin America. In 1960, Congress imported that condominium law from Puerto Rico, which was the beginning of federal legislation on condominiums.[84] In 1964, FHA was just beginning to finance condos, and only three states had their own laws authorizing them.[85] However, condos had a great future ahead of them. Thanks to condos, many more people could have beachfront dwelling units than if the beaches had remained the preserve of single-family homes.[86]

Residential associations go along with cooperatives and condominiums. They can be traced back in U.S. history to 1831, when wealthy people owning property fronting on Gramercy Park in New York City bought the right to run that fenced and gated urban square as their own private park. The influential English planner Ebenezer Howard proposed the residential association concept in 1898 as a way for "garden city" residents to manage their own private parks and streets.[87] However, the modern home owners association did not appear until 1928, when Charles Stern Ascher, a lawyer and planner, utilized the "covenants, contracts and deed restrictions" legal concept in property deeds to provide for owners in "common interest developments,"[88] where certain elements are owned collectively. The residential association was the legal means whereby the residents could manage those common elements. Nevertheless, residential associations were slow to appear. By 1962, the United States had only 500 home owners associations; but after that, their numbers mushroomed to 10,000 in 1970, 55,000 in 1980, 130,000 in 1990, and 230,000 by the early twenty-first century.[89]

These home owners associations can experiment with association-funded facilities, deciding what they want to maintain and how. As such, they can be both a creative and an efficient way to provide services to a specific population.[90] On the other hand, they can also open owners to various abuses. For example, someone delinquent by less than $900 in dues could find the home owners association forcing him or her into foreclosure and having to spend money on an attorney to keep the home. Issues can arise over hiring firms to do maintenance and even the size of the maintenance and replacement budgets. A resident who dislikes something his or her neighbor is doing can complain to the home owners association, which can handle the complaint, keeping the complainer's name anonymous. Resident associations that arrange for such services as exterior maintenance turned out to be ideal for the elderly and for second-home buyers and snowbirds.

Condos spread around the United States, but they became extremely popular in Florida. The pioneer Florida developer of condos, Sidney Colen, had prior experience with suburban tract development but decided that he wanted to tap into the market for elderly people and those who wanted to travel, so he built a 584-unit apartment complex in St. Petersburg in the late 1950s, Clearview Oaks, and called the units "ownership cooperative apartments," not condominiums, since very few people were familiar with that term at that time.[91] Basically, he started with the cooperative concept and modified it.[92]

As an early builder of condos, he may have walked into some pitfalls. One had to do with standard maintenance and whether the home owners association fee was adequate to cover it. Colen's On Top of the World massive condo complex north of Clearwater, Florida, has been the focus of several disputes. In one of them, the city of Clearwater threatened to take him to court in 1987 to get him to install "fire safety devices."[93] An adequate accumulation of reserve funds for maintenance as the buildings aged was crucial, too. As a very early seller of condo units, Colen arranged for his maintenance company to provide the ongoing upkeep of the buildings, and it would be his company that would set the fee for maintenance. The arrangement left Colen open to charges that while he had sold the units, he planned to continue to profit from their maintenance, with little that the owners could do about it. When a dissident group at Colen's On Top of the World complex charged his company with shoddy maintenance at excessive prices, his son, Kenneth Colen, then running the company, sued the dissident owners for tarnishing the company's reputation.[94] Most later builders of condos were likely to stay away from casting themselves in an ongoing maintenance role.

Problems did not interfere with the development of a million condominium units in Florida by 2000, then half the nation's total number of condos. The magazine *Florida Trend* helped to popularize the word "condominium" with a 1970 article extolling the lifestyle associated with their ownership. Terms like "condo mania" and "condo craze" followed the article's publication.[95] Two years earlier, Florida's most influential developer of condos for the elderly, H. Irwin Levy, had begun Century Village in West Palm Beach. Levy built small apartments; some units were accessed by outside stairs, not more expensive elevators. The units were modestly priced at around $9,000. What attracted retirees to Century Village were the amenities—swimming pools, golf courses, clubhouses, manmade lakes, and an active social calendar of adult education offerings and support groups. Levy successfully targeted elderly Jewish buyers from New York, used high-pressure sales tactics, and sold hundreds of units in a single day. Levy constructed 30,000 units in various communities in southern Florida and had a host of imitators.[96] Cooperatives and condominiums allowed many retirees "a slice of the Florida dream,"[97] and developers of major age-restricted, active adult communities like the Sun Cities and Leisure Worlds incorporated co-ops and condos in varying degrees as a way of reaching a mass market and making retirement in country club settings in the South widely affordable. These developers sold housing, but some developers just sold lots as a way to profit from people's retirement dreams.

Post–World War II Land Scams

Buying a condo was a relatively safe investment compared to buying a lot in a future development, where developers or scam artists marketed retirement possibilities that were often just dreams. The post–World War II land scams went on for decades and branched out from Florida to affect newer retirement areas such as Arizona. The elderly and even middle-age people thinking about retirement were especially vulnerable.

Often the sales promotion started with a free dinner meeting held a couple of thousand miles away from the land being sold. Prospective buyers were encouraged to plan for retirement but were also told that a lot in the development was bound to appreciate in value. They were not necessarily told about property taxes or the need to pay extra for utilities and road access, assuming those were even attainable, whether medical or commercial facilities were within a reasonable distance, and in some cases if, as in Florida, the land being sold was under several feet of water or, in Arizona, water was unavailable. If developers did acknowledge that the land was under water, they probably promised that a navigable canal would be built to drain it. The "navigable canal" was more likely to be a drainage ditch, if it materialized at all. Using high-pressure sales tactics, the diners would be encouraged to buy sight-unseen. After all, the lot was cheap, perhaps only $10 down and $10 per month on the installment plan. Since these land-scam artists frequently used sales contracts or deeds that did not allow for the accumulation of equity as payments were made, people stuck with such contracts had to either complete them or forfeit all they had paid if they chose to walk away from the deal. Misrepresentation was much more the rule than the exception.[98]

Since some buyers were cautious enough to want to see the land before buying it, a number of these land sale companies provided free or below-cost trips to the sites. The trips were carefully staged to keep the prospective buyers from independently inspecting the area. Furthermore, buyers rarely got the chance to view the actual parcel they were considering buying, often because it was inaccessible. A company might fly sales prospects over the planned community site in Florida. From the air, it looked lush and green, but a ground inspection, not available, would have revealed swamp underneath the greenery. A trip of several days allowed a certain amount of group camaraderie to emerge, which contributed toward the decision to buy. If family circumstances changed, perhaps the husband had a stroke, the purchase contract could not be canceled. As for reselling the lot, disappointed buyers typically found that no market existed.[99] The problem was not limited to Florida, but one historian of that state has commented, "Florida has attracted more than its time-share of bunko artists who sold land by the gallon and dreams for ten dollars down, ten dollars a month."[100]

One Florida land development scheme is worth a close look because it was also checked out by Del Webb's staff as part of the planning process for Sun City, Arizona; this was the Mackle Brothers Inc. community Port Charlotte. The Mackles had previously built several developments of homes priced for the mass market. When they ran an ad in 1955 in *Life* magazine for modestly priced homes on the east coast of Florida, the Mackles got 18,000 responses but only 127 buyers. That was when they decided to switch from home building to just selling lots. The number of buyers skyrocketed. In 1957, they formed the General Development Corporation, spent a great deal of money on publicity, and marketed relatively inexpensive houses and lots in Port Charlotte, a community they created out of ranch land. By 1959, when Del Webb's staff checked out the development, the Mackles had sold 65,000 lots, although the community had only 1,600 widely scattered homes. Lot sales spelled success for the Mackles, and they went on to market lots in other Florida developments. In some developments, it took twenty years after the lot sales commenced for a substantial population to arrive. At least their developments eventually amounted to something.[101]

Perhaps the most extreme case of sellers of lots and dreams, both in Florida and Arizona, was the story of Leonard Rosen, Gulf American, and the General Acceptance Corporation, or GAC. Leonard Rosen was a successful businessman in Baltimore in the mid-1950s when his doctor advised him to seek a warm climate for several months to help his arthritis. On arriving in Florida, Rosen was immediately attracted to the potential profits in land promotion. He organized the Gulf American Company, purchased a large tract of barren land on the Gulf coast, and named his project Cape Coral. That one was a legitimate community-building enterprise, with homes, commercial areas, schools, and churches.

However, bigger and faster profits could be made selling vast tracts of undeveloped land where the only improvements were drainage canals and dirt roads, which characterized Rosen's next development, the 113,397-acre Golden Gate Estates. There Rosen sold 1.25-acre lots for "investment." His third venture, the 63,000-acre River Ranch Acres in central Florida, lacked even dirt roads and drainage canals. Not only were large sections under water, but part of it was "within three miles of an air force practice bombing range." His fourth development, Remuda Ranch Grants, was 80 percent under water. Rosen had political connections. Florida governor Hayden Burns appointed Rosen to the Florida board set up to regulate companies like Gulf American. It took a new Florida governor, Claude Kirk, who appointed a new regulatory board, to crack down on Rosen. In 1969, Rosen sold Gulf American to General Acceptance Corporation. However, the new company continued to use many of the high-pressure sales tactics that the old one had pioneered, such as free dinner parties, fly-overs as substitutions for ground inspections of specific parcels, and misleading brochures in place of legally required property reports.[102]

With the legal noose tightening around GAC in Florida, the company shifted some of its land promotion efforts to Arizona, where it had 55,000 acres of grassland that it had subdivided into lots for a community called Rio Rico. In addition to the sales tactics it used in Florida, at least one account has GAC plying its prospective customers with drinks and finessing the local history of the area by claiming that remnants of an old town on the Rio Rico site were "where Cortez traded with the Indians." Salesmen would work the crowd of prospective buyers with announcements like "How about a nice, warm Arizona welcome for Mr. and Mrs. XYZ of Nebraska, who just picked up Lot No. . . ." Their purpose was "to create an atmosphere of carefree conviviality with an undertone of fear: If you don't buy, you're missing the opportunity of a lifetime."[103] Meanwhile, Arizona, other states, and the federal government increased the legal pressure on GAC. In 1977, the company filed for bankruptcy.[104]

Finding the tools to try to eliminate fraudulent interstate land sales was not easy. As part of the consumer protection movement of the 1960s, some states passed laws designed to protect their own residents in interstate real estate transactions. California and New York were in the vanguard. California's 1963 Subdivided Land Act required the state real estate commissioner to issue a report on a subdivision before lots could be sold, whether the transaction was intrastate or interstate. As part of the process, developers had to supply appraisals of their properties by independent, qualified appraisers.[105] California required out-of-state developers to bond themselves "for the completion of promised improvements within a limited time."[106] As a result, Florida developers avoided the California market.[107] GAC tried to circumvent the California law by luring prospective buyers to Las Vegas with free drinks, dinners, hotel rooms, and shows while promoting the sale of lots in Rio Rico. Since California's regulation of California-based developers was significantly less than its regulation of out-of-state developers, Californians could still be victimized in real estate transactions.[108] Other states likewise found it easier to get tough with out-of-state developers than with those within their own boundaries.

New York had a model statute dating back to 1936 and revised in 1963. The New York law required developers to disclose their financial status and provide roads to any lots marketed to New York residents as well as a bond or escrowing the money for any other promised improvements.[109] To advertise in the state's newspapers, send direct mail advertising within the state, or even respond to inquiries regarding an out-of-state development, the developer had to be registered with the state. One New York–based author of a 1973 book about interstate land fraud found that she had difficulty getting information mailed to her from certain developers because they were not registered to sell in New York.

I experienced a similar problem in Minnesota in 2005 when responding to an *AARP Bulletin* ad by WCI Communities for Sun City Center, Florida. WCI Communities (no connection with Del Webb) personnel answered that e-mail inquiry by saying they could not give out information about the location of its sales center because it had not registered to sell in Minnesota. As a Minnesota resident appearing in person at that sales center and model home park, I had no problem picking up informational brochures and touring the models in the company of a saleswoman. However, when the saleswoman sent a follow-up letter by mail to my Minnesota address, a Minnesota Department of Commerce analyst told me that the saleswoman had likely broken the law. As to why WCI Communities was not registered to sell in Minnesota, the commerce analyst noted that few developers bother to register to sell in all fifty states. It can still advertise in national publications but not in local ones.[110]

States did take actions against out-of-state developers for violating their laws. For example, in 1969 New York charged Florida condo developer Sidney Colen with failing to register in New York to sell, not filing the required information, and then running small classified ads in a New York newspaper that did not disclose that the condo development he was promoting had leased its utilities, buses, and recreational facilities from a corporation owned by Colen for the next twenty-five years, thus allowing Colen to collect potentially excessive management fees. New York's attorney general contended that Colen had been informed of New York's law but had failed to comply.[111] The attorney general also ordered out-of-state land sale companies to pay restitution to New York's victimized buyers. As of 1972, New Yorkers had obtained nearly $7 million in restitution.[112] Buyers themselves can also file individual and class action lawsuits to force a developer to comply with his promises.

In the late 1960s and early 1970s, fraudulent interstate land sales received intense publicity. Partly as a result, the number of states with some sort of regulatory control went from twenty in 1969 to thirty-five three years later. Typically, these laws are tougher than the federal legislation passed in 1968 that basically just requires interstate land sale companies to file property reports with the federal Office of Interstate Land Sales Registration and make the reports available to buyers.[113]

Publicity got to Florida and Arizona state governments, which eventually passed some very strong laws. One development company in Florida had convinced some local governments to finance improvements with the promise that buyers would appear to pay back the costs. The buyers did not materialize. That further motivated local politicians to pressure the state for tough regulation.

Some developments had water and sewer lines covering huge areas but almost no houses, such as a ten-block area with full infrastructure and only two houses. As the environmental movement gathered momentum, developers of some of these colossal paper communities found that they could not get permits for their land schemes due to local citizen opposition. That happened to the original developers of Rio Rico when they applied to a different county for a second community, and that county started asking questions about the adequacy of water resources, pollution of existing water supplies, and aesthetics as applied to the landscape.[114] Still another government problem occurred when the tax assessor for Rio Rico decided to assess that developer based on what it was charging for its lots, and GAC pleaded that they were only worth, for tax purposes, about $400 each, not the $5,000 apiece the company was charging its customers.[115] The Minnesota official in charge of examining interstate land sales in 2005 said he felt that state legislation was generally effective and that the situation with respect to interstate land fraud was nowhere near as bad as it had been in the 1950s and 1960s.[116]

Accounts of the interstate land-fraud business tend to focus on the initial marketing of these communities, various lawsuits, and state and federal actions. What has only been vaguely mentioned is the plight of the people stuck with lots on which they cannot build for decades, if ever. These people, many of them elderly, have been victimized also by unscrupulous real estate salespeople when they seek to resell their property. One anonymous source told the following story. An elderly farmer and his wife in Iowa in January 1972 were part of a free or below-cost bus trip with similar people from Iowa to a development between Phoenix and Tucson called Arizona City. There they succumbed to high-pressure sales tactics and bought a lot for $3,400 on the installment plan. They almost immediately regretted the purchase. Then the sixty-nine-year-old husband suffered a stroke, which eliminated any plans to build a retirement home there; but to them, a contract was a contract, so they completed the payments, paid taxes on the lot, and in 1996 paid for a sewage connection.

A 1988 appraisal valued the lot at $2,800, and the owners were told that a real estate agent would want a 10 percent commission to list it, and given the oversupply of lots on the market, that the realtor should be offered a bonus payment of $200 when it was sold. The wife did find a real estate agent to agree to list the lot but had to pay the agent $395 whether the lot was sold or not. It was not sold, so a couple of months later the wife engaged another real estate company by paying $695 when its agents offered to list the lot for $7,000. Again, it was not sold. Someone contacted the family in 2000 with an offer of $1,000 for the lot. The family rejected the offer but accepted one for $3,000 with the seller paying closing costs of $507. The family's tax loss was around $3,900. What was a retirement dream of playing cards with fellow Iowans under Arizona's winter sun had turned into an ongoing nightmare and source of family dissension. Only one member of the family paid a visit to Arizona City after the lot's purchase, and she could not find the lot due to the dusty street signs and a street name change.[117]

This author also visited Arizona City in March 2005. While numerous lots were still vacant, contributing to dust covering the street signs, a number had fairly new homes on them. Furthermore, because of the number of individual owners, the houses that were there exhibited quite a bit of variety for a moderately priced development.

With so many unscrupulous developers around, those developers who were honest had to separate themselves from the pack. Even then, they paid a price. The federal and state legislation that was passed as part of the consumer movement meant that all developers now had to comply with federal regulations as well as the regulations and registration fees of every state in which they were marketing their developments. Many developers chose to market only to certain states, thus reinforcing existing migration trends. For Del Webb in 1960, his problem was how to convince out-of-state buyers that his development was not just another land scam.

For example, Del Webb made a point of building his infrastructure, including recreational facilities, before selling houses. From the start of the first Sun City, he put his name on the towns he developed. In his ads, it was always "Del Webb's Sun City," to emphasize that he put his reputation behind the community. In the process, he built the "Del Webb" brand, a brand name that Pulte, which acquired it, uses today. However, the scammers had motivated various states to pass regulatory legislation, and that legislation applied to all developers. John Meeker, the president of the Del E. Webb Development Company, or DEVCO, the Sun City development division of the Del Webb Corporation, recalled that from the late 1960s into the 1970s, his company "received some static from certain states because it did not have their approval to advertise." As to why DEVCO had not registered to sell in certain states, Meeker recalled that California "wanted a fee for every recorded subdivision lot," and "New York required a yearly visit by an official with expenses paid for by DEVCO." As a result, Meeker confined DEVCO's advertising to national or regional magazines because they were not covered by state registration requirements.[118] On the other hand, the state of Arizona helped DEVCO by suing Phoenixaire in La Mirage for telling prospective buyers falsely that they could use facilities in Sun City. Marketers of that 40-acre development also claimed that it was 640 acres and advertised a nonexistent lake.[119] In the sleazy field of land development in the early 1960s, a builder with a good reputation stood out from the pack.

Age-Targeted versus Age-Restricted Communities: Youngtown, Arizona

Prior to Webb's first Sun City and even afterward, some developers marketed their communities as being for retirees, but they did not officially use age restrictions. Sidney Colen, who pioneered the condo concept in Florida, claimed credit for building Florida's "first planned senior community, Leslee Heights, in 1952" along with the United States' first condominium, the 584-unit Clearview Oaks, in 1957.[120] Both projects were marketed to retirees, but Colen did not institute specific age restrictions. In 1952, another Florida developer announced that the State Improvement Commission "endorsed as a retirement village" a projected 6,000-house development called Leisure City.[121] However, while targeting the retirement market, the developer also was allocating a site for a public school, which muddied the retirement village image.[122]

Still another Florida subdivision, Orange Gardens, was touted as the first to be architecturally designed for retirees. Begun in 1954, Orange Gardens was a 160-acre housing tract that was soon annexed to Kissimmee, near Orlando. The homes the developer built were barrier-free. One walked up a ramp, not steps, to enter these homes. Bathrooms featured special hand holds. Kitchens had higher than normal counters to minimize bending. Electrical outlets were twenty-six inches above the floor. Doors were wide enough to accommodate wheelchairs. However, the developer did not officially use age restrictions. The result was that

Orange Gardens by the 1980s blended into the larger community with an estimated 30 percent of its residents below age sixty-five.[123] Many other communities can be characterized as naturally occurring retirement communities, meaning that they have many retirees, but officially they are open to anyone without age restrictions.

From the viewpoint of some retirees, the problem with age-targeted communities was the occasional residence of children. A magazine for retirees, *Harvest Years,* reviewed Deltona, a Mackle Brothers community in Florida. Opened for lot sales in 1962, by 1968 Deltona had 4,000 people plus amenities that included a golf course and a community center complex with space for a variety of arts and crafts, dances, concerts, and adult learning classes that ranged from psychology to flower arranging. A popular two-bedroom, single-story home there sold in 1968 for $12,900. About 80 percent of the residents were retired, but another 10 percent were nineteen years old or younger. Some of the elderly complained about children yelling so loudly in the community swimming pools that they could be heard several blocks away. They also complained about minor vandalism and noisy vehicles. Deltona had much to recommend it as a retirement destination. However, in the retirement magazine's review, the presence of children along with a lack of more sophisticated urban facilities were considered negatives.[124]

To specifically require that all buyers belong to a certain age category was an innovative concept when real estate developer Ben Schleifer launched the development of Youngtown outside Phoenix in 1954. Youngtown was the first community to use specific age restrictions. Schleifer was a transplanted New Yorker who came to Arizona in search of a dry climate to help cure his asthma, and he went into the real estate business there. He said he acquired the idea for Youngtown after visiting a friend back in New York "who was living in a cooperative home for the aged." Schleifer was bothered by the rules that his friend had to endure, such as lights out and radio off by ten o'clock. As a result, Schleifer decided to create a place where old people could enjoy some autonomy, "stay active, live their own lives, and not lose their identity."[125] In a 1964 interview, Schleifer said the ideal retirement community should be a place "where the elderly can keep busy," be appreciated as individuals, and have their needs for medical services and personal security met. He said his inspiration for Youngtown came from having read Plato's *Republic* years earlier. According to Schleifer, Plato favored a cooperative community. Schleifer wanted to construct one where retirees could survive on Social Security payments and company pensions.[126] In other words, it was Schleifer's goal to create an affordable community where retirees would have autonomy as individuals.

Not only did Schleifer initially require that buyers be at least sixty-five,[127] but he also banned underage children as permanent residents.[128] His stated reason for excluding children was that he thought the ideal retirement community should be "a place where retired citizens can escape the whoop and croup of children, but still enjoy visits by them."[129] Since Schleifer was concerned that elderly people relying solely on Social Security could afford to live in Youngtown, that meant keeping taxes low. Popular writer Andrew Blechman notes that Schleifer realized banning children would eliminate large school taxes in Youngtown, although Schleifer subsequently said he was embarrassed when Youngtown's residents voted down a school bond issue.[130] Personally, Schleifer did not have negative feelings toward children. In fact, shortly after opening Youngtown, he married a woman with two young sons. Blechman reports that one of the stepsons, Paul Metchik, said Schleifer was primarily interested in creating a community for retirees. Excluding children as permanent residents was secondary to that objective. Metchik said his stepfather liked children and "was a wonderful father."[131]

Legally, once the development company sold property in Youngtown, the only way that age restrictions could be perpetuated at that time was through clauses in deeds. Furthermore, enforcement was basically left up to home owners since Maricopa County, where Youngtown is located, did not pass an age-restricted zoning overlay ordinance until the 1970s. The federal government did not define age-restricted communities, with fifty-five being the minimum for at least one resident in each dwelling unit, until 1988. Although Youngtown incorporated as a city in 1961,[132] its enforcement of the age restrictions was at times heated but at other times sporadic. No property owners association existed to provide enforcement, either. Consequently, things got to the point that in 1998 the Arizona attorney general canceled Youngtown's age-restricted status. Youngtown's city government lacked the financial resources to challenge that ruling.[133]

Developing a new community was a formidable undertaking for anyone with minimal financial resources. In raising the cash from a bank and other investors to launch Youngtown, Schleifer's group of investors started with only $48,000.[134] They constructed a number of small, single-family, ranch-style houses about fifteen miles outside of Phoenix on ranchland that had been owned by a widow, Frances Greer. Lots were a minimum of 100 by 60 feet, and maintenance was the buyer's responsibility.[135] Perhaps because of that motivating concern with preserving autonomy, the Youngtown Development Company chose not to construct any apartments or cooperative or condominium units.[136] Youngtown did give buyers who purchased lots the option of hiring their own builders, a practice that would not be allowed in its much better-known rival, Sun City.[137] Another example of more individual autonomy in Youngtown was that in the later Sun City, people who had RVs were required to keep them in the RV parking area. Sun City would not even allow an RV to pull up to an owner's house to be loaded for a trip. That was the reason Lucille Retheford gave for the decision she and her husband made to purchase in Youngtown rather than Sun City.[138] In general, Youngtown had fewer rules and restrictions than the other retirement communities that followed, perhaps primarily because of Schleifer's concern about maintaining the autonomy and respecting the individuality of its elderly residents.

The Youngtown Development Company built 125 modest houses on speculation in 1955, with 40 of them still unsold at the end of the year. Due to the limited financial resources of the development company, early buyers had to contend with dusty or muddy unpaved streets and inadequate utilities. Since the wiring that came with the houses could not handle an electric stove, early residents cooked on hot plates or coal burners until they could upgrade, at their own expense, their electrical capacity. Gas lines were slow in arriving, so the initial residents also had to cope with no hot running water or gas heat. In 1956, Congress made FHA mortgage financing available to those over sixty-two, which helped the sale of homes in Youngtown. In 1957, small, single-story, two-bedroom homes in Youngtown ranged in price from $6,800 to $6,950. With FHA financing, a buyer could purchase one of these houses for $500 down and $40 per month.[139] By comparison, the median price of a house sold in the United States in 1950 was $7,400.[140] Reliable median home prices are difficult to ascertain for the 1950s, but the National Association of Home Builders reported that the median price of a new home nationally in 1956 was $14,508.[141] Presumably, most of those homes were larger than Youngtown's small, two-bedroom ramblers.

The minimal financial resources of the Youngtown Development Company limited advertising, but the unique nature of the community brought it free national publicity. In 1955, Alistair Cooke's television show, *Omnibus*, did a segment on Youngtown.[142] Two years later, Dave Garroway gave Youngtown some more national exposure when his *Today* show featured Youngtown.[143] About this time, *Arizona Highways* magazine published an article on Youngtown. Schleifer's company did some radio and newspaper advertising and relied on satisfied buyers recruiting others.

Early buyers tended to come from the Midwest. In 1959, Youngtown had 363 households. Of these, 54 came from Illinois, 25 from Minnesota, and 24 from Michigan.[144] Youngtown encouraged state-of-origin identity with an annual all-states potluck dinner featuring friendly rivalry as to which state had the most residents there. The potluck provided an opportunity for new arrivals to connect with others from their home states.[145] Finally, many of the avenues in Youngtown were named after states or cities, such as Duluth Avenue. Thus, Youngtown reflected Ben Schleifer's own interstate, migratory experience. It also reflected some of the marketing techniques of the retiree trailer courts and earlier municipal campgrounds in Florida in the way it used state identity and the personal contacts of existing residents to recruit new buyers. Since the resources of the Youngtown Development Company were limited, it could not launch a major national advertising campaign, but its subsequent rival, Del Webb, did have those resources to promote Sun City, Arizona.

Youngtown in its early years included very minimal recreational amenities, commercial services, and medical facilities. The Youngtown Development Company did provide space for a small shopping center, but stores and other services were reluctant to locate there until the development had a substantial population. Youngtown reached a population of 1,400 in 1959,[146] but a major grocery store along with the rest of the shopping center did not open until 1961.[147] Residents in 1959 complained about inadequate medical facilities and public transportation as well.[148]

The major difference in the concept of Youngtown compared to that of Del Webb's Sun City and other age-restricted communities that followed was in Youngtown's relative lack of recreational facilities. Given Ben Schleifer's emphasis on the autonomy of the residents, Youngtown developers did not attempt to structure recreational activities for its residents. Schleifer contended that "older people wanted to develop their own activities and community organizations," and for that reason, "the Company did not provide golf courses, activity centers, or swimming pools." However, at least one historian of Youngtown said the lack of recreational facilities was primarily due to the development company's financial constraints and not philosophy. Apparently, the company's early advertising mentioned some recreational facilities that were never built. Mention of those was dropped in later advertising.[149] As a result, Youngtown did not promote the "active retirement" image that its next-door rival, Sun City, would begin doing in connection with its 1960 grand opening.

However, Youngtown did have some recreational facilities. Frances Greer, on whose ranchland Youngtown was built, donated her ranch house to the community for use as a clubhouse.[150] Her former house became a setting for club meetings, parties, and potlucks.[151] Her barnyard became the civic square of Youngtown, eventually containing a public library and other municipal buildings. Across the street from Greer's ranch house or community clubhouse was the shopping center. Greer remained in Youngtown, where she built another high-quality home at the end of Duluth Avenue overlooking the Agua Fria riverbed. She died in 1984.[152] Besides using Greer's original ranch house as a clubhouse, an amenity the developers provided was to take a Youngtown cattle watering hole and convert it into "the seven acre Maricopa Lake."[153]

Residents of Youngtown did organize a variety of groups in the early days of the community. By 1963, these included thirty-nine clubs, from bowling leagues to shuffleboard, horseshoes, card-playing, and social clubs.[154] The most significant of these groups was the Youngtown chapter of the American Association of Retired Persons, or AARP. Ethel Percy Andrus had founded the National Retired Teachers Association but wanted an organization open to all retired people. Therefore, in 1958, she established AARP. By 1960, that organization had more than one hundred local groups. Andrus decided that it was time to give the local groups chapter status. The national organization selected the Youngtown chapter of AARP to be officially designated as its first chapter. The Youngtown group coasted along with around thirty members until 1970. Then, with a new president, the Youngtown chapter began offering day trips to places like the Grand Canyon, then weekend trips to places like Las Vegas; by 1980, some chapter-sponsored trips were up to two weeks in length. The trip program built membership up to three hundred. Besides travel, the Youngtown chapter developed a variety of service activities, such as helping people with Medicare forms and assisting them in filing their income taxes, and it raised money for various causes.[155] As of December 2005, the Youngtown AARP chapter was still in existence.[156] However, the number of active clubs in the community had dwindled to three.[157]

As for Ben Schleifer, having successfully launched Youngtown, he decided in the 1960s to create another visionary community for retirees. Going twenty miles west where land was more affordable, he opened Circle City. Modeled on the Israeli kibbutz and affiliated with "the Workingmen's Circle, a Jewish society with socialist leanings," Schleifer marketed his community to "lower-middle-class Jewish retirees" but without much success. The community may have been too isolated for many prospective residents and Schleifer's financial resources too thin to sustain the effort. The failure of that vision left Ben Schleifer bankrupt.[158] Having originated the concept of the age-restricted community, he ceased to be a player in the subsequent development of that concept.

Between the elite wintering in the South in the late nineteenth century and the marketing of modestly priced single-family homes in Youngtown in the 1950s, a lot had happened. Initially, Florida was by far the favored destination, first of the elite but quickly also for people of far more modest means. Florida was fashionable and glamorous, with many miles of beaches and a warm climate. It was the land of the legendary Fountain of Youth and projected an image of being conducive to good health. Migration patterns meant that certain places in the South became hubs for later arrivals from the same places of origin. The strategies of people with more modest means allowed them to be able to winter in the South. In an era before Social Security and the prevalence of company pensions, these strategies included camping, usually in municipal campgrounds but also in private ones. A "tin can tourist" could live out of his "tin Lizzie" and an adjacent tent, eat out of tin cans, patronize the municipal recreation center, and enjoy the climate and social life while spending very little money. Those with more money might rent apartments. In the 1930s, trailer courts started to become an option. With the skyrocketing price of choice beachfront property after World War II, the development of the condominium helped those who were not rich split the cost of the site. Finally, some developers began to see a market for establishing tract subdivisions and promoting them as places for the elderly. Behind all these innovations were a number of creative businessmen, from St. Petersburg's gifted public relations man

John Lodwick to members of Bradenton's enterprising Kiwanis Club who organized its amenity-rich trailer court for retirees to Sidney Adler with his innovative "own your own lot" in the trailer court concept. All of these men as well as Sidney Colen, who pioneered the legal concept of the condominium, were Floridians. So, too, were the most notorious of the post–World War II land scammers, people who sold lots and retirement dreams, often fraudulently, to unsuspecting northerners. By the 1950s, they were exporting their retirement trailer courts and land scams to Arizona, which did not have the humidity of Florida. A latecomer as a retirement destination, Arizona was becoming the center of innovation, with Ben Schleifer and the first officially age-restricted community, Youngtown. As Arizona historian Thomas E. Sheridan puts it, "Youngtown (1954) might have been the first age-segregated 'geriatric ghetto,' but Sun City was the biggest and best-promoted. There would be many more."[159]

Del Webb's "Sun City" Concept

In 1972, developer Del Webb characterized the typical resident of his Sun City, Arizona, development as "the guy who worked for the power company in Chicago. He has a $50,000 house all paid for. He gets a touch of rheumatism. His doctor tells him to go to Arizona. He's never quite had the country club life. He comes out here and God, he's got something he never thought he'd have before."[1]

Webb opened his first age-restricted, active adult community in 1960 thirteen miles west of Phoenix and adjacent to Youngtown. Setting his minimum age at fifty, Webb promoted an active adult lifestyle with clubhouses, golf courses, swimming pools, craft facilities, an outdoor amphitheater, clubs, classes, and socializing. He billed this lifestyle as "active retirement," and he advertised it heavily. In a society with a strong work ethic and where social status tended to be grounded largely in a person's occupation, retirees had suffered from an image of being useless, stay-at-home persons to be pitied. Webb redefined that image as the "active adult" enjoying a country club lifestyle in the sun. It was a retirement dream worth pursuing. Just who was Del Webb? Why did he build a community that would not be marketed to the majority of the buying public but just to people over fifty? What sort of research and planning did his corporation do before risking millions of dollars embarking on its first Sun City? How was Webb's Sun City unique? How and why did people respond to it? Taking a concept like Youngtown, combining it with the amenity-rich appeal of retiree trailer courts, then building it on a huge scale, and finding phenomenal success in the process was something unprecedented in history.

Del Webb's Personal Background

Obviously, Del Webb was a creative, careful, and brilliant risk taker among American developers. Some of his interest in construction, his competitiveness, and his calculated approach to risk taking combined with a certain comfort with who he was can be traced back to his childhood. Delbert (he hated being called "Delbert," preferring "Del")[2] Eugene Webb was born on May 17, 1899, in Fresno, California. At the time of Webb's birth, Fresno was an agricultural service center and railroad town of 12,400. His family had some standing in the community. His paternal grandfather had been a preacher and had served in the California state legislature.[3] His maternal grandfather farmed and "built one of the first irrigation systems" in California.[4] His father, Ernest, was president of a sand and gravel company and doubled as a board member of another gravel company.[5] His father was also an amateur baseball player and dabbled in construction. Del was the oldest of three sons.[6] Before Del was ten, his father taught him how to use various carpentry tools and instilled in him a love of baseball.

Del's comfortable childhood was shattered when he was fourteen. His father suddenly went bankrupt. The details are unclear, but it appears that his father was constructing a major building, either Fresno's first skyscraper or a hotel, when a dishonest subcontractor pulled out, bringing the Webb family "close to ruin."[7] Apparently, his mother also owned some land in Fresno that in 1972 became the site of the twenty-one-story Del Webb Fresno TowneHouse. Webb recalled that, ironically, his mother had lost ownership of that parcel because she could not pay the taxes on it.[8] Webb had to drop out of high school to help support the family, which was living in much reduced circumstances.

The lessons Webb seems to have learned from seeing his father near ruin was to have a "five-year plan" and to keep close track of things.[9] As his company grew in size by the mid-1930s, he practiced diversification into various types of construction in different states and invested in professional sports in the 1940s with part ownership of the New York Yankees. He drove himself hard and was constantly on the go from Phoenix to New York to Los Angeles. His father never recovered financially. As for Del Webb in the risky business of construction, he once admitted that perhaps 80 percent of his own decisions were mistakes, "but the other 20 percent were good enough to overcome them."[10] One way he had of expressing his appreciation for his executives was to frequently remark to them, "If I lost everything, I could make it all back with good people."[11] Insecurity from the childhood trauma of his father's business failure was a motivator that stayed with him throughout his life.

Webb's family background influenced his personality and character in other ways as well. He did have some rough edges. Jerry Svendsen, who did public relations for Webb from 1961 to 1982, recalled that Webb talked "blue collar" and that Webb's English was not polished.[12] A reporter in 1964 referred to Webb's "country boy touch" and quoted Webb saying in a speech, "When I come to Arizona, this here fella learned me. . . ."[13] Webb, who was already a public figure when Sun City opened due to his co-ownership of the New York Yankees, professed shyness when it came to public speaking. However, he probably enjoyed the attention, even if he did not admit it. He was willing to use himself and his image to promote Sun City. Fracturing his grammar may have made him a more interesting speaker in a folksy sense.

As a major figure in both construction and the sports world and as head of a firm that had done very well by government contracts since the beginning of World War II, Webb was at home interacting with leading politicians and entertainment figures. In fact, he boasted about being on a first-name basis with every president from Franklin Roosevelt onward. Gregarious, he enjoyed meeting all sorts of people.[14] While at times he may have exaggerated some of his characteristics or feigned shyness, he had a kind of comfort level in who he was that may have come from his grandfathers' accomplishments and his father's position prior to his financial reverses. Webb's physical appearance was also impressive. He was often the tallest in the crowd, usually wearing a hat that added to his six feet four inch height. He might have appeared aloof and arrogant at times, but he also came across as a warm, sincere individual who "was disarming and persuasive in conversation."[15]

Del Webb was a frustrated professional baseball player, but his experience with baseball contributed to his success as manager of a large corporation. Having quit school at fourteen, he sought out carpenter jobs during the week and semi-professional baseball games on the weekends. At thirteen he was six feet three inches tall, weighed 130 pounds, and occasionally earned $2.50 playing a semi-professional game.[16] He was a right-handed pitcher but a left-handed batter, eventually pitching for a couple of teams in the Pacific Coast League. In his early twenties, with his weight up to 200 pounds, he was not afraid of a collision with another player at home plate. In one such collision, though, he sustained some permanent damage to his right shoulder, which made him better suited to playing the outfield than pitching. His real downfall as a professional ballplayer came when he participated in an exhibition game at San Quentin Prison. A convict holding a glass of water with his fingers near the rim gave it to Webb to drink. While that may not have been the cause, two weeks later Webb was seriously ill with a severe case of typhoid fever. Webb's weight fell to ninety-nine pounds before he recovered.[17]

In the meantime, friends recommended that he relocate to Arizona because of the climate.[18] Still hoping for a career in professional baseball, Webb headed for Phoenix. He got a ball-playing job with the Industrial League but was not supposed to play until he had been in Arizona for thirty days. Unfortunately for his baseball career, he agreed to pinch hit on day 29, got caught, was suspended for thirty days, and never went back to baseball as a professional player.[19] With an ailing arm, he decided to refocus on a career as a contractor. He was twenty-eight.[20]

Love of sports remained with Webb throughout his life and may have made him health-conscious as well as contributing to his business success. In an era when smoking was very common, Webb neither smoked nor tolerated secondhand smoke in his offices. All his desks had "No smoking" signs front and center. One of his top executives, R. H. Johnson, thought Webb may actually have been "the first to put a 'No smoking' sign in corporate offices."[21] He apparently developed a taste for whiskey as a ballplayer, but when his consumption in the 1940s got up to twenty bourbons a day, his doctor suggested he cut back. Webb went one better and cut out alcohol altogether. No longer an active ballplayer, Webb improved his golf game. By 1962, he was scoring in the high 70s and a member of fourteen golf clubs in various locations around the United States. The golf course proved to be a relaxing place to discuss business deals and develop relationships that could be useful in getting the necessary permits for some construction projects. His co-ownership of the New York Yankees also meant that he had free passes to use in cultivating business contacts, and it did make him nationally known.[22] He would make golf courses central to planning his Sun Cities.

Many executives will look back on their participation in sports when explaining where they got their management skills, and Del Webb was no exception. He knew "the value of having a happy team."[23] In addition, he picked up a sense of showmanship, boldness, and the ability to turn in a steady performance under pressure.[24] Webb himself once remarked,

"I just apply baseball to business and it works."[25] He could spot talented people, promote from within his company, and give these people the freedom to be creative. In the end, it was his trust in their plans backed by his money that would pay off with Sun City.

Webb's personal life played a role in the Sun City concept. The emphasis on "active retirement" at the opening of Sun City may have had something to do with Webb's memory of his grandfather Jimmy Webb complaining "about being old with nothing to do."[26] Del Webb's marital history may have been a factor as well.

He was married twice. In 1917, Webb had obtained steady work in the Oakland, California, shipyards.[27] Two years later, he married Hazel Church, a tall, dark-eyed woman who "was trained as an operating room nurse." He described her "as a childhood sweetheart."[28] In some ways, they were opposites. She appears to have been something of a homebody, while her husband liked to be constantly on the move. Their happiest years may have been their first years in Phoenix. Webb needed office and storage space for his fledgling construction company, so he bought and remodeled a building to include living quarters upstairs for himself and Hazel. Hazel occasionally helped out in the office, but as the work increased, Webb hired a secretary/bookkeeper.[29] During the 1930s, Del and Hazel were among the couples who enjoyed going out for evenings to dance to swing music.[30] However, as the Del Webb Corporation expanded, the two drifted apart. Hazel did not enjoy the constant travel, although she occasionally accompanied her husband on his business trips.[31] Those trips increased. They had two different lifestyles. Del grew intellectually and socially as his corporation expanded, while Hazel remained a very private person.[32] They had no children. Eventually, after thirty-three years of marriage, they divorced in 1952.[33]

Following the divorce, Del continued to meet his obligations to Hazel. Eighteen years after their divorce, Hazel wanted a place to live where she would feel secure. Del Webb at that time was building some single-story condos that were the ultimate in privacy with all rooms opening onto inner courtyards, no windows to the outside, and solid brick walls six feet high enclosing the patios. These were in Phase 2 of Sun City, Arizona, within about a half-mile from a first-class hospital that he was also building. He gave Hazel one of these condos on the corner of 107th and Del Webb Boulevard. She had a Del Webb street sign outside her door. She was around seventy when she arrived in time to be listed in the 1971 Sun City Directory. In the directory, she listed her former state of residence as Arizona. She declined to list a former occupation. She did not become involved in her ex-husband's community, spending most of her time within the walls of her condo. She hired people to do her shopping and cleaning. Del apparently told his company staff that if she needed something to help her out. When he died in 1974, he left her an income of $75,000 per year for the rest of her life. She continued living in her Sun City condo until around 1989. At that point, her health was failing. A nephew came to take her to California, and she died shortly thereafter. She had never remarried.[34] Del Webb himself never lived in his flagship community of Sun City, Arizona, but it is worth noting that he did make that personal use of his community.

At the time that Del Webb gave that condo to his ex-wife, he had been married to his second wife, Toni Ince, for around nine years. Toni was very different from Hazel. Del met Toni on a blind date that one of his executives arranged. Their courtship lasted seven years.[35] Twenty-two years younger than Del, attractive, and outgoing, she would become his regular travel companion after their low-key marriage in 1961 in a hotel suite in Reno, Nevada.[36] At the time of their marriage, she was a buyer for Bullock's Wilshire Department Store in Los Angeles and a millinery designer.[37] Travel with Del was constant.

Del Webb had an extremely migratory lifestyle. He maintained three hotel suites on a full-time basis at fashionable addresses—in Los Angeles at the Beverly Hilton and in Phoenix at the Mountain Shadows Resort, both of which his firm had built, as well as in New York at the Waldorf Astoria. To avoid packing, he maintained complete wardrobes in all three places.[38] Since the success of Sun City, Arizona, was based on a belief that a significant number of retirees would migrate to a new location, Webb's own penchant for moving around may have reinforced that insight. His preference for living in hotels also may have contributed to an appreciation that some potential buyers would look for homes with amenities.

A picture of how Toni was an asset to Del on his travels occurred in connection with two weekend visits the pair made to Sun City, California, to celebrate its opening in 1962. A reporter described her as "charming" and chatting easily with various people, including visitors. When her husband temporarily turned to confer with his executives, she continued to work the crowd. She identified with the locals by recalling her days as a drama student at Valley Junior College in fairly nearby San

Bernardino.[39] It was Toni's second marriage as well. Again, no children resulted. When Del died in 1974, he left Toni $1.5 million. By far the bulk of his estate went to his foundation to further his charitable interests, largely in health care.[40] For some reason, when a building at Sun City, California, was dedicated in her husband's honor following his death, Toni Ince failed to appear.

What may be most significant about Del Webb's personal life was how he felt about not having any children, given the fact that Webb's Sun Cities banned children as permanent residents. In an interview about a year and a half before his death, Webb said he had no regrets about not having children. He admitted that he occasionally wondered what his life would have been like had he had a family. He concluded that he might have remained a carpenter. Without children, he said, he was "freer in moving around." He added, "I'm not saying it's the best way to live. But I'm used to it."[41] In deciding to ban children as permanent residents of Sun City, Webb was betting elderly couples who had raised one generation of children did not want to raise another generation.

Webb's Construction Company

Webb's construction career in Arizona began with a variety of small carpentry jobs. As an employee of someone else, he hung doors for the Westward Ho Hotel.[42] He then helped another contractor build some modest houses. Webb went to work for a small contractor who was doing some construction for a Bayless grocery store. Webb's paycheck bounced, and the contractor disappeared. J. B. Bayless wanted his store completed before that of a rival. Webb agreed to take over, met the deadline in twenty-seven days by working around the clock, and founded his own company in the process. The firm's initial inventory of equipment, inherited from the disappearing contractor, was a cement mixer, ten wheelbarrows, ten picks, and twenty shovels. However, Webb now had the backing of Bayless for future jobs. Besides the Bayless stores, Webb did alterations and remodeling for a variety of other stores. Gradually, the jobs got bigger.

Webb began to accumulate a staff of talented future executives. One of his earliest hires was R. H. Johnson as timekeeper. Three decades later, Johnson would become president of the Webb Corporation. Webb became highly regarded "as a keen judge of human nature." He was also known for paying "better than average salaries," for working hard and insisting "that his men do likewise," for having a "quiet yet firm manner," and for generating "harmonious cooperation."[43]

In some ways, his corporation was like a family to him. When he died in 1974, Webb named R. H. Johnson to be the executor of his estate, the bulk of which went to Webb's charitable foundation. In his will, Webb also left $150,000 to Johnson and $100,000 each to five other executives.[44] Ten years after Webb's death, executive Fred Kuentz called him "my friend, boss and father rolled into one." Another longtime executive, Owen Childress, remembered Webb calling him on a Sunday to inquire about his cancer-stricken father. R. H. Johnson recalled Webb "calling his executives constantly on weekends 'just to talk.'" Webb had hired many of these men when they had little in the way of credentials, then taught them the business, kept them on for decades, and virtually made their careers. He was repaid with much loyalty, even years after his death.[45]

In spite of the Great Depression, Webb's construction firm expanded. In 1936, he opened a branch office in Southern California. Also in the 1930s, Webb began to cultivate government officials in both Washington and Sacramento who had the power to award construction contracts. He even met President Roosevelt. Apparently, the two shared a bond in that both had been bedridden for some time, an experience that turned out for both to be career-altering. Roosevelt is reported to have remarked to Webb, "An illness can be a turning point for a man. I was laid up for four years and those years changed my thinking; in fact, changed this country's thinking."[46] The corporation's next big step in expansion would be government contracts during World War II.[47]

The first of these major federal government contracts was to build an Army post, Fort Huachuca. The contract called for completion within ninety days and a budget of $3 million. Webb did the job, reinforcing his reputation for bringing projects in on time and within budget. A number of other contracts for military installations, bases, compounds, airfields, and hospitals in Southern California and Arizona followed.[48]

The project that Webb later recalled as "one of the highlights of [his] company's accomplishments" would turn out eventually to be the most socially controversial.[49] In February 1942, the federal government made a quick decision to relocate Japanese and Japanese Americans from their homes and businesses in California and western Arizona into hastily constructed relocation camps in isolated locations in the West.

Since the federal government was forcing those to be relocated to move within weeks, it needed to construct the relocation camps fast. Webb got the contract in March 1942 for the Japanese Relocation Camp at Poston, also known as the Theater of Operations at Parker, Arizona. Parker was the major community in the area. Webb immediately pulled heavy equipment away from a California project to Poston, had the mesquite plowed under the next day, and hired 5,000 men using a double-shift schedule. The job did not just involve the construction of barracks but of an entire community. Besides housing, Webb built roads, schools, and other community facilities. He completed the job in three weeks. He then signed a second contract to expand the camp to house 25,000 more.[50] At completion, the camp, about twenty miles south of Parker, housed 36,000 internees.

Webb may have seen this camp as a "highlight" because it was his first experience building a complete community. However, even toward the end of his life, he regarded that job with pride, calling it "one of the most patriotic things" his company had done.[51] Some of his executives came to feel differently. After R. H. Johnson retired, he recalled that conditions at the Poston camp were "not very nice." When the camp was under construction, Johnson spent several nights there. Dust swept through cracks in the walls of the hastily constructed temporary buildings to the extent that when Johnson awoke, he found "it piled on his face." Johnson said he did not think the internees were well treated, but it was the firm's job to get the camp built fast and not to question federal policy.[52] The firm's success with the relocation camp led to a number of other military construction projects, including Luke Air Force Base, which was very close to the future Sun City.

Today, Pulte, which owns the Del Webb company and brand, tends to downplay its subsidiary's relocation-camp past. A web site history of Webb notes that the firm "was offered numerous defense contracts to help the country prepare for war. Several contracts called for building entire cities, foreshadowing the kind of development work that would make Del Webb famous in the years to come."[53] The absence of any mention of a Japanese relocation camp stands out in this particular company history. As one of the nation's leading home builders in the twenty-first century, Pulte undoubtedly sells some housing to people of Japanese background plus a great many others who find the relocation camps a deplorable episode in American history.

Del Webb did not shrink from doing business with some very colorful and controversial clients. One of these was Howard Hughes. Over a span of some thirty years, Webb built manufacturing facilities, office buildings, and other structures for Hughes. That meant Webb was available to meet him at odd hours, usually during the four hours after midnight, and in isolated locations.[54] Webb delighted in placing telephone calls to Howard Hughes while reporters were present. He publicly referred to Hughes as "one of my closest friends." While Webb acknowledged Hughes' "peculiarities," he also called Hughes "one of the shrewdest fellows I've ever known."[55] Webb's last secretary, Maxine Newman, said Hughes had a private telephone number for his own line to Webb's office. If Webb answered that telephone, everyone else in the office was supposed to leave. She recalled once meeting Webb at the airport when Webb appeared to be quite tired. When she inquired, Webb responded with "that goddam Howard Hughes and his late night phone calls."[56] Webb and Hughes seem to have had frequent telephone conversations.[57]

One reason for those telephone conversations was that both moved into the casino business in Las Vegas. Del Webb's initial involvement was when he built the first casino on the Las Vegas Strip, the Flamingo. His client for that construction job was the notorious mobster "Bugsy" Siegel. Much later, Webb decided that in addition to construction, his firm should diversify by actually owning Nevada casinos. Although the FBI maintained a file on Webb, he and J. Edgar Hoover became friends, with Hoover penning him "Dear Del" notes. In 1968, Hoover praised Webb and Hughes "for fighting organized crime in Nevada."[58] Both Webb and Hughes discovered that it was not easy. Eventually, years after Webb's death, the Webb Corporation exited the casino business to concentrate on what it did best—building age-restricted, active adult communities.

Perhaps the building project most relevant to the future Sun City was Webb's construction of Pueblo Gardens, a postwar suburb outside Tucson. The construction of the massive tract suburb Levittown, which opened in 1947 on Long Island and within a few years consisted of 17,400 houses on 4,000 acres, all based on just a couple of models and built using assembly-line techniques, inspired a number of builders.[59] The Levitt company did not invent using power nailers and other tools or materials like plywood, but Levitt was so well publicized that the firm had imitators across the country. One of these was Del Webb.[60]

In 1948, Webb acquired 1,500 acres in the desert outside of Tucson and designed a community of affordable, FHA-financed homes using mass-production methods like assembling roof trusses and wall frames off site. The result was five hundred detached "cookie cutter" houses and one hundred duplexes. Webb included a strip shopping center and built sewage and water systems. The firm built a total community, not just houses. Webb followed that experience in community building with the construction, beginning in 1953, of a company town, San Manuel, for Magma Copper. That project involved constructing houses, shopping facilities, parks, and utilities.[61] In the late 1980s, the Webb Corporation officially referred to San Manuel as a "master-planned" community.[62] In the late 1950s, Webb's Housing Division built Clairemont Estates near San Diego and several hundred houses in north Phoenix.[63] By 1957, the firm was beginning to prepare for yet another challenge in creative community building.

Originating the Sun City Concept

Sun City historian Jane Freeman wrote that it was not the case that part of the Del Webb "legend was that the concept of Sun City was Webb's own." Webb had gathered around him a number of creative, talented executives. One of these was L. C. Jacobson, who by 1959 was supervising the day-to-day operations of the company.[64] It was Jacobson who gave the approval to explore new retirement concepts.[65]

Vice President Tom Breen took charge of researching the feasibility and concept of such a community for the Webb Corporation. Breen had grown up in Hollywood. His father worked on film production crews and in the Hays censorship office, which enforced certain moral standards for films. As a teenage actor, Tom Breen had acting roles in a couple of films that starred Elizabeth Taylor. After serving as a Marine in the South Pacific during World War II, Breen resumed his film career. Working for MGM as both a writer and actor, his movie career peaked in 1951 with a starring role opposite Jane Powell in the movie *Luxury Liner*. The following year, he abandoned Hollywood for a job as an assistant advertising director for Webb's housing subdivisions. His explanation for why he left Hollywood was, "I liked the work but not the life." He then went on what he called "the cactus circuit" as Webb's manager of housing developments in Casa Grande (about eight miles north of Arizona City), plus nearby Eloy, and Coolidge.[66] While other company officials took part in researching a potential Webb retirement community over a period of four and a half years,[67] Tom Breen, who became vice president for development, was the most heavily involved.

The Webb firm's research effort began shortly after the opening of Youngtown, the first retirement community to be officially age-restricted. In 1955, Tom Breen caught Alistair Cooke's report on Youngtown on the *Omnibus* television show and, later, Dave Garroway's 1957 coverage of Youngtown on the *Today* show.[68] Owen Childress, then a young member of Webb's company, later recalled that some staff wondered why they had not thought of the Youngtown concept themselves. However, at least one employee thought Webb could improve on Youngtown by building houses that were better than the small, plain, "chintzy" houses in that development. Webb's staff concluded that many retirees would spend more for a nicer product.[69] Specifically, Youngtown appeared to serve the lower end of the middle-class retirement market, and Webb's staff decided to aim for the next level up while still keeping the homes widely affordable.[70] In creating a retirement community for middle-class retirees, Webb was, in popular writer Andrew Blechman's words, creating "a new version of the American dream, designed exclusively for the nation's fastest-growing leisure class."[71]

Breen turned to the academic community for research. He contacted the prominent sociologist Robert Havighurst, who with Eugene M. Friedmann wrote *The Meaning of Work and Retirement*, published in 1954. In this book they argued that upon retirement, workers missed the structure, status, and extra income that their jobs provided. However, to some extent, "organized leisure activities" could provide retirees with a substitute for work, a concept soon dubbed the "activity theory." As for segregating the elderly into their own communities, Havighurst was among those academics who thought that the activity the elderly wanted involved contact with other generations. Breen was not so sure.[72] He then hired Western Business Consultants of Phoenix for $10,000 to research the issue. Their report was based on a number of government pamphlets that generally echoed Havighurst's views, which were "of little value" to Webb's executives.[73] Havighurst had taken issue with other sociologists at that time, such as Elaine Cumming and William E. Henry, who subscribed to what they termed the "disengagement theory," meaning that the elderly wanted a quiet life as they became progressively more "disengaged" from their surroundings.[74] Also, Breen's financial consultants warned him that the elderly would have more difficulty in securing home financing through such programs as FHA.[75]

Breen's supervisor, L. C. Jacobson, decided to consult with other top developers through the Urban Land Institute. The Webb Corporation paid for a half-dozen developers to hold a three-day seminar at the Mountain Shadows Resort for Webb executives. These developers generally echoed the academics. The refrain, "Old people want to be with their families, not together in an isolated community," characterized their response. They predicted such a project would fail because more residents would die than would move in to take their places.[76] They advised the Webb Corporation to drop the idea of an age-restricted community.[77]

Not discouraged, Breen took the next step of hiring his friend Lou Silverstein, "a local radio personality," to research the retirement-community concept while Silverstein was visiting Florida to assist in establishing his brother's radio station there. Florida was a well-known retirement destination. When Silverstein returned after interviewing Florida retirees, he reported that they enjoyed their grandchildren but did not want to raise "someone else's children." Silverstein also mentioned some of the abuses in the sale of Florida real estate. Intrigued, Breen decided to check out Florida for himself. What struck Breen on his visit was the number of retirees who appeared to be sitting around with nothing much to do.[78] It is unclear if Breen visited St. Petersburg, then known for lining its downtown streets with green benches, which were popular sitting places for the elderly. However, Breen and Silverstein did reference the Mackle Brothers development Port Charlotte, south of St. Petersburg, in a three-and-a-half-page memo, "Recommendations for Retirement Living."[79] Breen and the other executives apparently concluded that their own informal research, their gut feelings, and the nearby success of Youngtown were worth more than the academic research and advice of expensive consultants.

The "Recommendations for Retirement Living" memo was significant in part because within months the Webb firm not only would have its concept for Sun City in place but would begin construction on the community. The memo, dated 16 March 1959, covered housing, lot sales, and the nature of the community itself. With respect to housing, Breen and Silverstein recommended building two-bedroom and three-bedroom homes, each with one bath. They raised the possibility of including a swimming pool with one model. Their suggested price range was between roughly $7,500 and $12,000. Most homes would be single-family, detached ones, but they did suggest some construction of row houses. As for style, they advised the Webb firm to avoid contemporary in favor of "something that would be reminiscent of construction in the East and the North, the type of thing that the retirees have been used to all their lives." Their lot size recommendations varied from 50 by 80 feet up to 80 by 120 feet.[80]

Breen and Silverstein's recommendations for the physical town planning and the social engineering concept of the community were most interesting. Nervous about refusing to sell to buyers under a certain age, they envisioned a community that would have housing for retirees on one side of a major highway, another area for families on the other side of that highway, and possibly a small area for retirees with families. (In 1962, Webb would actually open Sun City, California, as a retirement community on one side of a highway; years later, an intergenerational community, Rancho Ramona, opened on the other side of the highway.) As for amenities, Breen and Silverstein had Florida-like visions of a large lake, a network of canals, or one large, horseshoe-shaped canal, stocked with fish and able to, if possible, handle power boats and water skiing. A more practical suggestion was a nearby stable. They had checked out recreation centers in Florida, the largest being 1,500 square feet, which they thought should be included in the Webb retirement community with a nearby swimming pool, preferably heated, and shuffleboard courts. They recommended inclusion of a post office and direct delivery of mail to homes. Another feature present in some retiree trailer courts that they thought Webb should include was a community newspaper. They recommended a library, too, although the pair admitted that they felt more research was needed as to the type of books likely to appeal to "old people." They guessed that mysteries would be popular. The two made no recommendations on public transportation within the town, but they did recommend a bus for sightseeing and trips to a larger nearby community. As for financing these facilities, their memo suggested that a monthly fee be added to each household's mortgage payment. Most of these facilities they had seen in retiree trailer courts in Florida, with the exception of the stables. To their knowledge, Webb would be pioneering with stables.[81]

Based on their Florida findings, Breen and Silverstein had some significant recommendations on land acquisition. They pointed out that the Mackle Company paid a bargain price of forty dollars per acre for its initial land purchase for Port Charlotte. As the development succeeded and the Mackles decided to expand, they ended up paying considerably more for adjacent land. The moral of the story was to buy a very large tract of land at the start. Furthermore, if Webb did plan a development on a very large scale, the two suggested it could be located "anywhere, out in the desert, perhaps 50 or 100 miles from any town." They mentioned keeping land costs "as low as possible."[82] Smaller developments, on the other hand, should be closer to a town with necessary facilities. The pair thought Arizona offered excellent possibilities. One problem they spotted in Florida and recommended that Webb avoid was where lots were sold over a large area but only a few scattered homes were built. They commented, "It looks bad and very unappealing." They predicted some major public relations problems for the Mackles as a result.[83]

Finally, they made a number of marketing recommendations. Because the Mackles were so successful at selling lots for $10 down and $10 per month, Breen and Silverstein suggested that Webb do the same. With Mackle selling Gulf coast lots for $995, the pair suggested that Webb consider $795 per lot. They even pushed the use of the Mackles' Miami advertising agency. The two considered it possible to extend the $10 down and $10 per month installment program to the purchase of a house as well as a lot, with a housing area reserved for those paying the full cash price. Advertising should be in national publications along with "saturation type promotions going from city to city." The two actually envisioned "a sales office with a cactus, perhaps a papier-mâché horse, or palm tree." They were concerned that buyers would arrive only to discover that their lots were a "sand dune." To reassure these buyers, the pair recommended that "the name and reputation of the Del E. Webb Construction Company . . . be exploited to its utmost."[84]

Since Webb was a construction company, not a land sale company, it never did embark on a plan to sell lots only. However, it did implement this last recommendation. From the very beginning, it was always "Del Webb's Sun City." Initially, this was Webb's way of saying that he stood by his product. Emphasizing Del Webb the person in promoting Sun City had the effect of personalizing a large corporation. In the process, the corporation created a brand name that is still used in the twenty-first century.

Joe Ashton, vice president of land development for Webb, asked Breen to produce his own, two-page memo recommending "an age-segregated retirement town organized around three principles: 'activity, economy, and individuality.'"[85] The activity would revolve around a recreation center and golf course. The homes would be affordable, with the cost of the recreational facilities incorporated into the pricing of a large number of homes. The minimum age to purchase would be lowered from Youngtown's then sixty to fifty. As for individuality with respect to resident activities, Breen recommended that the Webb Corporation not do a lot of organizing of activities but leave that to the residents. The Webb Corporation would have to risk $2 million at first, but company executives liked the demographics.[86] More people with Social Security, pensions, and paid-up houses back home were living longer, healthier lives. Furthermore, many of the retirees' grown children were part of the migration to the Sunbelt.[87] And while post–World War II suburbs were certainly not marketed as age-segregated communities, developers often did have a certain typical buyer in mind, such as the returning veteran just starting his family and making his first move to the suburbs. Some of Webb's executives had probably lived in new suburbs where there was a fair amount of de facto age segregation, just not of the elderly variety.[88] Before taking the gamble on an age-segregated retirement community, Joe Ashton and Tom Breen made a visit to a state mental hospital in Phoenix to consult with Dr. Robert L. Beal. Beal liked the idea.[89]

Then there was the example of Youngtown, at that point the only officially age-restricted retirement community in the country. Breen's research included a survey asking Youngtown residents "what they liked and disliked about their community." Although it is unclear just what the survey results were, Breen's public thanking of Youngtown residents for their advice included the statement that Webb was beginning construction of a neighboring, age-restricted community of at least 1,600 homes that would include medical facilities and shopping.[90] While not totally absent in Youngtown, both shopping and medical services there were extremely meager. The Webb firm was well aware of the scarcity of recreational facilities in that earlier community along with its unimpressive infrastructure.

Webb executives "had been looking for something out of the ordinary, with a special 'eye' on what it termed the 'retirement market'" for four years.[91] Their research had produced conflicting results. As Tom Breen put it, "Turning our backs on 80% of the potential housing market was a big gamble." Webb's partner, L. C. Jacobson, was inclined toward the experiment. Joe Ashton would become "the prime mover" with the "initial drive" to make it happen.[92] Other executives were nervous about whether a sixty-five-year-old man could get a thirty-year mortgage or even if anyone would bother to come to the official opening of the community. As for Del Webb, who was willing to provide the financial backing, he was somewhat skeptical. As the community was being constructed in late 1959, he periodically called Tom Breen to ask him if "he was sure he knew what he was doing with that old folks home."[93] It is to the Del Webb Corporation's credit that, in spite of conflicting research, it took the gamble and made history in the process.

Implementing the Sun City Concept

Having made the decision to proceed with an age-restricted community, the next major step was land acquisition. Meanwhile, James G. Boswell II, president of the Boswell Company, which owned 20,000 acres west of Phoenix that it was using for growing cotton, had become concerned about whether the water table in the future would continue to support cotton cultivation. He had already sold about 480 acres to the developers of Youngtown for $1,500 per acre, but he wanted to sell more. Boswell had known R. H. Johnson, then senior vice president in Webb's Los Angeles office, for several years. They belonged to the same investment group and were members of the Annandale Country Club. Boswell approached Johnson on 5 February 1959 to inquire whether Webb would be interested in purchasing his ranchland near Phoenix. Johnson passed that inquiry on to Webb.[94] Breen and Silverstein produced their recommendations in their memo of 16 March 1959.

On March 25 Boswell reached an agreement with Webb Executive Vice President L. C. Jacobson and Senior Vice President Joe Ashton to form a joint venture. Boswell and Webb would each own half. Webb agreed to a twenty-year arrangement to purchase the 9,000-acre Marinette Ranch, the 998-acre Heading Ranch, and the 10,000-acre Santa Fe Ranch, all in close proximity to each other about thirteen miles west of Phoenix. The price was $15 million, with Boswell to release acreage to Webb only as needed over a twenty-year period.[95] That arrangement was very advantageous to Webb because Boswell agreed to pay rent equal to taxes and most assessments on the acreage until Webb needed it. As for Boswell, he could continue to grow cotton on most of the land, gradually releasing acreage for development. The arrangement also meant Webb could pay for the land in installments over time, and Boswell could work out a measured winding down of his agricultural activities.

The joint venture became the Del E. Webb Development Company, or DEVCO. Technically, Webb had formed the DEVCO subsidiary in 1953 to build housing projects. Originally, DEVCO built in various Arizona communities, from Tempe to Casa Grande to Yuma, and in Brawley, California. Tom Breen had been the sales manager for these. From 1954 to 1957, DEVCO built 650 homes for another developer in San Diego's Clairemont Estates, this time with Tom Breen as community development manager. Finally, DEVCO built 350 slab-on-grade homes in Cedar Rapids, Iowa, in 1956–57 but met with sales resistance due to the lack of basements and for being an out-of-state contractor. DEVCO exited that project.[96] When the DEVCO-Boswell agreement was finalized on 22 July 1959, Boswell's share was reduced to 49 percent, with Webb's at 51 percent, apparently for tax reasons.[97]

The Golf Course Community of Middle-Class Homes

Five days after reaching the initial agreement with Boswell in March 1959, L. C. Jacobson, who was Webb's partner and who owned 25 percent of the corporation, ordered that the master-planning process begin for "an active retirement community" on the Marinette Ranch land. The plan was to include "an entrance way," motel, shopping center, nine-hole golf course, "community facilities and the very lowest cost house buildable plus several upgraded plans." The Webb Corporation had previously used planner Ken Mitchell of Los Angeles and retained him to master-plan this retirement community. For some reason, Mitchell became enamored with the water well sites throughout the project and proposed a series of Venice, Italy–type canals. At that point, DEVCO decided to take a pass on Mitchell's design and do its own plan.

A unique feature of DEVCO's physical plan was the golf course curving through the community in order to maximize the number of house lots backing directly onto the course. Given the lack of early planning maps, it is impossible to know how similar the route of this meandering golf course was to Mitchell's series of canals. The actual route of the golf course was worked out by DEVCO and Sparling Engineering, a firm DEVCO hired to work on the community plan. A local golf professional, Milt Coggins, designed the traps, tees, greens, mounds, and a small lake.[98] Certainly a golf course was far more practical than canals in the desert. Furthermore, Webb and some of his executives were golfers. Emphasizing golf fit in with their projected theme of "active retirement." Since golf is an expensive sport associated with country clubs and high social status, its emphasis certainly put Sun City on a higher social plane than neighboring Youngtown, which lacked a golf course. However, DEVCO was not building for the country-club set but rather for those middle-class retirees who aspired to that lifestyle and so far had not been able to afford it.

DEVCO officials believed they were the first in the United States to offer a moderately priced home on a lot that bordered a golf course. Their lowest-priced model with a lot bordering the golf course was initially priced at $9,750.[99] That modest home consisted of a living room, eat-in kitchen with linoleum flooring and Formica countertops, pink tile in the only bathroom, two bedrooms, and a single-car carport.[100] For comparison purposes, in 1959 the National Housing Conference said that $10,990 was the median price in the United States for a three-bedroom tract home.[101] DEVCO may well have pioneered the concept of moderately priced, residential, golf course communities. Certainly developers before them had occasionally offered expensive homes backing onto golf courses. Furthermore, the typical golf course had fairways doubling back on each other rather than meandering through a community. The usual design of golf courses before the development of Sun City, Arizona, gave priority to the golfing experience. Webb's planners, on the other hand, gave priority to maximizing the number of golf course lots, which meant stretching out the length of the fairways. Fairway frontage could have a sale value approaching that of waterfront property.

Recent research dates golf course communities from the 1950s, at least in terms of "earnest development."[102] Following Sun City's successful opening in 1960, the golf course community quickly became popular in other retirement and resort developments. It spread rapidly around the country, with increasing numbers of developers stretching golf courses through their communities. Between 1972 and 1984, more than a thousand such courses were built.[103] The plan of Sun City did not include any public parks, green belts, or open spaces. It did include paved sidewalks along the streets but not exercise paths. The golf courses in Sun City would fulfill these functions of open space and exercise. DEVCO underscored the golf theme of its community by naming a number of streets after famous golf courses and golfers.[104] Examples are Cherry Hills Drive, Pebble Beach Drive, Augusta Drive, St. Andrews Drive, and Snead Drive. Webb did not lay claim to beginning this type of community planning. Instead, in his recollections about building that first golf course, future company president John Meeker recalled that DEVCO was the first in Paradise Valley to use "the golf course quick coupler sprinkler system [with] PVC plastic pipe laterals with asbestos cement pipe main lines." The company also imported mature palm trees from California to dress up the golf course and make the main entrance to the community more impressive.[105]

The golf course was important to the success of Sun City in a number of ways. Apparently, DEVCO designed the golf course first, then had the streets parallel that course, and repeated the process with additional golf courses as Sun City expanded. Again, streets paralleled the new golf courses. About the farthest anyone was from a fairway was around a half-dozen houses as the crow flies. The golf courses were the means whereby DEVCO brought green grass to the desert landscape, something appreciated by a number of migrants from the East and Midwest. Golf gave substance to Webb's "active retirement" concept. The sport was growing in popularity and could be played by all ages. With the invention of the electric golf cart in the 1940s, extensive walking was no longer necessary to participate.[106] On the public streets of Sun City, the golf cart soon became an alternative mode of transportation to the automobile. That practice would be adopted in other golf course communities as well. Because Webb chose to construct small, low-cost homes initially, the golf course did much to give Sun City a luxury feel or country-club image.[107] Webb had started out as a carpenter and had become an avid golfer. Had he remained a carpenter, Sun City was the kind of golf community that he could have afforded.

The golf image was heavily emphasized in DEVCO's advertising, whether local or national. For example, a May 1960 ad began, "The fairways wind all around . . . this remarkable community for active retirement." Among the photos of house models and the recreation center was one showing the newly planted palms on the fairways.[108] Most sports facilities, such as tennis courts, swimming pools, and shuffleboard courts, could be built indoors for year-round use, but the golf experience was impossible to duplicate satisfactorily indoors. In emphasizing golf, Webb was telling golf fanatics as well as people just plain sick of long, cold, snowy winters in colder sections of the country that a warm climate year round had its advantages.

DEVCO advanced the concept of the amenity-rich development with Sun City's emphasis on community centers, recreation and craft facilities, and meeting spaces for social gatherings and events. Back in 1959, they called these "facilities," not "amenities." DEVCO implemented the concept on a scale that went beyond the amenities at those Florida retiree trailer courts and condominiums. The company's first sales brochure contained a one-page essay, "The Philosophy of Retirement," that mentioned not only outdoor sports but also a Creative Activity Center that had the necessary equipment and space for a variety of crafts.[109]

As for social life, this essay told prospective buyers that they would not have to deal with their contemporaries living "clear across town" or with being "busy baby-sitting." Sun City was just for senior citizens. Written as if it was Del Webb himself speaking, the essay claimed that "while senior citizens look back on their years of raising a family as wonderful . . . they don't want to have to raise the neighbors' children with attendant skates and bikes and torn-up flower beds." Therefore, Webb "designed a community exclusively for senior citizens where the 'under-age' may visit, of course, but never take up permanent residence." The essay concluded with the claim that Del Webb had "completely changed the meaning of the word 'retirement.'" At Sun City, retirees enjoyed "days . . . over-flowing with interesting activity" and continual companionship with like-minded people. This Webb-scripted lifestyle added up to "active living" and "a heart-warming, soul-satisfying New 'Way-of-Life.'"[110]

The phrase "active living" would soon become "active retirement." In emphasizing activity and sociability, Webb sensed what gerontologists a generation later would affirm as contributing to the health and well-being of the elderly.[111] Back in 1960, Webb got a strong, positive response from the elderly themselves; many were grateful for the "new way of life" and new image of retirement Webb was promoting. As one person who flew from Chicago during a snowstorm and landed in Phoenix just in time to buy a home at Sun City's opening expressed it: "The sun was shining . . . birds singing and flowers blooming. I thought I'd died and gone to heaven."[112] From Sun City's beginning, DEVCO was not just selling the houses it had built; it was selling a lifestyle that it had scripted.

In planning Sun City, DEVCO went for what became known as the "village concept."[113] The idea was to avoid strip malls by using small shopping centers as neighborhood anchors. At the time it opened, Sun City was thirteen miles from Phoenix and not near any major community. DEVCO believed that to succeed, the community had to be self-sufficient. Webb would have a golf course and a community center with craft facilities ready to go on opening day. The firm would also build space for shops and a supermarket, but finding tenants without any current residents was not easy. Fortunately, Boswell was on the board of Safeway, a major supermarket chain in the West. Safeway agreed to take a gamble on Sun City in return for getting the "first right of refusal on future [supermarket] sites" in Sun City.[114] With Safeway arriving, some small businesses quickly opened. Del Webb was determined that potential buyers, jaded by promises accompanying the notorious land scams of the era for future golf courses and/or other amenities that often never materialized, would have no such worries when making a commitment to buy in Sun City. Before the first house was sold, the recreational amenities and essential businesses would be up and running. By using small shopping centers as neighborhood anchors, DEVCO was at the forefront of another planning trend.

One innovation that was just starting to appear in community planning but that Webb eschewed was the gated community. Anyone could move freely in and out of Sun City. Webb did erect a cement-block wall around the community, but it was to serve as a "barrier against hot, dry winds and the dust they carry." With no gate, there was no pretense of walled security. One could argue that the wall set Sun City residents apart, just as it marked the line between desert and town.[115]

However, that sense of apartness was more due to the psychological effect of special landscaping, an asset Webb favored. Webb provided for wide, grassy medians down the middle of major streets in Phase 1 of Sun City. These grassy medians defied the desert climate. In the twenty-first century, landscaping tends to feature plants native to the desert to conserve water, and plans are to redo the landscaping of these grassy medians, which have gotten rather scraggly due to maintenance problems. As for the first houses in Sun City, about 80 percent of the original owners opted for grass lawns as opposed to gravel. Ten years later, only about 10 percent of new home buyers were installing totally grass lawns.[116] The landscaping of Sun City reflected Webb's belief in the value of quality infrastructure, which immediately set Sun City apart from neighboring Youngtown. It also reflected an attitude common in 1960 that money and modern technology could do much to defy and remake something other than the natural environment.

DEVCO spent more than $1 million on infrastructure, the golf course, a recreation center, and a shopping center before actually selling a single house.[117] Unit 1 in Phase 1, with its nine-hole golf course, was scheduled for 400 dwellings, and the second nine holes of the golf course were in the planning stage by the end of 1959.[118] When Sun City opened in 1960, DEVCO did not have a complete plan for the community. Instead, the company expected it to "grow in accordance with the desires and tastes of the residents and prospective consumers."[119] The community was experimental. The executives were unsure what the response would be. They essentially adopted a wait-and-see attitude. They really could not predict, even after a very successful first year, that this age-restricted community, when it reached build-out in 1979, would number around 46,000 elderly people. In geographic terms, Sun City would be about a mile and a half wide and eight miles long, covering some 9,000 acres at completion.

In 1960, the company was moving into uncharted territory, with conflicting research and the one example of Youngtown, whose growth was slow. That may explain why an early, possibly 1963, DEVCO plan for Sun City included a residential area designated as a "working community" plus six elementary schools, a high school, and an industrial district with a modified gridiron street pattern.[120] The family section and the industrial district were never built. The formulation of this plan, though, indicated that the tremendous success of Sun City took even the Webb Corporation by surprise. That DEVCO took a $2 million gamble at the start also said something about the firm. Webb's partner, L. C. Jacobson, stated, "We tried to be a cut above anyone else in the business . . . and we wanted to maintain that."[121] DEVCO succeeded so well that Sun City became "a prototype for other American retirement communities" and an influential community in the history of city planning in the United States in general.[122]

Selling "Active Retirement"

Much of Sun City's success and influence was due to the very heavy advertising that accompanied its opening. DEVCO did not have a name for its retirement community until several weeks before its official opening. Thus, one national advertising ploy was a contest called "Name the Active Arizona Retirement Community." These ads appeared in national publications such as the *Saturday Evening Post* in November 1959. They mentioned the fifty-year age limit and affordable homes starting at $8,000 and listed such amenities as a "Championship golf course," an

"Olympic Size Swimming Pool . . . Shuffleboard—Horseshoes—Croquet—Archery," and a "Creative Activity Center" along with a community center. The pitch was "Win a New Way of Life," and the ad included directions on how to enter the contest.[123]

Webb hired a Chicago company, Reuben Donnelly, to handle the contest. The winner was to get a house in the new community. Donnelly staff and Webb staff were reviewing the entries on 8 December 1959 when Del Webb arrived at the agency. He looked at some of the choices, announced that he favored "Sun City," and left. Donnelly staff thought the choice was theirs to make. Webb executive L. C. Jacobson corrected them. Since five different people had submitted the "Sun City" name, Webb's staff contacted all of them, getting them to agree to a drawing as to who would get the house, valued at $8,750. Webb added a second prize of a golf course lot, and the remaining three would each receive a two-week vacation in Phoenix. The winning couple was from Eugene, Oregon, and simply sold the house, never moving to Sun City.[124] It is unclear if the officials who participated in the selection of the name realized that it was already the name of a community in Florida that was a result of land speculation there in the 1920s and also the name of a 1950s land speculation scheme in the Rio Grande Valley in Texas. However, the Webb Corporation did much to make the name Sun City its brand. By the 1990s, the company was using names like Sun City Vistoso, Sun City Hilton Head, and Sun City Huntley for its largest, full-service, master-planned, age-restricted, active adult communities.

An even more important part of the advertising process that dated from the beginning of the first Sun City was turning Del Webb the person into Del Webb the brand. When advertising for the first Sun City began in 1959, Del Webb was nationally known as the co-owner of the very successful New York Yankees. In addition, Webb had a prominent reputation as a contractor. The main reason for initially putting Del Webb's name on Sun City was to tell the public that Sun City was not the usual land scam. Del Webb was up front in standing by his community with his reputation. Hence, advertisers and public relations personnel were told that it was never to be just "Sun City" but always "Del Webb's Sun City."[125] The first sales brochures featured Webb's photograph along with this quote: "Concrete, steel and lumber can make buildings, but people make the community. Together we can realize a Way-of-Life unprecedented in America." The quote continued to be used in sales literature even at the time of Webb's death in 1974.[126] Developers of age-restricted, active adult communities in the twenty-first century still occasionally use the phrase "way of life" or "new way of life."

Advertising tended to personalize Del Webb's involvement in the community as well. Future Webb president John Meeker recalled that many Sun City residents thought of Webb as personally building their homes and that he "would personally take care of any problems." Actually, Webb in practice distanced himself from Sun City management, leaving most of the decision making to the DEVCO staff.[127] Except for public appearances connected with the opening of various facilities, Webb spent little time in the community. In fact, his public relations director for Sun City recalled that when Webb was in the community, he needed to have a staff member with him so he would not get lost. Some residents said they saw Webb on the golf course, but it was probably another DEVCO executive.[128] In 1961, when Webb spoke to the Women's Club in Sun City's first recreation center, the local newspaper headline, "Love at First Sight," captured the audience's reaction to him. Webb claimed to be somewhat embarrassed by the attention he received when in Sun City; still, he was an ardent clipper of newspaper stories about himself, finding some that even his clipping service missed.[129] Much as he might profess shyness and embarrassment, he was definitely willing to use himself to promote Sun City. In the twenty-first century, Pulte, which owns the Del Webb brand name, continues to use "Del Webb" to denote its age-restricted, active adult communities.

Webb had the resources for a very expensive and extensive early advertising campaign to sell the country on the idea of "active retirement." The firm used full-page ads in color in such magazines as *Life, Look, Saturday Evening Post, Holiday,* and *Ladies Home Journal.*[130] Webb's reward for advertising in *McCall's* was to receive a special certificate from its Congress on Better Living in July 1960.[131]

The themes of these 1960 ads stressed the "Active Retirement" lifestyle, not the actual houses. What the company was selling was a "Unique way-of-life" featuring "Country Club Living" with "fairways," a "Club House and Riviera-Size Swimming Pool," and "Activities unlimited," all with "Small Town Friendliness and Freedom with Big City Convenience." One ad noted that since Sun City had opened four and a half months earlier, 1,600 people "from 31 States (and 3 Foreign Countries)" had bought homes in the community.[132] The advertising presented an image of the Sun City retiree as a person to be envied. Historian John Findlay looked at a number of ads in the early 1960s and concluded that their message was that "the elderly would spend the best years of their lives in Sun City," both in terms of "greater individual fulfillment and a more supportive environment that would actually prolong life."[133] One early ad featured a photograph of three men in the woodworking shop and a story about a wife who complained that her retired husband was under foot all the time. However, with their move to Sun City, the husband now had a life beyond sitting at home, and "she belongs to a dozen clubs."[134] It may be only a slight exaggeration to note that "the opening line of every advertisement included the word 'active.'"[135]

An early (and ongoing) way to get prospective buyers out to look at the model homes was to offer entertainment, which was also available to residents of Sun City. An ad on 31 January 1960 mentioned a "Special Gem and Mineral Showing" at Sun City while also indicating that the cheapest house price had risen to $8,500. An ad dated 13 March 1960 announced a free synchronized-swimming exhibition and vintage auto display at Sun City with attendees encouraged to then tour "This Remarkable Community for Active Retirement."[136] A week later, an ad touted a free art show complete with complimentary pencil sketches of attendees. A June 1960 ad mentioned a free organ recital "in the Air-Conditioned Community Center Club House."[137] By this time, the cheapest house had increased in price to $8,750.[138] While most of the dwellings were single-family, detached houses, some were condominium apartments. The ad featuring these asked, "Weary of Weed-Pulling . . . Lawn Care . . . Fence-Mending . . . and Home Maintenance?"[139] Promoting "active retirement" and a "way of life" over the actual homes, which were quite simple and conventional, was the key to Del Webb's early success with Sun City.

Webb's extensive advertising paid dividends when reporters for several magazines and newspapers wrote stories on Sun City. During its first and second years, Sun City's corporate sponsors arranged for quick fly-in trips for reporters from around the United States. During the second trip, seventy reporters got to compete with Del Webb in hole-in-one and putting contests. They also heard Tom Breen claim that the firm owned or controlled 30,000 acres in the area. In 1961, Breen predicted "a potential Sun City population of 150,000."[140] Comedians made some good-natured references to the community on national television. Webb himself made the cover of the 3 August 1962 issue of *Time*. In 1965, *The New Yorker* ran a forty-page story on Sun City. Webb generated additional publicity for the community when Sun City sponsored a car at the NASCAR races in Daytona Beach.[141] Within a couple of years, "Del Webb's Sun City" and "active retirement" had become household phrases.

The best known of the advertising jingles or songs promoting Sun City revolved around the theme of active retirement. Written by Robert Garland of the Garland Advertising Agency, it began: "Wake up and live in Sun City For an active way of life."[142] The company used this jingle in radio advertising and on a record that it distributed at the 1961 grand opening of Sun City's second recreation center, with its second nine holes of golf and 1961 model homes.[143]

Presumably, all of this advertising and publicity had a major impact on how Americans perceived retirement and retirees, even with those individuals who had no interest in relocating in their retirement. The image of Grandpa in a rocking chair had become Grandpa on the golf course. Sun City was presented as "the reward for a life time of hard work, meetings, and schedules." It became "the location in which retirement fantasies would be fulfilled. At the same time, it established what those fantasies would be."[144]

The Official Opening of Sun City

In spite of all the preliminary publicity, the tremendous response to the official opening of Sun City on New Year's Day 1960 took Webb executives by surprise. During construction in 1959, Del Webb had repeatedly called Tom Breen to ask, "Do you know what you're doing out there?" After doing a final check on the recreation facilities, shops, and five furnished model homes the day before the opening, Breen and other top executives went out to relax. As each silently wondered if anyone would come to the opening the next day, Owen Childress, who later became the chief financial officer for DEVCO, finally voiced his worries, exclaiming, "How am I going to get a 30-year mortgage on a guy who is 65 years old!"[145]

Their anticipated target number of opening-day visitors was 10,000. When 100,000 turned up on the three-day opening weekend beginning 1 January 1960, they were unprepared. However, the story that such a huge traffic jam developed on Grand Avenue leading to the entrance at 107th that it was necessary to drive the guest of honor, Del Webb, over irrigation ditches and cotton fields was mere legend. Webb's business diary proved that he spent Sun City's official opening in Las Vegas, returning to Phoenix nine days later.[146]

It was fact that the firm did not have enough contract forms for buyers to sign. Eventually, someone ran to a local store to buy a receipt book so buyers who put down $500 on homes would have something to take with them. DEVCO sold 237 houses that first weekend and more than 400 by the end of the first month.[147] The homes came with Frigidaire appliances. DEVCO's order to Frigidaire for those appliances indicated the firm only expected to complete around 200 houses its first year. Instead, it sold 1,301 houses.[148] The first 400 homes was the entire number planned for Unit 1, so the firm quickly put together Unit 2 with 675 homes. Originally, its three-year projection was 1,700 homes, but it had sold 2,000 homes by the end of its first year. That kind of success added to the national attention that came Sun City's way. In 1960, the largest number of buyers, 172, came from Arizona, and it and California, Illinois, Colorado, and Minnesota constituted the top five states of origin. Some of the initial buying frenzy was the result of investment buying when buyers bought two or more homes at once.[149]

Early Residents Buy into the "Active Retirement" Image

The most significant attraction of Sun City for buyers was the image it projected of "active retirement." One satisfied resident wrote a letter to Del Webb thanking him for changing the couple's "way of life." They had escaped the cold winters and icy roads of Michigan for "a lovely home in an ideal climate. . . . The country club atmosphere [was] an additional bonus." She and her husband were "in the retirement class, but [were] actually more active . . . than ever before." Her husband enjoyed "his daily round of golf." He square danced, played bridge, and provided "keen competition on the shuffleboard court." The wife praised Webb's activity coordinator for providing them "with a round of entertaining events" that helped them feel welcome in their new community, and she praised Webb's "warm, friendly" staff.[150] Webb himself remarked, "When some Sun City resident, perhaps a total stranger, buttonholes me on a visit to say that life in Sun City has made his or her retirement years well worth living . . . well, to me, that says it all."[151] By redefining retirement as "active," it was as if Webb had given the retirees their lives back.

Some observers thought that usually "husbands were more enthusiastic about" moving to Sun City than their wives. Husbands might channel their energies into golf, but some eventually got bored with it and had difficulty finding other hobbies. On the other hand, wives in the early 1960s typically had not had careers from which they had just retired and may have adjusted better. Sun City was a new community, and early residents, both male and female, thought of themselves as "pioneers." It could be a very satisfying experience to get in on the ground floor organizing basic services, such as a church, a charity, and Sun City Civic Association.[152]

With home prices starting at $8,500, Webb had made that active, country-club lifestyle affordable. Low property taxes were also part of the affordability appeal. A retired community-planning consultant who moved to Sun City remarked, "This was about the only place where you could buy a house and become a member of a golf or tennis club. . . . There were opportunities you never had all your life."[153] Other developers were promising plenty of amenities, but in 1960 many of those promises had not materialized. As another early Sun City resident recalled, "We'd been around the country, looking. Every place told us what they were going to have. You'd go back in a year, and still they didn't have it. But this was all here."[154] Those with whom they shared the amenities, or "facilities," were "racially and economically homogeneous,"[155] and as a longtime resident put it, "They had all come from somewhere else and they had that in common. They bonded."[156]

Youngtown aside, an aspect unique to Sun City was DEVCO's requirements that the homes be occupied by at least one person over the age of fifty and that no one under age twenty be allowed as a permanent resident.[157] The firm established this policy prior to advertising the community. However, its legal counsel advised against incorporating those age restrictions into the property deeds, partly because of enforcement problems.[158] Predictably, advertising produced expectations that led to some strong social pressure generated by residents amounting to fairly effective enforcement when two families with underage children moved to Sun City.

Because Sun City was a relatively isolated community, DEVCO executives found it desirable to have certain essential people there as residents, specifically a medical doctor and an air conditioner repairman. Therefore, DEVCO had made two exceptions to its policy of no children as permanent residents. One was in selling a home to an air conditioner repairman with two small children. He wanted to live in Sun City to more easily handle emergency calls. The firm made its second exception to get a doctor to locate in the community. The doctor had a grandson permanently living with him.

As one of the DEVCO executives recalled, when the neighbors saw the school bus stop to pick up the children, "all hell broke loose." Sun City residents threatened both the bus driver and the children. These people were living in the desert, but they drove the air conditioner repairman out of town. However, the ringleaders of the anti-children campaign called off their verbal attacks on the doctor's grandson after the wife of one of them suffered a heart attack. The doctor saved her. A DEVCO executive regarded the anti-children campaign as "an indication of the strong attitude of older people toward children." Seniors were happy to have children come for a visit "and just as happy to see them leave."[159] In banning children as permanent residents along with restricting buyers to a minimum age of fifty, Webb had dared to go against the advice of leading sociologists. The firm's instincts, based on some unprofessional interviewing, had proven correct, at least for a significant segment of the retiree population.

Given the tremendous success of the opening of Sun City, DEVCO immediately began to plan for expansion outside of Arizona. Webb was already advertising nationally. Why not add Sun City communities in the popular retirement states of Florida and California? By standardizing these communities, using the same house plans and materials, the same designs for recreation centers and motels, and the same national ads, the firm could achieve additional economies of scale while expanding. Interested persons seeing the ads could then choose which location most appealed to them and request further information on that community. Developing standardized retirement communities in different locations simultaneously was another Webb innovation and an important part of Del Webb's initial concept of the affordable, active retirement community. Preliminary land acquisition and planning for these communities got under way the same year Sun City, Arizona, officially opened. Also that year, the parent company of DEVCO, the Del E. Webb Corporation, went public with its initial stock offering on the NASDAQ exchange.[160]

Additional Sun Cities Soon Open

The first of Webb's retirement community projects outside Sun City, Arizona, was Kern City, near Bakersfield, California. The Kern City project was something of a flop. As to why Webb got involved with it when no marketing survey had been done, one of his executives said Webb may have done it as a favor to George Montgomery, head of the Kern County Land Company. The latter company was involved in a major Santa Monica urban renewal project. Webb may have negotiated a construction contract in connection with the Santa Monica effort as part of the Kern City project. In any case, Webb and Montgomery formed a joint venture, the Stockdale Development Corporation, to build Kern City. The project encompassed 6,000 acres. Webb used the same people who had planned Sun City, and the joint venture built six single-family model homes and two garden apartments ranging in price from $10,650 to $17,550, a nine-hole golf course, recreation center, and small shopping center. Even after Webb abandoned trying to market Kern City for retirees and opened the development to conventional housing, it still failed to attract many buyers. John Meeker, soon to become president of DEVCO, said Kern City failed "because most Californians have a low opinion of Bakersfield with its oil refinery odor, Thule fog and high summer time heat." Kern City did appear in some Sun City ads and brochures along with other Sun Cities in the early 1960s. By 1965, when Webb sold his interest to Montgomery's company, buyers had purchased only 314 homes, of which 214 were for retirement.[161]

The remaining two communities, one each in Florida and California, were both initially called "Sun City." Both opened in 1962. Copying what he was doing in Sun City, Arizona, the California and Florida Sun Cities used the same house plans, the same recreation center plans, the same motel plans, and even some of the same street names. The communities featured golf courses winding through them to maximize the number of house lots backing onto the fairways. The natural environments of all three communities varied widely, from desert in Arizona to wetland in Florida to semi-arid valley in California. Nevertheless, in all three communities, Webb built the same wide, grassy medians studded with palm trees down the main thoroughfares. Webb used manmade lakes in the Florida and Arizona Sun Cities. It was as if, with the exception of temperature, he could defy local environmental conditions and topography with modern construction and earth-moving equipment. He also standardized the product. No regional variation existed in the design of the small, ranch-style homes and condominium apartments or single-level townhouses and duplexes in these developments. One could drive down Pebble Beach Boulevard or Cherry Hills Drive, swim in the same angular pool, stay at the same Kings Inn, and choose from among the same house models in all three Sun Cities—Arizona, Florida, and California.

Webb envisioned large communities and wanted a lot of land, which led to some real regrets in Florida. When Webb officials scouted out large blocks of land for sale in Florida, they did consider a 5,000-acre site in Sarasota that had water access to the Gulf of Mexico and already possessed some infrastructure and amenities. Again, without "any in depth site location marketing research," they rejected that site in favor of a 12,000-acre, swampy site inland, about midway between Tampa and Sarasota, probably because of the desire for more land. DEVCO executive John Meeker recalled the attitude that "the Sun City name would be enough to sell a project so long as it was located in the Sunbelt states of Arizona, Florida and California."[162]

Webb paid $8,950,000 to the Universal Marion Corporation in staggered payments for the inland site. The model home park at Sun City, later called Sun City Center, Florida, opened in January 1962. The reason for the name change was that the remnants of a 1920s town development scheme, Sun City, still existed. It even shared the same zip code as Del Webb's Sun City. The post office would not allow "Del Webb's Sun City" as a location, so Webb was forced to use a different community name. Hence, the name of Webb's active adult development in Florida became Sun City Center.[163] Sales were slow.[164] An early 1960s plan reminiscent of one for Sun City, Arizona, and published in the nearby Ruskin, Florida, newspaper, indicated a possible intent to incorporate housing for all generations with school and industrial sites, but Webb never implemented it.[165] By 1970, Webb had developed only 1,400 acres and sold 1,550 homes. At that point, Webb reconveyed all unreleased land back to Universal Marion Corporation. In 1972, Webb sold the remainder of his company's interests in Sun City Center to the Walter-Gould Corporation. A few years later, that corporation filed for bankruptcy. It is unclear if the Webb Corporation ever received full payment from Walter-Gould.[166] Among the reasons for the failure of Webb at Sun City Center, another developer suggested that Webb erred in placing the community between two major highways but not near neither. Consequently, the model home park and shopping center were not built "where people could see them."[167] Interestingly, the developer of Sun City Center in 2007, WCI Communities, had a model home park right off Interstate 75, although it was a bit of a drive into the heart of the community. That interstate was not there in Webb's day.

For his third Sun City, Webb chose a 14,000-acre site in the semi-arid Perris Valley, about twenty miles south of Riverside, California. The firm began selling houses there a few months after opening its Florida Sun City in 1962. Initially, sales were brisk, with nearly 1,200 homes sold in the community's first nine months.[168] Home prices were similar to those in the other Sun Cities, with the smallest two-bedroom, one-bath, ranch-style house selling for $11,950.[169] Sales were also strong the following year, but then a seven-month carpenters strike led hundreds of buyers to cancel their purchase contracts. Meanwhile, a rival retirement community, Rancho Bernardo, opened near San Diego. In addition, the costs associated with carrying undeveloped land at Sun City, California, especially property taxes, were substantial. Sales settled down to less than 200 homes per year. As early as 1964, Webb began selling off land parcels at the California Sun City. The Webb Corporation completed its exit when it sold its remaining holdings to the Presley Development Corporation of California around 1970.[170]

One can cite a number of other reasons for Webb's disappointment with the pace of sales in these communities and his decision to get out of both at about the same time. The home office was in Phoenix, which may be why that Sun City got priority. Also, around 1970, DEVCO was approaching build-out on Phase 1 of Sun City, Arizona, and facing the prospect of moving across Grand Avenue for Phase 2, with major expenditures needed for infrastructure, a recreation center, and another golf course before homes could be sold there. Then, too, there were individual circumstances at each of the Sun Cities. One thing they had in common, though, was an isolated location, a byproduct of Webb's desire to purchase at least 10,000 acres. To get that much contiguous land at a reasonable price, he did have to go far out of urban areas. Sun City Center was about twenty miles from both Tampa and Sarasota. Sun City, California, was more than twenty miles from Riverside, the nearest major community. While Sun City, Arizona, was thirteen miles from Phoenix, the expansion of Phoenix was headed in its direction. Not so with Tampa, Sarasota, or Riverside. Neither the Florida nor California Sun City was near a major city. Thus, Webb's concept of a minimum of

10,000 acres may have been the major flaw in the California and Florida communities. As relatively small developments, they would have been better located closer to cities.

While other developers took over both communities, neither has flourished anywhere near the extent of the original Sun City. Part of the reason has to do with Del Webb's concept of how to implement an active retirement community. Recreation centers formed the nucleus of each neighborhood in Sun City, Arizona. DEVCO stayed with that community until it reached build-out in 1979. As it built each new phase, it continued to add recreation centers, golf courses, and shopping areas. Each year it added new house models while carefully watching the market for trends in their design. For residents at Sun City, Arizona, watching the continual expansion of their community reinforced their sense that they had picked a winner. Given Webb's phenomenal success at the original Sun City, other developers quickly began to build what eventually amounted to hundreds of retirement communities.[171] However, more so than the others, Webb set the standard for success with his first Sun City.

Del Webb never saw the 1979 completion of his most significant creation, Sun City, Arizona. During the construction of Phase 2, he was diagnosed with prostate cancer, received conflicting recommendations with respect to surgery, and so decided against an operation. Even though Webb was a nonsmoker, the cancer then spread to his right lung. The Mayo Clinic removed that tumor in March 1974. Four months later, Webb returned for exploratory surgery and died following it.[172] He was seventy-four. He left behind a talented group of executives, such as John Meeker and Fred Kuentz, who not only carried Sun City, Arizona, to completion but subsequently launched a series of other active adult, age-restricted communities. In addition, Del Webb left behind the "Del Webb" brand name, which he had made into a valuable asset. It was one of the reasons Pulte Homes bought the corporation in 2001. Pulte routinely puts the "Del Webb" label on its active adult, age-restricted communities. Decades after Webb's death, the "Del Webb" brand name is still regarded as the leader in the retirement community business. Finally, Webb left most of his personal fortune to the Del E. Webb Foundation, which emphasizes medical research.[173]

Del Webb was the most influential individual in shaping American attitudes toward the elderly with his concept of "active retirement" and his development of a new urban form, the amenity-rich, active adult, age-restricted retirement community that bans children as permanent residents. He succeeded because he had the ability to assemble a creative staff and the instinct to back their plans with his money and business resources, even when years of research had produced conflicting results. He essentially took the amenity-rich retiree trailer courts of Florida, combined them with Youngtown's policy of selling only to those of a minimum age, and then very heavily and nationally advertised the concept of "active retirement" communities. Retirees responded for a variety of reasons, one being that Webb's image of the active retiree playing year-round golf, exploring new interests, and socializing with his peers was such an appealing one. Up to around 1960, most people pictured retirees as sitting at home bored and with nothing to do. Webb made retirement attractive, with its affordable country-club lifestyle. Retirement was something to anticipate. Even among the vast majority of retirees who chose not to relocate, the image of the retiree had changed. There were some retirees who felt that Webb had given them their lives back. With Sun City, Arizona, Webb was a social engineer, and he had changed the social landscape of America. Among developers, Webb had many imitators, but one, Ross Cortese, who created the Leisure World concept, was far more than just an imitator of Webb.

Ross Cortese's
"Leisure World" Concept

3

At the start of the 1960s, an employee in FHA's cooperative housing program rushed into his boss's office to inform him that "some lunatics on the West Coast were thinking of using our program to isolate thousands of senior citizens by actually walling them up in a slum in Seal Beach."[1] That was an unflattering reference to Ross Cortese's pioneering efforts with relatively compact, gated communities. When Cortese opened his first Leisure World the year after Webb opened Sun City, Cortese said his concept was "to supply the basic needs of life for people aged 52 or older, create a serene atmosphere of beauty, provide security, recreation and religious facilities . . . then leave the living to the individual."[2]

Cortese was an innovator, not just an imitator of Del Webb. Certainly the two had a lot in common. They were aware of and somewhat influenced by each other. However, Cortese seems to have arrived at his concept of the ideal age-restricted, active adult community on his own. How did he do it? In California, home of the first two Leisure Worlds, Cortese became better known than Del Webb. And unlike Webb in the 1960s, Cortese built retirement communities on the East Coast. While his Leisure Worlds reinforced the "active retirement" image that Webb was promoting, Cortese spotted some of Webb's mistakes and avoided them. Just who was Ross Cortese? What innovations did he bring to city planning in general and to retirement communities in particular? Finally, what were Cortese's specific contributions to changing attitudes toward and images of the elderly?

Ross Cortese's Background

Cortese was a much more private individual than Del Webb. Cortese shunned the limelight and rarely gave interviews. He did not function to the degree that Del Webb did as a public spokesman and promoter of his communities, nor did he succeed in turning his personal name or the name of his company, Rossmoor, into a brand like Webb did, although the name Leisure World does function as a brand name somewhat like Sun City. Because of the kind of person he was, not as much is publicly known about Ross Cortese compared to Del Webb. No book-length biographies exist about him. Thus, it is harder to tell his story with much detail.

In the twentieth century, a college degree became almost mandatory for success, but neither Webb nor Cortese even graduated from high school. Cortese was a generation younger than Webb. Instead of his parents and grandparents having a prominent place in the community, Ross Cortese was the son of an Italian immigrant, Salvador Cortese, and his wife, Frances.[3] He was born on 19 November 1916 in East Palestine, Ohio. His family, which included three sisters and a brother, moved to Glendale, California, near Los Angeles, where Ross's father had a push cart from which he peddled fruits and vegetables.[4] During the Great Depression, it was a real struggle to just subsist. To help the family make ends meet, Ross dropped out of Glendale's Hoover High School in his sophomore year to peddle fruits and vegetables. He was seventeen. A Glendale school official recalled how Ross went door to door with his small truck.[5] Years later as a very successful builder, Cortese admitted to being "kind of embarrassed" by his lack of formal education. He explained to a Los Angeles Times reporter, "I'm afraid that I won't say quite the right thing in the way I want to say it." One result of this embarrassment over his lack of educational credentials was his practice of distancing himself from outsiders.[6]

His daughter Heidi Cortese described him while he was a teenager as "the breadwinner of the family." She recalled his generosity. At one point, instead of spending some of his meager earnings on himself, he bought dolls for his sisters. As she expressed it, her father "had a heart the size of the universe; [he] was the most tender hearted person I ever knew." Apparently, he retained that sense of personal generosity as a successful builder. Heidi Cortese told how people would come up to her and "explain that when they were late on a [house] payment, mysteriously it was made for them. Or when a dog would die, a new puppy would anonymously appear." Her father had known real poverty growing up and, in Heidi's eyes, his generosity was remarkable. His impoverished youth stayed with him in other ways as well. For example, when his accountant told Ross Cortese that he owed a huge amount in taxes, Heidi said he responded, "Imagine, a poor fruit farmer being able to afford to pay all those taxes! What a gift."[7]

Ross Cortese soon moved from peddling produce to selling real estate. One of his produce customers, Ben Weingard, wanted to sell a run-down house near the Los Angeles working-class suburb of Compton. Cortese agreed to fix up the house so it would be marketable. Specifically, he painted, repaired, and landscaped the property. Weingard was sufficiently impressed with the transformation Cortese had wrought to lend him the money to buy some income property in Culver City.[8] In 1939, Cortese paid $400 for two vacant lots, then began building houses himself, selling them at a profit.[9] He would be in a position to benefit from the postwar housing boom in the Los Angeles area.

Prior to developing his Leisure World communities, Cortese acquired substantial experience as a builder of houses in various Los Angeles suburban tract developments, including the largest tract development in the United States—Lakewood, California. Developed at about the same time as the better-known Levittown in New York, Lakewood within a few years replaced bean fields with 20,000 houses using only a couple of models. Cortese's firm built 200 of these homes. Another contractor, Murray Ward, was a subdivision chief who built 4,000 homes in Lakewood. In 1952, Ward joined Cortese's firm. Together, they built another 750 homes in Lakewood plus 700 in Anaheim. When Cortese embarked on his experiment building Rossmoor, a walled and gated tract subdivision in 1957, Ward was there. At the time Cortese was building his California Leisure World communities in the early and mid-1960s, Ward had the title of executive vice president in charge of construction at Cortese's company, then called the Rossmoor Corporation.[10]

Part of Cortese's success was due to his ability "to surround himself with experts in all fields: land evaluators, architects, builders." He had a reputation as "a hard taskmaster with a low boiling point but he paid top dollar."[11] His "low boiling point" at times erupted into a "legendary temper" that he occasionally directed at buyers who found fault with his homes, but he did not see his temper as a major problem. While Cortese admitted to being disturbed by occasional buyer hostility, his attitude was, "That's life."[12] He could lose his temper with business associates, too. Tracy Strevey, academic vice president at the University of Southern California, recalled being on an advisory board for the Rossmoor Corporation. At a meeting of that board in Cortese's corporate headquarters, Strevey witnessed Cortese explode at someone on one occasion. While Cortese's "explosion" did clarify things and move the meeting forward, Strevey concluded that Cortese had a "short fuse."[13]

Other aspects of Cortese's character contributed to his success. He was creative, tenacious, a good salesman, a tough negotiator, and a person who having once agreed to something stuck with it. His creativity came through when in 1957 he pioneered the walled and gated community concept for a development of relatively modest homes. Several years later, Cortese applied that concept to his Leisure World retirement communities. He demonstrated his tenacity numerous times when he encountered major obstacles, such as no nearby water and sewage facilities for Leisure World Laguna Hills. He built those himself.[14] His head civil engineer, Alton "Jack" Fowler, recalled that "Cortese moved and thought fast and was a super salesman."[15] Al Hanson, a former president of the Golden Rain Foundation, which was involved in managing Leisure World communities, recalled that Cortese fought hard in negotiations, "but once he made an agreement, he'd stick to it." He also did high-quality work.[16]

With respect to his employees, he was a "stickler for loyalty."[17] Another aspect of how he treated his employees, though, was evident when he invited all those who had worked on his Seal Beach Leisure World to a sit-down dinner with prime rib at the newly completed Clubhouse One in Laguna Hills on Christmas Eve 1963.[18] Like Webb, Cortese had some men in key positions in the 1960s who had been with him from the early days of his firm. In writing about his employees, Cortese called them "a team that has learned to function as smoothly and efficiently as a machine. The difference, though, is this big machine has always been more of a family."[19] Like Webb, he stressed loyalty and job longevity among his employees and seems to have regarded them almost like family. Rossmoor Corporation would build a number of Leisure Worlds plus other housing developments. By 1982, his company had built more than 50,000 housing units, of which about half were in the Leisure World communities.[20]

Cortese won several housing awards in the early 1960s as his first Leisure World reached completion. They included Builder of the Year in 1963 from the National Association of Home Builders and *House and Home Magazine*'s Award of Merit in 1964. Cortese attributed his success to "work."[21] To do what he did, he needed the confidence of banks in order to borrow money and the confidence of other businessmen to enter into joint ventures. His reputation was one of "straightforward business dealings,"[22] another key to his success.

Cortese's Personal Life

Cortese's interest in real estate led to his meeting his first wife, Alona Marlowe. Nearly eight years older than Ross, she was born in St. Cloud, Minnesota, on 21 July 1908 with the name Ilona L. Goetten.[23] As a youngster, she enjoyed the Minnesota outdoors, fishing, duck hunting, and ice skating. When she was a teenager, her family moved to the Los Angeles area, where the youngsters attended Hollywood High School. All got jobs in the motion picture industry. The most successful was her sister, June Marlowe, who played opposite such famous actors as John Barrymore Jr., Laurel and Hardy, and Jackie Cooper and was featured in *The Little Rascals* films. Her brother Louis Marlowe was a film and early television commercial director, working with such stars as Ronald Reagan, Loretta Young, and Jean Harlowe. Armour Goetten, another brother, became a set designer who worked on such television shows as *Green Acres* and *Petticoat Junction*. Gerald, her youngest brother, for a time had a contract with MGM. Since acting jobs could be sporadic, Alona decided to take an evening course in real estate at Hollywood High School. That was how she met her future husband, Ross W. Cortese. She obtained a license as a real estate broker. Her 1948 marriage to Cortese lasted for decades and produced one child, Heidi, born in 1953, before ending in divorce.[24]

Cortese also had a daughter, Jade (Hillary Jade), as a result of a seven-year affair with his company's interior decorator, Ruth Elaine Hall. The affair began in the late 1950s. Jade was born in 1961. According to Bill March, who began working for Cortese in 1964, Jade's existence was fairly common knowledge among company employees. In the 1970s and 1980s, when Jade was in high school, Cortese gave her "a monthly allowance of about $500." During the 1980s, Jade Pedersen met Heidi Cortese. The latter offered "to set up a trust that gave Pedersen up to $3,000 a month" on the condition that Jade Pedersen not have contact with her father. Pedersen agreed, "received money for a couple years," then subsequently regretted her choice. When Ross Cortese died in 1991, he stated in his will, "I have no other living or deceased children" than Heidi Cortese. His heirs were his daughter, Heidi; his ex-wife and

Heidi's mother, Alona; and his second wife, Eloise Cortese. Furthermore, almost all of his assets were placed into trusts that excluded Jade Pedersen. Nevertheless, Jade Pedersen, then with three children of her own and married to her second husband, attending school full time, and with her mother suffering from emphysema and cancer, decided to sue for a portion of his estate. However, she did not prevail before the Orange County, California, Superior Court in September 1993. She described her father as "eccentric" and "tough" and said she was "just tired of being second class."[25]

Ross Cortese was a strong Catholic. It was possible that his Catholicism was a factor in his decision not to divorce Alona at the time of Jade's birth. Also, had he divorced her when he was about to open his first Leisure World, at Seal Beach, it is possible that he would not have had the financial or perhaps even psychological resources to embark on Leisure World Laguna Hills and the other Leisure Worlds that followed.

Alona Cortese's family-provided obituary describes her as the "co-developer of Leisure World." In the Los Angeles area, she and her husband developed apartments and built Marlowe Homes before embarking in 1957 on the innovative gated community, the "Walled City of Rossmoor." Her obituary notes that "Rossmoor was the first housing tract in the nation to be wholly surrounded by walls and the first to so strongly emphasize security. The Corteses and the community were honored at the 1964 World's Fair in New York for the creativity of the development."[26] The obituary refers to Alona as "a successful female in the then male dominated construction industry," but it does not specify just what Alona's contributions were other than that she joined her husband in applying the walled and gated community concept to retirement communities "featuring a country club way of life."[27] These were the Leisure World communities in California, Arizona, Florida, New Jersey, Maryland, and Virginia. As she was knowledgeable about real estate, perhaps her husband listened to her ideas or bounced some of his ideas off her or both. It is reasonable to assume that she gave him the encouragement or reinforcement to take some very creative risks in anticipation of positive outcomes. In 2000, *Builder Magazine* included Alona Cortese and her deceased ex-husband on its list of "the 100 most influential persons in the real estate industry for the 20th century."[28]

On her own, Alona Cortese's business interests and skills also became apparent. She became so knowledgeable about stocks and bonds that the Pasadena office of Dean Witter Reynolds used her to advise recently widowed and divorced women. She earned the respect of bankers at the United California Bank and later, Wells Fargo, with her investment skills. Her concern for seniors who could not afford legal representation led her to endow Chapman University law school's Alona Cortese Elder Law Center. That organization provided free legal representation for needy seniors and watched out for exploitation of the elderly. She was also a strong Catholic. Cardinal Roger Mahoney presided over "a private family ceremony" marking her death and interment at the Cathedral of Our Lady of the Angels Mausoleum.[29] She never remarried.

In 1972, when asked what his "most interesting experience" was at Leisure World Laguna Hills, Ross Cortese mentioned seeing the community grow and seeing the churches expand.[30] The comment reflected Cortese's strong religious values. Those values along with the private nature of his personality probably contributed to his desire to keep his divorce as discreet as possible. He apparently gave Alona and their daughter, Heidi, a good financial settlement, and Heidi became his primary heir. Cortese then married Eloise. In the mid-1990s, Eloise Cortese appeared at a meeting of the Leisure World Historical Society of Seal Beach, the first of the Leisure World communities. The vice president of that group in 2006, Tom Barratt, recalled Eloise as an attractive woman who appeared to be around seventy in the mid-1990s.[31] The main relative representing Ross Cortese following his death, however, was his daughter Heidi Cortese. While sources do not give the date of Ross and Alona Cortese's divorce, it may have been in the early 1980s, when Ross Cortese chose to liquidate his company. No major creativity followed. In fact, Ross Cortese's most creative years were the late 1950s and the 1960s, indicating that Alona Cortese indeed may have played an important role in his accomplishments. One would like to know more.

Possibly in part because of his immigrant father, his impoverished childhood, his failure to earn even a high school diploma, and then his divorce, daughter out of wedlock, and remarriage, Ross Cortese never seemed as comfortable with himself in public as was Del Webb. Yet, except for not having an immigrant father and being childless, Webb had experienced all those circumstances as well. Heidi Cortese remembered her father saying such things as, "If you want to be successful, you cannot be self-conscious." She said he "was adamant about 'leaving room for mistakes, believing in oneself, and being incredibly observant.

When life goes down, you must adjust to the circumstances.'"[32] Given the cyclical nature of the construction business, both Webb and Cortese no doubt felt the need to be cautious, but that did not stop either from engaging in cutting-edge, very expensive, high-risk experiments. Whether it was a middle-class gated community or a middle-class golf course community, both developers had an instinctual sense of what would appeal to the public. As such, the two men left their mark on subsequent middle-class housing developments, not just those that were age-restricted.

As a "rags to riches" person, Cortese may be forgiven some of his rather pretentious indulgences. These included building an imposing corporate headquarters building with white columns just outside Leisure World Laguna Hills. His employees dubbed it "the Taj Mahal." They and the nearby residents of Laguna Hills were well aware of Cortese's arrivals and departures because he was making them in a helicopter. The housing slump in 1966 and 1967 meant that his company had to sell off assets, including some land acquired for future development and "the Taj Mahal." Subsequent corporate headquarters were more modest.[33]

Cortese's personal lifestyle reflected a love of luxury. While stories were told about Del Webb's numerous suits and shoes, Cortese in 1973 made the Association of Custom Tailors' list "of the 10 best-dressed men for 1973." Other names on that 1973 list included Prince Rainier of Monaco, then governor of California Ronald Reagan, and the famous actor Sir Lawrence Olivier. Cortese had his public relations department publicize his selection by the association.[34] Cortese hired the Center of Heraldic Genealogic Research in Florence, Italy, to determine his family's crest or coat of arms. The center produced the Cortese Crest, dating from 1619, certified the family as nobles, and mentioned a Cortese who was a mathematics and physics professor in 1554, another who was a prominent soldier in 1648, and a third who achieved "the highest rank of the clergy." Ross Cortese then had this heraldic crest emblazoned on the tower of the Mediterranean-style Clubhouse One at Laguna Hills.[35] Still another example of his taste for opulence was the 12,000-square-foot mansion that he left his second wife. Located on 2.5 acres in North Tustin, Orange County, the home featured a pool, wrap-around terrace, and 360-degree view that took in the ocean, mountain peaks, and city lights.[36] Cortese's personal indulgences may have been compensatory behavior for an impoverished childhood with an understandable desire for luxury or resulted from other causes. In any case, some of his pretentious indulgences contrasted with the down-to-earth style of the better-known Del Webb.

Ross Cortese aspired to an image as a philanthropist; but given the ups and downs of the housing industry, he was not always able to follow through on promises. Like Webb, Cortese did extensive research before building his first retirement community, including consulting some academics at the University of Southern California. A 1965 article in the company-sponsored *Leisure World News* stated that Ross Cortese gave $4 million to the University of Southern California "to establish the Rossmoor-Cortese Institute for the study of retirement."[37] (Webb in 1962 met with "a group of medical researchers about the establishment of a research center for gerontology at Phoenix' Sun City,"[38] but nothing seems to have happened as a result. Webb, who never had any children, left the bulk of his fortune to his foundation, with directions to focus on medical issues.) However, the Cortese donation was reported as $250,000, not $4 million, in a memorial service pamphlet printed for the dedication of a posthumous plaque in Cortese's honor affixed to Clubhouse 3 at Laguna Hills. The University of Southern California by this time had changed the name of the Rossmoor-Cortese Institute to the Ethel Percy Andrus Center, after the woman who founded AARP. The only family member to speak at this plaque dedication was Heidi Cortese. Interestingly, the memorial service program stated, "The camaraderie, friendship, partnership and love of Alona Cortese and Ross W. Cortese produced Leisure World. Their stunning achievements revolutionized the housing industry, as well as enriching the quality of life for Seniors. Their mutual respect for, and integrity towards each other are eternal." There was no mention of their divorce, let alone Cortese's second wife, Eloise. However, Heidi did make special mention of her "sweet aunt" Colleen Cortese Covelli "for her constant joyful love."[39] It was an understandable attempt to rewrite some history and an indication of a family rift that hadn't healed.

Heidi Cortese also sponsored the Ross W. Cortese Memorial Golf Tournament and banquet the year after her father's death.[40] The event raised more than $20,000 for the Laguna Hills Senior Center, which ran activities such as a Meals on Wheels program. Rossmoor Partners was helping the center with $3,200 per month toward its monthly $6,400 rent. The center depended on donations. Heidi Cortese talked about making the golf tournament an annual event,[41] but that apparently did not happen.

Heidi Cortese's attempts to maintain a positive presence at Leisure World Laguna Hills subsequently went sour when she sued the community, claiming her right to royalties for the use of the name Leisure World. She may have been hoping to gain some revenue from advertising on the community's closed-circuit television station. Her attempt did not work. Leisure World Laguna Hills changed its name to Laguna Woods Village.[42] The episode undermined Heidi's role as the keeper of the Ross Cortese legend; but as of August 2006, the plaque still remained affixed to Clubhouse Three.

At the time of Ross Cortese's death, his sister Colleen Covelli was living in the adjacent community of Laguna Hills with another sister, while a third sister, Pauline Sugarman, was a resident of Leisure World.[43] Sugarman was not the only member of Cortese's family to live at Leisure World Laguna Hills. When talking about how he came up with the concept for Leisure World, Ross Cortese occasionally mentioned thinking about what the ideal community would be like for the elderly. That included his own parents. In 1972, he admitted that his mother and father were living in Leisure World Laguna Hills with their small dog, whom Ross called "our watchman." He acknowledged that his parents did not attend any classes in the community, explaining, "Dot hasn't been feeling too well, so they stay kind of close to home." Ross told the interviewer that he was influenced by his parents and by watching other elderly people "in this age bracket that are bored no matter what kind of life they lead or what section of the country they live in. . . . Activity is the most important thing to them—keeping busy, keeping your mind very, very active. . . . People are beginning to realize this, and this is why it's so successful."[44] Both parents lived at Leisure World Laguna Hills until their deaths. His mother died in 1991 and his father in 1976.[45] Thus, both Webb and Cortese had relatives living in their flagship communities; and in both cases, the relatives stayed "close to home," avoiding the "active adult" lifestyle these developers were promoting.[46]

Another curious parallel between Del Webb and Ross Cortese was that both publicly expressed admiration for one of the more enigmatic recluses of their time, Howard Hughes. In 1981, five years after Howard Hughes' death, Ross Cortese told a reporter that Hughes was "'a great man,' who did 'an awful lot to benefit the future of America.'" This reporter asserted that Hughes was Cortese's "idol—and an apparent inspiration for [Cortese's] walled-in, guard-gated community." Not only had Cortese built Rossmoor as the first tract subdivision to be walled and gated, but all of his Leisure World communities were walled and gated as well. Some observers have regarded Cortese "as the unchallenged king of guard-gated retirement communities in America." In spite of Cortese's prominence as a developer, he was rarely seen in public. In fact, the reporter noted, "Some people call the reclusive millionaire Ross W. Cortese 'the Howard Hughes of Leisure World.'" While the reporter did not mention it, the photograph of the sixty-four-year-old Ross Cortese accompanying the article also bore some resemblance to an elderly Hughes, with Cortese's similar mustache, receding hairline, steely expression, and lean build.[47] Although he publicly expressed admiration for Hughes, there is no record of Ross Cortese ever having had a business relationship with Hughes. Furthermore, it does not appear that the reclusive Ross Cortese ever personally met either Hughes or Del Webb.

Even though Ross Cortese experienced considerable success early on as a developer, he seems to have gotten more reclusive as he aged. In the mid-1960s, the "dapper and energetic" Cortese could be seen scurrying around Leisure World Laguna Hills and its adjacent "Taj Mahal" headquarters building. By 1980, mid-1960s headquarters staff of around 350 had shrunk to 50.[48] He was maintaining a low profile, not making public appearances, and only granted an interview to a reporter in 1981 because he was liquidating his company.

However, like Webb, Cortese never fully retired. He remained as board chairman of two Rossmoor subsidiaries, Laguna Hills Utility Company and RCC Inc.[49] In the twenty-first century and following Ross Cortese's death, RCC Inc. was still building Rossmoor Leisure World in Silver Spring, Maryland, as a joint venture with IDI, International Developers Inc., founded by Giuseppe Cecchi.[50] By 1981, the other Leisure World developments had reached build-out or Cortese had sold his interest in them. Unlike the more gregarious Webb, though, Cortese failed to maintain a personal image or presence in his flagship community. Coincidentally, both men died at the age of seventy-four. Also, prior to their deaths, both men suffered from prostate cancer.[51] The immediate cause of death for both was complications following surgery.[52] In spite of all the two had in common, they had very different personalities.

Gated Communities of Middle-Class Homes

Besides popularizing the age-restricted, active adult community, Webb's major contribution to city planning was the golf course community of modest homes. Cortese's primary contribution to city planning in the United States was the walled and guard-gated community of middle-class homes. Granted, precedents existed, historically and internationally, for these communities and with respect to certain elite developments. During the colonial period of American history, such famous settlements as Jamestown, Spanish military settlements, and the Dutch city New Amsterdam, soon to become New York, were all initially gated. So was the landmark, elite suburb Llewellyn Park, built in Eagle Ridge, New Jersey, in the mid-nineteenth century.[53] Internationally, in 1837, some wealthy businessmen pioneered elite suburban development with Victoria Park outside Manchester, England. Their 140-acre enclave was walled and guard-gated on the model of an English country estate.[54] Walled and gated communities have also become very common throughout Latin America.

Ross Cortese opened his first gated community, Rossmoor, in 1957. Located in Orange County north of Seal Beach in the Los Angeles, Long Beach, Los Alamitos area, it was an intergenerational development of around 3,500 tract houses on tree-lined streets and entirely surrounded by a distinctive red brick wall.[55] The average price of a house in that guard-gated community originally was $13,000.[56] Cortese's gamble that middle-class buyers would respond to a gated community paid off. By 1960, the Walled City of Rossmoor, as it was first called, reached build-out. His success at Rossmoor not only gave Cortese the money to acquire 541 acres nearby for what would become Leisure World Seal Beach, his first retirement development, but it also influenced his planning of subsequent Leisure Worlds, all of which would be guard-gated communities.[57]

In the United States until very recently and then primarily in the Sunbelt, gated communities had remained very much the exception. Americans preferred "the wide open spaces of the western frontier" and "the fenceless landscapes of suburbia."[58] In 2007, Minnesota had only one gated community, Bearpath Golf and Country Club in Eden Prairie, with a second one planned for development in another Twin Cities suburb, Blaine. For about twenty-five years, the exclusive St. Paul suburb of North Oaks had guarded gates but ceased to man them in 1981. As for California and Florida, attitudes were very different. In 2006, "40 percent of new homes in California [were] in gated communities." In Florida, it seemed like most communities, including trailer parks, were gated. Nationally, approximately 6 percent of homes were within gated developments.[59] In terms of numbers of gated communities, California and Florida are in the lead, with Texas coming in third.[60] With respect to retirement communities, Del Webb did not favor gates, and his Sun Cities were open communities. However, in the mid-1990s, about twenty years after his death, the Del Webb Corporation opened its first gated communities, Sun City Palm Desert in California and Sun City Hilton Head off the coast of South Carolina. The Webb Corporation may have been using gates to signal that these communities were for the elite.[61] By the 1990s, it is possible that as many as one-third of gated communities were retirement communities, including both age-restricted and naturally occurring ones.[62]

The reasons for the appeal of the gated community have been debated. The most obvious reason for buyers preferring them has been fear of crime. Whether gates really do deter certain types of crime is somewhat controversial. One researcher has found that in a given suburban, low-crime area, no significant difference existed in the amount of crime in a gated community compared to a nearby community without gates.[63] Another claimed that gates did have the effect of shifting crime to nearby neighborhoods without gates.[64] Gates apparently give residents of the community an enhanced sense of security, enough so that they are willing to pay to man them and even supplement them with private security patrols.[65] Elderly people, particularly elderly women, feel especially vulnerable to violent crime. In a gated community, they may feel freer to take a walk at night than they would in a neighborhood without gates. Another concern of people who travel a lot or who maintain second homes, such as snowbirds, is burglary.[66] Whatever individual buyers' reasons were, when Ross Cortese decided to gate his communities, he found a market.

One reason some people prefer gated communities has more to do with social exclusivity and status than security. As a knowledgeable observer put it, gates reinforce "the sense of exclusivity" that is part of the active adult retirement community lifestyle.[67] Another observer tied in the popularity of gated communities with the increasing heterogeneity of urban neighborhoods and a corresponding tendency to emphasize one's racial, ethnic, and gender identification instead. People who chose a gated development were looking for a sense of community. Some of that sense of community was based on white privilege, such as "education, elite taste cultures and behaviors."[68] Some of it was also based on protecting one's social status as a retired person. Maintaining one's social class identity after having retired from one's job could be difficult.[69] A study of retirement communities in California pointed out that in the retirement community, "the elderly can create a social order wherein their individual statuses are secure.... The old can have self-respect and honor."[70]

Accompanying the gates in the retirement lifestyle community were privatization and exclusive use of amenities for the residents such as the recreation centers and golf courses. To keep outsiders out, pass keys or pass cards may limit access to the clubhouse, and an internal gate may further limit access to the golf course.[71] But have all these measures to keep outsiders out really fostered a sense of community inside the gates? In one sociological survey, only 8 percent of gated residents regarded their communities as "neighborly and tight-knit."[72] Neither in California nor nationally did a majority of gated-community residents find their developments "particularly friendly" or even having "a sense of community." However, as this expert concedes, "*Community* is a slippery term."[73]

What gating does to the planning or physical layout of the development has gotten surprisingly little attention in the literature. That may be because most gated communities are strictly residential neighborhoods around some recreational amenities within a larger community. However, that was not so with major, master-planned retirement communities intended to provide not just housing but churches, commercial businesses, medical facilities, and occasional cultural events. Except for the housing and recreational facilities, the churches, stores, banks, hospitals, and clinics need to serve people both within and outside the gates. To do so, the community has to be planned so that all these facilities will be located outside the gates while being convenient to those inside the gates.

Probably the single largest gated community is Leisure World Laguna Hills in California, now called Laguna Woods, which has around 12,000 housing units and 18,000 residents.[74] There Ross Cortese originally owned land within and outside the gates. He did provide for the location of churches, a hospital, and various commercial developments adjacent or very close to the walled and gated residential areas. One result was a dozen gates that continue to be staffed at considerable expense to the residents. In 2004, the monthly home owners' fee at Laguna Woods averaged close to $400 per dwelling unit, although it included much more than just staffing the gates.[75] Another problem in some gated communities is the traffic jam at the gates when a number of people are leaving or entering at the same time. In the case of a popular synchronized-swimming show at Laguna Woods, outsiders lined up at Gate One to enter. Security guards did not even ask to see tickets, partly because ticket sales were still going on inside at the clubhouse. Anyone could enter.[76] In gated communities that are not age-restricted, gates can get jammed at popular commuter times for people driving to work or dropping children off at school. One gated-community resident commented, "The irony is that we are trapped behind our own gates, unable to exit. Instead of keeping people out, we have shut ourselves in."[77]

Some retirement community developers have chosen not to use gates or have used what may be termed "fake" gates. A "fake" gated community is one with walls and a gate or gates, but they are not manned. For residents who want the look of exclusiveness that gates provide but not the ongoing expense of staffing gates with guards, this may be the ideal solution.[78] An example would be Sun City Grand, begun in the mid-1990s near the original Sun City, where the Del Webb Corporation did provide for manning the gate while selling homes, perhaps partly to give directions to people looking for the model home park. Once Sun City Grand reached build-out, the live guards disappeared, although the gate house remained. In much smaller developments, a keypad entry system may be used, again to get around the expense of paying guards. Another problem with a serious gate at Sun City Grand was that the clubhouse complex included a restaurant that was open to anyone. At Sun City Huntley, Illinois, also opened in the mid-1990s, both a restaurant and a pro shop were in the clubhouse and served outsiders.[79] Going back to the early 1960s, retirement communities varied, with Leisure Worlds being guard-gated, while the Sun Cities founded in that era were, and still are, completely open.

It has become quite common for researchers to make the claim that retirement communities pioneered the gated development. Edward

J. Blakely and Mary Gail Snyder in their 1997 book, *Fortress America*, wrote, "Gated communities remained rarities until the advent of the master-planned retirement developments of the late 1960s and 1970s. Retirement developments like Leisure World were the first places where average Americans could wall themselves off. Gates soon spread."[80] That statement gets quoted by both Marc Freedman in his 1999 book on retirement, *Prime Time*,[81] and Setha Low in her 2003 book on gated communities.[82] Historians of suburbia Rosalyn Baxandall and Elizabeth Ewen in 2000 wrote that gated communities were "originally designed for retirees in the Southwest and West."[83] It was not so, although Blakely and Snyder were close to the truth.

The Leisure World Concept

In 1966, Michael Barker called attention to the fact that most developers who created retirement communities built conventional suburban tract housing first.[84] That was the case with both Del Webb and Ross Cortese. Cortese's 1957 gated community, Rossmoor, was both experimental and successful. In some ways, Cortese regarded Rossmoor City, as it was later known, as his signature community. He named his firm the Rossmoor Corporation. He also at times called his Leisure World communities "Rossmoor Leisure World Laguna Hills," or "Rossmoor Leisure World Seal Beach."[85] However, Cortese was not nearly as strict as Del Webb in putting his corporate name on his communities; Rossmoor failed to evolve into a brand name. In the late 1950s, while building and selling Rossmoor, Cortese "watched and listened, asked questions and studied statistics and came to the conclusion that builders were not meeting the needs of the middle aged would-be residents." For Cortese, middle age began at fifty-two.[86] The success of Rossmoor led Cortese to take a second gamble and experiment with an age-restricted, active adult community.

Like Del Webb, Cortese spent a couple of years carefully researching the concept of a retirement community before beginning to build one, in 1960. He talked to all sorts of people, from psychologists to Catholic clerics to individuals. What type of community did mature adults want and need? What were their aspirations and their fears?[87] He met with senior citizen groups in the Los Angles area and with Cardinal James Francis McIntyre. Cortese seems to have met McIntyre while the latter was an archbishop. Cortese's original goal was to build a Catholic hospital in the Long Beach area, but Long Beach medical personnel opposed it as unnecessary competition. McIntyre was influential in refashioning Cortese's goal to that of building a retirement community featuring medical care. McIntyre helped Cortese connect with Lewis Letson, then a hospital administrator.[88] In addition, Cortese began talking with an attorney and former congressman, A. Oakley Hunter. Cortese's original goal had been to construct a hospital near Rossmoor, but he ran into problems getting federal funding for that project.[89] It was probably with that intention in mind that he was interested in Letson and Hunter. However, those two also played a role in redirecting his efforts toward a retirement community with medical services.

Putting together the retirement community concept and then deciding to proceed was what Cortese called "shoe-leather research." Letson encouraged him to incorporate a medical services program into the structure of his retirement community. Hunter alerted Cortese to the recently passed Section 213 cooperative housing program under FHA. Cortese decided to work with this FHA program so he could market his future retirement community as eligible for low-interest, FHA-insured home mortgages. Cortese hired Hunter to secure this FHA eligibility and kept Hunter as his attorney for the rest of the 1960s. Letson also became a Rossmoor employee.[90] Another Rossmoor employee, L. H. "Bud" Davis, thought up the name "Leisure World."[91] Cortese's actual planning staff consisted of only about seven or eight people, but he had his carefully worked-out plan in place when he acquired the land for Leisure World Seal Beach.[92]

Some biographers of Cortese credit him with creating the concept of "the successful adult community,"[93] even though he did not begin construction on his first one, Leisure World Seal Beach, until 1960, when Webb was already selling houses in Sun City, Arizona. Cortese and Webb seem to have done their research and planning at about the same time but independently. Cortese's concept differed significantly from Webb's Sun Cities, where the vast majority of the housing was of the single-family, detached variety. All the housing at Seal Beach originally was cooperative, attached, townhouse units. Although Webb would later advertise some townhouse units at Sun City, California, as cooperatives, they were really condominiums. At Leisure World Seal Beach, buyers owned a share in the cooperative, which gave them the right to occupy a specific unit; technically the cooperative was the owner, collected payments for the mortgage and taxes, and paid them for the member units. The cooperative also was responsible for exterior maintenance and owned, furnished, and replaced the interior appliances. Seal Beach consisted entirely of these cooperative units.

No single-family, detached housing was ever built at Leisure World Seal Beach. Furthermore, the units, dubbed "manors" for sales purposes, were actually back-to-back apartments, which limited the ways they could be expanded. However, that meant that Cortese, keeping most units on ground level, could squeeze more than 6,000 units onto a 541-acre site—about one square mile—that had been beet fields. The compactness would be advantageous for a community bus system. It also meant that the community could get by with just two guarded gates.

Like Webb, Cortese included recreational facilities in the form of clubhouses and a nine-hole golf course. However, recreation, exercise, and entertainment came in second on Cortese's list of objectives for his retirement community. His first objective was the most innovative part of Cortese's original concept. It was the provision of a free medical clinic within the community to serve its residents.[94] Hobbies, including golf and clubhouses, came in third on his list.[95] He carried over to Leisure World Seal Beach what he had learned about the value of walls, guarded gates, and exceptional landscaping in developing Rossmoor. To summarize Cortese's concept, he wanted to develop an age-restricted community for people over fifty-two where the residents would have gated security, access to an on-site medical clinic with doctors and nurses, freedom from exterior maintenance, clubhouse facilities to develop hobbies and other interests and to socialize, and, finally, country-club amenities such as a golf course and pool. He also wanted to create "a serene atmosphere of beauty" and provide space for several churches.[96]

In an 8 October 1961 interview with a *Los Angeles Examiner* reporter, Cortese ignored the Youngtown and Sun City precedents, saying, "For years. . . . I assumed someone would launch a major housing program for [the elderly], but nobody did."[97] It is hard to imagine that when he began construction of Leisure World Seal Beach in 1960 he was totally unaware of Sun City, which was then open. However, Cortese's concept was quite different. At the time he made his decision to proceed with Leisure

World Seal Beach, he may well not have known of the significance of Sun City, let alone the poorly publicized Youngtown.

Because Cortese decided that he wanted Leisure World Seal Beach, originally called Rossmoor Leisure World (the name was changed in 1967),[98] to qualify under the FHA's newly passed Section 213 cooperative housing program, that gave FHA considerable leverage in shaping the development. Winning FHA approval meant that buyers could qualify for government-insured, forty-year mortgages at 5.25 percent interest. Since the initial price of housing units at Rossmoor Seal Beach was $9,000–$11,000,[99] FHA-insured mortgages would keep monthly payments as low as $93.[100] Given that the youngest a buyer could be was fifty-two, that meant the mortgage might not be paid off until the buyer was at least ninety-two. Because Rossmoor Seal Beach was a major project under a new program, FHA gave it considerable scrutiny, both in Washington, D.C., and in Seal Beach. When Congress passed Section 213, FHA officials had not expected it to fund a project anywhere near as large as the more than 6,000 housing units proposed for Seal Beach.[101] Legend has it that the paperwork involved in launching the development eventually measured 13.5 linear feet of documents.[102] For Cortese, whose company was not as large, financially sound, or diverse as Webb's, securing FHA backing made it easier to obtain bank financing, while Webb was able to self-fund much of his initial costs and use conventional mortgage financing.[103]

One of FHA's specific requirements was that Rossmoor Leisure World be annexed to the existing community of Seal Beach. While Del Webb's three Sun Cities all were and remained unincorporated and Ross Cortese's next Leisure World at Laguna Hills would be unincorporated for decades, Rossmoor Leisure World from its start became a neighborhood of the existing community of Seal Beach. Today, Seal Beach has a population of around 30,000, of which about 10,000 are residents of Leisure World Seal Beach. The latter usually elect two out of five members of the Seal Beach city council.[104] However, one Leisure World council district is shared with an outside neighborhood. In 2009, the council member from the combined district was from outside Leisure World, meaning only one council member was a Leisure World resident.[105] Thus, residents of Leisure World Seal Beach, which maintains its own roads and community facilities and does not send children to the local schools, pay taxes to support a municipal government where their community is a distinct minority.

Another major difference between Cortese and Webb was in their philosophies regarding the amount of land acquisition and the location of their retirement communities in relation to major metropolitan areas. Webb liked to have at least 10,000 acres, while Cortese was willing to go with 541 acres for Seal Beach and 2,000 to 3,000 acres for his subsequent Leisure World communities.[106] That reflected Cortese's vision of a more compact community consisting primarily of apartments or townhouse units. Cortese was more concerned than Webb about locating close to a metropolitan area, which meant that his per acre land prices were higher and larger tracts more difficult to obtain. Thus, Cortese's communities were less isolated than Webb's. In the early 1970s, when Del Webb decided to sell his Sun Cities in California and Florida, one reason was slow sales due to their relatively greater distances from cities. Cortese's sales were initially more rapid than Webb's, which may indicate that Cortese had a better sense of location, although Sun City, Arizona, was a significant exception. That development reached build-out at 46,000 people, while Laguna Hills, the largest Leisure World, came in at around 18,000 people. Given that Cortese found himself hemmed in by other development, expansion for him meant going to other metropolitan areas to develop more Leisure Worlds. In 2007, Pulte Homes, which by then owned Del Webb, seemed to be following Cortese's philosophy of smaller developments closer to metropolitan areas. However, Pulte was still following the original Del Webb approach of emphasizing the single-family, detached home in most of its twenty-first-century retirement community developments.

Cortese's relatively small amount of acreage compared to Webb's Sun Cities influenced the physical planning of Seal Beach. The community opened with a nine-hole golf course as its centerpiece. Apparently, Cortese originally planned a second nine holes but decided that he could make more money by putting housing in that area instead. At build-out, with around 10,000 people, Leisure World Seal Beach had about half the population of Cortese's next community, Leisure World Laguna Hills, but only about a quarter of the acreage. The Laguna Hills development ended up with a twenty-seven-hole golf course and riding stables, which were not present in Seal Beach. However, some Seal Beach residents preferred the coolness associated with their proximity to the ocean. It is adjacent to Pacific Coast Highway, which parallels the coast. Laguna Hills, on the other hand, is on the bluffs about seven miles inland from Laguna Beach and averages about 14 degrees hotter as a result.[107]

Still another difference between Cortese and Webb was in the attention Cortese gave to incorporating design elements for the elderly in his housing units. Almost all units at Seal Beach were single-story, ground-floor units with grab bars by the tub or shower and toilet, raised electrical outlets, wide hallways, and other features meant to make the units livable for the elderly as they became less mobile. While Webb kept most of his housing single-story, he did not bother with such signs of limited mobility as bathroom grab bars. On the other hand, Cortese did not allow any space within the walls of Seal Beach for a nursing home. Webb initially avoided nursing homes as well, but within about five years they began to spring up in the much more fluid and open to development Sun City. Both developers saw their market as being the "active adult" or those elderly persons in relatively good physical condition.

Also, both developers initially kept their units small. At Seal Beach, a two-bedroom unit was 759 square feet,[108] about the size of Webb's smallest two-bedroom house. Keeping the units small was one way of keeping interior housekeeping easier for the occupants. In Webb's case, however, his houses were on lots that did require homeowner maintenance but made remodeling and enlarging the houses much more feasible. At Sun City, a home owner typically enlarged the living space by adding an Arizona room on the rear of the house. At Seal Beach, many owners have enlarged the spaces off the front by enclosing covered patios and have added skylights to compensate for the lack of light in the interiors of the back-to-back units.[109] Still another major difference was that Seal Beach reached build-out within three years, whereas it took Sun City at least eighteen years to be completed. The greater amount of time evolving over the years meant a much greater variety in the types of housing at Sun City as well as the total number of houses.

Developing Rossmoor Leisure World Seal Beach

Cortese may have been inspired by some early Del Webb advertising when he titled a 1961 advertising brochure for Seal Beach "Rossmoor Leisure World: A New Way of Life." Also reflecting Webb advertising, Cortese referred to his Leisure World Seal Beach as "this country club city." However, Cortese's advertising called attention to the fact that his housing units had a number of features "specifically designed for the comfort of happy people over fifty-two." His sales brochure went on to list extra-wide doorways, no stairs in any of the buildings within the walls of the community, "rolled" curbs on the streets, electrical outlets two feet above the floors, night lights toward the bathrooms, sidewalk lights, an intracommunity bus service, and buses to nearby Long Beach. He described the medical plan with its clinic and medical personnel on call that came with the housing units. As for the "active retirement" image that Webb was promoting, Cortese included a half-dozen pages describing the social and recreational facilities that came with a "full-time Recreation Coordinator."[110] While Cortese was pitching Webb's formula of affordable country-club living with a slightly higher minimum age, fifty-two as opposed to Webb's fifty, Cortese was also realistically addressing issues of aging such as potentially impaired mobility, greater concerns about physical security, and pre-Medicare worries about the availability of affordable medical care.

Rossmoor Leisure World at Seal Beach had its grand opening on 18 October 1961. Cortese had gambled the money he made on the Walled City of Rossmoor development on the very new concept of an age-restricted retirement community and was pioneering by adding to the concept gated security and onsite medical services. His competitors were skeptical.[111] How would the public respond? Cortese was so nervous that he chose not to personally be present at Leisure World Seal Beach's opening. Cortese's explanation for his absence was, "You can be the brightest person in the world and still be stupid. . . . You never know the public."[112] He need not have worried. Like Webb, Cortese's staff had underestimated the crowd of potential buyers who came. The Leisure World staff put in a quick call to Abbey Rents for more tables and "a tent to shelter the milling throng." Cortese's biggest problem would be accelerating the pace of construction to meet the demand. Seal Beach's 6,740 "manors," as Cortese dubbed the single-story, back-to-back, townhouse units, all sold within two and a half years of the grand opening.[113] One of Webb's executives recalled Cortese's emphasis on medical coverage and said Cortese would take anyone no matter how old or what the ailments were. The Webb executive wryly noted that Seal Beach Leisure World was "moderately successful."[114]

That Cortese had set a minimum age of fifty-two for buyers and built on the outskirts of the expanding Los Angeles–Long Beach metropolitan area are indications of just who the initial buyers were. By far, the majority came from California. However, among the first-year home owners were 257 buyers from elsewhere. Most numerous were the thirty from Illinois, followed by twenty-two from Iowa, eighteen from Washington, and sixteen from New York, where cooperatives were relatively common. Tying for fifth place among states represented were Minnesota and Colorado, each with fifteen buyers. Five buyers came from foreign countries.[115] While Cortese targeted a local market, his development did receive national attention. To buy at Seal Beach, at least one member of the household had to be fifty-two, and no minor children could be permanently present. The year after the community opened, the average age was sixty-one.[116] Among these initial buyers was Ross J. Kidder, who moved from Sun City, Arizona. There Kidder had been "the first City Manager of the Sun City Civic Association,"[117] an early organization of residents. It is unclear why Kidder moved from Sun City to Seal Beach. However, the ocean breezes must have been a welcome relief from the summer desert heat.

Life at Leisure World Seal Beach

The Rossmoor Corporation worked to develop a sense of community. It sponsored a community newspaper, *Rossmoor Leisure World News,* that publicized community activities and published occasional photographs and brief biographical sketches of some residents, such as where they were from, their former occupations, and their hobbies and interests. The age-restricted nature of the community gave the residents another bond. So did the experience of migrating to a new and innovative community.

Organized activities at Leisure World Seal Beach furthered resident interaction and promoted the "active retirement" concept. A year after opening, the community had twenty-three clubs or interest groups. Besides the golf course, informal clubhouse activities ranged from shuffleboard to swimming in the pool to use of the woodworking shop.[118] Rossmoor's professional activities director announced that Orange Coast College of Costa Mesa would be offering adult education classes in the Leisure World clubhouse. These would include conversational Spanish and sewing and would be taught by instructors from the college. Finally, volunteers were busy organizing a bowling league, hiking clubs, and special events trips, such as to an Ice Follies performance.[119] Six months later, the Rossmoor events coordinator exclaimed, "Active retirement [the Del Webb phrase] is a particularly appropriate term for the literally hundreds of dancers at Leisure World." He went on to list at least a half-dozen types of dance classes, from square dancing to ballroom dancing, plus a regular, weekly schedule of ballroom dances.[120]

By the summer of 1963, stories featuring "the Leisure World way of life" had appeared in *Time, Newsweek,* and *House and Home* with future stories expected in such publications as the *Christian Science Monitor.* The news services United Press International and Associated Press also covered the new Leisure World.[121] In some ways, the activities available surpassed those at Sun City, probably because of the availability of community college instructors in the area and the proximity to Los Angeles. Also, the "active retirement" publicity that Rossmoor Leisure World generated on a national level reinforced Del Webb's advertised image of Grandpa on the golf course enjoying himself.

Of the two major features of Cortese's concept that differed from the Del Webb concept—guard-gated security and on-site medical services—the one to really prove itself was the gated security. Leisure World Seal Beach's main gate was manned twenty-four hours a day. The community only staffed its second gate from 8 A.M. to 8 P.M.[122] With no other gates, the expense of staffing them was reasonable. As for the medical clinic that was supposed to be built into the services the community provided its residents, Rossmoor in 1963 pictured a medical center with twenty-six nurses, ten physicians, a pharmacy, and a laboratory with X-ray capabilities.[123] However, incorporating the cost of that kind of clinic into the operation of Seal Beach was not feasible in the long term. Fortunately for Cortese, in 1965 Congress passed the Medicare program, which soon gave his communities a graceful exit from the medical care business. Twenty-five years later, Seal Beach still had a medical clinic and pharmacy, but Los Alamitos Medical Center, not Leisure World Seal Beach, was operating them. The later medical facilities were only for those residents who chose to use them. Predictably, the population had aged. Twenty-five years after the opening of Leisure World Seal Beach, the average age of residents had advanced to 77.6 years.[124]

The management of Leisure World Seal Beach turned out to be different from what Cortese originally anticipated. Apparently, Cortese had planned to carry out the maintenance of the common areas, such as the golf course, through the nonprofit Golden Rain Foundation, which he initially controlled.[125] The problem was that he would be setting the resident fee not only for routine maintenance but also for upkeep as time took its toll. In Pinellas County, Florida, some residents of retirement cooperatives complained loudly that where this type of arrangement existed, they felt it was a scheme of the developer to continue to make money off the buyers. At Seal Beach, FHA as well was questioning the nature of future management.[126] The director of FHA's Division of Cooperative Housing decided to call a conference to resolve this issue at Seal Beach.[127] At this meeting, the FHA administrator there made it clear that FHA would not tolerate "owner-management of Leisure World then or in the foreseeable future." Instead, FHA insisted that "the services of a strong professional management organization were necessary to the economic stability of Leisure World."[128] While the name of the management group, Golden Rain Foundation, continued, it became administratively separate from Ross Cortese.

Leisure World Seal Beach reached build-out in 1965. A portrait of the community at that time showed that among the residents, women outnumbered the men almost two to one; 60 percent of those women were single, widowed, or divorced. Women were more attracted to "the social aspects of the community." On the other hand, men made greater use of the recreational facilities. When both men and women were asked what feature of Leisure World Seal Beach was most important to them, 45 percent said the medical plan, 18 percent the social activity, 16 percent the exterior and common-area maintenance, 10 percent the recreational facilities, and coming in last at 8 percent, the community's bus system. When asked what facilities they actually used, club rooms had the highest percentage of users at 78 percent, followed by 56 percent taking advantage of bus trips outside the community, and use of the pool in third place at 38 percent. Only 18 percent used the golf course. Least used was the sewing shop at 8 percent. In 1965, with Lyndon Johnson having won the presidency by a landslide the previous year, seniors at Seal Beach were out of step: 55 percent said they were Republicans, while 30 percent called themselves Democrats. Altogether, only 4 percent described themselves as "politically active."[129] The heavy preponderance of women and the political conservatism were characteristics that would become relatively common among most retirement communities, not just at Leisure World Seal Beach.

Cortese originally estimated that it would take five years to reach build-out at Seal Beach.[130] Selling approximately 6,500 housing units in less than three years meant that Seal Beach was a phenomenal success for Cortese, and it launched him "on a land buying spree from coast to coast." Besides Seal Beach, by 1989, he would build or have been responsible for a total of seven Leisure World communities across the United States.[131] His land acquisitions included 2,500 acres for Leisure World Laguna Hills; the Robert Stanley Dollar estate for Leisure World Walnut Creek, near San Francisco; 1,000 acres in Olney, Maryland, near Washington, D.C.; 600 acres for Leisure World Coconut Creek, near Fort Lauderdale, Florida; land for Leisure World Maryland; 3,700 acres for Leisure World Golden Hills, in Mesa, Arizona;[132] and eventually a Leisure World in Virginia.

When it came to the architecture of homes in these communities, Cortese would differ from Del Webb in that Cortese from the start favored following regional styles rather than the standard, nondescript tract housing styles of the 1960s. Consequently, Cortese used some Spanish tile and stucco elements at Laguna Hills while doing colonial-style buildings at a Leisure World near Princeton, New Jersey.[133] Some of these Leisure Worlds were joint ventures in which Cortese was an initial partner before others took over his interests. Nevertheless, with the success of Seal Beach, Cortese had a viable retirement community concept plus the energy and resources to take it across the country. His success attracted imitators or developers who rated his approach above that of Del Webb.

Leisure World Laguna Hills

Of all these Leisure Worlds, the largest and the one that he considered his flagship community was Leisure World Laguna Hills, opened in 1964. Cortese figured that the growth of the Greater Los Angeles area would extend to southern Orange County. He knew that he was unlikely to be able to acquire any property from the Irvine Company, but adjacent to its land was the Moulton Ranch, with more than 3,000 acres.[134] In 1961, Nellie Moulton, the widow of Louis Moulton and in her early eighties, was open to selling some of her land. She and Cortese drove over her hills as Cortese decided what acreage he wanted to purchase.[135] The land was arid and had only deep wells for water and no sewage disposal system other than cesspools. However, Cortese knew that the congested Highway 101 between Los Angeles and San Diego was scheduled to be upgraded to freeway status. (Eventually, it became Interstate 5, sixteen lanes across, as it passed very close to what became Leisure World Laguna Hills.) He also had the ability to look at barren land, assess its future potential, and envision a lush, populous settlement on the site.[136] He bought 3,568 acres from Nellie Gail Moulton for $2,300 per acre.[137]

Moulton was so intrigued with Cortese's development of Leisure World Laguna Hills as an age-restricted community that she moved into one of the early units. While a resident, she joined the Laguna Hills Art Association, which was formed in 1965. An amateur painter, she and some other members would pack their art supplies and box lunches in cars for day trips to paint outdoors at nearby scenic spots. In 1967, the Art Association invited Nellie Gail Moulton and Ross Cortese to be guests of honor at a dinner. On that occasion, Nellie Moulton gave a speech about her life on the Moulton Ranch, displayed some of her paintings, and read another person's poem about her deceased husband. She also expressed her admiration for Ross Cortese and "said she liked the way he conducted business matters."[138] However, while she thought living at Leisure World was nice, she also felt hemmed in by "too many houses and too many people." She eventually moved out in favor of living at her beach house, which gave her more of a sense of the wide open spaces to which she was accustomed. Nellie Moulton died in 1972 at the age of ninety-three.[139] Like Frances Greer, a widow who sold her ranchland for Youngtown, Nellie Moulton may also have been motivated to sell her land in part by a personal interest in possibly living in the projected community herself.

Having acquired the land for Leisure World Laguna Hills, Ross Cortese's challenges were only beginning. First, he needed to figure out how he was going to get water and sewage lines to his development site. The only procedure in place in Orange County at that time was for a developer to annex to an existing community with those systems. Therefore, in 1962, Rossmoor Corporation applied to Santa Ana, about fifteen miles north, for strip annexation along the freeway in order to tap into that community's water and sewer system. Initially, Santa Ana was receptive. However, part of Cortese's land lay under the flight path for the El Toro Marine Naval Air Station. The Marine Corps vociferously objected to Cortese's building plans, with the result that Santa Ana rejected Cortese's annexation request.[140]

Fortunately for Cortese, Orange County then came through with a procedure that would allow planned communities with their own water and sewer systems. To finance these systems, Rossmoor again applied to FHA for financial backing. Now the Marine Corps, with some success, was going after both Orange County and FHA to block Cortese's plans. For Cortese, it must have been nerve-wracking because he had paid development prices for more than 3,500 acres, and now he was being denied the development permits he needed. To get the backing of FHA, Cortese had to reach an agreement with the Marine Corps that would protect a 4,000-foot-wide landing flight path for the El Toro air base. What the Marine Corps wanted was no housing on 709 acres.[141] That meant that Cortese had to rework his community plan. For example, the golf course got relocated under the flight path, eliminating a "considerable number of golf course-oriented units" that could have sold for more money in that location than elsewhere. The compromise did clear the way for FHA and Orange County approval.[142]

Rossmoor went on to create two subsidiaries, Rossmoor Water Company, later known as Laguna Hills Water Company, and Rossmoor Sanitation, later known as Laguna Hills Sanitation. Both companies built systems designed to serve more development than just Leisure World.[143] As for the 1963 compromise that imposed development restrictions on Cortese, in 1972 he successfully sued the Marine Corps for compensation of $4.2 million on the lost value of the land plus interest. The development restrictions remained.[144]

In the physical planning for Leisure World Laguna Hills, Rossmoor had to satisfy the demands of the Marine Corps with respect to its flight path, and at the same time this was to be a tremendously large, gated community. Cortese was not just planning housing and recreational amenities; he was also planning for the location of churches and commercial facilities to serve people both inside and outside the gates. Thus, the gated-community concept applied to a total community meant that Leisure World would have to be configured in such a way that the churches and commercial facilities would be located adjacent to the community but outside its gates. Another planning constraint was the flight path. It basically went north/south straight through the middle of the community, bisecting it. A third planning constraint was El Toro Road. The major route through the foothills down to Laguna Beach, it cut through Leisure World Laguna Hills in an east/west direction, almost at a right angle to the flight path. One result was fragmented neighborhoods and the impossibility of driving through the entire community without having to exit through one gate and reenter through another. Had Cortese not been strongly committed to a gated community and had the Marine Corps closed its El Toro base in the early 1960s rather than later, Leisure World Laguna Hills would have had a very different plan.

The Marine Corps literally dictated what would be in the center of the community in a north/south direction under its flight path. For example, it appears from the comments of a former Rossmoor president that Cortese had wanted to construct a golf course winding through the community to maximize the number of housing units facing the golf course, probably similar to what Webb was already doing at Sun City. Webb had demonstrated that buyers would pay a premium for golf course lots. Instead, the golf course was placed in the center of the community with fairways doubling back and forth on each other. A short distance south of that golf course, Cortese eventually added a second golf course. In between were the community's riding stables, tennis courts, two community garden areas so residents could have their own fruit and vegetable plots, and RV storage. Like Webb, Cortese did not want residents parking RVs near their homes. Cortese also located a community center and administration buildings and eventually two small shopping centers in this corridor, and he donated sites for five churches and a synagogue.

Leisure World Laguna Hills ended up consisting of neighborhood clusters bisected by a wide swath of north/south public space in one direction and an east/west ribbon of what has become a very heavily traveled El Toro Road in the other direction. To assist golf carts in crossing El Toro Road, Cortese added a tunnel under it, thus separating golf cart and regular highway traffic. The dispersal of seven clubhouses throughout the community provided anchors for the various neighborhoods. However, because the clubhouses specialized in certain activities, such as a large theater in one, a party rental facility in another, the largest pool in a third, and so on, residents did sometimes have to pass through guarded gates even when staying within the community.

Designing for inside and outside the gates was another matter. Part of the planning process meant some of Cortese's 3,500 acres would be outside the 2,200 acres enclosed by walls and guarded gates that constituted Leisure World Laguna Hills. Soon after Leisure World opened, so did an adjacent 120-acre shopping center with a supermarket, gas station, the Leisure World Medical Center, the Leisure World resales office (the company also sold used units within the community, as did Webb in his Sun Cities), and other services.[145] Cortese eventually was involved in the development of the regional Laguna Hills Mall adjacent to Leisure World that Penney's and Sears would anchor. On completion of this mall, he sold his interest in it to his co-developer, Ernest W. Hahn Inc.[146] As for the neighborhood shopping centers and churches below the flight path, the community's walls and a dozen gates for vehicles had to go behind them so that these facilities would also be accessible to the general public, not just Leisure World residents. Giving priority to guarded gates and the Marine Corps flight path, Cortese managed to put together a complete community for what eventually proved to be 18,000 people, although he initially projected more.

Cortese's persistence in the face of adversity also paid off in the land-scaping of Leisure World Laguna Hills. From his very first house reha-bilitation project, Cortese had paid attention to landscaping. At Seal Beach, he initially filled the grounds with golden rain trees, which he had seen in New Orleans and admired for their drooping golden blos-soms. Unfortunately, virtually all of these trees planted at Seal Beach died. That did not turn off Cortese's interest in luxurious landscaping. In 1963 at Laguna Hills, he personally began working with a landscape architect, Rey Forsum of R. W. Forsum, Dana Point. The following year when the first residents moved in, the semi-arid landscape had become lush with green grass, trees, and blooming plants. From the start, this very attractive landscaping was a feature turning viewers of Leisure World Laguna Hills into buyers. In 1978, the American Association of Nurserymen selected that development "as one of the best in the nation for design and construction." The following year, the California Land-scape and Irrigation Council praised the community "for sixteen years of 'landscaping excellence.'"[147] To a greater extent than most develop-ers, Cortese recognized the value of a beautiful, association-maintained landscape.

Cortese's vision extended beyond physical planning to include social planning. Like Leisure World Seal Beach, Laguna Hills also began with a medical plan as part of the package offered buyers when the commu-nity opened in 1964. In the early years, this medical feature included "80% payment of retail value of in-home nurse's calls, doctor's office calls, prescription drugs and Christian Science practitioner fees."[148] The health care aspect related to the fact that Cortese was targeting "ac-tive mature adults" with substantial recreational amenities. While Cor-tese may never have required medical exams of buyers to be sure they were in reasonably good health, a 1966 study of California retirement communities found that some of them "tried using medical examinations to determine whether a particular prospect was 'active,' and also to determine the degree of risk the prospect placed on the community health plan." This study reported that the communities soon dropped the medical examination requirement because those who did the best on the examination "were also those most likely to suffer strokes."[149]

Cortese was concerned about health needs but planned Laguna Hills initially without any nursing home or assisted living facilities. Then, in 1974, The Towers, twin fourteen-story condominium buildings opened, offering meals in common dining rooms and a registered nurse on duty.[150] Cortese subsequently wanted to include more assisted living facilities within the gates of Leisure World, but, interestingly, given the medical services aspect in the initial concept, residents of Leisure World objected. Instead, several assisted living facilities were built immediately outside the gates. Residents also successfully objected to a proposed continuing care facility within Leisure World. For the residents, the active retirement image was more important than living arrangements that incorporated ongoing medical services.

The last cooperative housing units at Leisure World Seal Beach provided the model for the first housing units, also called "manors," at Laguna Hills.[151] These units were two-story, walk-up ones, but Cortese quickly reverted to single-story units for subsequent housing. In both Leisure Worlds, the bulk of the housing was back-to-back apartment units ranging in size from 800 to 2,250 square feet.[152] Parking in both places was in banks of carports, necessitating some walking. In some of the early neighborhoods, called mutuals, at Laguna Hills, the laundry facilities were in separate buildings a short distance from the apartment buildings. The high quality of the landscaping and the greater space plus some more elaborate architecture in the units built later definitely made Leisure World Laguna Hills more attractive than its slightly older forerunner at Seal Beach.

From "Active Retirement" to "Active Adult"

While Ross Cortese borrowed some advertising themes from Del Webb to publicize Leisure World Seal Beach and used them again to publicize Leisure World Laguna Hills, Cortese contributed a new phrase to the advertising rhetoric that Webb and other developers have subsequently used. From Leisure World Laguna Hills' opening in 1964, Ross Cortese, like Del Webb, stressed the word "active" in his advertising. A full, double-page ad in a local newspaper in February 1964 touting the opening of Leisure World Laguna Hills was headlined, "For you *active, interesting people over 52.*" The 1964 ad also borrowed a phrase from Del Webb as it promoted a "new way of life."[153] Meanwhile, Webb was continuing to use the phrase "active retirement," which was something of an oxymoron. In 1966, Cortese used the phrase "active adults" in a sales brochure.[154] Since then "active adult" has become standard in the retirement community industry to denote elderly people still in relatively good health and/or potentially interested in communities with extensive recreational amenities.

Retirees responded to the "active adult" pitch. Milton Plotnick retired as a controller at Saks Fifth Avenue. When he was fifty-seven and his wife, Bess, fifty-four, in 1971 the couple left Beverly Hills for Leisure World. Milton decided that retirement was their "opportunity 'to live it up.'" At Leisure World, they enjoyed theatrical productions, Saturday-night dances, line dancing, tap classes, aerobics, swimming, biking, and bridge parties. Bess commented on how friendly and supportive their friends were at Leisure World and summed up their eighteen years there by saying, "It's a marvelous time of life." When Dr. Bernard Friedman first heard about Leisure World, he did not like it, telling his wife, "You'll never get me in there with a bunch of old folks. All you'll see is heart attacks and ambulances." However, at the age of sixty-seven, Friedman retired as a dentist and actually bought two Leisure World "manors," one in New Jersey and the other in Laguna Hills. After ten years of the snowbird lifestyle, Mrs. Friedman commented, "It was the best thing we've ever done." The Leisure World Laguna Hills recreation director in 1989 said, "Some people come here, get involved in activities they've never tried before, and are more active than ever. . . . It's like a second life."[155]

In summary, while Webb preceded Cortese in developing his "active retirement" community concept, Cortese was an original thinker who apparently arrived at his initial concept without the knowledge of what Webb was doing. However, once the two began to market their initial communities, each had to have been well aware of what the other was doing. To a certain extent, they do appear to have borrowed from each other. Yet, Cortese's Leisure World communities remained distinct from Webb's Sun Cities. The Leisure World communities were all more compact than Webb's, were closer to major metropolitan areas, featured a much higher percentage of multifamily units, had guard-gated security, provided bus service within the community, and incorporated a pre-Medicare health plan. Both Webb and Cortese favored officially age-restricted communities barring children as permanent residents, but they differed slightly as to what age. Webb had a minimum requirement that the buyer be fifty, Cortese fifty-two. Both also designed their communities to have very extensive recreational facilities to be financed through a community association; and through their advertising, both promoted the concept of the "active" elderly. They had their imitators, and both men were extremely influential in reshaping the image of the elderly person from someone who was withdrawn and sedentary to someone who was out on the golf course or in the clubhouse, socializing and enjoying life.

Above: Figure 1. The first home occupied in Youngtown (1954). Youngtown homes were quite modest. Photo by the author.

Left: Figure 2. Del Webb was responsible for the first active adult community. Webb was an early advocate of not smoking. Ironically, he died of lung cancer, which had metastasized from prostate cancer. By permission of the Sun Cities Area Historical Society.

Figure 3. Sign at one of the entrances to Sun City, Arizona. During the first half of the 1960s, the phrase used was the oxymoronic "active retirement community." After the mid-1960s, these communities became known as "active adult" ones. Photo by the author.

Figure 4. Priced at $8,500 during Sun City's grand opening in 1960, this model home with two bedrooms, one bath, a kitchen, and a living room was Del Webb's cheapest. Gravel has since replaced the original grass turf. Photo by the author.

Figure 5. The sign marks the dividing line between the lot that went with the original model home and the adjacent golf course. Webb charged extra for lots that backed seamlessly onto a golf course. Photo by the author.

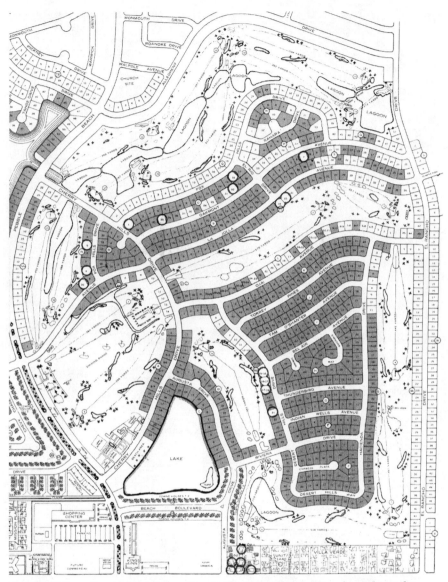

Figure 6. Plan of a section of Sun City Center, Florida, showing how the eighteen-hole golf course snaked through Phase 1 of that Del Webb community. One of the goals was to have numerous house lots backing onto the course. This plan was included in a sales brochure in the possession of the author.

Figure 7. Golf course homes at Sun City Center. Models were virtually identical to those Webb built in the 1960s at Sun City, Arizona, and Sun City, California. Photo by the author.

Figure 8. Residents of golf course communities soon discovered that golf carts made excellent transportation vehicles within their communities, as seen in this drugstore parking lot in Sun City, California. Photo by the author.

Figure 9. All three of the original Sun Cities had the same clubhouse and pool design. Sun City Center's pool was largely unchanged as of 2006. Photo by the author.

Figure 10. Volunteers at Sun City Center drive these security patrol cars. Volunteer neighborhood watch groups have become fairly common. However, Sun City Center is unusual in that it also uses volunteers as first responders in medical emergencies. Photo by the author.

Left: Figure 11. Ross Cortese pioneered the first gated community of modest homes, Rossmoor, in 1957, then successfully applied that concept to active adult communities with his first Leisure World in 1961. By permission of the Historical Society of Laguna Woods.

Below: Figure 12. In 2006, Kenneth Walker was president of the Leisure World Historical Society, Seal Beach. He is shown standing in front of his unit, which his parents purchased in 1962 for $11,000. The unit had been enlarged by enclosing a portion of the patio. By permission of Terry Walker. Photo by the author.

Figure 13. These two-story condos were the last units Ross Cortese built at Leisure World Seal Beach. He then used these plans to build the first units at Leisure World Laguna Hills. He did not include elevators, although since then they have been added to some buildings. Photo by the author.

Figure 14. The largest pool at Laguna Woods formerly Leisure World Laguna Hills was at Clubhouse 1. The Aquadettes, a group of women residents, put on a popular annual synchronized swimming show. Photo by the author.

Figure 15. This exercise group at Laguna Woods met from 8 to 9 A.M. Bob Ring, president of the Historical Society of Laguna Woods, is shown talking with the fitness manager. Photo by the author.

Figure 16. The clubhouse at Century Village, West Palm Beach. Like the Leisure World communities, Century Villages were gated communities of relatively compact condominium units, which facilitated the use of vans for intracommunity transportation. Photo by the author.

Figure 17. Shuffleboard courts at Century Village, West Palm Beach, in 2009. Originally, this community had even more shuffleboard courts, but shuffleboard is no longer as popular as it was in the 1960s. Photo by the author.

Figure 18. The west gate at Century Village, West Palm Beach. Residents have an electronic device that allows them to pass, but all others must identify themselves to the guards who man these gates. Photo by the author.

Figure 19. Plan of Century Village, West Palm Beach. Gated communities present several planning problems. First, it is desirable to limit the number of entrances in order to limit the number of guards to be hired. This community has only two entrances, the east gate and the west gate. The second problem is how to locate those establishments that will serve both community residents and outsiders. Century Village handled that by leaving Okeechobee Boulevard open for commercial development and moving the west gate a block behind that strip.

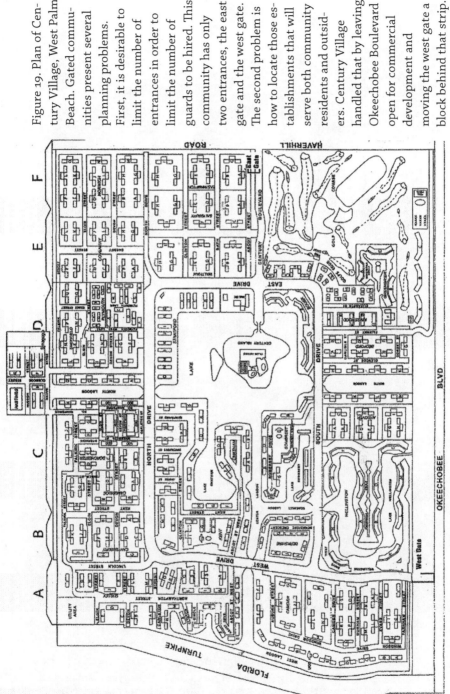

Figure 20. Housing in active adult communities becomes more elaborate as time passes. This three-bedroom golf course "spec" home with a golf cart garage in The Villages was listed at $456,000 in the depths of the 2009 housing crisis. By then, The Villages had around 70,000 people in different neighborhoods. House prices ranged from $65,000 for a used manufactured home in the oldest neighborhood to more than $1 million in the most exclusive areas. Photo by the author.

Figure 21. This home includes an in-ground swimming pool protected by a Florida "bird cage." The author was tempted to give the salesman a check for $2,500 to hold the home and chuck this book project, but she resisted. Photo by the author.

Figure 22. The Villages has a couple of commercial squares with "faux history" themes. The plaque on this bar and restaurant with a risqué floor show tells the story of Katie Belle Van Patten, a successful pioneer hotel operator of somewhat questionable repute. Other buildings at this Spanish Springs Square also have amusing, historically themed plaques, as does the Sumter Landing Square. The squares offer free entertainment on a nightly basis and lend a Disneylike atmosphere to the community. Photo by the author.

Figure 23. Because of discrimination and poor treatment, African Americans tended to be substantially underrepresented in active adult communities in the past. However, by the twenty-first century, most developers now regard African Americans as a segment of the population that they would like to attract. This Del Webb advertising photograph of a racially mixed group of residents centering on an African American is typical of other developers' occasional use of multiracial images in advertising as well.

Creating Community

The Developers' Script

The initial sales brochure for Sun City, Arizona, began with Del Webb saying, "Concrete, steel and lumber can make the buildings, but people make the community. Together we can realize a Way-of-Life unprecedented in America."[1] That quote appeared repeatedly in Sun City sales promotions up to Webb's death in 1974.[2] Webb, like most housing developers, was used to delivering houses to buyers, then walking away. In the words of John Meeker, who in 1965 became president of DEVCO (the Webb Corporation's retirement community subdivision), "The developer never wanted to see or hear from the buyer again."[3]

However, Sun City was different. Webb was not so much marketing houses as he was marketing a way of life for "active retirees." So was Ross Cortese with Leisure World Laguna Hills. It would take both communities around eighteen years to reach build-out. Both developers realized that they could not just build houses and let their buyers take it from there. They would actually have to implement the lifestyle they were touting. Just how did the developers do that? How did the residents react to this advertised and scripted lifestyle? What roles did the residents of these communities play in shaping or modifying the developers' image of an "active adult" lifestyle? What were the residents' politics, needs, values, and demands? Overall, for an age-restricted, active adult development, what was the process of creating community?

Webb and Cortese began with advertising strategies that were designed to target a particular kind of buyer and to give that buyer a certain identity or image that in turn would define the community. Early brochures pictured relatively youthful retirees, invariably white, and often as couples, engaged in a variety of crafts and recreational activities, socializing around the recreation center pool or enjoying a backyard barbecue with friends. From the start, Webb and Cortese made frequent use of the word "active" in defining their buyers and used the phrase "new way of life" to provide a script for their buyers' expectations of life in Sun Cities and Leisure Worlds. In the early 1960s, Webb launched a very expensive national advertising campaign designed to motivate young retirees to leave the North for one of his Sun Cities in Arizona, Florida, or California. Cortese put more emphasis on the use of local advertising, encouraging retirees in Southern California to first consider Leisure World Seal Beach and later, Leisure World Laguna Hills. For northern Californians, Cortese offered Leisure World Walnut Creek near San Francisco. Cortese had a national impact when he opened up Leisure Worlds on the East Coast to attract New Yorkers and other easterners to his nearby retirement communities in New Jersey and Maryland. Advertising was expensive. Developers varied, but each tried to assess the most likely market, present an image with which prospective buyers would want to identify, and hand them a script for a lifestyle they would want to buy.

Snowbirds and recent migrants to the Sunbelt were among the more likely prospects. As seasonal visitors or new migrants, they were already familiar with and drawn to various places in the South and Southwest. For example, Pete and Effie Whiting were successful Montana ranchers who decided to sell out in 1955 and move to Mesa, Arizona. When Sun City opened in 1960, Pete was attracted to the golf courses there and Effie to the new community's proliferating social organizations. She became the first president of the Sun City Women's Club and active in the local hospital auxiliary. Fred and Norma Millard moved in the 1950s to Youngtown, Arizona, from Davenport, Iowa, where Fred had been a carpenter. When Sun City opened, the Millards seized the opportunity to own a home backing onto a golf course, something not possible in amenity-starved Youngtown. Accomplished musicians, the Millards took part in a number of musical performances.[4] Golf and lots of social life were advertising themes, and many buyers were attracted to Sun City because they wanted such a lifestyle.

Preserving Home-State Identity

Trailer courts continued to attract almost entirely seasonal residents, but in the new retirement towns, the majority of the residents were permanent. However, some retirement-town residents continued their pattern of snowbird migration in various degrees. A 1975 survey of Sun

City showed 75 percent living there for twelve months, 17 percent nine to twelve months, 7 percent six to nine months, and 4 percent under six months. Four years later, in 1979, when Sun City reached build-out, only 60 percent were twelve-month residents; 28 percent were there from nine to twelve months and 10 percent from six to nine months. Those under six months or lacking legal residency there (minimum six months and one day, hardly a burden for those from states where winter seemed seven months long) in 1979 were just 2 percent.[5] The figures may reflect that most migrants came from high-tax states and found legal residency in Sun City a tax advantage. On the other hand, at California's Leisure Worlds, nearly everybody lived in those communities all year.[6] Possibly reflecting California's relatively high tax status, the bulk of those communities' residents already hailed from that state and wanted to remain reasonably close to their home communities.

For Arizona and Florida migrating retirees, some incentives existed for "permanent" residents to return to their states of origin in the summers. First, for many, the summer climate in their home states was cooler. Second, the annual return trips allowed them to maintain ties with friends and family back home. In other cases, some friends and family followed the migrants to the Sunbelt; in still other cases, with the passage of time migrating retirees lost touch with those back home and developed closer ties with people they got to know in their new retirement communities.[7] In any case, year-round residents in popular retirement areas in Florida and Arizona noted the increase in traffic and congestion during the winter months. Historian Daniel Boorstin maintains that transiency is part of the American character, and new cities with no history have been part of the pioneering experience.[8] Boorstin does not touch on migrating to a new retirement community, but these communities may well be a recent version of the pioneer trends influencing the American character and the decisions of some retirees in the past half-century.

Webb, Cortese, and other developers quickly learned how to use state identity to assuage some anxieties associated with migrating and to make their recruits happy and keep additional recruits coming. From the point of view of those who chose to buy into these new retirement communities, motivating factors often involved such state-related issues as a warmer, healthier climate and financial issues such as the relative price of housing, cost of living, different state tax structures, and differing states' philosophies as to whether it was better to have low taxes in a community and rely more on volunteers for services or higher taxes and more paid services. Whether snowbirds, who returned to their states of origin during the summers, or year-round residents, many would seek out others in the retirement communities from their home state and maintain a certain amount of that state identity. Developers used this desire for state identity as a recruiting tool to get existing residents to recruit others. Also, emphasizing the migrant identity of residents was a way of fostering sociability in their new communities.

In some ways, the tendency of the "active adults" in these communities to seek out others from their home states may be a kind of aging in place in spite of their temporary or permanent change in residence. Developers knew that most retirees would be reluctant to migrate but that there was a definite niche market among retirees who would respond. In 1960, Webb estimated the size of that niche market as 2 percent of retirees. By 1972, his estimate had grown to 10 percent of retirees.[9]

While developers emphasized ties to one's state of origin as a way of encouraging people to migrate and of creating a sense of community, recipient states sometimes expressed concern about lack of loyalty to them. For example, U.S. Senator Bob Graham of Florida coined the phrase "Cincinnati factor," meaning people from Ohio might transfer their legal residence to Florida, but emotionally they were still in Ohio. Florida was simply a way station between their work life in the Midwest and, as one writer, John Rothchild, put it, "the Pearly Gates."[10] The fact that retirees from elsewhere in these retirement communities had a different way of relating to their adopted states certainly contributed to their own sense of community within the retirement developments.

Webb's choice of states with low cost of living for his retirement communities was conscious, particularly with respect to the Arizona and Florida Sun Cities. In 1964, Webb told a Honolulu reporter that his firm had considered Hawaii as a location for a Sun City, but the cost of living was too high for the "middle income group—doctors, lawyers, retired army officers" who made up the typical clientele for a Sun City. He did not think that a Hawaiian Sun City would generate "enough volume" for the type of community he was building. Furthermore, while retirees were willing to travel, Hawaii's distance from the mainland was too much. Finally, Webb conceded the need to be near a large city.[11] It is possible that when he made that statement about being near a large city, Webb was indirectly indicating his awareness of the phenomenal success of Ross Cortese's Leisure World Seal Beach in the Greater Los Angeles area. Developers did keep track of their competition.

Some of the state differentials in taxes and home prices were not as pronounced in the early 1960s as they would become later. California did have a state income tax, but in the early 1960s, it did not have a reputation as a state with relatively high home prices. Webb built nearly identical homes in all three Sun Cities—California, Florida, and Arizona—and the prices of those homes were all fairly comparable. For a buyer coming from a northern climate that necessitated additional construction costs, however, Webb's homes looked very reasonably priced. By emphasizing affordability, both Webb and Cortese attracted residents who valued keeping costs low. That value would influence their unfavorable attitudes toward incorporation of their communities. In some cases, it also influenced their politics when it came to school bond issues and the use of volunteers to provide services that people elsewhere were willing to pay professionals to provide.

State background also involved a lot of intangibles, such as familiarity with the state's politics, support for local sports teams, and just a sense of what it meant to be from a particular place. Almost from the beginning, DEVCO used its first residents to attract others from their home communities. Typically, the earliest residents saw themselves as pioneers in their new communities and were willing participants.[12] DEVCO's public relations department employees interviewed many of them to get their stories and take their photos, then mailed the material to their hometown newspapers. DEVCO estimated that the hometown newspapers used more than 80 percent of these stories. Another tactic was to comb the Sun City telephone directory, which listed the previous businesses or occupations of the residents. If DEVCO employees spotted a number of residents who had worked for the same company, such as Quaker Oats, the public relations department would arrange a barbecue and some entertainment, "take a group photo, write up a story and send it to the company publication." It was a great way to get those current company employees fantasizing about possibly retiring in Sun City.

Although DEVCO's primary purpose in using home-state identity in these ways was to sell homes, such sales tactics also helped new residents get to know each other. In addition, the residents developed a sense of common identity based in part on being migrants from elsewhere. The elderly who chose to migrate to an active adult community generally shared relatively good health plus the financial means to relocate,[13] not to mention the psychological energy or sense of adventure that it took to risk moving to a new location. Furthermore, as retirees, they were free from "factors pertaining to the workplace" and could indulge in picking a social environment that suited their interests.[14]

Developer-sponsored newspapers and newsletters were another community-building device that doubled as a sales tool. DEVCO sent a biweekly newsletter to buyers who had returned to their home states to sell their homes, keeping them psychologically tied to Sun City and fending off "buyer remorse." This newsletter was designed to be shown to the buyers' friends and relatives back in the home states, along with other promotional material. DEVCO even provided its residents with free Christmas cards picturing the community to send back home.[15] Although Leisure World Laguna Hills was drawing more of its residents from the local area, it too began publishing a weekly community newspaper that it sent to residents in the community,[16] as well to future residents.[17] The other Leisure World communities of Seal Beach and Walnut Creek in California had their own versions of this newspaper.

To implement their advertised "active retirement" lifestyle, from the start the major developers hired activities directors for their communities. Longtime Del Webb public relations director Jerry Svendsen recalled, "The activities department and the marketing department were related."[18] These activities directors also used home-state identity to foster sociability among the new residents. In Sun City's early days, Webb's activities director ran monthly dances at which all the new arrivals from that month were "introduced by their former state of residence."[19] One of the first ministers in Sun City began the practice of asking new residents "to stand on a large map of the U.S. within the boundaries of the borders of their previous state of residence. They were then joined by more established Sun Citians from the same states, who welcomed the newcomers."[20]

With a larger population by the mid-1960s, DEVCO began its State Days promotions with food and entertainment.[21] It celebrated a different state or group of states each Sunday, bringing together Sun Citians from that state for socializing.[22] DEVCO continued its State Days promotions until Sun City reached build-out in the late 1970s.[23] Supplementing the State Days were state clubs, which have continued down to the present, long after DEVCO personnel withdrew from promoting community activities and events in Sun City once it reached build-out. As time passed, the original home buyers aged; as their homes came up for resale, that kept the flow of out-of-state migrants coming, continuing the "migrant" identity of the community and replenishing the state clubs.

State identity was also a way for residents to come together at Leisure World Laguna Hills. In February 1965, thirty-seven former Minnesotans formed the Minnesota Club with plans to hold monthly meetings open to all former residents of that state.[24] The next month, former residents of Iowa came together to organize an Iowa Club.[25] However, Leisure World Laguna Hills was drawing a lot of residents from its own state of California. So as not to be left out, these people soon formed a Native California Club.[26]

As time passed, California state taxes rose, and so did the price of California real estate. Increasingly, movement to a California retirement community became an in-state thing as opposed to a financial draw for out-of-state prospects. For example, a 1977 study showed the property taxes on a $62,000 home in Sun City, Arizona, to be $470 compared to $2,200 for property taxes on a similar home in Palm Springs, California.[27] Shortly after build-out in the early 1980s, about two-thirds of Leisure World Laguna Hills residents had lived in southern California prior to moving into that community.[28] While both the Minnesota and Wisconsin clubs were still around in 1989,[29] by 2006 they had become part of the Midwest Club. Among those Laguna Hills clubs persisting into 2006 were the New Jersey Club, the New York Club, and the Chicago Club.[30]

The Leisure Worlds tended to draw many residents from their local areas, while Sun City, Arizona, attracted most of its residents from out of the state. However, migration patterns there shifted somewhat over time. During its first year, more people (20 percent) came from California than any other state. Arizona contributed 17 percent, and 10 percent were from Illinois. The majority, 54 percent, were from the West. Ten years later, Illinois was in the lead as the state of origin for 14 percent of Sun City's residents. Arizona contributed only 4 percent. By region, the North Central, or Midwest, was the most prominent former place of residence, with 47 percent coming from there.[31]

That shift reflected Del Webb's policy of aiming advertising largely at the Midwest. For example, a 1962 full-page ad headlined "Vacations Last a Lifetime in Del Webb's Sun City—California, Arizona, Florida" ran in the newspapers of ten medium-sized towns. Four of these were in Illinois—Decatur, Springfield, Galesburg, and Elmira. Another four were in similar towns in neighboring states—Muncie, Battle Creek, Lafayette, and Saginaw.[32] Retirees from the Northeast, Indiana, and Ohio were more likely to head for Florida.[33] However, whether they were moving across the country to Sun City, Arizona, down to Florida, or relocating from a nearby metropolitan area to Leisure World, the vast majority made their retirement communities their permanent homes, unlike those in retiree trailer courts, which were practically empty of residents during the hot summer months.

Ethnic, Racial, and Religious Diversity Issues

In creating a sense of community, developers stressed how much the residents had in common. These communities placed far more emphasis on home-state identity than they did on ethnicity. However, with so many residents from California and given the ethnic diversity of that state, ethnicity did take on added importance with the passage of time at Leisure World Laguna Hills. Groups meeting in mid-August 2006 included a Chinese Club and a Korean American Club, various Jewish groups, and the local chapter of the Daughters of the American Revolution.[34] This ethnic diversity exhibited in the twenty-first century tended to go against the stereotyped image of active adult, age-restricted communities being for whites only. When it came to civil rights and diversity issues, just how open were these communities?

A few critics from the 1970s and 1980s contended that anti-Semitism was present in these communities. In the early 1970s, Maurice Hamovitch, a University of Southern California researcher, alleged that anti-Semitism and racism were common in retirement communities in California.[35] However, Miriam Goldstein, mother of the famous feminist Betty Friedan, lived at Leisure World Laguna Hills for more than two decades. Goldstein had been active in Jewish groups while her daughter was growing up in Peoria, Illinois.[36] Cortese followed a policy of making free building sites available within his communities for churches and synagogues as one way of developing complete communities and also because these institutions added to the community facilities for only the cost of the land to the developer. Furthermore, a year after opening and before a synagogue could be built at Leisure World Laguna Hills, Jewish residents were holding Sabbath services in a clubhouse dining room.[37] In her 1983 article profiling Sun City Center, Florida, that is reprinted in her *Cities on a Hill*, journalist Frances FitzGerald remarks that anti-Semitism was widespread. However, the 2005 telephone book for Sun City Center listed a Jewish Reform Synagogue. Furthermore, a 1980 survey of Sun City, Arizona, revealed that 4 percent of the community's residents were Jewish, which at that time was twice the percentage of Jews in the Phoenix metropolitan area.[38] Miami Beach developed the reputation of being the Jewish retirement destination, but Jewish retirees chose a variety of other places as well. Historian Gary Mormino has credited retirement communities for doing a lot to bring other ethnic groups and Jews into Florida, substantially diversifying that state's population.[39] That diversification extended to other retirement destinations as well. Since all organizations supported by local residents' associations had to be open to everyone in the community, inclusion based on residence in the community, not ethnic or racial background, was built into the formal social structure of these communities.

Webb's policy on church sites was to sell them at a "moderate" price and "on an as needed basis." The company promoted having as many denominations present as possible. The main concern seemed to be that some of the first church buildings were quite plain and lacked landscaping. Hence, the company began adding landscaping costs to the sales price. The result was more attractive churches in Phase 2 of Sun City, Arizona, something that DEVCO president John Meeker referred to as "an even better sales tool for DEVCO."[40] Churches turned out to be more important to Sun City residents than to those in other communities in the area. According to a 1980 poll, 62 percent of Sun City residents considered themselves "church oriented" compared to 41 percent for the Phoenix metropolitan area as a whole.[41]

However, a significant discriminatory problem existed with the lack of African American retirees living in active adult retirement communities. One observer said that in 1990 less than 1 percent of the residents of Sun City and Sun City West in Arizona were black, Hispanic, or Asian.[42] Communities appear to have differed with respect to a sizable contingent of Asian residents, but African Americans appear to be virtually absent from all of these communities. In 1950s Florida, blacks were supposed to stay off the beaches unless they were working there in a service capacity.[43] That prejudice seemed to carry over into the new retirement communities in Florida and elsewhere. The 1970 Census for Sun City, California, listed 5,519 residents, of which none were African

American and only three were other races.[44] Furthermore, since Sun City, California, was drawing its residents primarily from the Greater Los Angeles area, where blacks were 18 percent of the population, place of origin was hardly an explanation.[45] Instead, these very "clubby" communities were guilty of quite pervasive, but subtle, discrimination.

The developers set the tone. Jerry Svendsen noted that it was "a Caucasian thing to do" to move to a retirement community; Webb, who began selling homes in Sun City in 1960, never intentionally said, "Come out to our white community."[46] Tom Breen, an early Webb executive, told a reporter in 1964 that salesmen were told "to assure 'Negro' customers that they could buy any house they wanted." An African American woman took the firm up on that offer at Sun City, California. According to Breen, Webb staff then contacted her future white neighbors on each side of her house, giving them the option of switching lots. Even though one neighbor "said it made no difference to them," Breen claimed, "We were just one step short of a revolution out there." Breen added, "What would happen if she should want to have a swimming party and invited all her colored friends from Los Angeles out there a couple of nights? It would amount to having the swimming pool taken over by colored people a couple of times a week." The African American woman never moved into the community. While salesmen for Sun City were told not to discriminate, according to Breen as quoted by the reporter, it was the sales manager's job to explain to prospective African American buyers "what they are getting into because, let's face it, a Negro would be miserable in Sun City."[47] Looking back, Jerry Svendsen emphasized that neither the Webb Corporation nor Tom Breen "was racist." Instead, they were responding to the attitudes of those who wintered "annually in the sun states and marketed to that cohort."[48] At build-out in 1980, less than 1 percent of Sun City, Arizona's, population of 46,000 was African American.[49]

The residents in general tended to reflect the attitude that Svendsen noted. As time passed, outside salespeople handled an increasing number of resales. According to a sociologist writing in 1974, salespeople were quite willing to show prospective African American buyers homes in a community like Sun City, California. However, their message, reinforced by residents there whose heads turned at seeing an African American in the shopping center or clubhouse, was that African American buyers "would be happier elsewhere." The sociologist called what was going on "genteel discrimination."[50] As for African Americans, one Sun City, Arizona, critic cited several of his African American acquaintances saying they "wouldn't be caught dead in that Whitie-land."[51]

An Arizona-based scholar in 1992 predicted, "Retirement communities in the future will have to face the same requirement for racial and other integration as other neighborhoods within the city."[52] Webb and other developers, in their twenty-first century advertising, were including photographs picturing African Americans as residents. In chapter 6 I further discuss how the developers reflected the growing egalitarian attitudes of buyers and have attempted to exploit the African American market in recent years. With the developers' heritage of stressing the commonality of residents, implementing racial diversity would not be easy.

The Middle Class and the Affordability Pitch

Just as residents of these communities shared overall homogeneity in terms of age and race, they also had a lot in common in terms of their former occupations and financial status. At the end of the Arizona Sun City's first year of existence, one-sixth of the residents mentioned sales as their former occupation, 15 percent indicated a blue collar background such as carpenter; 7 percent had been managers, and another 7 percent were health care professionals.[53] Leisure World Laguna Hills had a number of former blue-collar workers as residents initially as well, although the majority of early residents were professionals or business managers.[54] Likewise, Sun City, California, had a similar mix of former professionals, military personnel, and "skilled blue collar workers."[55]

These former occupations meant that those moving into the communities typically had above-average but not lavish incomes. In 1960, the median income for people over sixty-five in the United States was $3,671. In Sun City, Arizona, it was $6,850.[56] However, it is important to remember that many of those at Sun City, Arizona, were actually younger than sixty-five since the minimum age was fifty. By 1970, the mean income in Sun City, Arizona, was $11,113, about the same as the mean income nationally for those ages sixty to sixty-four. What made Sun City, Arizona, different at that point was that only 10 percent of residents had incomes under $4,000 per year compared to 28 percent nationally.[57] Again, with relatively few residents who were very rich or very poor, what stood out about the active adult, age-restricted communities and what, presumably, many of their residents appreciated was the relative social class homogeneity.

This social class homogeneity was somewhat undercut by the trend among developers to build more expensive houses as time passed. A usual explanation was the growing affluence of retirees. However, developers soon found themselves competing with resales of their earlier houses. Consequently, the pressure was there to make the newer models fancier and more expensive. At Sun City, Arizona, several years after build-out at the end of the 1970s, the average income for a two-person family who had lived there a couple of decades was $14,000, about the same as for similar households nationally.[58] Some of the earlier residents traded up as the newer, fancier models became available.

To put a face on these statistics, Ina and John Dodt were fairly representative of the early residents. Ina Dodt had been a Champaign-Urbana, Illinois, department store model. Her husband had worked as a salesman. On retirement in the mid-1950s, they moved to Scottsdale, Arizona. Both were avid golfers. Attracted by the "active retirement" advertising of Sun City and the lively social life, they moved in during the community's first year. Thirty-some years later, Ina Dodt praised the community's "close-knit atmosphere," its recreational opportunities, and the warm climate. For her, the community met its advertised expectations.[59] DEVCO was not just selling houses; it was scripting and selling an "active adult" lifestyle. The Dodts were typical of buyers who were attracted by the advertised script.

Ina Dodt's interviewer did not mention the affordability of the homes as a reason for the Dodts' move to Sun City, but affordability was one of the main themes in the design as well as the advertising of both Webb's and Cortese's communities in the first half of the 1960s. A 1963 Del Webb sales brochure led with the statement "ANYONE who can retire CAN AFFORD Full-time living in any of Del Webb's Beautiful Cities." The brochure went on to list "6 reasons why many folks live on less than $300 a month in any of these Del Webb cities." They included use of the recreation facilities "for just a nickel a day. . . . low, low rates" on the golf course, "very modest prices on the homes and cooperative apartments," and "low property taxes" due to not having to finance school buildings.[60] Del Webb kept his homes affordable by constructing large numbers of them based on just several models and replicating them in retirement communities in three states. In a sense, where Levitt and Sons was building suburban communities on a mass scale with the young veteran in mind after World War II, Webb was building ex-urban communities for retirees on a mass scale beginning in 1960. His executives kept the comparison in mind. In 1976, R. H. Johnson, chair of the Del Webb Corporation, sent a note to DEVCO president John Meeker that Sun City, Arizona, was surpassing the 17,000 dwellings in Levittown, New York, with nearly 21,000 units, making Sun City the largest city to be constructed by one company.[61] In terms of number of homes, Sun City also surpassed the larger but less publicized Los Angeles suburb of Lakewood, with its 17,500 homes.[62]

Lakewood and Levittown had larger populations because they were intergenerational communities. Lakewood at build-out in 1954 had 57,000 residents compared to Sun City's approximately 46,000. Lakewood occupied 3,500 acres compared to Sun City's 10,000, indicating that Webb was using land for golf courses, recreation centers, and other nonresidential uses that were absent in Lakewood. Finally, both Lakewood and Levittown were built within a few years using only a couple of basic house models. Sun City was developed over nearly two decades and had a much greater variety of housing. However, that is not to say that Webb did not derive some inspiration from the large tract suburbs of the postwar period. Webb had kept his land costs reasonable by purchasing large tracts from thirteen to thirty miles from metropolitan areas. Distance from cities would prove to be a drag on sales for Sun Cities in Florida and California, but the Arizona Sun City soon became contiguous with the rapidly expanding Greater Phoenix metropolitan area.

Cortese also aimed for the mass market with affordable retirement homes. His land costs were higher because he built closer to metropolitan areas. However, he built more compactly. In the early 1960s, all of his units were cooperative apartments in the back-to-back configuration, with the first units averaging around 900 square feet.[63] While the designs were Cortese's, he relied heavily at this time on FHA financing, and FHA used its clout to dictate some design changes. For example, FHA was responsible for the addition of two closets, one for linen and the other storage, in two models, the substitution of an iron railing for a stucco wall encasing outdoor balconies, and the centering of stairways to second-story apartments in the breezeways between the buildings, allowing for wider kitchens and larger windows.[64] The sales price of a typical Leisure World unit in 1962 was around $11,000. With FHA guaranteeing an interest rate of 5.25 percent for forty years with just 3 percent down, it made the Leisure World communities affordable.[65] Thus, FHA had a lot of clout.

The advertised theme of affordability was reflected in the actual design and construction of Sun City's houses in the first half of the 1960s. Webb's first houses ranged in size from 850 square feet in the Kentworth model to 1,600 square feet,[66] were built with cement block, and had ceramic tile in the kitchens and baths, carports, concrete patios, and landscaping. In the early 1960s, landscaping included palm trees, orange trees, and cacti plus green grass surrounding about 80 percent of those early homes. Grass was what most buyers were used to back home, but it was not very practical in the arid Southwest. However, overspray from the golf course sprinklers created some problems for residents whose yards backed onto the fairways, so Webb switched to gravel yards for those lots.[67] By 1970, the firm was using full or partial "rock lawns" for more than 90 percent of its new homes.[68]

Sun City buyers in 1960 could choose from five single-family detached home models with three exterior treatments or apartments. Options included upgrading from evaporative to refrigerated air conditioning, going from a single to a double carport, and a lot backing onto a golf course. Desiring more space, many of the early buyers converted their patios into glassed-in Arizona rooms.[69] A number of Florida buyers did the same thing in Sun City Center, calling the enclosed patio a Florida room.[70] Webb had deliberately hired a Denver architect who had experience designing homes for clients in several midwestern states. His idea was to give out-of-state people a home in Sun City that would resemble what they knew in their home states.[71] The Arizona and Florida rooms are good examples of buyers responding to their new climates and adapting the developers' homes more to suit themselves. The patio conversions also sent a message to developers that buyers wanted larger homes.

While Webb did not emphasize townhouses and apartments, he did offer them from the start at Sun City. Webb even pioneered the condominium legal concept in Maricopa County, Arizona. DEVCO convinced the county to adopt "a new type of apartment zoning" for its garden apartments, giving "apartment and duplex owners fee title to the property the unit was built on and a share of the common area. It also allowed each unit to be taxed separately."[72] Since the public in the early 1960s was more used to the word "cooperative" to denote a residential association to maintain the common areas of the apartment complex, Webb's ads at this time used the word "cooperative" for what was legally a condominium.

The Middle Class and the "Resort-Retirement Community" Pitch

In the early 1960s, Cortese built affordable units in part because he was participating in FHA's cooperative housing program. However, in the late 1960s, conventional mortgage rates skyrocketed while FHA rates remained fixed. That meant that banks charged discount points to FHA buyers, which made FHA financing so expensive that Cortese dropped it in 1968. At the same time, he switched from cooperative to condominium ownership.[73] At first, the apartment units were the same, but condominium buyers had more freedom in selling or renting units they owned individually. If the appliances broke down, replacement was the condominium owner's responsibility, but cooperatives still had the responsibility for appliances in those units. The advantage to the condo owners was that they had more choice in deciding which appliances they wanted. Thus, FHA financing of cooperative ownership fell victim to rising interest rates.

Cortese realized that buyer demand was moving in the direction of larger units. By the early 1970s, his condominiums and attached townhouses "averaged 1,200 square feet, and by the late 1970s, they were typically 1,600 square feet." He did not include single-family homes at Leisure World Laguna Hills until it was about to reach build-out around 1980, but those were luxury homes averaging 2,400 square feet.[74] While Webb did offer some condominium apartments and townhouses, the majority (70 percent) of his units at Sun City, Arizona, were single-family, detached houses.[75] With more compact communities, Cortese continued to provide an intracommunity shuttle bus service and guarded gates, amenities lacking in the Webb developments. Initially, Webb's and Cortese's pricing was similar for both the homes and the residential association fees, partly because Cortese provided an initial subsidy of more than $2 million to support maintenance and various community services.[76] However, with the passage of time, the gates and buses made the Leisure World residential association fees substantially greater than those of the Sun Cities.

Retirement incomes continued to rise, just as house prices in general rose nationally and the average house got larger and more expensive.

Around 1965, Webb dropped the affordability advertising theme and stopped building for "the lower end of the housing market."[77] Houses became more expensive. Webb added fancier features such as courtyards and atriums and began experimenting with Mediterranean designs. The first project of this type opened in 1966 with flat-roofed villas sporting columns, friezes, arches, decorative tile, ornamental ironwork, and a second-story room to serve as a retreat for the husband. At first sales were slow, but the popularity of this style increased over time as buyers began to look for more Mediterranean character in their housing.[78] As for handicap-accessible features, DEVCO president John Meeker continued to eschew them. In his view, buyers did not want wheelchair ramps as standard, nor did they like prominent bathroom grab bars, so these were only included at the buyer's request.[79]

In addition to watching its sales figures, DEVCO had several other ways of trying to anticipate and then accommodate buyer preferences. One was to reasonably price buyers' change orders, keep track of them, and then include the most frequently requested ones as standard on future models. A second way was to be alert "to any negative feedback" and adjust the designs of the next models accordingly. Likewise, the firm kept track of favorable comments. Among items that got good reviews were windows over the kitchen sink, good "carpet so the buyer did not have to automatically upgrade, and high quality kitchen appliances."[80] John Meeker, who became president of DEVCO in 1965, was known to actually call or drop in on Sun City home buyers to solicit feedback on what they liked and disliked about their homes along with how those homes might be improved.[81] On at least one occasion when a resident complained that the flat roof on his house was not built properly, Meeker arrived at the man's house with a ladder, went up to the roof, decided that the man was right, ordered the repair, then returned afterward with his ladder to be "sure it was fixed."[82] A more organized approach to getting feedback occurred in the early years of Sun City when Meeker's office mailed 1,100 questionnaires to Sun City home buyers and got 1,000 of those returned. The high return rate may reflect Meeker's reputation for taking buyer feedback seriously and trying to incorporate that feedback into the firm's latest models.[83]

A third strategy for getting buyer feedback, used in 1967, was to build an experimental home to sample public reaction to a variety of new features. Among other things, this home had a central courtyard with a fountain, masonite siding to reduce maintenance, an automatic garage-door opener, a whirlpool bathtub, a double fireplace serving both the leisure room and sunken living room, and a centrally controlled music and intercom system. DEVCO sought opinions from potential buyers for which innovations they would be most willing to pay. The company then offered some of these innovations as options on subsequent homes and discarded others as either too expensive for their potential market or "ahead of their time."[84]

Finally, there were the models themselves with their available options. At Sun City, the most expensive model group appeared in 1974. Options included an indoor swimming pool and a sunken tub and bidet. Apparently, the buyer response was less than enthusiastic. The 1976 models were less expensive and more traditional in design.[85] As for the residents at Sun City, the annual updating of the models and the continual expansion of the amenities until build-out at the end of the 1970s reinforced their sense of pride in being part of a growing community.

In 1969, DEVCO ran an ad characterizing Sun City as a "Resort-Retirement Community."[86] About that time, the firm crossed Grand Avenue, the major highway into Sun City, to begin Phase 2. Phase 3, which included the model with the optional indoor pool, was north of Phase 2. Hence, the more expensive, newer models undercut some of the earlier economic homogeneity of Sun City, with the area north of Grand Avenue being decidedly more expensive than the older section to the south. As one observer put it, "Older residents came to regard Grand Avenue as a class divide."[87] The firm introduced new models about every two years. For current residents, viewing the new models "became the social event of the year."[88] Some of the viewers turned out to be buyers, eager to trade in an older model for a newer one, perhaps crossing the class divide to a fancier neighborhood. For the developers, much like the automakers, changing models was a way to keep sales moving.

Another result of the constantly changing models over the nineteen years that it took to build Sun City was an unusually wide variety of housing for a community built entirely by one firm. For example, while the standard lot size was only 7,000 square feet, Webb developed Rancho Estates as part of Phase 1 with one-acre lots connected to bridle paths for horse enthusiasts.[89] Phase 2 included some houses backing onto manmade Viewpoint Lake. The typical home had an open yard with no privacy walls allowed; for those who wanted privacy, Sun City offered townhomes surrounded by brick walls six feet high and rooms opening onto interior patios. It was one of the latter that Webb gave to his reclusive ex-wife, Hazel Church Webb. While the dominant script was the highly social, active adult lifestyle for middle-class retirees, the company provided a variety of options—but no slums and not many really expensive homes, either. Even though the firm dropped the affordability theme from its advertising in the mid-1960s, that image lingered and did hamper the company's occasional attempts to tap into a wealthier market. Buyers limited some of the firm's options, but DEVCO, with its early emphasis on affordability and a mass market, was the dominant player in shaping the social characteristics of Sun City.

While they did not serve the very wealthy, Webb, Cortese, and other developers did note the trend toward buyers preferring more expensive, larger, and more elaborate homes. Besides the growing wealth of retirees, DEVCO president John Meeker theorized that "it took buyers with financial stability to relocate from their present home in another state," and they wanted more than just a basic house.[90] Tax laws and skyrocketing home prices also became a factor. By the early 1980s, retirees selling their original homes often faced big tax bills on their capital gains. However, they could take advantage of a one-time rollover to shelter that gain by purchasing another home of equal or greater value within two years.[91] The "Resort-Retirement" sales pitches for these more elaborate houses contributed to the impression that these were communities for the well-to-do.

The older neighborhoods did not deteriorate into slums. However, as time passed, some poverty, though largely invisible, did exist in Sun City, Arizona. The early buyers tended to have fewer financial resources than the later ones. Furthermore, inflation eroded fixed incomes. The death of a spouse could also reduce income. By 1975, 20 percent of Sun City residents had "incomes of less than $8500 per year," the majority living in Phase 1 south of Grand Avenue. Sun City churches and philanthropic organizations reached out to those in need. However, when promoting charitable activities as an option with Sun City's active adult lifestyle, DEVCO personnel talked about those organizations helping people outside the community, not within its borders. Poverty was not part of the image of "paradise" in the DEVCO script.[92]

Affordability through Resales

Finally, within a few years of the opening of their communities, developers began to experience the effect of the resale market for their earlier homes. In fact, for a time both Cortese and Webb operated resale businesses in their communities. By making their new houses more elaborate than their resales, they were able to differentiate the products. From the viewpoint of the buyer with a limited amount to spend, the resale market maintained the initial affordability of these communities.

From the developers' viewpoint, the resale market was the answer to their concern with the mortality of buyers and those houses coming on the market and the related concern in the early 1960s that the demand for housing in an age-restricted, active adult community was limited. Webb entered the business of reselling its homes in Sun City, Arizona, in 1964, handling about 250 such sales that year.[93] The following year, Webb executive Joe Ashton produced a memorandum he called "A Matter of Life and Death." After selling nearly 1,300 homes in Sun City, Arizona, in 1960, sales had declined to around 600 in 1963. The other Sun Cities and Kern City, California, showed similar declines. Hence the concern about the future demand. At the same time, the population of Sun City, Arizona, was aging. Ashton estimated that deaths would put around 100 houses on the market each year, which "could provide a negative influence on the new house sales." This memo had an actuarial table attached projecting the timing of deaths of the 1963 residents of Sun City.[94]

DEVCO's resale business continued to expand even as the firm added more new homes to Sun City. The real estate market was cyclical. While Sun City was expanding, there were years when resales outnumbered new home sales. In 1973, DEVCO sold 382 new homes and handled 426 resales of its older homes.[95] That year "the turnover rate on Sun City homes . . . was a low 7.7 percent, about half the national rate for FHA housing." Furthermore, it was not just deaths of residents behind the resales. More than 40 percent of Sun City residents selling their homes did so to buy new homes in the community.[96] That high number indicated significant resident satisfaction with Sun City, even as residents sought to move up to better homes. In 1976, DEVCO had five real estate offices located in Sun City shopping centers, all handling resales. When the firm reached build-out at Sun City in 1979, one of its final projects was a 5,000-square-foot resale office at a prime intersection between Phase 2 and Phase 3 of Sun City.[97] Years after build-out, Webb was still in the resale business in Sun City.[98]

Other developers also found themselves in the resale market of their homes. In 1968 in Leisure World Laguna Hills, the resale price of a two-bedroom, two-bath, unfurnished "Majorca" unit was $5,850. The following year, a new one-bedroom, one-bath condo was $15,900.[99] Eventually both Cortese's and Webb's firms exited the resale business, perhaps because of some conflicts of interest in dealing with potential buyers. While the Webb and Cortese firms were in the resale business, sellers always had a choice of going with the developer's resale operation or listing with an independent broker. The persistence of resales, however, kept these communities more affordable than the new home ads after the mid-1960s indicated.

Sun City Amenities versus National Advertising

Given the recession of 1965, sales of new homes at Sun City, Arizona, were about half what they were in 1960, and sales at the other Sun Cities were also lagging. While DEVCO was still operating in the black, Del Webb had to put some of his own money into the parent Del Webb Corporation to stabilize it financially.[100] The time had come for a re-evaluation, a new direction in marketing, and an administrative reorganization. Webb had begun Sun City, Arizona, to the tune of a very expensive national advertising campaign. With the addition in 1962 of the Florida and California Sun Cities, the firm adopted a policy of very substantial opening-year advertising on both the national and local levels, then "writing it off over a five year period."[101] Obviously, those heavy advertising expenditures could not go on indefinitely. Furthermore, by 1965, the heavy national advertising campaign had achieved its objective of letting the public know that a new kind of retirement community had come into being.

Credit for putting together the Sun City concept and then making it a reality belonged to three executives, L. C Jacobson, Joe Ashton, and Tom Breen.[102] With the 1965 reorganization, all three of those men were out—along with the entire fifty-person marketing group. Survival as a financially sound company meant staff cutbacks had to take precedence over keeping the corporate "family" together, and the former ways of doing business needed to be reassessed. The new marketing staff consisted of only three people. With them came a shift in emphasis away from major advertising and toward an emphasis on greater company involvement with the community "instead of just 'sell the house and forget them.'"[103] Support for the community, in the words of the new president of DEVCO, John Meeker, "became a most powerful sales tool."[104] That strategy meant cultivating the residents who in turn would sell the community to their friends, relatives, and prospective visitors to Sun City. John Meeker, who now had responsibility directly under Del Webb for all the Sun Cities, was a major advocate of this new direction, and it worked.

Meeker would remain head of DEVCO through the build-out of Sun City and the launching of Sun City West, eventually leaving the company along with a number of other staff members during the 1981 recession. His long tenure made him extremely influential in the development of both communities. Meeker was born in 1926, attended public schools in Phoenix, and at the age of twelve began working as a golf caddy at a public course. Two years later, he was a caddy at the Phoenix Country Club, where he met construction company head Del Webb. Webb began to regularly ask for his services.[105] Meeker's family circumstances were modest. His father had died by the time Meeker met Webb. Webb had no children of his own. Meeker recalled that he considered Webb his friend. The two liked each other.[106] In 1944, at the age of seventeen, Meeker joined the Air Force. Discharged in 1946, he considered college but took a position that Del Webb personally offered him with his corporation. He started at the bottom as an errand boy and moved up rapidly. In 1955, he transferred to Webb's housing division. The firm had built a number of conventional subdivisions, including five in the Phoenix area. Meeker got experience working with the salesmen to improve the house designs and keep sales moving. A married man, he moved his family into one of those Webb homes.[107]

Meeker was an avid golfer whose resume listed only two hobbies, "golf and development planning."[108] In 1959, Meeker became the person responsible for the city plan for Sun City along with the design of the homes, public facilities, and golf courses.[109] Meeker deserves "major credit for the concept of circling Sun City avenues and boulevards around the golf courses,"[110] or winding the golf courses through the community with modest homes on lots backing up to those courses. It was a very innovative concept at the time and probably the first use of that concept in a development of modestly priced homes. Meeker also picked the names for Sun City's streets. He used golf as a theme, naming streets after famous golfers such as Hogan and Snead and famous golf courses such as Cherry Hills Drive and Pebble Beach Boulevard.[111] He standardized the street names in all three Sun Cities so one could turn left onto Pebble Creek Boulevard, then right onto Cherry Hills Drive in each one. Meeker shared Del Webb's passion for golf and translated that passion into a theme for Sun City.

Meeker's impact on the development of Sun City increased when he became the president of Del Webb's retirement community subsidiary, DEVCO. It was Meeker's policy to spend much less on advertising and a lot more on "community activities and promotions in an effort to get residents to become supportive and be a stronger source of referrals." DEVCO had always had an activities director to organize events and bring the residents together, which was a major difference from the first age-restricted community, Youngtown. That older development's founder, Ben Schleifer, avoided doing that on the theory that residents should organize their own activities.[112] Sun City retirees had proven that they wanted activity direction. Meeker ramped up the activities. Through a series of actions in the latter half of the 1960s, DEVCO showed the residents that it "truly cared about [their] security, happiness and the Sun City way of life."[113]

Foremost among these actions was the implementation of the Sun Bowl, Meeker's idea for an outdoor amphitheater featuring big-name talent at low cost for Sun City residents as well as prospective buyers. DEVCO brought in national entertainers like Lawrence Welk for Sunday-afternoon shows, charged only $1.50 per ticket, attracted audiences of around 7,000, then invited those present to tour the model homes after the show.[114] At the time, Sun City, Arizona, had around 8,000 residents. While Meeker wanted to apply this policy of support for the community to the other Sun Cities, their populations were deemed too small to support a Sun Bowl. Meeker called the Sun Bowl "Webb's first major effort in promoting companionship."[115]

Still another example of the company literally "promoting companionship" among Sun City residents was when it became concerned that attendance at some recreation-center clubs was declining. To spark renewed interest, DEVCO began offering expensive door prizes to someone attending a randomly selected club meeting. When around ten people showed up for the meeting and discovered that one of them would walk away with a color television, attendance was much larger at the next meeting. Instead of a door prize, though, those people found, in Meeker's words, "friendship and companionship." Meeker regarded companionship as "a most important human need," and "promotion of companionship . . . became a valuable sales tool for DEVCO."[116]

Putting resources into Sun City, Arizona, also meant that the company lent material assistance to a variety of community and charitable projects. Among these was the company decision to join with a group of residents to form a nonprofit corporation to build and operate a hospital. Initially, plans called for a 61-bed facility, but when Walter O. Boswell Memorial Hospital opened in 1970, it was a high-quality, 355-bed facility. The company helped a group of Sun City residents form a fire district for the community as well. Not only were fire insurance premiums lower for residents as a result, but the fire district provided professional first responders in emergencies. To assist the Maricopa County Sheriff's Department in Sun City, residents formed a neighborhood watch group, the Sun City Posse. DEVCO gave the Posse land for members' vehicles and activities.[117] DEVCO donated land and then built at cost a structure to house the medical equipment, such as wheelchairs, that the Sunshine Services charity ran. The wheelchairs and other equipment were then lent to Sun City residents on an as-needed basis. To try to make public transportation viable in the sprawling Sun City, DEVCO leased a bus at low cost to the owner of a bus franchise in Sun City.[118]

Meeker also had a policy of renting company-owned office space to charitable groups for a token one dollar per year. When he left the firm in 1981 and the company was selling off some of its buildings to new, less generous owners, the charities suddenly had to find realistic rent money in their tight budgets. While DEVCO did not actively publicize its charitable office rentals, encouraging charities strengthened the volunteer side of the "active adult" community.[119] Of all these charitable activities, the construction of Boswell Hospital probably paid the biggest dividends in attracting buyers. The company owned the land north of the Southern Pacific Railroad tracks and Grand Avenue that it hoped to develop into housing for Phases 2 and 3 of Sun City. To quote Meeker, with the hospital, "DEVCO had its anchor" across the tracks and the Grand Avenue highway.[120]

Investing "in more community activities" meant beefing up the recreational and cultural facilities of Sun City. DEVCO built the Sun City Stadium, which eventually became the spring training home of the Milwaukee Brewers, and hosted some semi-professional women's softball games. The company supported a number of community events, from a Mothers Day Strawberry Festival to a Fathers Day Root Beer Bust. The sixty-five-member Sun City Symphony received company sponsorship for a concert series. DEVCO also helped form the Sun City Art Museum.[121]

Perhaps DEVCO's most visible gift to the residents and the core element in the "active adult" lifestyle was not only to continue to build recreation centers and golf courses as the community expanded but to keep building better and more elaborate facilities. At first, the company operated under the policy that people buying in a particular neighborhood would have control over that neighborhood's recreation center, which the company turned over to them. When a second recreation center opened in 1964, residents from the older neighborhood wanted to use it, but the newer neighborhood opposed their use of it because the fees were different. The situation escalated into what Meeker termed "a mini Berlin wall." DEVCO intervened, with the result that all residents of Sun City would have the use of all existing recreation centers and those yet to be constructed.[122]

Furthermore, Meeker fought within the company for more and more elaborate facilities. The Sundial Recreation Center got an Olympic-size, indoor swimming pool. Lakeview Recreation Center was adjacent to a thirty-three-acre manmade lake with a hilltop gazebo and waterfall. Bell Center became the largest and included a building for a public library. In spite of cost overruns on the Bell Center, Meeker also approved the small Marinette Center on the north edge of the community.[123] All of these were open to all Sun City residents. However, for those residents fed up with the difficulty of getting tee times during the popular winter months, he did go along with the creation of a couple of private country clubs and a private dining club. Most residents were content to just use the public facilities.

When he was fighting hard within the Webb corporate structure to get the money for all these projects, one of the arguments Meeker used was that they would help increase the sales of homes. To demonstrate these amenities and the resort lifestyle of Sun City to prospective buyers, Meeker developed a new sales tool, the vacation special. Previously, the company had offered a Try Buy Vacation Program in which sales staff could make available to selected prospects one of twenty-two apartments for $50 per week or $150 per month. If the prospect bought a dwelling in Sun City, the cost of the vacation rental was deducted from the escrow account. The program did not include any other incentives, was not advertised, and was eventually dropped due to a lack of results.

Meeker revived this program, adding incentives and national advertising. Among other enticements, it included two free rounds of golf, "a western style dinner with entertainment by various Sun City groups," and a bus tour of the Greater Phoenix area with Sun City residents acting as bus hostesses. The emphasis was on contact with residents and experiencing the active adult lifestyle of Sun City, not contact with salesmen, who were told to avoid high-pressure sales tactics. Participants could win door prizes in the form of crafts that Sun City residents made utilizing the recreation center facilities. Sales prospects did pay for the program, but the charges were below cost. Meeker's verdict was that "the public relations host, resident bus tour hostesses and resident entertainers proved . . . to be more than adequate spokespersons for the Sun City way of life."[124] In 1972, DEVCO opened the posh Lakes Club as a private dining and social club. However, it also used that facility to entertain its vacation special prospects.[125] By 1975, DEVCO was utilizing 309 apartments in its "vacation special" program.[126] The program paid off. In 1977, people utilizing the vacation special program bought 1,495 homes.[127] Furthermore, at build-out in 1978–79, DEVCO put the vacation special units up for sale.[128] They commanded a premium price due to their location.

At build-out, Sun City represented quite an accomplishment. It consisted of 25,419 homes plus 304 vacation apartments. Meeker estimated its population at around 48,000. The community boasted seven recreation centers, eleven golf courses, three private country clubs, the Sun City Stadium seating 4,000, the Sun Bowl seating 7,500, twenty-nine churches and synagogues, 300 organized clubs, six shopping centers, various private businesses, and the signature item—"5000 Privately owned golf carts."[129] Webb had died in 1974, five years before the completion of Sun City. However, one can imagine the sense of satisfaction his protégé, John Meeker, must have felt when describing the completed community he did so much to create.

How did the residents feel about Meeker's efforts? Longtime Sun City resident and historian Jane Freeman commented, "He gave us what we wanted before we even knew what that was." Mediating among different groups, he helped to make the community cohesive, and he made it a community, "not just a lot of houses."[130] In spite of the generally warm feelings residents had for DEVCO, they did differ with the wishes of the developer on some issues and through their own needs and efforts helped shape the community in ways that were not always in keeping with the active adult, country club, and later resort lifestyle that Webb executives promoted.

Developers Create Resident Associations

The Del Webb Corporation had significantly more financial resources than did Cortese's Rossmoor Leisure World, which limited Cortese's generosity and made him more subject initially to the influence of FHA's 213 cooperative housing program. For example, FHA insisted that an entity other than Ross Cortese, the developer, manage and market the Leisure World communities. Thus, the Leisure World Foundation came into being to manage the various Leisure Worlds. Almost all the units during the first few years were cooperatives in which residents elected officers of the mutuals governing their group of units. Initially, Cortese's corporation played a leadership role in getting leaders of the mutuals to come together into resident associations. The year after Leisure World Laguna Hills opened, the head administrator, Robert Price, began meeting informally with small groups of residents. His purpose was to recruit leaders to form the resident association that FHA required.[131] When condos replaced cooperatives, some reorganization occurred with the residents' governance mechanism.

Meanwhile, all the Leisure Worlds except Laguna Hills had replaced the Leisure World Foundation with management that was more local. In 1972, the resident directors at Leisure World Laguna Hills decided to replace the Leisure World Foundation with its reconstituted successor, Professional Community Management Inc., or PCM.[132] Professional Community Management also became the management arm of a number of other communities in the area with resident associations.[133] Thus, FHA kept Cortese from earning profits through managing his communities, but FHA policy insulated Cortese from charges that he was taking advantage of the residents in a management role. In addition, it empowered the residents.

Like many other active adult retirement communities, neither Leisure World Laguna Hills nor the Sun Cities were incorporated. Webb believed that the residents would create the community, but it was necessary for his corporation to provide some sort of structure so the residents could make and enforce rules and oversee the management of the extensive amenities. Thus, the corporation quickly created the Sun City

Home Owners Association to enforce deed restrictions, which ranged from policing exterior paint colors to dealing with what one observer called "contraband children." Webb was eager to extricate the corporation from recreation center and golf course maintenance. To do that, the firm created a nonprofit group, Recreation Centers of Sun City Inc., and gave it the ownership of the amenities. That group also got the controversial task of setting the residents' annual fees for use of the facilities. As for updating the centers and other capital improvements, the Recreation Centers of Sun City began charging new residents, even if they purchased a resale home, "a onetime impact fee of a few thousand dollars."[134] The amount of the annual fee tended to generate controversy, with older residents who used the facilities less wanting to keep the fee low and younger residents willing to pay much more to have "all the bells and whistles."[135] The situation was similar at Leisure World Laguna Hills.

Since FHA was providing the financing for the Leisure World cooperative units, it specified the monthly income that a person needed to buy into the community.[136] In spite of a somewhat different product and different financing, Cortese used a lot of Webb's promotional language and sales techniques, and Webb used some of Cortese's as well. For example, both men had professional activities directors in their communities from the start. Both put more emphasis on promoting a lifestyle than on promoting the actual dwellings that they were selling. When Cortese in a 1967 brochure touted Leisure World Laguna Hills' "multi-million-dollar resort facilities," he sounded very much like Webb.[137] Cortese even had his own version of Webb's Vacation Special. Besides the living units for sales prospects to sample life at Leisure World Laguna Hills for a week or two, Cortese built a small clubhouse that became the community's sixth clubhouse on build-out. Since one of Cortese's selling points was no exterior maintenance or gardening responsibilities, he originally did not include garden plots for residents, but he changed his mind and added two groups of garden plots for those who wanted them.[138] Cortese listened when the Golden Rain Foundation, the entity that owned the common facilities, became concerned that a proposed manmade lake would be difficult to maintain. That group convinced Cortese to substitute a nine-hole golf course for the lake.[139] While residents did have some input, the basic plan was Cortese's.

Like Webb, Cortese discovered that the majority of his buyers first became interested after talking to friends or relatives.[140] While not on

Del Webb's scale, Cortese did practice some community philanthropy. After selling land to Orange County for a fire station, Cortese then donated a fire engine.[141] On the other hand, he was unable to keep the promise he made in early sales brochures to construct a hospital. One opened in 1974 adjacent to Leisure World Laguna Hills with a variety of other financing, some of it from the residents themselves.[142] As for the amenities, Leisure World Laguna Hills at build-out had a similar number of clubhouses as Sun City for fewer than half the residents. Occupying less than a quarter of the land of Sun City, Cortese's community had to make do with only two golf courses compared to the eleven at Sun City. Both communities had spectacular landscaping. These communities attracted people who appreciated the amenities but could only afford them through shared ownership and resident association fees.

Residents Oppose Developers' Plans for Assisted Living Facilities

Ross Cortese tried to exert some community control in ways that for the most part Del Webb avoided. Both corporations initiated community newspapers, but only Cortese had a regular column. Cortese used his space, "It's a Great World," to promote various aspects of the growing community. One of these was the fourteen-story Towers, independent-living condominiums with features such as three meals per day in the common dining rooms and maid service.[143] However, when Cortese proposed a continuing care facility within the community, residents balked.[144] Apparently, he bought the argument "You won't sell if people think this is a place for old people." Feminist Betty Friedan's mother supported the decision, saying, "This place has a stigma as it is."[145] After Friedan's mother broke a leg, though, she sold her apartment and moved into the Towers. While still at Leisure World, she found herself cut off from her former friends and activities. Then, when the time came for her to move into a nursing home, she, like so many others, had to leave the community. In her case, being near a Milwaukee granddaughter was a factor in relocating halfway across the country.[146] Other types of assisted living and extended care facilities and even a mortuary soon sprang up just outside Leisure World's gates.[147]

The opposition to continuing care and assisted living facilities as the communities and their residents aged was quite common. It underscored generational differences among the aged. In 1993, with an average age of seventy-seven at Leisure World Laguna Hills, those in their sixties were part of the community's "younger generation." They wanted "a veritable theme park for recreation-oriented retirees," according to a *San Francisco Chronicle* reporter. He quoted University of Southern California gerontologist John Pynoos as saying, "These communities weren't designed with the aging process in mind." At Leisure World Laguna Hills, some of the younger residents actually nicknamed it "Heaven on Hold." For the older residents whose health had declined, what they needed was nutrition and nursing services, "not another square-dancing or sculpture class." Arthritis got in the way of an active adult lifestyle, and Alzheimer's made the sameness of the housing and size of the community additional problems. Granted, Leisure World Laguna Hills had its intracommunity buses, but as late as 1993, the buses were not equipped to handle wheelchairs. In opposing developer Ross Cortese's proposal for a continuing care facility, the younger generation showed its prejudice against the older one. At Leisure World Laguna Hills, the younger ones won the battle against the developer. However, they could not keep additional facilities for the older generation from springing up just outside the gates. Some people blamed the presence of the older generation for making it harder to sell their homes in the community. However, a man who was moving out of Leisure World Laguna Hills after living there for twenty-four years commented, "What good is a twenty-seven-hole golf course if you can't even get on a bus?"[148]

Webb was more successful with integrating facilities for the older generation of the elderly, allowing the first nursing home in Sun City to open in 1965.[149] However, its presence was not part of Sun City's publicized image. Neither did he publicize the cemetery that he opened in 1962 in what would become Phase 2 of Sun City. Subsequently, a variety of independent and assisted living facilities sprang up within Sun City. Neighboring Youngtown did get a continuing care facility, but both Webb and Cortese focused on the "active adult" image in their advertising. Their typical buyer preferred it that way, at times refusing to face the likelihood of eventually needing some sort of extended care facility. Nevertheless, Sun City did a much better job than Leisure World of integrating these facilities into its community and providing access to its clubhouses and activities for the residents of these care facilities. That may reflect Webb's greater resources in terms of land, his open community (as opposed to gated community) philosophy, and his greater independence from the residents than Cortese in being able to exploit market opportunities.

Developers' Influence on Residents' Behavior

To foster community at Leisure World Laguna Hills, Cortese from the beginning had the homes hooked up to a closed-circuit television channel.[150] The bulk of the programming concerned activities within the community, although a regular feature was *Administrative Chat*, a program that management staff used to promote its views, answer questions, and let the community know about changes. The Leisure World Foundation, the residents' management group, controlled the station until an independent company took it over in 1969. Webb never bothered with closed-circuit television.

Both developers were interested in curbing inappropriate behavior among their residents, especially on the links. In Sun City and Leisure World, many residents were new to golf and needed some education about the basic rules and etiquette of the game. *The Leisure World News* became one vehicle for communicating how to do things, for example in a two-page article, "Golf Is a Science, A Study," that appeared in 1965.[151] Golf lessons were also available in Leisure World and Sun City communities.

Sun City had the added problem of large numbers of houses whose rear yards backed onto the golf courses. With so many amateur golfers, stray balls frequently ended up in residents' backyards. Some home owners did not appreciate trespassing golfers retrieving balls on their property, though most embraced the open nature of Sun City. One couple even put up a sign saying, "Welcome fellow golfers. If your ball lands in this yard retrieve it and take one from the box. You have been our guest.—A fellow golfer."[152] The claim that in the early years some Sun City golfers just simply walked through the rear doors of adjacent houses to use the bathroom or get some water to drink may have been an invention or exaggeration to get Webb to include restroom facilities and water fountains on subsequent golf courses. Home owners themselves could solve that problem by locking their rear doors.[153] While the story about Sun City golfers helping themselves to facilities in adjacent homes is probably more legend than fact, it captures the spirit of openness in Sun City.

Use of golf carts on city streets was another innovative area. The golf cart was relatively new in the 1960s; early models had three wheels rather than four and so were less stable. Nevertheless, Sun City residents quickly discovered the convenience of using their golf carts on city streets for short errands. They had to remember to use hand signals and not leave anything of value in the completely open vehicles. Other drivers did not always treat them very well. One resident remembered feeling especially vulnerable when stopping at intersections because "someone had once thrown an empty soda can at [his] mother" while she waited for traffic to pass in her three-wheeler.[154] The popularity of using the golf cart on regular streets grew as four-wheelers replaced the older models. This use of the golf cart became quite common in active adult, age-restricted communities, so common that residents took to calling them golf cars instead of golf carts because, within their communities, they were using them like cars.

The Sun City and Leisure World communities had different cultures when it came to the choice of using volunteers or paying to have professionals perform jobs. Both communities had the traditional volunteer activities of hospital auxiliaries and other charities and nonprofits. However, when it came to security and "first responders," there was a big difference. Most of these communities were unincorporated, which meant that they depended on the county or special districts for services like law enforcement and street maintenance. In Sun City, Arizona, DEVCO maintained the street medians until build-out, and then it was up to the residents. Rather than hire people to maintain the landscaped medians, Sun City chose to form the Prides, a group of volunteers who did the job. At Leisure World Laguna Hills, El Toro Road carried heavy through-traffic. However, the residents hired large numbers of workers to maintain their very beautiful, award-winning landscaping including along the segment of El Toro Road that cuts through their community. Likewise, to staff the security gates and patrol the streets, Leisure World used relatively high association fees to hire a large number of residents on a part-time basis to staff its twelve gates and to teach some craft and hobby classes. In 1984, 360 residents were holding these jobs.[155] Sun City had lower association fees, but its residents formed the Sun City Posse, a neighborhood watch group with patrol cars that supplemented county law enforcement.

Perhaps the most extreme use of volunteers occurred at Sun City Center, Florida. There volunteers drove ambulances and acted as first responders in medical emergencies. If, in the opinion of the volunteer, professional help was needed, then the volunteer called for it.[156] As of 2009, Sun City Center was one of only two communities in Florida to have an all-volunteer community ambulance squad. On each ambulance "run," two of the volunteers had to have passed Florida's "First Responder" exam, and the third volunteer on the ambulance crew had to have passed "the more stringent licensing requirement as an Emergency Medical Technician."[157] At Sun City, Arizona, DEVCO helped a group of residents form a fire district, perhaps because the company was headquartered there. The emphasis on paid staff at Leisure World reflected developer Ross Cortese's concern about gated security, while the extensive use of volunteers at the Sun Cities mirrored Del Webb's more open and casual approach to creating community along with a desire to keep costs low.

Low Taxes and Anti-Union Policies

The "keep taxes low" attitude was especially strong at the Arizona and Florida Sun Cities and not so much at the California one, perhaps because California did not attract out-of-state residents seeking lower taxes. The most notorious evidence of this anti-tax attitude were the numerous school bond issues that the residents of Sun City, Arizona, voted down. With the expansion of suburban Phoenix, enrollments were burgeoning in the Peoria School District, which originally encompassed Sun City. However, over a twelve-year period beginning in 1962, Sun City "voted down seventeen out of eighteen school bond issues."[158] In 1969, the *Arizona Republic* carried a story on the situation with the headline, "Peoria schools victim of Sun City."[159] Students had to attend school in shifts while nonessential programs fell by the wayside.[160] The local school superintendent charged that Webb salesmen were telling prospects that Sun City did not have a school tax. That was incorrect because Sun City residents did pay into a general state fund covering some school expenses. The Webb firm subsequently instructed its salespeople to use the "pitch that the area has the lowest tax rate in Maricopa County."[161]

The issue came to a head in 1974. DEVCO and other builders met with the school board and worked out a compromise whereby the builders, including DEVCO, would donate land for schools and Sun City would have its own school district. Sun City residents were up in arms. They discovered a law that would allow Sun City to become an unorganized school district. That meant that if both Sun City and the Peoria School District agreed to the arrangement, Sun City would not have to build a school for what was then 105 students. The Peoria school district had

had it with Sun City blocking bond issues for much-needed schools. Thus, Sun City became an unorganized school district and paid for those 105 Sun City students to attend Peoria schools while escaping local school taxes.[162] At times when Sun City residents felt strongly about something, they could trump the developer.

Meanwhile, the residents of Leisure World Laguna Hills were reacting very differently to their local school district. Part of the answer as to why may lie with their very different experience with adult education. In 1965, some of the Leisure World residents asked their community activities people for some classes. Those people approached the local Tustin Unified School District, which launched an ambitious program of classes within Leisure World. Since Tustin had to serve all the people in the district and Leisure World was a gated community, a system of special security passes for outsiders was instituted. Then California had its own anti-tax rebellion with the passage of Proposition 13 in 1978. The local school district announced that it could not afford to continue the classes. Luckily, at that time, Saddleback Community College was beginning a program of classes in the Leisure World churches. Saddleback agreed to take over the school district adult education classes, applying college standards to such issues as instructors and courses. Furthermore, Leisure World residents got earlier registration times than outsiders, some of whom still attended. Finally, Saddleback took feedback from a council of Leisure World residents as to what courses the community wanted.[163] That initial, very positive experience with the local school district was probably a factor in predisposing Leisure World voters to "more strongly support Orange County's predominantly heavy education-oriented taxes than any other community."[164]

A factor in retirement community support for public education was the local system of funding. In California, school taxes were spread over an entire city, with schools receiving one-half to two-thirds of the residential property tax revenue. Since retirement communities do not require schools but can be taxed to support them, retirement communities have been welcomed because they reduce property and school taxes for the entire city.[165] Given that situation, organized opposition to increased school funding was unlikely.

Sun City had a very different experience with adult education. The community did find a professor to teach a world issues course in 1960, but it was unable to arrange with an outside educational institution for adult education at the college level until Glendale Community College came along in 1971. (Adult education had not been an option with the financially strapped Peoria School District.) Then in 1981, Arizona State University began special lectures and acquired an office and classrooms the following year. When scholar Marc Freedman listed the reasons for lack of support among some retirement communities for schools, one was retirees lacking a connection to the local schools.[166] Adult education provided that connection at Leisure World Laguna Hills but not at Sun City, Arizona.

Just as the concern for tax relief led to lack of support for school bond issues in some communities, concern over taxes also contributed to opposition to incorporation in a number of these communities. None of the Sun Cities of the 1960s or Leisure World Laguna Hills was incorporated. Leisure World Laguna Hills changed its stance on this issue in the twenty-first century. In chapter 6 I examine the future of the nearby abandoned air base to understand why the community reversed itself on incorporation. Another reason for the opposition to incorporation may be that local politics focused on the resident associations that were responsible for the common areas and for activities within their communities.

In any case, at Sun City, Arizona, incorporation was another issue in which the majority of residents trumped DEVCO. In 1964, the Webb Corporation not only endorsed the idea of incorporating Sun City but offered the residents a free site for a city hall if they would vote for it. DEVCO offered to build a new city hall at cost, meaning that it would forgo a profit on the project.[167] The voters did not go for it.[168] The issue resurfaced as the community approached build-out in 1978. Some of the residents formed the Charter Government Association of Sun City to push for incorporation. At the time of build-out, Sun City had a population of 47,500.[169] It had more people than any other of Arizona's unincorporated areas. However, except for special districts such as the fire district and the services performed by the Sun City Homeowners Association and other resident groups, it depended on Maricopa County. Sun City residents "voted down incorporation several times,"[170] as did residents of the later Sun City West.

After retiring and assessing his accomplishments and mistakes, DEVCO president John Meeker wrote that the company "should have pushed harder for incorporation. The tax money that Sun City would have received exceeded the cost [of running a city government] by a substantial figure. This excess money could certainly be used . . . to solve some of the social problems of an aging community."[171] By not incorporating, Sun City lacked the right to levy a local sales tax and could not apply for federal and state grants.[172] Sun City relied on the county for all sorts of services, including planning and zoning.[173]

Perhaps Del Webb's early 1960s affordability pitch contributed to getting a low-tax culture going in Sun City. Taxes have remained artificially low. One observer has noted that for Sun City residents, the tax rate was less than half what families in surrounding communities with school districts pay.[174] The difference was even more dramatic for someone moving to Sun City, Arizona, from a high-tax state. A migrant from Michigan had property taxes there of $5,000; at Sun City, they were about $750. The man commented that when he received his first Sun City tax bill, he "thought it was a monthly payment."[175]

As DEVCO approached build-out at Sun City, Arizona, its management shifted attention to planning the next venture, Sun City West, on the opposite side of the Agua Fria riverbed from Sun City. One way DEVCO was able to be competitive in the housing market at Sun City West was that its executives decided to use non-unionized construction workers in the field in 1976, although the company stayed with union workers at a plant where it did some prefabrication of building components.[176] DEVCO's head, John Meeker, recalled the various craft unions "making outrageous demands" on contractors that year. Some contractors settled, but DEVCO remained steadfast in the face of a long strike and numerous lawsuits brought by the unions. The situation reached the point that some picketers were dropping nails around DEVCO construction sites, causing flat tires. When DEVCO representatives went to the county attorney's office, they were told they needed proof that it was the picketers who were dropping the nails. Therefore, DEVCO hired a private detective "to do camera surveillance. It showed the nails in the roadway after the picket walked by; but since he was dropping the nails through a hole in his pocket, it wasn't considered conclusive." Then, a "sheriff's patrol car received four flat tires and the deputy who happened to be 6'6" tall and mad as hell got all over the picket suspected of causing the problem. It ceased."[177]

Most Sun Citians were politically conservative and supported DEVCO's decision to go non-union. However, in any community with thousands of people, there will be dissenters. In 1977, Larry Spitz, a former union organizer for United Steelworkers, bought a house in Sun City. Two years later, he organized the Union Club for retired union members seeking to help out local unions with their battles.[178]

In 1977, with 42,000 people in Sun City, the company ceased constructing recreation centers and announced that it would no longer maintain the landscaped street medians or subsidize Sun City's bus system. Predictably, residents objected. John Meeker had to remind them that the Webb Corporation was a business accountable to its stockholders. It could not permanently provide various community subsidies because, as Meeker put it, "Frankly the bottom line would not give a just and reasonable return on our investment to our shareholders."[179] For the first time, Sun City would be on its own as the construction company reached build-out.

The Webb Corporation left behind the largest retirement community up to that point in the United States. It was a complete community with churches, shopping centers, medical facilities, and local newspapers. Running the community were the home owners association and the management group for the recreation centers. Looking back on the reasons for the success of Sun City, John Meeker listed first its location "near dynamic Phoenix with its warm weather" and its reputation "as a destination winter tourist resort." He also cited "low taxes," Boswell Hospital, the variety of religious facilities, and the neighborhood shopping centers. In addition, the firm's policy of adding "different facilities within each new recreation center" and building the Lakes Social Club and Dining Facility contributed to Sun City's success. Certain of the firm's sales tactics made Meeker's list, too, including the Vacation Special program and the involvement of residents with the Sun Bowl outdoor amphitheater and Sun City Stadium.[180]

With hindsight, he then identified a list of mistakes. Besides not pushing harder for incorporation, he regretted not responding to residents' insistence sooner that the advertised Marinette recreation center be built and some industrial zoning decisions and activities that eventually were overcome; interestingly, he added that "more recreation facilities and activities for women should have been included."[181] The emphasis on golf appealed more to the men than to the women; and in the early years of the community, "generally the husbands were more enthusiastic about the move."[182] Sun City opened in 1960, several years before the beginning of the modern women's movement and at a time when wives tended to defer to their husbands. Granted, women also had their golf leagues; but Leisure World, with its emphasis on bridge and crafts such as jewelry making, may have had a more gender-balanced appeal. Just how Webb and Cortese learned from their original communities as well as how other developers sought to imitate them will be covered in the next chapter. So will the demographic issue of the appropriate minimum age for at least one resident in each housing unit. The preponderance of women residents as these communities aged will be covered in chapter 6.

To sum up, Webb and Cortese were not just pioneers in building a new kind of active adult, age-restricted community. They were also treading on new ground for developers in that they discovered that creating a community was more than just putting up masonry blocks and mortar. They had a script to implement, so they hired staff to get activities going, recruited resident leaders to take over the management through residents' associations, and attracted certain necessary institutions such as churches, medical facilities, financial services, and supermarkets. The developers also discovered that the major key to sales was satisfied residents who would recommend the community to their friends and neighbors back home. That may be why the developers did not fight their residents very hard when they and their residents were on opposite sides of incorporation or school bond issues. The developers had their script, and for the most part, the residents literally bought it. In spite of the control exerted by the developers, when they left at build-out, they were sadly missed. Together, they and their residents had created complete communities. The residents were now on their own.

Proliferation and Standardization

"We have a 93 or 94 year old gal . . . she's out there every afternoon making her laps in the swimming pool, slow as she goes, so slow that we have our own name for her—but she couldn't do that if there were children laughing and splashing and playing," explained the president of the Florida West Coast Condominium Association to a 1987 congressional committee concerned with discrimination against children in housing.[1] This testimony helped to convince Congress to legalize nationally the age-restricted, active adult communities that were proliferating. The phenomenal success of Webb and Cortese had motivated a host of other developers to build their own versions, often with different minimum ages than Sun City's fifty or Leisure World's fifty-two. Success, plus reaching build-out on their flagship communities, also encouraged the companies the original developers founded to embark on new communities. To exempt age-restricted, active adult communities from legislation designed to bar discrimination in housing with respect to the presence of children under nineteen, Congress had to give them a precise definition, which resulted in some standardization. Meanwhile, these communities had continued to evolve and proliferate, challenging and redefining attitudes toward aging.

Arizona's "Active Adult" Communities Proliferate

In 2002, a PBS series on Arizona in the 1960s featured Sun City as "a standard bearer for thousands of retirement and family developments for the next 40 years." The Sun City trademark was that its amenities, such as a golf course and craft facilities in a recreation center, were operating when the first homes were sold.[2] Sun City had opened to phenomenal success in 1960; by 1961, other developers already were putting together their own versions of Del Webb's age-restricted retirement community.

For example, Sun City was the model for Green Valley,[3] also in Arizona; its developer, Maxon Construction, initially proposed the development in 1961 with Dartmouth College listed as a sponsor.[4] Green Valley began with 1,000 single-story apartments, had FHA funding, and was built twenty-five miles south of Tucson. It later included single-family homes and a golf course.[5] Forty-five was the minimum age required for its residents.[6] Due to slow sales at first, Webb was approached in 1964 to take it over. Webb refused because of its location. Green Valley was very close to some missile silos, one of which was about a hundred yards from the entrance to the community. Also, extending along one entire edge of the development "was a major open pit mining operation." Eventually, the Air Force removed the missile silos, but the community changed hands a number of times until Fairfield Development Company acquired it in 1972. Fairfield made the community successful, selling around 6,000 homes by 1993.[7]

Another Arizona company that began doing its own "take" on Sun City was the Farnsworth Development Company. About the same time Sun City began, Farnsworth opened Dreamland Villa in Mesa. While that community had affordable housing, the developer took a "spartan" approach to the amenities. The president of DEVCO, John W. Meeker, called Dreamland Villa's success "marginal."[8] However, it was successful enough for Farnsworth to build a second, nearby development in 1974, Sunland Village, which had a golf course and auditorium but no clubhouse or recreation center. Farnsworth's third development in the Mesa area, Sunland East, opened in 1987 and did include a recreation center.[9] A sample house in this development was a spacious, single-story, brick rambler with a family room and its own backyard swimming pool, perhaps reflecting fewer community amenities than in a development like Sun City.[10]

By 1975–80, Arizona was the third most popular state for migrants over the age of sixty and was rapidly gaining on the number two state, California.[11] The Phoenix, Mesa, Tempe, and Scottsdale areas were experiencing mushrooming growth and leapfrog development. Most of the new developments were not age-restricted, even though many became popular with retirees. The McCormick Ranch property in Scottsdale was marketed to the affluent.[12] Generally, the more affluent the development, the less likely it was to be age-restricted, even if the developer was marketing it primarily to retirees. Closer to Sun City was middle-class Litchfield Park, an intergenerational community that one guidebook described as popular with the "many retirees who prefer living in a mixed rather than an all-adult community."[13] This study is focused on those communities that are specifically age-restricted, but it is important to note that the expansion of these age-restricted communities occurred in the midst of the expansion of intergenerational communities that were often marketed primarily to retirees. However, for a retirement community to ban children as permanent residents, it had to be specifically marketed as age-restricted.

Sometimes a developer attempted to create an age-restricted community, failed, and then redefined the community as an intergenerational, or conventional, development. Some developers attempted to straddle the age-restriction issue by building both age-restricted and conventional housing in different sections of the same development. In 1971, the Presley Company, which took over Sun City, California, when Webb sold that development, decided to open Ahwatukee south of Tempe, Arizona. Initially, the major part of this development was to be retiree housing and the rest intergenerational. However, with fewer retiree home buyers than expected, Presley eventually redefined the entire development as conventional housing.[14]

Another example occurred in 1976. A Phoenix area developer, Designmaster, opened a community adjacent to Sun City's southern border. One section was for adults only, the other intergenerational. However, Designmaster did not build separate golf and other recreational facilities for the two groups. They clashed, with the presence of children an issue. Webb executive John Meeker called this development "barely successful."[15]

The age-restricted development with the youngest minimum age in the Phoenix area was Sun Lakes, which opened in 1971; it required at least one home occupant to be forty. Sun Lakes, south of Chandler, Arizona, began as a mobile home, or manufactured home, community. Its circular golf course layout was imitative of that in Phase 2 of Sun City, which was being developed about the same time. In fact, the developer of Sun Lakes, Ed Robson, was "a former Del Webb executive" and one of the builders who "attempted to copy the Sun City model" with competing, amenity-rich, retirement communities in the same general area as Sun City, Arizona.[16]

Just as Webb discovered a market for better homes among relocating retirees, so did Ed Robson. He quickly switched to more expensive, stick-built homes, as opposed to manufactured or prefabricated homes. Robson also followed the Webb policy of mandating that buyers of lots build homes constructed by his company within a relatively short time frame.[17] Besides the golf course, Sun Lakes had "four lakes, a 144 acre 'commons,'" and a commercial area. Since children under nineteen were not allowed to live there, that meant no school building taxes.[18] One effect of newer, more affluent housing at Sun Lakes was that the older residents in the trailer park section, while technically eligible to join in community activities, apparently kept pretty much to themselves, resulting in a social class divide.[19] With the exception of its trailer park beginning, Sun Lakes was very similar to Sun City and was probably the most serious competitor of Sun City and the nearby Sun City West in the 1970s and 1980s. One authority in the field called Sun Lakes "one of the largest and most successful [active adult retirement communities] in the nation."[20] By 1992, it was the third largest age-restricted development in the Phoenix area, at 9,500 residents, compared to 46,000 for Sun City and 19,000 for Sun City West, which had not yet reached build-out.[21]

With the success of Sun Lakes, in 1986 Robson began to purchase land fourteen miles north of Tucson for his next age-restricted, active adult community, Saddlebrooke. Like Webb, he was willing to go some distance outside a metropolitan area to get enough land to accommodate a minimum of 2,000 homes, an eighteen-hole golf course, and other recreational facilities. In his view, he needed that many homes to support the cost of the amenities. Starting with 1,100 acres, Robson eventually accumulated 2,100 acres at that location.[22] On average, homes at Saddlebrooke were slightly larger, a little classier, and a bit more expensive than those in the Del Webb developments.

Sun City's and Leisure World's Influence on Retirement Developments in Florida

The boosters of retirement living in Arizona emphasized that Arizona's heat did not come with Florida's humidity, but they could not match Florida's abundance of waterfront locations or Florida's long history as THE retirement destination.[23] During 1975–80, Florida was still the clear frontrunner among states attracting migrants over the age of sixty. Specifically, Florida was the destination for 25.9 percent of those migrants compared to Arizona's 5.7 percent and California's 8.8 percent.[24] Trailer courts and beachfront condos continued to be very popular, especially among snowbirds seeking second homes. While many Florida developers preferred to market to retirees, they were more reluctant to adopt specific age restrictions or specifically bar children. Nevertheless, Webb's success in Arizona did have some impact on Florida.

An early example was the 1961 advertising for Ridgewood Mountain Village, a community of moderately priced, single-family homes near St. Petersburg, Florida. The ad borrowed Webb's phrase "'Active' Retirement." It pictured seniors dancing at the Ridgewood senior activity center. It listed amenities such as shuffleboard, "Olympic Swim Pool" (not pictured), and golf (no mention of how many holes in the course). The developer may not have followed the Webb principle of getting the recreational facilities in before selling the homes, but the 1961 ad did proclaim, "Ridgewood Senior Citizens are the 'Activist'!!!!"[25]

H. Irwin Levy Develops Florida's Century Villages

One of the most successful Florida developments was more in the condominium tradition of Ross Cortese's Leisure World. In the 1950s, Florida had pioneered the beachfront, high-rise condominium development, which was very popular with retirees. Then, in 1968, H. Irwin Levy became the developer of Century Village in West Palm Beach. Since 1951, Levy had been a real estate attorney in Palm Beach County. His only experience with development prior to 1968 was when he was representing the owners of a project whose management team walked out. Levy stepped in on a temporary basis and managed the project until it was sold.

Levy got involved with Century Village when the original developer decided that the market for amenity-rich communities was shifting away from trailers to condominiums. Consequently, the developer had to come up with construction financing, which could be difficult to obtain. That developer approached Levy, who liked the concept. Levy proceeded to put together a group of investors who became the board, with Levy as chairman. Two to three months after they launched the project, units were selling much faster than the couple of hundred per year that the company was capable of building at that time. The developers were concerned that when they actually delivered some of the apartments they had already sold, construction costs would be more than their sales price. The original owner at that time was more comfortable running a "'mom and pop' operation" than a big company and opted to leave. That put Irwin Levy in charge of actually running the new development. Not only did Levy discover that he loved the work, but he added to the "active adult" concept and refined the marketing approach along with finding a solution to speeding up the construction of units.[26]

Century Village did not originally have a minimum age requirement for buyers. It just excluded children under the age of sixteen as permanent residents.[27] Levy's target market was retirees who were working-class or less affluent than Webb's Sun City buyers. His condos were small, unadorned, simple concrete-box apartments; elevators were deemed too expensive, so residents of upper units had to access them by stairs. In 1968, these units sold for $9,000, less than the cheapest units at both Sun City and Leisure World. Sun City Center, Del Webb's Florida development that opened in 1962, was mainly single-family homes but did have some single-story condominium units initially priced at $7,000. Those were probably selling for around $11,000 in 1968.[28]

After becoming involved with Century Village, Levy personally visited a Leisure World community in California.[29] He did take a cue from Webb and Cortese with his inclusion of generous, upscale amenities, such as a large clubhouse, golf course, swimming pools, and manmade lakes. Like them, his focus was not on selling housing but telling people of modest means that they, too, "could have country club facilities."[30] In fact, he took the active adult concept even further by featuring frequent and affordable theatrical entertainment at Century Village. Eventually, he was scheduling 120 to 150 professional shows per year for Century Village's auditorium. Ticket prices for individual shows were in the five- to ten-dollar range. Because the community was gated, performances were limited to residents and their guests. His inspiration for offering plentiful and affordable entertainment was the Catskill Mountain resorts popular with Jewish vacationers in New York.[31] However, Levy did take another cue from Cortese when Century Village provided its residents with bus service. In addition, he recognized that the external environment was important. Century Village's residents would want to be near shopping facilities, a hospital, and government offices like Social Security.[32] By 1974, Century Village had close to 8,000 condo units.[33]

Levy had a much more specific target buyer in mind for Century Village than Cortese or Webb had for their developments. Del Webb seemed to have had a generic, middle-America image of his potential buyer. Ross Cortese assumed that his Leisure Worlds would appeal to middle-class retirees from the larger cities near them. In Levy's case, he recognized that the area from Palm Beach to Miami already had a strong appeal for Jewish retirees from New York City and the Northeast, so much of his early advertising was in that coastal stretch of southeast Florida. Traditionally, the Gulf coast of Florida is more popular with midwesterners. Irwin Levy's son's mother-in-law was from Detroit and chose to live in Sarasota. Another of his target groups was retirees who were already wintering in Miami's South Beach. Levy recognized after going to the beach that those retirees had nothing to do. He would take busloads of retirees from South Beach, show them the facilities and active adult lifestyle of Century Village, then sell units to about two-thirds of them. He successfully targeted vacationers visiting the area as well.[34]

Levy had a much more specific image of his potential buyers than some other developers, and he adjusted that image as times changed. In 1970, the average retiree was truly retired. Century Village was likely to be their second retirement place. Average buyers were closer to seventy-five years old. That meant that they were born around 1895. Many were first-generation Jewish immigrants, were not overly educated, and were likely to speak with a slight accent. They had worked hard as teachers and firemen and in other civil service or unionized jobs. They were in their thirties during the Great Depression, had young children, and probably struggled more than many others to support their families. After World War II, they bought houses for around $300 down, continued to work and save, and did fairly well down to their retirement. At that point, typically they had $30,000–$40,000 in savings and could sell their houses for around $30,000. They could then buy condos at Century Village for $10,000 and live on $500 per month. They actually had an improved, wealthier lifestyle in Century Village than they did where they lived before. The wife in such a couple often did not drive, which made the husband her chauffeur. However, husbands needed time away from their wives. Century Village provided transportation with its bus service plus activities for the wives. The recreation building had a 1,200-seat theater, a party room that could hold 800–900 people, a card room that could accommodate a huge number, small craft facilities with jewelry-making equipment and kilns, and thirty sewing machines with instructors. Inside the building were Ping-Pong tables and outside, shuffleboard and tennis courts plus boats for use on Century Village's manmade lakes.[35]

Early residents translated Irwin Levy's picture of his typical buyer into reality. In 1970, Ed Levy bought a one-bedroom unit for $18,990. Born in 1909 in Brooklyn, Ed Levy was a copyboy for a New York newspaper, then opened his own "business as a food purveyor." He had lived in Brooklyn for thirty-one years and owned a home there. He and his wife initially planned to use their Century Village condo only during the winter months. However, after ten years of the snowbird lifestyle and a bad cold Ed Levy caught in Brooklyn, the couple sold that home and became year-round residents at Century Village. Ed Levy was fairly typical of middle-class, Jewish buyers from New York.[36]

Goldie Schaefer, an Army wife, and her husband were spending the winter on Miami Beach when they decided to take an excursion bus to Century Village. Goldie Schaefer recalled that it "looked like an Army post" to her, but she "fell in love with it." The Schaefers bought. Two decades later and by then a widow, Goldie Schaefer said she had "no regrets about their decision." Lea Dobkin, an AARP housing specialist, explained the appeal of Century Village: "It fulfills the goal of keeping people active. There are an incredible number of groups there. It turned the idea that retirement is stagnation on its ear."[37] By the early 1970s, Century Village was the largest active adult, age-restricted condo community in Florida.

Del Webb may have inspired a couple of other Century Village marketing ploys. Like Ross Cortese, Levy had his own version of Del Webb's vacation special for prospective buyers. In Levy's case, prospective buyers could get free transportation, lodging, and some meals.[38] Also, to distinguish Century Village from copycat developments that sprang up, often with "Century" in their names, Levy decided he needed a famous spokesperson for his community, which was somewhat reminiscent of Sun City being advertised as "Del Webb's Sun City." Levy wanted someone with a "family guy reputation," perhaps a little younger than prospective buyers but someone who would appeal to them. He passed on Jackie Gleason, who became the spokesperson for another community in the area, because of Gleason's image as a drinker and womanizer. Instead, Levy hired Red Buttons, who had been a popular borscht-belt comedian and was originally from New York City's Lower East Side when that neighborhood was known as a heavily immigrant neighborhood for Jews from eastern Europe. Levy thought Buttons would appeal not only to Jewish buyers but to others as well. As it turned out, the original buyers at Century Village were 90–95 percent Jewish.[39]

Century Village's working-class retiree image continued into the twenty-first century. The median age of residents in 2008 was 77.7 years. Women outnumbered the men by nearly two to one. Median household income in Century Village in 2005 was $20,000, compared to Florida's average of $42,433. An even greater disparity existed in the average condo price in 2005 at Century Village of $57,700, compared to $189,500 for the average house or condo in Florida as a whole. Century Village in 2008 was 95.6 percent white and 3 percent Hispanic.[40] However, it was no longer 90 percent or more Jewish. Among the more recent buyers were a number of French Canadians. By 2009, about half the buyers of resales at the original Century Village and also at Century Village, Pembroke Pines, were Hispanic.[41] Florida historian Gary Mormino exaggerated when he called Levy "the first to create a modestly priced retirement complex,"[42] but Century Village was slightly more affordable than either Sun City or Leisure World.

With the original Century Village in West Palm Beach reaching build-out around 1974, Levy opened a second Century Village that year in Deerfield Beach, Florida. This time he not only included the guarded gates and community bus service that Cortese had pioneered, but he also included the closed-circuit television channel that Cortese had first used at Laguna Hills. Levy was shrewd enough to realize that his target buyer was somewhat different. Those who were of retirement age in 1974 had been born around 1910. Some were only teenagers when the crash came. The Great Depression had not affected them as much as it had the original buyers at the first Century Village. Some were World War II veterans who had used the G.I. Bill to get a college education. They had held higher-level jobs than the first group of buyers. Levy decided to drop the sewing center, emphasize clubs based on former jobs and former states or neighborhoods, included Canadian clubs, built lots of meeting rooms, and offered educational classes and lectures. At 8,500 units, Century Village, Deerfield Beach, was a little larger than his first development.[43]

Levy opened the third Century Village at Boca Raton, Florida, in 1979. By the early 1980s, the average prospect was around sixty years old. That meant that he had been born around, or before, 1925 and was probably a well-educated professional. With its canals and waterways, 65 percent of the Century Village units in Boca Raton had waterfront. At 5,700 units, this Century Village was the smallest, but it was also the most upscale. The last Century Village, at Pembroke Pines, opened in 1984. By this time, Levy had adopted another of Ross Cortese's innovations, closed-circuit television, and added it to all of the Century Villages.[44]

In 1997, Irwin Levy sold the right to use the name Century Village to another development company, Avatar Holdings Inc., which did not appear to make subsequent use of it. As for Irwin Levy, even though he discontinued opening new Century Villages, he remained involved in managing recreational facilities and booking their entertainment. Having four communities, all close together, was an asset in negotiating for entertainers. In fact, Century Village became known among entertainers as the "anchor of the condo circuit."[45]

With the success of the Century Villages, several rival developments came along. However, Levy had maintained his edge because of the number and size of the Century Villages. The more residents, the lower the per unit fee for maintenance and amenities. In 2009, it was possible to live in a Century Village community with only a little extra income beyond Social Security. Levy's smaller rivals had difficulty delivering the same value for the money.[46] Nevertheless, Century Village spawned so many spin-offs and rival developments that southeast Florida came to be know as the "condominium belt."

Sidney Colen Takes On Top of the World from the Gulf Coast to Ocala

The Gulf coast of Florida has historically been regarded as more affordable than the state's Atlantic coast. Some have theorized that the 1970s completion of Interstates 75 and 95 tended to channel East Coast migrants to Florida's Atlantic coast and Midwest migrants to Florida's Gulf coast. Migrants like to settle near others like themselves, a phenomenon sometimes called "chain migration."[47] The Gulf coast does have its ritzy locations such as Naples and Sanibel Island, and the east coast of the state has its Century Villages along with Palm Beach. The generalizations have plenty of exceptions.

Developer Sidney Colen began building conventional housing in the St. Petersburg area, then became one of the early pioneers of condominium units as opposed to cooperative ones. High-rise condominium apartments helped to keep the west coast of Florida affordable since hundreds of people could now own property on the beach where before just a couple of houses were feasible. While Colen was reluctant to adopt age restrictions, he was very interested in the retiree market. In 1967, he started building his "first all-inclusive active adult community, On Top of the World, in Clearwater." These were high-rise buildings on the Gulf coast, yet the complex was rich in amenities. It offered "the active, fulfilling lifestyle" of golf and swimming. On completion of the last building in 1999, On Top of the World had a total of 4,966 units.[48]

By the 1970s, the Colens (Sidney and his son, Kenneth) perceived the opportunities for a townhouse and single-family-home type of retirement community in inland central Florida. In 1975, the family acquired 12,900 acres southwest of Ocala, Florida. Its first homes were attached villas, but by the 1990s, it too had moved toward more upscale, concrete-block, single-family homes in the spirit of Del Webb's Sun City. Like the Webb developments, On Top of the World near Ocala was amenity-rich and age-restricted. As of 2002, it featured a recreational complex with an indoor pool, an outdoor pool, tennis courts, golf course, fitness center, and adult learning opportunities. It followed the Leisure World principles of maintenance-free living and gated security. In 2005, it had more than 8,000 occupied units and was still growing.[49]

Harold Schwartz and Gary Morse Develop The Villages

Still another Florida developer, Harold Schwartz, decided in 1982 to take advantage of the evolution of trailers into manufactured homes with an extensive, amenity-rich community. Because land was cheaper away from the coast, he purchased acreage about two dozen miles south of Ocala, added a trailer park and more land amounting to a total of 26,000 acres,[50] converted it into The Villages, and quickly switched from manufactured to wood-frame and masonry homes. In 2005, out of 27,000 homes, only 3,000 were manufactured housing.[51] The developer really emphasized the recreational amenities. By 2007 The Villages was up to twenty-five golf courses, more than ten recreation centers, dozens of public swimming pools, bowling alleys, a polo field, and extensive club, craft, and recreational facilities.[52]

When The Villages reached a population of 36,000, the developer got approval to build an additional 21,000 homes, potentially doubling The Villages' population to more than 70,000. Writer Andrew Blechman reports that for three straight years beginning in 2003, more homes were sold in The Villages than in any other planned community, including 4,263 in 2005 alone.[53] Some have called The Villages "a Disney World for adults." Others have dubbed it "Sun City on steroids."[54] By 2007, The Villages claimed a population of 63,000,[55] and by 2008, AARP reported it was 68,000,[56] making it the largest community of its type. When this author visited The Villages in June 2009, a salesman put the population at 70,000 and a tour bus hostess at 75,000. For comparison purposes, Sun City, Arizona, had 46,000 residents and the nearby Sun City West 31,000; the Agua Fria riverbed kept those two communities from being contiguous. None of these communities, Sun City, Sun City West, or The Villages, was incorporated. Because of its size and the rapidity of its growth, The Villages was in a class by itself.

What did the developer of The Villages do to out-compete the originators of Sun City and Leisure World? Like Ross Cortese, Harold S. Schwartz, the colorful founder of The Villages, came from an impoverished immigrant family. In Schwartz' case, his grandfather was a Hungarian Jewish immigrant who had to place Harold's father and two brothers in an orphanage because he could not support them. Harold himself grew up in a tenement on the South Side of Chicago. As a young man, he worked as a salesman for his father's clothing business and married Mary Louise, a woman who lived in his tenement building. Harold developed a small mail-order business; his marriage to Mary Louise lasted about ten years. Both remarried. Mary Louise's second husband was Clifford Morse. They resettled with her daughter and son, both Harold's children, in the resort town of Central Lakes in northern Michigan. During World War II, she and her young son began selling honey from a roadside stand. That stand soon evolved into a souvenir store, then a restaurant and historical museum complex. Meanwhile, her son, Gary Schwartz, changed his last name to that of his stepfather, Morse. He inherited his birth parents' entrepreneurial spirit but overexpanded the Morse family's Michigan restaurant, which only had sufficient clientele in the summers.[57]

At the same time, Harold Schwartz was prospering, buying commercial real estate and radio stations. According to writer Andrew Blechman, two of Harold's radio stations were "border blasters," located in Mexico to circumvent the federal rule that limited the number of stations one person could own. Schwartz went into the mail-order land speculation business, peddling lots and dreams of retirement in Florida and elsewhere to buyers in both the United States and the United

Kingdom. These were quarter-acre lots in central Florida that had been used to grow watermelons and for pasture. Harold paid $150 per acre, then sold them for what amounted to $1,180 per acre. When mail-order land sales became illegal, Harold's business partner put a trailer court on the property. With little demand, the partner wanted out. Harold then happened to visit his sister, who had just moved to Sun City, Arizona. Like his trailer court, Sun City was in a relatively isolated location, but Del Webb was successfully promoting its "active adult" lifestyle with abundant amenities. As Blechman notes, "Webb's vision soon became Harold's road map." Harold himself was retirement age at seventy-three in 1983, but he decided to buy out his partner, sell everything else that he owned, and start marketing the "active adult" lifestyle. At his urging, his son, Gary Morse, became his partner.[58]

Father and son had a lot to do. Their trailer park, called Orange Blossom Gardens, had only 400 manufactured homes and a small recreation center. Morse turned a watermelon field into a nine-hole golf course and started using "free golf" as a major selling point. In reality, the only "free golf" was on modest, nine-hole courses and then only if one did not use a golf cart. Furthermore, residents paid for the maintenance of the "free" courses through their monthly amenity fees. Sales immediately soared. Gary added more and better golf courses, recreation centers, and other amenities. He also succeeded in attracting a supermarket and other businesses, all accessible to residents by golf cart. To facilitate the use of golf carts on the streets when crossing major thoroughfares, he incorporated golf cart overpasses and underpasses plus special golf-cart paths, essentially designing The Villages for golf cart transportation. In fact, The Villages made the *Guinness Book of World Records* for staging "the world's largest golf cart parade."[59]

As for the housing, Morse and Schwartz followed the Sun City pattern of centering each neighborhood on a recreation center. Both the Del Webb Corporation and The Villages offered new housing at various prices, but in general the later housing was somewhat more upscale than the earlier housing. The Villages even copied Webb's practice of naming some streets after famous golf courses, such as Pebble Beach Lane. It was Schwartz' idea to give names to each new neighborhood, calling the total development The Villages.[60]

Along with "free golf," a slogan contributing to the success of The Villages was "Florida's Friendliest Hometown," meant to assure migrants from elsewhere that they would feel at home with many sociable neighbors in The Villages. Gary Morse did take a cue from Ross Cortese, however, when he surrounded the residential neighborhoods with walls and guarded gates. Some residents even added security cameras. The walls and gates served to mark off the gradations in the prices of the homes in what eventually became at least fifty neighborhoods or residential "villages." Homes ranged from very affordable in the oldest neighborhood, at just under $65,000 for a used, manufactured home in the oldest neighborhood, to more than $1 million for some deluxe homes on choice golf course lots in June 2009. By sorting the homes into neighborhoods by price, residents could be assured that their immediate neighbors paid about the same for houses similar to theirs. At the same time, the developers emphasized that regardless of the neighborhood in which one lived, all residents of The Villages had equal access to the golf courses and most of the other recreational facilities.[61]

While residential neighborhoods at The Villages are gated, the gates do not seem to be the main reason for a minimal crime rate. To an outsider faced with a guarded gate every couple of blocks, The Villages may not look so friendly. (Visitors whose appearance fits the demographic profile of a potential resident and who drive into the visitors' lane at the main gates will probably just have the guard wave them through, no questions asked. So much for "security.") On the other hand, to those living inside the gates, they seem to emphasize the homogeneity of their "friends" and neighbors. The very exclusive neighborhoods take their gates more seriously and do not have the visitors' lane option. Furthermore, to emphasize neighborhood homogeneity, the homes come with numerous deed restrictions, such as no hedges taller than four feet, no outdoor clotheslines, no lawn ornaments, no portable window air conditioners, and a limit of two pets per household.[62] The residential neighborhoods are all devoid of commercial options such as gas stations and convenience stores, but they are accessible nearby.

Unlike developers Del Webb and Ross Cortese, Harold Schwartz and Gary Morse chose to live in their development. Schwartz built a modest ranch-style house on the edge of a lake in the original neighborhood, Orange Blossom Gardens. He added a short dock with a small gazebo at its end perched over the lake. Harold enjoyed walking around the neighborhood, chatting with residents and, according to some people, "was a heck of a ladies' man." While he was still alive, a bronze statue of him was erected in the Spanish Springs downtown area of The Villages. It depicts him in a sports coat with an arm outstretched in welcome. The statue is reminiscent of one of Walt Disney. It is also reminiscent of a statue of Del Webb erected on the grounds of one of the recreation centers at Sun City. Schwartz' descendants have engaged in a personality cult featuring his image on everything from promotional paper money to a billboard announcing construction of a hospital. In fact, the use of Harold Schwartz' persona as the "kind-hearted founder of The Villages" is also somewhat reminiscent of the use of Del Webb's persona to personalize the history of Sun City.[63] The family of Harold Schwartz has followed the practice of the Del Webb Corporation in making donations of land for worthy causes. For example, Gary Morse donated land for a hospice in the community.[64]

Gary Morse and son, Mark Morse, have been considerably more reticent while living on their private land in the center of The Villages. Neither Gary nor Mark, the current head of the company, gives interviews. Gary Lester, who heads public relations for the community, also has a reputation for being extremely noncommittal about matters of substance. Author Andrew Blechman has reported that he spent a month in the community and never managed to get an interview with any member of the Morse family and only a very brief and uninformative one with Gary Lester. Blechman reports only one sighting of Gary Morse. That was when he appeared with a bunch of rambunctious children, probably his grandchildren, in a glass-walled enclosure at the movie theater in The Villages. Blechman also reports that Gary Morse apparently enjoys polo, which is the reason that The Villages has a polo field. Residents do not play polo on the field, nor do they have an equestrian center in The Villages, but they can watch Morse and his wealthy friends with their horses.

Given the Morse family's extreme control over the community's communications, zoning, and building permit apparatus, it is possible their low public profile may be motivated by a desire to minimize controversy. It can be difficult for a community just beginning to develop to attract a variety of businesses to meet the future residents' needs. The Morse family solved that problem at The Villages with family members themselves opening a variety of businesses within it, ranging from a Laundromat to a liquor store.[65] The Morse family went on to own the community newspaper, called the *Daily Sun,* the local radio station, and The Villages' closed-circuit television station. The last was also a feature of Leisure World Laguna Hills and the Century Village communities but not of the Sun City communities. The newspaper reflects Gary Morse's conservative politics, printing conservative columnists, but one will not find *Doonesbury* with its liberal satire in it. Morse has made some very substantial political gifts, including a $500,000 donation to Florida's Republican Party, the loan of his private jet to former Republican governor Jeb Bush, and major donations to George W. Bush's presidential campaigns. Most age-restricted retirement community residents tend to have conservative politics, and that has been especially true of the Morse family at The Villages.[66]

The control that the Morse family exercises over The Villages may only be possible in Florida and reflects a quirk in Florida law that originated with the Walt Disney Company and its development of Disney World in Orlando. First, it was Walt Disney's philosophy that a large amount of land should be acquired for Disney World and that it should straddle two counties. That was a way of reminding politicians of one county that if necessary, the Disney company could move to the next county, although company officials maintain that economic considerations, not political ones, were behind its very large land holdings.[67] The Morse family's land holdings for The Villages sprawl over three counties—Sumter, Lake, and Marion—with most of the community located in Sumter.

Prior to embarking on Disney World construction, Disney got the Florida legislature to create the Reedy Creek Improvement District, which would have certain government functions such as issuing building permits and some policing of its property. The company wanted the ability to cut through the red tape of the permitting process, and it wanted flexibility. The improvement district would also control the rest of Disney World's holdings. To be sure Reedy Creek residents supported company policy, only a few trusted corporate officials were allowed to have homes within it.[68] Gary Morse copied that practice at The Villages when he created the "downtown" areas of Sumter Landing and Spanish Springs, both of which have restaurants, boutique shops, and nightly entertainment in their open squares. These "downtowns" give residents a place to go where they can mingle informally. However, because Spanish Springs serves as the holding entity for The Villages and no one lives there without the Morse family's approval, the Morse family is able to exert control over certain government functions, just as the Disney Company was able to bypass local permitting authorities with its Reedy Creek Improvement District.

Both "downtowns," Sumter Landing and Spanish Springs, are themed entertainment areas designed by a firm that had worked for Universal Studios.[69] Sumter Landing used Key West as its architectural inspiration. St. Augustine inspired Spanish Springs. Each downtown has an open square featuring nightly music and social dancing. Both downtowns have buildings with phony facades, like Disney World's Main Street. These buildings also sport fake historical markers. For example, one marker honors "'Maria Sanchez, 1770–1873, the first female resident of Spanish Springs.'"[70] The line between reality and fantasy is not always crystal clear. For example, the author spotted a quaint "Please don't feed the alligators" sign on an ice cream shop next to a lakeside dock. That one was for real. The blurring of reality and fantasy is part of the appeal of The Villages.

The impact of the Morse family and the residents of The Villages was felt on Sumter County. Geographically, The Villages is just a small corner of northeastern Sumter County, but it soon outnumbered the rest of the county's population. With county commissioners being elected at large, it was difficult for county residents who did not live in The Villages to have a voice in Sumter County government. The Morse family uses its control of the local media to back candidates who will support what it wants. Since The Villages also bans door-to-door soliciting, standard door-knocking campaigns have been impossible within its limits.[71] It appears that the rest of Sumter County will just have to live with its poor roads to keep the tax rate low for residents of The Villages.

The Villages is the prime example of a huge, active adult, age-restricted community displacing the previous local power structure. Hal Rothman in *Devil's Bargains* argues that communities that successfully developed their tourism industry were making a bargain with the devil because tourism would supplant the local power structure and redefine the identity of the place, especially if it is a small place at the start.[72] The largest age-restricted communities have often had even greater impacts on the local areas around them, like the voting-down of school bond issues by residents in Sun City, Sun City West, and others. When the Sun City West expansion area could not get out of its school district, it had the votes to control the school board and keep school costs and services low, as discussed in chapter 4. At The Villages, those residents living in the portion of the community in Lake County contributed to the initial defeat of a sales tax increase to fund schools, although it passed three years later.[73] As mentioned, most of The Villages is in Sumter County.

There The Villages resident and school board member Haydn Evans proposed moving some school board meetings into one of The Villages' recreation centers so they would be more accessible to other residents of The Villages. A major realignment in Sumter County's school districts was anticipated as a result of the 2010 Census.[74]

At the state level, seniors represent a substantial voting bloc. One result is that Florida exempts retirement communities "from paying new-housing impact fees designed to help fund school districts."[75] Even more than tourism, an age-restricted community numbering in the tens of thousands could impact an area and displace its existing power structure.

Within the past couple of decades, The Villages has been the single most successful active adult, age-restricted development. While the Morse family was inspired by amenity-rich Sun City and utilized gated neighborhoods reminiscent of Leisure Worlds, it did significantly better than those developers. The initial reason seems to have been the marketing ploy of "free golf." As the community's population expanded, its numerous walls and gates divided up a community with widely varying house prices into small, homogeneous neighborhoods, allowing the developers to continue to use the "friendliest hometown" slogan. As Webb and other developers struggled to attract commercial businesses to their developments, the Morse family, when it encountered the same problem, turned to supplying the necessary businesses itself. Furthermore, while the small "downtown" of Spanish Springs was serving as the means for the Morse family to maintain control, it was also an amenity not present in many other developments. Residents were attracted to the opportunities for informal mingling among its shops and restaurants, a central space that had a somewhat different quality from the golf courses, recreation centers, and formal shopping centers of other developments. Even if they did not golf, the ease of using a golf cart to get to these amenities suited the mobility needs of the elderly.

Finally, the control of the Morse family meant that it could build a continuing care facility within The Villages and not worry about opposition. In a departure from the earlier developers, the Morse family has incorporated advertising for that facility into its overall promotion of The Villages.[76] While the community began as an imitation of Sun City, it has reached the point that it may be cutting-edge and, in some ways, a model for other developers.

Del Webb's Sun City Center in Florida

While Del Webb had some influence on Florida developers, his concept differed in several important ways from the established style of retirement development in the state that had pioneered retirement housing. His own Florida development, Sun City Center, failed to meet his expectations for sales, and he sold it in 1972. A critic of the notorious land scams in Florida mentioned that Webb would not allow speculation on the part of purchasers, meaning that if one bought at Sun City Center, the buyer had to build one of Webb's model homes almost immediately. That did not suit the dreams of those who envisioned retirement as being some years away. Also, Webb did not just market to retirees in general. He insisted that at least one member of each household buying into Sun City Center had to be at least fifty, and no underage children were allowed as permanent residents. Visiting underage children or grandchildren could use the pool, but only during certain hours. Finally, his inland location seven miles from Tampa Bay and about twenty-five miles south of Tampa, was a negative.[77] Webb's concept took a while to succeed in Florida.

Webb's executives cited much the same reasons for Sun City Center's failure as a Del Webb development. Webb's general manager for community development in 1971, David F. Ward, also expressed the opinion that restricting sales to those over fifty might be "wrong for Florida." The Webb Corporation had halted the construction of new homes in its Florida community the year before and was having some difficulty finding buyers for those homes it had already constructed.[78] Another Webb executive, Ken Parker, who was vice president for sales in 1984 and who had worked at Sun City Center in the mid-1960s, recalled that the firm's Florida community was "not necessarily competitive to the marketplace." It was "remote in location" and "remote from the corporate structure."[79]

DEVCO president John Meeker faulted his company for becoming overly confident with the success of Sun City, Arizona, and as a result not doing "any in depth site location marketing research" for the Florida and California Sun Cities. The firm could have purchased a 5,000-acre site in Sarasota that had water access to the Gulf of Mexico but turned it down in favor of the 12,000-acre inland site that became Sun City Center.[80] In retrospect, Meeker noted that in the early 1960s, "the west coast of Florida simply did not have the drawing power of developments on the east coast. . . . Tampa was an industrial port city, and St. Petersburg was a haven for minimal income retirees."[81] While the Del Webb concept of how to do a retirement community may have been a bit advanced for Florida in the 1960s, the fact that Phoenix was the location of its corporate headquarters was also of major significance.

From the perspective of Sun City Center residents, the Webb Corporation neglected their community. According to Sun City Center historian and resident John Bowker, when the popular restaurant in Webb's motel, the King's Inn, burned down in 1971, not only did the company not rebuild, but it took them months just to clean up the rubble from that disaster. Also, when the population was under 4,000, Webb had promised to build a new recreation center once the population reached 5,000. The next construction phase would take the community south of the major highway leading into it, again requiring a significant expenditure for infrastructure since Webb was committed to getting in the amenities before selling additional homes.[82] However, the residents blamed the Webb Corporation for its lack of commitment to Sun City Center.

Meanwhile, back at corporate headquarters in Phoenix in 1970, Webb was preparing to expand that Sun City north across Grand Avenue and the railroad tracks. That year saw substantial expenditures for a luxurious recreation center, manmade lake, and other infrastructure at the Arizona Sun City. Also in 1970 in connection with that expansion, the firm estimated that it needed $15 million for a hospital and clinic, a supper club, apartments for its "vacation special" marketing program, and a shopping center, not to mention some new homes.[83]

Webb liked to raise cash within his company if possible. At Sun City Center, Webb had developed 1,400 acres out of the 12,000 originally purchased. The corporation that had sold Webb 10,000 acres, Universal Marion,[84] bought them back in 1970 for the same price Webb originally paid.[85] From the Del Webb corporation's standpoint, other factors were the slow sales at Sun City Center combined with the high costs of carrying undeveloped land. Based on its Sun City, Arizona, experience, DEVCO had projected sales of 800 homes per year at Sun City Center; but instead, sales were around 450 per year.[86] In an interview in 1972, Webb explained that, with respect to both Sun City Center, Florida, and Sun City, California, "the taxes were going up faster than the revenue coming in." He said that it was time for his "corporation to 'get out.'"[87]

Sun City Center then went through several different developers. Its first owner after Webb was the Walter-Gould Corporation.[88] Prior to 1968, Gerald Gould had been president of the company developing Lehigh Acres, one of the massive Florida land developments of the era—98,000 lots platted on 58,000 acres, with more than 50,000 of the lots sold.[89] Apparently, this was one of those developments where the developer sold mostly dreams. The population in 1970 was only 11,250, about three-fourths retirees.[90] Clearly, Gerald Gould was not a Del Webb type of developer.

The Walter-Gould Corporation began with high ambitions but soon got caught in the energy crisis and economic downturn of the mid-1970s. It started by buying additional land, increasing its Sun City Center acreage to 12,000; but then, to repay a bank loan, it sold some of that acreage to one of the Century Village spin-offs, Kings Point, for a condominium development, Kings Point West, that would have its own separate recreational facilities. Furthermore, Kings Point West was not technically age-restricted. As the population in Sun City Center grew, Walter-Gould, under pressure from its bank, did honor the Del Webb concept of constructing additional community facilities, specifically expanding space for crafts, a library, a building to house the residents' association, and an indoor pool.[91]

However, Walter-Gould ended the age-restricted policy of Del Webb while still using the billboard slogan "Sun City Center, the town too busy to retire."[92] That did not do much to help sales. Gerontologists were pointing out that as people age, they tend to disengage from intergenerational society and that society tends to disengage from them. One response of the elderly was to seek out more association with their peers. Also, this generation was familiar with large postwar suburban tract developments marketed primary to young married couples. Therefore, why not a similar tract development marketed to retirees?[93] An age-restricted community not only had a minimum age requirement to purchase, but these communities barred children under the age of nineteen as well. Many of the Sun City Center residents were grandparents, but as the 1979 president of Sun City Center's resident association put it, "Your grandchildren can stay with you as long as you can stand them."[94] Joking aside, it was a reference to the fact that much as they loved their grandchildren, those children can get on the nerves of the elderly. Furthermore, their presence became a community issue with shared facilities like the swimming pool. Walter-Gould's ambiguity on the issue of age restriction and being overly ambitious at the wrong time eventually led to failure. The partnership filed for bankruptcy, and the bank was later forced to sell Sun City Center.[95]

The new owner, Victor Palmieri, who arrived in 1981, did go back to the age-restricted policy of Webb, but he had little interest in honoring the original Webb concept of additional community facilities as the population increased. Therefore, the residents' association announced that it would not allow his buyers to use their recreational facilities. With his home sales falling, Palmieri agreed to construct a large, multipurpose community hall. Then, in 1987, he sold his interests in Sun City Center to Al Hoffman, the current developer. Along the way and with the changes in ownership, much of the original Del Webb concept that each new group of 5,000 residents would surround additional recreation and shopping facilities got lost.[96] By the twenty-first century, Sun City Center residents numbered around 11,000, and another 5,000 lived at Kings Point West.[97]

Del Webb in California

During the 1960s and 1970s, California was also considered a retirement mecca; Del Webb paralleled the development of Sun City Center, Florida, with Sun City, California. This community was relatively isolated, again because Webb wanted a very large amount of land. In this case, his purchases amounted to 14,000 acres, located inland in the Perris Valley about twenty-five miles south of Riverside.[98] During the mid-1960s, Webb ran national ads touting his three Sun Cities and offering interested readers his "Vacation Special" (lodging, meals, entertainment, and the opportunity to buy a Sun City home) in the Sun City of their choice. Of those who responded, about 50 percent chose the Arizona Sun City, 40 percent went to the Florida development, and only 10 percent wanted to visit the California Sun City. Furthermore, in analyzing the states of origin of their Sun City, California, buyers, almost all were from California, indicating that the California retirement market was largely an in-state one.[99]

When a slump in housing sales hit in the mid-1960s along with a prolonged strike that halted home construction at Sun City, California, sales lost their original momentum. Webb may have expected its Sun City, California, to be an even bigger success than the Arizona Sun City because it initially projected California sales of 3,000 houses per year, while only 2,200 homes were sold in the Arizona community in its first two years.[100] The estimate was way overblown. The 1970 Census showed a Sun City, California, population of 5,519.[101]

The following year, 1971, Webb sold 390 vacant lots, the house models, and its sales building to the Presley Corporation.[102] With Del Webb paying high, development-level taxes, not agricultural ones, on thousands of acres of land that he could, at the time, only rent to farmers, he decided as early as 1964 to begin selling excess land. The buyer of 4,000 acres of his land that year was another land developer.[103] The original Webb plan for this Sun City was to use 5,163 acres for retirement housing, another 5,781 for conventional housing, and 914 acres as an industrial area. However, the conventional housing did not appear on the site until the 1980s, about twenty-five years after Webb's land purchases and over a decade after Webb exited the area.[104] As Webb sold out, the firm allowed a mobile home park to be constructed within Sun City's boundaries,[105] something that it avoided in its other communities and that lowered the general image of Sun City, California. While some people blamed Del Webb for the community's problems such as the lack of a public transportation system and no nearby hospital, others thought of him as a Santa Claus who agreed to subsidize the residents' association for several years after he ceased to actively develop the community.[106]

In some ways, the subsequent history of Sun City, California, was similar to that of Sun City Center, Florida. Presley was the major developer after Webb, but other developers helped to expand the town. However, without Webb, there was not the same commitment to building additional recreation facilities as the population grew. In 1978, Presley agreed to replace an old shuffleboard court with a 7,700-square-foot building by paying $100,000 of the anticipated $180,000 to $200,000 cost of the building. As of 1992, that project was still uncompleted.[107] That same year, the residents association refused to allow another developer, Carlsberg Construction Company, which was building 476 housing units, to let its buyers use the association's community facilities.[108] With more than one developer expanding the unincorporated community at the same time, the residents of Sun City, California, had even less control over the nature of development than did their counterparts in Florida. The growth of the community was slower and the planning more fragmented.

The Del Webb Corporation was involved at different times in some other California retirement communities. Kern City near Bakersfield opened in 1961, the year before Sun City, California. Kern City did not develop to any significant degree and ended up on the Webb selling block.

Webb's influence on California was limited. The year Kern City opened, so did a rival retirement community, Palm City, at Palm Desert, between Palm Springs and Indio. The developer was Nels Severin, who was active in the leadership of the National Association of Home Builders. In Meeker's view, Severin "pretty much duplicated Sun City, Arizona's amenities except for the shopping center." However, within a few years, the Palm City project failed.[109]

It would be another couple of decades and long after Del Webb's death in 1974 before the Webb Corporation returned to California with an age-restricted, active adult development. The firm had avoided the gated communities that were the trademark of the Leisure Worlds; but in the mid-1990s, the Webb corporation reversed itself and opened its first gated retirement communities at Palm Desert, California, and at Hilton Head, South Carolina. They joined the more traditional Webb communities of Sun City Roseville, California; Sun City MacDonald Ranch, Nevada; and Sun City Georgetown, Texas.[110] The firm was targeting more elite buyers than Century Village did in Florida, branching out beyond the traditional retirement states of Arizona, Florida, and California, and with the use of gates, co-opting an important characteristic from the other leading type of age-restricted retirement community, the Leisure Worlds.

Ross Cortese Expands Leisure Worlds across the United States

Like Webb, success in the early 1960s with age-restricted communities motivated Ross Cortese to develop additional age-restricted communities, first in California, then the Atlantic coast, Arizona, and Florida. Almost simultaneously with the opening of his flagship community, Leisure World Laguna Hills, Cortese opened Leisure World Walnut Creek near San Francisco, officially called Rossmoor Leisure World at Walnut Creek. By 2007, it was known as Rossmoor in Walnut Creek, California. Just as Del Webb put his name on his Sun Cities' advertising, Cortese tried to use Rossmoor, the name of his corporation and his innovative first development, originally called Walled City of Rossmoor, to brand his communities. However, he was not as successful in elevating Rossmoor to brand status, perhaps because he was not the celebrity that Del Webb, co-owner of the New York Yankees, was; but also, his company lacked the financial strength and staying power of the Del Webb Corporation. In any case, by the spring of 1965, Cortese said that with more than seven hundred residents at Rossmoor Leisure World at Walnut Creek, it was "northern California's largest self-contained adult community."[111]

A survey of rather loosely defined retirement communities in California in 1966 numbered more than sixty developments, including the three Rossmoor Leisure Worlds—Seal Beach, Laguna Hills, and Walnut Creek. It listed Webb's developments; the imitation of Sun City, Palm City; and the highly regarded Rancho Bernardo in San Diego.[112] In California and on the East Coast, Cortese's concept of guard-gated communities relatively close to cities, compact enough to support intracommunity bus systems, and in varying architectural styles reflecting the heritage of the region where he was building was more influential in the next couple of decades than was the Del Webb concept of more open communities of single-family homes on much larger sites somewhat further from cities and with identical architecture whether they were in California, Arizona, or Florida. Both developers built age-restricted retirement communities with similar "active adult" amenities such as golf courses and clubhouses. While California's reputation for setting future trends may have helped Cortese win acceptance in the East,[113] the practical aspects of his concept of the ideal retirement community were probably more important.

By 1966, Cortese was selling "manor homes," as he liked to call his modest cooperative apartments, at both Leisure World Maryland and Leisure World New Jersey. Like the California Leisure Worlds, Leisure World Maryland required that the buyer be at least fifty-two. Located in Olney, Maryland, within commuting distance to Washington, D.C., the community featured an on-site medical clinic as part of its service package. Activities planned in 1966 included adult education in coordination with the local school district, golf, horseback riding, and the closed-circuit television that had been so useful in developing a sense of community at Leisure World Laguna Hills.[114] Leisure World Maryland attracted "a few private businesses."[115] However, the community did not match the success of the California Leisure Worlds. By 1982, the smallest California one, Walnut Creek, numbered 3,122 housing units, compared to the 1,995 that Cortese built at Leisure World Maryland.[116] The New Jersey Leisure World was even less successful. Located near

Princeton at Cranberry and featuring colonial-style architecture, it had only 534 units.[117] Cortese originally planned to have 19,000 housing units at the New Jersey community and 10,000 units at his Maryland Leisure World. The problem with the small number of units actually sold was that it meant fewer people to support the commonly owned recreational and other facilities and hence higher homeowner fees.

Due to a decline in sales with a tight mortgage market around 1967, Cortese sold the New Jersey Leisure World to Solomon Eisenrod and his associates, who completed the community known as Rossmoor, bringing it up to 2,000 homes. In the 1970s, Eisenrod began another active adult community of 2,000, Clearbrook, which reached build-out in 1993. Meanwhile, Eisenrod added a third active adult community nearby, the Ponds. All three communities were in Monroe Township, with freeway access in a little over an hour to midtown Manhattan. Eisenrod attributed his success to the location of the communities, his addition of more recreational amenities, and the faith he had in the active adult community concept when these communities were a novelty in the 1960s.[118] Since Eisenrod began in the active adult community business by taking over a Ross Cortese community, Cortese was clearly his inspiration.

However, Cortese's view on the disappointing sales in New Jersey and Maryland was that the climate was not as benign as it was in California. He had made some tentative moves to bring a Leisure World to the Chicago area in the late 1960s. He bought 3,000 acres but ran into problems with permits, tight money, and high interest rates.[119] Abandoning plans for an age-restricted community, he eventually built 299 units of conventional housing at Woodridge, Illinois.[120]

Nevertheless, Cortese was very much in an expansionist mode, perhaps more so than was wise given his financial resources. In 1962, Western Savings and another bank had begun the Golden Hills retirement community in Mesa, Arizona. They put in some recreational facilities, including a golf course, and opened the development to local home builders, all without much success. Then, in 1971, Western Savings partnered with Ross Cortese to turn the community into a Leisure World.[121] Cortese and Western Savings came up with a ten-year development plan for the 2,200-acre site that called for an active adult community of 17,000 and a family area to house 10,000. The architectural style was predominantly Spanish; 60 percent of the site was to be open space, with a thirty-six-hole golf course, lakes, and streams. The development would have Rossmoor's signature guard-gated security with a wall six feet high surrounding the entire community. A residents' association would do all yard maintenance.[122]

Leisure World Golden Hills put Ross Cortese in Del Webb's backyard. Some interesting competition in advertising ensued. Golden Hills actually used billboards in the Phoenix area with the slogan: "Sure, visit Sun City, but then come to Leisure World and buy." Ross Cortese even bought advertising space in Sun City's newspaper and used it for a column touting Leisure World's advantages, such as gated security. Sun City executive John Meeker called Leisure World's efforts "the best free advertising Sun City ever received."[123] In 1973, Leisure World tried to get Sun City residents into its community with free bus trips. As Meeker put it, "They got a few takers but not many sales."[124] In fact, Cortese sold only 362 units at Leisure World Golden Hills before exiting the project.[125] Golden Hills continued as a Leisure World active adult, age-restricted development. So did its attempts to reach the Sun City market. In 1988, as people drove toward Sun City, some substantial billboards advised them, "See Leisure World First."[126] However, as a compact, guard-gated community of condos, Leisure World Golden Hills was very different from the open, sprawling community of predominantly single-family homes that was Del Webb's Sun City.

Finally, Ross Cortese tried his luck in the leading retirement state of Florida. In 1974, a Fort Lauderdale newspaper featured a half-page ad for Leisure World Coconut Creek near Pompano Beach north of Miami. Units ranged from studios to three-bedroom apartments. Even though 1974 was well into the Medicare era, his ad mentioned "24 hour health services." This ad called Coconut Creek "a Caribbean paradise filled with golf, swimming, clubhouses, gardens and more," but the ad used drawings of the amenities, not photographs, indicating that they had yet to be built. Coconut Creek was age-restricted, but perhaps to try to stimulate sales, Cortese lowered his minimum age from his usual fifty-two to forty-five.[127] Cortese eventually sold 432 units at Coconut Creek. In addition to his age-restricted, active adult communities, Ross Cortese continued to build a number of conventional developments in most of these states.[128] While his Leisure Worlds outside California met with mediocre success under his management, he deserves a lot of credit for promoting an alternative version of the age-restricted, active adult community in other parts of the United States than that advertised by Del Webb. Cortese's main problem seems to have been generating the volume of sales to make the common-interest amenities affordable for the people interested in buying his condos.

Irwin Levy, the successful developer of the Century Village communities, and his son, Mark Levy, had some interesting opinions as to why Cortese failed at Coconut Creek. Cortese was a Californian and, to use Irwin Levy's words, "was a very successful and excellent developer" there. However, Irwin Levy noted, "The Florida market was very different from California," and in Levy's estimation, Cortese "did not understand the Florida marketplace."[129] Irwin Levy knew that part of Florida was very popular with Jewish retirees from the Northeast, having specifically defined his target buyers. Cortese, who had a number of partners, had a policy of building near major cities, in this case Miami, apparently with the idea of appealing to local retirees. Since the early history of Florida was Spanish, Cortese used Spanish-style architecture at Coconut Creek; it was a style associated with Catholics. Thus, he aimed for the wrong ethnic group.[130]

With only thirty-two sales in two years, Cortese's partners got upset, took control, and ousted him. The partners then needed another developer. H. Irwin Levy had already successfully completed his first Century Village and begun launching the second. He succeeded Cortese at Coconut Creek,[131] and Levy successfully revamped the development. Leisure World Coconut Creek became simply Wynmoor and had a more upscale appeal than the Century Villages.[132] With Levy handling Wynmoor, by the mid-1990s all 5,260 units were sold.[133] Apparently, Webb, who had nationally advertised all three of his Sun Cities in the same ads, and Cortese had a generic retiree image in mind, were very successful when they were in their home territory but failed to appreciate how varied the retirement market was in other parts of the country. That contributed to, if not failure, less than stunning success with some of their later developments.

Ross Cortese decided to liquidate his development company in 1982 after Leisure World Laguna Hills reached build-out. Other developers and joint-venture partners who succeeded Cortese, such as in the Maryland and Arizona Leisure Worlds, eventually made those communities successful. These included Giuseppe Cecchi, whose company, International Developers Inc., or IDI, added more than 2,700 units, some of the high-rise apartment variety, to the Maryland Leisure World.[134] As for Leisure World Coconut Creek becoming a success as Wynmoor, Irwin Levy knew that the coastal area of southeast Florida was very popular with Jewish retirees from northeastern states, and marketing should be targeted to that area.[135] While Cortese may not have had the financial capacity or the marketing savvy to always carry out his vision, it was basically his concept that shaped those communities.

Leisure World's East Coast Imitators

Just as Webb had his imitators, so did Ross Cortese. In 1962, New Jersey's first retirement community appeared in Ocean County. Other retirement developments quickly followed, partly due to the relatively low cost of the land along with the proximity to New York City and Philadelphia. By 1976, Ocean County had twenty retirement communities, representing more than half of the state's 30,000 units of retirement-village housing. All of these communities had clubhouses and shuffleboard courts, 60 percent had golf courses, and another 60 percent had swimming pools. Like Ross Cortese, these developers targeted a local market of retirees who wanted an amenity-rich, age-restricted community but did not want to move far from home.[136] In fact, a 1976 survey showed that 84.4 percent of those living in New Jersey retirement communities moved into them from elsewhere in New Jersey or were from the New York City and Philadelphia areas.[137] Retirement communities continued to expand in Ocean County. During the 1970s, the county's population increased by 66 percent, with people over age sixty-four accounting for more than half that increase. Middlesex County, where Ross Cortese started a Leisure World, had the most new home construction during the early 1980s, due in part to the growth of active adult communities. That made New Jersey the fifth most popular state for migratory retirees and the only one outside the Sunbelt. The states that outdrew New Jersey were Florida, California, Arizona, and Texas.[138]

Residents of New Jersey retirement communities chose them for a variety of reasons. House prices were relatively low. The recreational amenities, clubhouses, golf, and exterior maintenance were popular. The communities were within an hour or so from New York City, making cultural excursions very feasible. Some retirees wanted to remain reasonably close to their grandchildren. Other residents had not actually retired. In 1984, Manchester Township had a minimum age of forty-eight for residents in that municipality's retirement communities. After Joseph Famoso moved into Crestwood, New Jersey's largest retirement community, with 15,000 residents and ten clubhouses, he continued to work for two years. At Crestwood, he and his wife took part in bowling, bridge, art classes, and group trips to New Orleans, Alaska, and Bermuda. A resident of another active adult community was commuting to his accounting job in New York City with a one-hour bus ride on the New Jersey Turnpike. As for developers, they liked the relatively cheap land in that part of New Jersey that was also fairly close to Philadelphia. Existing communities welcomed the retirees because, while they might vote against school tax increases, in New Jersey, the State Department of Education could overrule those votes. Finally, some year-round residents preferred the varied climate over Florida's summer heat and humidity.[139]

One of the most successful developers of these New Jersey communities was a company called Leisure Technology. The success of Leisure World Seal Beach directly inspired the company's founder to build a downsized version of that community in New Jersey in the 1960s. He saw the large Italian and Jewish populations of Philadelphia and New York City as having strong family ties. His target market was retirees who wanted an age-restricted community of their own with amenities but close enough for frequent visits with their children and grandchildren.[140]

Leisure Technology chose Ocean County for its first three Leisure Village communities, including Leisure Village West, which opened in 1972. Leisure Technology did not try to copy Cortese's inclusion of some on-site medical services, but it did create a walled and guard-gated community of townhouse condominiums. As in the Leisure World communities, exterior maintenance was provided. Leisure Technology also used Cortese's minimum age of fifty-two for this age-restricted community and barred children eighteen or under from permanent residence. Most Leisure Village West residents lived there year-round, but about one-quarter wintered in the Sunbelt, especially Florida. Some of these had second homes. In 1981, most Leisure Village West residents were middle or upper middle class, retired, with an average age in the early 60s, and in good health. In fact, deteriorating health was one reason to leave the community.[141]

As of 1981, Leisure Village West numbered around 2,600 residents on 800 acres. On completion, the community was planned to have 3,200 housing units. Besides golf, swimming, and other recreational activities, Leisure Village West featured a variety of adult education classes and field trips to New York City for theatrical productions. The developer even copied the closed-circuit television station that Cortese used at Leisure World Laguna Hills. He used some of Cortese's advertising themes, as well, such as "freedom from loneliness, fear, and boredom: freedom to choose from a multitude of leisure activities; and freedom from home maintenance." Using the Leisure World model, Leisure Technology dominated the Ocean County retirement market into the 1970s.[142]

During the late 1970s, Leisure Technology began to experience serious competition from other retirement community developers in New Jersey. By this time, the company founder, who had been so inspired by Ross Cortese's Leisure World model for retirement communities, had died. In 1977, Leisure Technology decided to switch from condominium townhouse units to single-family detached homes, thus becoming more like Del Webb's Sun Cities.[143]

Among Leisure Technology's competitors on the East Coast was U.S. Home, which opened Heritage Harbor in the Annapolis, Maryland, area in 1979. Like other developers, Leisure Technology executives discovered that more and more retirees were opting for smaller houses in amenity-rich communities. Furthermore, these were buyers with equity in their existing homes, which they could sell to finance a moderately expensive, new, retirement home. Generally, they had more money to spend than first-time home buyers, a fact not lost on the developers. For tax reasons, many elderly buyers took out mortgages on their retirement homes and invested the money from selling their former homes to add to their incomes. By the mid-1980s, the Washington, D.C., area had three active adult communities. Ross Cortese had pioneered in that area twenty years before with his Leisure World at Olney, Maryland. He had provided a model for other East Coast developers of active adult communities in emphasizing "personal security, social/physical amenities and attractive, smaller dwellings that are better suited to the aging resident than old houses with two levels of living plus a basement and an attic."[144]

Sun City West, Arizona

Elsewhere, condos and gated communities characterized the retirement market, but by the 1970s, the Del Webb model of the amenity-rich retirement community was definitely dominant in Arizona. A 1975 survey of dwelling units in various types of retirement communities in

Arizona found that 53 percent of the units were in "retirement villages/towns." Another 33 percent were in mobile home parks. The remainder were in retirement hotels and "life care facilities."[145] In 1985, Don Tuffs, head of marketing for DEVCO, noted that in just Arizona, there were "over 100 adult-type communities, varying from the small basic low amenity mobile-home park all the way to the likes of Sun City and Sun City West," but the resale of homes in Sun City was what he considered the strongest competition to sales of new homes in Sun City West.[146] What allowed for the continued construction of what might be termed the second-generation retirement communities was that the size of the niche market of "retirees willing to move more than 200 miles from their hometown" had grown from what Tuffs estimated at 3 percent of all retirees in 1960 to 8–10 percent by the 1980s.[147] As Sun City reached build-out in 1979 with around 46,000 residents, DEVCO crossed the nearby Agua Fria riverbed to begin marketing its new community there, Sun City West. As the second-generation successor to Sun City, the differences in this development were indicative of the trends in the 1980s and early 1990s in age-restricted, active adult communities in general.

Just as John Meeker, who became president of DEVCO in 1965, redirected the development of Sun City, so too his vision was crucial to the launching of Sun City West. As early as 1971, company executives realized that Sun City would reach build-out within seven years and began buying additional land for a new community. By the end of 1979, the company had accumulated a total of 12,611 acres for Sun City West. Actual planning of the community began in 1974, was halted due to the 1974–75 recession, then resumed in 1976 with sales expected to start in 1980. However, Sun City sold out faster than expected, so the opening date for Sun City West was moved up to 1979.[148]

Meeker attempted to draw lessons from Sun City. For example, one of the criticisms of Sun City's golf courses was that they were designed to maximize the number of golf course lots for sale and not to enhance the golfing experience. Therefore, Meeker determined that Sun City West would have a golf course capable of hosting Professional Golf Association (PGA) tournaments. And in place of Sun City's outdoor amphitheater, the Sun Bowl, Meeker planned a giant auditorium, eventually known as the Sundome. Sun City West would have a social and dining club similar to Sun City's Lakes Club. Meeker decided that the community's first recreation center would be "the largest private facility for recreational and creative activities in Arizona." In place of Sun

City's small, neighborhood shopping centers, Sun City West would have space for a regional mall. At this point, the company was planning for an eventual Sun City West population of at least 70,000.[149] Much about Sun City West's initial planning was meant to make it larger and better than the original Sun City.

Sun City West never came close to reaching 70,000 population, nor did a regional shopping mall develop in the community. One factor was the severe recession of 1980–82 that sharply curtailed sales. Potential buyers had difficulty selling their existing homes in order to purchase ones in Sun City West. DEVCO dealt with the recession by cutting back on home construction, curtailing administrative costs—both president John Meeker and public relations director Jerry Svendsen left the company at this time—and selling off assets, including a large portion of the land that had been intended for the development of Phase 2 of Sun City West.[150] In order to get a supermarket to open in Sun City West, DEVCO had to promise Safeway that it would not have to pay rent until Sun City West had 5,000 occupied housing units.[151] Even with the return of prosperity, the sale of about half the land intended for Sun City West meant that the community would not be able to support a regional mall.

A second reason for the smaller size was the growing tendency to question whether bigger meant better. A 1980 poll of area residents published in the *Arizona Sun* newspaper showed that growth was their biggest concern, followed by traffic congestion.[152] Later, in 1992, when the corporation acquired 1,335 acres for added housing for at least 6,000 more people at Sun City West, community residents raised concerns again about traffic congestion and about crowding at the existing recreation centers and golf courses. DEVCO answered the latter complaint with plans for another recreation center and golf course plus a promise to not increase the existing housing density of Sun City West in what became known locally as the Sun City West "expansion area."[153] It took Sun City West twenty years to reach build-out in 1998, with approximately 31,000 residents on 7,100 acres. At that point, the community had nine eighteen-hole golf courses, four recreation centers, the 7,100-seat Sundome (too large for most community events and thus donated to Arizona State University), and a 203-bed hospital. Known for seamless transitions from one retirement-community project in the area to the next, in 1998 DEVCO was already two years into selling homes across the road from Sun City West at Sun City Grand.[154]

Standardizing the Minimum Age for Active Adult Communities

Unfavorable attitudes toward the aged in a youth-oriented culture in part reflect the ideas that the aged are financially dependent, physically infirm, and mentally in decline. Feminist Betty Friedan thought a great part of the appeal of age-restricted communities was their "promise to separate old people from the prejudice and discrimination of young people."[155] Some retirement destinations, but not active adult communities, became associated with disparaging images of the elderly. For example, St. Petersburg, Florida, for decades attracted retirees with limited funds to its downtown residential hotels. Many elderly enjoyed sitting on the green benches lining the downtown sidewalks. However, if a wealthy retiree left his beachfront condo to go to downtown St. Petersburg and sat on one of those benches, he would be regarded as "just another 'old' man."[156] When St. Petersburg decided to gentrify, it got rid of its trademark sitting places for the elderly, the sidewalk green benches. One way for the elderly to insulate themselves from negative and patronizing attitudes was to segregate themselves in age-restricted communities.

In addition to some of the harsh views that society has of the aged are the views of the aged toward themselves. It is common for the elderly to think of themselves as younger than they really are. That tendency affected advertising for age-restricted communities. For example, the photographs of "residents" used to advertise these communities commonly featured "people ten to fifteen years younger" than the developer's target market.[157] Longtime Sun City public relations director Jerry Svendsen recalled that when asked the average age of people in the community, Webb's staff would respond by shaving a few years off what they really thought it was.[158] By using the "active adult" theme, developers played to the self-image among prospective buyers as younger than their chronological ages.

With active adult communities proliferating but using varying minimum ages for eligibility to buy into the community, the question arose of what age was appropriate for retirement, for labeling someone as "elderly," a "senior citizen," or an "active adult" old enough to move into an age-restricted community. Chronological age does not reflect an individual's employment status or health but is used when an easily identifiable attribute is needed. For example, AARP uses fifty as its minimum age for seniors to become members. The Social Security system has sixty-two as its minimum age for seniors to begin receiving retirement benefits.[159] A 1987 Del Webb survey of baby boomers about when they fantasized retiring had almost half thinking about retiring before the age of sixty.[160] By the mid-twentieth century, many corporations had selected sixty-five as the age for compulsory retirement.[161] However, increased life expectancy, strain on the Social Security system, and the recognition that chronological age does not necessarily reflect individual ability or productivity led to the Retirement Age Act of 1978 severely restricting the use of a mandatory retirement age.[162] Consequently, with these varying ways of defining the elderly, it was not surprising that age-restricted communities would vary their minimum ages all the way from forty at Sun Lakes to sixty-five for both spouses during the first two years of Youngtown.[163]

An important part of the concept of the age-restricted community was banning the permanent residence of children under the age of nineteen. One study of retirement communities in the greater Phoenix area concluded that 25 percent of the adults in these communities were childless, which was somewhat above the norm.[164] Another study of the first group to move into Leisure World Laguna Hills revealed an even higher proportion, one-third, to be childless.[165] Other observers have made references to intergenerational tensions, not that residents do not miss their grandchildren but that they prefer to spend most of their time around their peers and neighbors.[166] Perhaps the best way of summing up the attitude toward grandchildren was that most residents were glad to see them come for a visit and glad to see them leave. They liked children, but they did not want them around on a permanent basis. As to how long a visit from grandchildren could be before an age-restricted community resident wanted them to leave, that certainly varied. Stanley Hauseman, who described the woman over ninety doing laps in his condominium's pool, told a congressional committee holding hearings on banning children in age-restricted communities, "after five or six days, love them as I do, I don't feel too bad when I have to say goodbye and I get rid of the confusion and the disturbance that they have brought into our little household." When he apologized for his frankness, a congressman responded, "That's all right. I have grandchildren, too."[167]

At a time when most social scientists were saying that the elderly wanted intergenerational contact, Del Webb Corporation executives had sensed something different. Writing about Phoenix-area retirement communities, one observer listed a series of advantages for the elderly in an age-restricted community, including reducing the "pressures of a youth-oriented culture," developing closer relationships with their elderly peers, having local political power by concentrating their votes geographically, and having more resources at hand for dealing with the problems of aging.[168] For age-restricted communities in their first couple of decades, the problem was how to protect their age-restricted status and enforce the ban on underage children as permanent residents.

When Youngtown and Sun City were established, there was no legal framework for banning children as permanent residents in those communities. Without a law, those determined to keep children out could try vigilante action. The adults who yelled taunts and threats at the school bus driver and the children of the air conditioner repairman in Sun City were successful. The repairman took his children and moved.[169] At the FHA-financed Leisure World communities in the early 1960s, FHA had a regulation banning children under eighteen from its housing projects for the elderly.[170] By 1963, the Webb Corporation was including a ban on underage children in its Sun City deed restrictions, and Sun City had a homeowners association to enforce them.

However, government enforcement was preferred. In 1976, Sun City, California, residents applied to Riverside County for their community to be zoned for senior citizens.[171] While some residents regarded the absence of children as unnatural, others had chosen the community because they preferred "peace and quiet, law and order and company of their own choosing."[172] Sun City, California, received its requested senior zoning overlay and got county enforcement. In 1988, Riverside County's Building and Safety Department sent letters to seven alleged violators, and the matter was resolved in all cases.[173] However, the county became increasingly reluctant to approve new age-restricted projects.[174]

In the Phoenix area, residents of some retirement communities in east Mesa led the charge for a county-enforced senior zoning overlay ordinance for their active adult developments. They were successful in 1979. The ordinance had such requirements as elevators for buildings over two stories, and it completely banned underage children. However, it did provide that under extraordinary circumstances, such as a grandparent bringing up a grandchild, a person could apply "for a temporary use permit" or exemption.[175]

The local senior zoning overlay solution was undercut in California with a 1983 state supreme court ruling that said a California civil rights law barring various types of discrimination, including age discrimination, made these senior zoning ordinances invalid. That court decision prompted the management company of Leisure World Laguna Hills to form a group of retirement communities for the purpose of legalizing their age restrictions.[176] A resident wrote in a letter to the editor of the *Leisure World News*, "We love children. . . . [but] some residents are required to walk a certain distance daily, some take naps, many retire early. Imagine youngsters playing, skate boards, roller skating, tossing a ball, in short just being children, clearly a hazard to an elderly resident."[177]

They were successful in getting a bill that said if a community required that one resident in all units be fifty-five, the community could ban underage children. Residents of these communities then tried to use this legislation to ban couples in which one spouse or co-habitant was substantially younger. The Leisure World group coordinating this effort to ban what might later be called "trophy wives" in their retirement communities estimated that it generated perhaps as many as 9,000 letters and other contacts to the governor, pleading for a bill that would require all residents, spouses and co-habitants included, to be forty-five.[178] Governor George Deukmejian rejected their plea and signed the bill stipulating that only one occupant be at least fifty-five; he acknowledged that "although the bill does not go as far as some advocates wanted," he thought it would "enable most senior communities to maintain the kind of lifestyle that their residents desire."[179] The California law, including the veiled battle over significantly younger wives, portended the legislative efforts to legalize these communities at the national level within a couple of years.

The passage of the federal Fair Housing Act in 1988 settled the question of the legality of age-restricted communities and gave them a national standard minimum age. At the hearings, Stanley Hauseman, president of the Florida West Coast Condominium Federation, provided numerous examples of why the elderly need the peace and quiet of an age-restricted community that banned children. These were common-interest communities with shared facilities such as pools, billiard rooms, and walkways and had the "closeness" of condominium living. He talked about the elderly losing their ability to deal with the noise, confusion, and disturbances that children brought. He described a blind person not having to worry about avoiding skate-boarders and bicyclists. Prior to the institution of age restrictions at the condominium complex where he lived, the developer had sold a unit to a divorcee with a fourteen-year-old-son. Hauseman told the subcommittee the boy not only was addicted to playing the drums but had organized a rock band. Another couple with teenage children attracted motorcyclists. Hauseman mentioned his own desire for peace and quiet as he cared for his wife, who had just been diagnosed with inoperable cancer.[180]

In drafting the bill, the House committee started out with a minimum age of sixty-two for one resident in 90 percent of the units in the community. When the bill passed, the minimum age for one resident had been lowered to fifty-five, and the proportion of units covered had been lowered to 80 percent. The reason 20 percent of the units were exempt was that Congress, like the male-dominated California legislature and male governor, was concerned about the presence of substantially younger family members, such as adult children, live-in caregivers, or much younger spouses. Without the exemption, once the resident who met the minimum age requirement died, the younger resident would have to move. Congress' problem was how to estimate the number of significantly younger spouses, including occasional other adult residents and caregivers. The committee came up with 20 percent. Legalizing their presence, however, did not eliminate substantial "emotional discord" within the communities over the issue of much younger wives. As it turned out, though, Congress vastly overestimated the percentage of significantly younger wives and other adult household members under fifty-five within this population. What some communities actually chose to do with the generous 20 percent exemption during times of slow home sales was to temporarily lower the minimum age of a certain number of buyers to forty-five. That was not the intent of Congress.

The federal law did allow states and local communities to pass stricter legislation if they so chose. With the passage of the federal law, Maricopa County, with its minimum age of fifty in its senior zoning overlay ordinance, did bring its minimum up to fifty-five; other local governments similarly changed their ordinances, as well.[181] Thus, the federal law brought some minimum age standardization to these age-restricted communities.

Originally, Sun City and Leisure World were two rather distinct ideas as to what constituted the ideal age-restricted retirement community. However, by the mid-1990s, their influences were merging as those developers borrowed from each other and as other developers borrowed from both. H. Irwin Levy added to the "active adult" concept with frequent and affordable theatrical shows. Some of the first communities were aging. At the same time, The Villages in Florida was breaking new ground with its promotion of "free golf," variety of gated neighborhoods, informal "downtowns," and streets designed to accommodate golf carts—allowing it with around 70,000 residents to still proclaim itself "Florida's friendliest hometown."

While some developers preferred to market to retirees but not specifically age-restrict their communities, they could not ban children as permanent residents. For age-restricted communities, once the civil rights issue of age discrimination against children in housing emerged, their many residents provided a powerful lobby to legalize these communities at the national level. Since the law needed to be specific to be enforced, Congress in 1988 arbitrarily decided that the minimum age for one resident in 80 percent of the units in an age-restricted development must be fifty-five if that development was to ban children as permanent residents. For the first time, these communities had a common, national definition, and the merging of developer influences as time passed further standardized them. "Active adult" and "resort" lifestyle still characterized their advertising, even as these communities aged, and a distinct resident subculture emerged.

An Active
Adult Subculture

The Residents' Script

"Could a vital age be built around such games [as bridge] in a community walled off from the rest of the world?" asked the famous feminist and social critic Betty Friedan. Her own mother had spent a couple of decades at Leisure World Laguna Hills. Friedan concluded that while many residents, especially new ones, were often very busy going to clubs and classes and participating in a variety of recreational activities, few had a real sense of purpose or passion about what they were doing. She referred to an age-restricted, active adult community as an "adult playpen."[1] Writing in 1993, Friedan was only one in a long line of critics of these communities, which also had their defenders. Maggie Kuhn, activist leader of the Gray Panthers, was calling age-restricted communities "playpens for the elderly" back at least as far as 1982,[2] long before Betty Friedan picked up on the analogy. Meanwhile, as the pioneering communities aged, so did the residents themselves. Some old problems persisted, and new social, cultural, recreational, and health care trends emerged. Developers had supplied an active adult script, but it was the residents who gave it substance, filled in the gaps, and modified it, creating a subculture to suit their needs. What was life really like in these evolving active adult, age-restricted communities?

Sun City West: A Second-Generation Community Subculture

Youngtown and Sun City were the first of these communities to be established. With the addition of the second-generation community, Sun City West, they provided researchers with the longest time span for analysis of the residents and how their social lives, recreational and cultural activities, and health care evolved. A 1983 survey revealed that almost 24 percent were childless, a high percentage that may be related to a preference for a community banning children as permanent residents. This survey showed that 79 percent made that area their home for at least ten months of the year. The communities were stratified by income, with no one in Youngtown making more than $25,000 annually, but 57.6 percent in Sun City West had at least that income, and so did 29.2 percent in Sun City. As for their health, nearly half over age sixty-five said it was "good," and another 28.6 percent rated their health "excellent."[3] The high number of childless people meant that the average area family had 1.56 living children, compared with 2.07 nationally. Most also migrated into the area from elsewhere, which may be an indication that those elderly who do migrate "are healthier, better educated, and more affluent than older adults" who stay in their hometowns. In fact, the residents of retirement towns were so affluent that one writer described such a community as "an oasis of greenbacks in the desert." As of 1989, Sun City had 46,000 residents and Sun City West 25,000, making the combined communities at that time "the largest retirement development in the world." They were "active," supporting more than 400 clubs. As the Del Webb spokesperson that year said, "Anybody can sell a house. We sell lifestyle."[4]

That lifestyle was documented in Sun City West in polls of the late twentieth and early twenty-first centuries. A 1992 poll showed that 88 percent lived there at least six months out of the year, only half golfed regularly, less than half bowled, about 20 percent played tennis, two-thirds used the community's fitness centers, a similar number belonged "to an arts and crafts club," and 89 percent had library cards. Almost 45 percent were at least seventy.[5] A similar poll in 2001 showed a somewhat older population, with 40 percent being over seventy-five. Under one-third golfed regularly, although most appreciated the sweeping greenery of the golf courses in a visual way. Like Sun City, Sun City West supported the neighborhood watch group, the Posse, and the group maintaining the landscaped medians in the thoroughfares, the PRIDES; but volunteers were harder to come by with an aging population.[6]

Buried within the survey statistics was a range of individuals with varying motivations for moving to Sun City West. Among the first buyers were Loise Copes and her husband, who came to Phoenix in 1978 to attend a postmasters convention. Since the Sun City West Vacation Special cost considerably less than the convention hotel, they opted to stay in Sun City. Loise remembered enjoying dining at the Lakes Club in Sun City and some of the local residents who put on a square dance performance and who "looked so much younger" than she and her husband. When their friends decided to buy a home there, the Copes bought one a week later at a $5,000 price increase. In 1984, the ten-thousandth buyers in Sun City West were John and Hazel Telin from Freeport, Illinois. More buyers came from Illinois than any other state. The Telins said they chose Sun City West because they wanted a warm climate, a friendly place, and recreational activities.[7] Luman Wicks and his wife were looking for a warmer climate where he could exercise outdoors in the winter following his open-heart surgery. Edward and Clarice Uhl had settled in California following Edward's 1962 retirement from the Navy but had come to regard that state as overcrowded. They made their move first to Sun City, then to Sun City West, because they discovered that they could get much more for their money in the Sun City area than they could in California.[8]

Sun City West was a second-generation community for the Del Webb Corporation, and some of the buyers were second-generation as well. In 1984, the company began its "Refer-A-Friend" program, which offered large prizes if the friend bought into the community. The "friend" Helen Morgan, who had lived in Sun City for seventeen years, referred was actually her daughter and retired naval officer son-in-law, who were visiting from their home in Hawaii. Helen took them to see the Sun City West model homes. They bought one, and the company gave her a new refrigerator as her reward.[9] The 2007 president of the Sun Cities Area Historical Society, Edson Allen, who spent winters in Sun City West and summers in Wisconsin, mentioned that his parents back in 1975 had bought a Sun City home, hence his familiarity with the Sun City and Sun City West area and his own decision to purchase a home there.[10] Similarly, the volunteer office manager at the Sun Cities Area Historical Society remembered visiting her parents at Sun City in the 1960s, and the historical society's volunteer newsletter editor inherited a condo built in the 1970s at Sun City.[11]

Interestingly, in 2006, the president of the Leisure World Historical Society, Seal Beach, Kenneth Walker, was living in a cooperative garden apartment (manor home) that his parents purchased around 1962. When he inherited it in the early 1990s, he could not sell it for what he thought it was worth, so he and his wife decided to make that apartment their home.[12] Second-generation buyers in Florida retirement communities also were fairly common. For example, journalist Frances FitzGerald mentions a seventy-three-year-old woman at Sun City Center whose mother was in her nineties and had her own home a block away from her daughter. As these active adult communities aged, their populations in general were of two generations of the elderly and occasionally even in the same family.[13]

Another type of resident that appeared with the passage of time was the one who wanted to trade up to the latest model or newest community. This type of person in particular encouraged the Del Webb Corporation to continue building in the original Sun City area. However, there was a type of buyer that the Webb Corporation did all it could to discourage. Those were the "investment" buyers or speculators, who also often lived in the area.

The home construction business was cyclical. Investment buyers were attracted in 1978, a strong year for home sales and rising prices. These individuals did not plan on occupying the unit or units they bought but instead expected to resell within a relatively short time for a profit. The Webb Corporation only was asking for a $500 down payment to hold a lot and 20 percent down before beginning to build a house in Sun City West; and, consequently, it got many investment buyers from Sun City. Many never moved into their completed homes, with the result that Sun City West opened with a lot of "For Sale" signs.[14] The DEVCO sales manager at that time, Ken Parker, was aware of what was happening. During 1978–79, home prices were increasing by as much as 25 percent annually, and interest rates were relatively low. Some buyers wanted to purchase as many as a dozen garden apartments or eight homes. He knew that once the housing market turned, the company would be stuck with quite an inventory of unsold homes as the investment buyers defaulted on their purchases. Therefore, in 1977, the company adopted a policy of only one house for personal use to a customer and no speculation or plans to rent the unit. Even then, some buyers circumvented the rules by changing their names or putting home purchases in the names of relatives. Even with this tough policy intended to curb home speculation, when interest rates in 1980–81 went into double digits and the market suddenly turned, DEVCO still had around 600 completed homes on its hands and very few buyers.[15] The company would reinstitute policies similar to Parker's to curb investment buying at Sun City Festival during the hot housing market of January 2006.[16]

One of the most obvious trends in age-restricted, active adult communities was toward more upscale housing. Paul Tatz, president of DEVCO in 1987, attributed that trend to the growing affluence of retirees. In the mid-1960s, "retirement communities catered to former middle-class workers, the butchers and bakers"; by 1987 it was "upper-middle-class business owners and executives" who were buying the new homes. What that translated into in terms of the houses was that in 1987, the majority of new Sun City West houses had ceramic tile floors and mission-tile roofs, luxuries that were rare in the early 1970s.[17] However, in trying to compete with more upscale communities like Scottsdale, DEVCO overreached in 1981. It built two very large and luxurious model homes, one with 4,200 square feet and the other with 4,680 square feet. Options included a maid's quarters, a butler's pantry, a library, a sauna, and an exercise room. The homes drew 25,000 lookers within three weeks but no buyers.[18] While age-restricted retirement communities tended to be characterized as more or less affluent, how much retirees were willing to spend also reflected whether they were making a year-round commitment to a home or if it was to be a second, seasonal home. The Sun Cities were stuck with a middle- and upper-middle-class image but not a wealthy one.

Other trends of the 1980s and early 1990s reflected both the aging nature of these communities' facilities and their physically aging populations. One advantage of age-restricted, active adult communities was that they did a better job of attracting both leisure activities designed for retirees and health care facilities to meet the needs of the elderly than did the so-called naturally occurring retirement communities.[19] Among some of the recreational trends of this period were the growing popularity of fitness centers and the decline but not total disappearance of shuffleboard. Many of the clubs at Sun City West duplicated the early clubs at Sun City, but some reflected changing times. For example, Sun City West got a water fitness club in 1980, a general fitness club in 1983, a computer club in 1984, a line dancing group in 1993, and a yoga club in 1994.[20] The older communities modernized their activities as well.

The "active adult" characterization of these communities continued to attract people who wanted to be active, with the Webb Corporation in 1974 adopting "resort-retirement living" in place of a "country club" lifestyle as its advertising theme.[21] The company had experimented with the phrase "Resort-Retirement Community" in its advertising going back to 1969,[22] and that more relaxed but friendlier pitch continues to be used in the twenty-first century by both Webb and its competitors in the age-restricted community business. An example of a couple who bought the "active adult" or "resort-retirement" script in 1979 was Roger and Althea Curfman, retirees from Cleveland, Ohio, who moved that year into Sun City West. The Curfmans may have exaggerated when they recalled that "everyone was active and took part in everything" as Sun City West welcomed its first group of residents, but that statement reflected the spirit of the community. Roger taught CPR and swimming at the recreation center. Althea became one of the first library volunteers, joined the Bicycle Club, was active in many other clubs, and eventually became head of the Pioneers Club of early residents.[23]

As the communities aged, some became conscious of their history, producing publications commemorating their pioneering communities' early years and establishing historical societies. A group began working on Sun City's historical book, *Jubilee,* in 1982 and in doing so stimulated the collecting of historical materials that were first housed at the Sun City Library.[24] Then, in 1989, Jane Freeman, the co-author of *Jubilee,* and others founded the Sun Cities Area Historical Society,[25] which encompassed Sun City West. That year they also acquired the first Sun City, Arizona, model home, the two-bedroom, one-bath Kentworth next to the first recreation center and backing onto the first golf course. The historical society used this home as an archives and museum.[26] Combining forces from the two Sun Cities also strengthened some other endeavors, including some of the state clubs that persisted with new arrivals continuing to come into both communities. Meanwhile, Sun City, California, residents published a book chronicling its first thirty years in 1992.[27] As for Sun City Center, Florida, its historical society in 2005 acquired the original Kentworth model home in its community to house that society's activities.[28] The historical society at Leisure World Laguna Hills was fortunate to have donors provide the money to construct a building to hold its archives and published a history of its first twenty-five years in 1989.[29]

School Issues Continue

The 1980s and early 1990s saw the extension of some previous trends. The residents of Sun City placed a lot of emphasis on religion, and more churches were built in Sun City West plus a synagogue.[30] In fact, churches formed at Sun City on the average of one a year, so that by 1984, Sun City had twenty-nine churches and synagogues. The pace continued at Sun City West.[31] Adult education, including college-level courses, was becoming more popular. Originally, Sun City had problems accessing educational resources, but increasingly residents enrolled in the nearby Rio Salado College, accounting for most of this community college's 1,400 students by 1978.[32] That did not affect its political stance on school bond issues. Sun City West followed the example of Sun City in voting down school bond issues and, in 1981, got ejected from the Dysart School District, allowing the retirees to escape some school taxes.[33] However, to get out of the school district, Sun City West did allow its commercial core to remain within the district.[34] Like Sun City, Arizona, Sun City West, which eventually had a population of 31,000, rejected incorporation. That was also true of Sun City, California; Sun City Center, Florida; and until the twenty-first century, Leisure World Laguna Hills, not to mention The Villages, Florida. The goal of retirees with both the school issue and incorporation was to keep taxes low.

The school issue resurfaced at Sun City West in the late 1990s. The area immediately to the north of Sun City West remained within the school district. The Webb Corporation then acquired that land, added it to Sun City West, and sold homes there. The so-called Sun City West expansion area was within the school district, which set the stage for an encore to the deannexation battle. The expansion area residents in 1998 voted 2,059 to 306 to get out of the school district, but residents outside the expansion area voted 2,327 to 127 to keep the area in the district.[35] In 1997, expansion area residents were paying a school tax rate that was three times what residents in the rest of Sun City West were paying.[36]

With the expansion area remaining within the school district, its residents had the votes to control the school board and keep expenses low. For the students within the Dysart School District, that meant no public funding of the schools' sports programs. Some Sun City West residents and a local real estate agent donated enough money so Dysart could have a varsity football team, but without junior teams feeding into it, the Dysart team "was outscored by a combined 84-6 in its first two games."[37] The school board cut music, art, and physical education.[38] Residents of the Sun City West expansion area continued to have the power to elect three of the five school board members, and those three continued to keep school expenditures low. Locally, the leading Phoenix newspaper ran a cartoon picturing the Dysart School Board as "Retirees Running from Responsibility,"[39] while nationally the retirees were labeled "child haters."[40] The situation was somewhat alleviated in 2001 when the Arizona legislature added 0.6 percent to the state sales tax to fund schools.[41]

Some of the fallout from the well-publicized school controversies has affected developers of large retirement communities around the country. Developers need zoning changes and permits to proceed. Nearby communities may be concerned that a large active adult retirement development will make trouble for its local schools, and their local governments might not grant the permits the developer needs to proceed. Some developers have offered free school sites to allay that anxiety, but if the retirees who move into the community vote down school bond issues, the problem remains.[42] On the other hand, small developments of retirees that will not dominate the local school board may be more than welcome because they can be taxed to support the schools without adding any pupils to them. That was the experience of Cambridge Homes, the largest developer of retirement communities in the Chicago area and a division of D. R. Horton, one of the nation's biggest home builders.[43]

It is also important not to overgeneralize and assume that every large retirement community will be self-serving and withhold support from public schools. Besides the earlier example of Leisure World Laguna Hills, which initially benefited from its local school district's adult education program, Wynmoor, the remade Leisure World in Florida, had enough residents by the early 1980s to dominate Coconut Creek's city council. Nevertheless, Wynmoor supported "a new elementary school" and other community issues, such as annexations, that were not directly in Wynmoor residents' own self-interest. However, Wynmoor did fight a losing court battle to keep Broward Community College from installing a campus entrance opposite Wynmoor's main gate. Wynmoor residents' concern on that issue was traffic.[44] Nevertheless, one of the important effects of large age-restricted communities was that by concentrating the votes of the elderly, they did make it possible for older voters to have a controlling voice on various local issues.

In the area of politics in general, again it is important not to overgeneralize. The majority of active adult communities tend to be Republican, but they also have their Democratic voters; and Democrats have definitely had a majority in some retirement communities. The best example may be Century Village in West Palm Beach. Because most of the early residents were Jewish and from the Northeast, liberal Democrats dominated that community. Furthermore, with Palm Beach County electing all of its commissioners at large, they had the votes to dominate county politics as well. The retirees when they relocated simply transferred their liberal politics to their new community. That set the stage for a clash with the more conservative powers that were native to southern Florida. In 1990, Palm Beach County replaced its at-large commissioners with ones representing specific districts, "in part to break the retirement communities' stranglehold on local decision-making."[45] The conservative natives also "gerrymandered, divided Century Village into two voting districts, thereby diluting Democratic Party votes."[46] Since these communities ban underage children as permanent residents, their residents do cast more votes than intergenerational communities of the same population. While they do not always prevail politically, their residence in a large, active adult, age-restricted community can be politically empowering for the elderly.

Elder Care Facilities Proliferate

The Webb Corporation had promoted both Sun City and Sun City West as "active adult" communities so that, with the exception of the hospitals, its promotional efforts skipped over the increasing number and variety of health care facilities for the aged that cropped up in both communities. Also contributing to the omission was the idea that as the health care needs of the elderly increased, residents would move back to their home states to be nearer their children. Some did follow that scenario.[47] However, many frail elderly either lacked close relatives elsewhere or had developed support networks within their retirement communities. In some cases, providers of health care services sought to enter these communities. At Sun City, Arizona, churches provided support for the initial development of services such as nursing homes, day care centers, and other forms of assistance to the frail elderly.[48]

The 1970s saw a growing interest in these facilities. At Sun City Center, Florida, in 1973, W-G Corporation, which had just bought out Del Webb, sold ten acres to a group that built Trinity Lakes, a life care facility with apartments and a nursing home wing. A second facility with independent and assisted living apartments and an Alzheimer's unit opened in 1992. That facility added a hospice in 1997.[49]

Meanwhile, the first nursing home had opened in Sun City in 1965, and the community's health facilities continued to expand there and in other active adult communities. The Webb Corporation wanted a quality company and got Beverly Enterprises in the mid-1970s to agree to locate a care facility in Sun City, Arizona.[50] Out in Sun City, California, the Meals on Wheels program began in 1977.[51] Back in Sun City, Arizona, Beverly Enterprises opened its nursing home in 1978 and then began proceeding with what were then called "catered living units," or assisted living apartments.[52] In 1980, the Webb corporation was in negotiations with another company for a combination nursing home and condominium facility and with yet another company for a continuing care facility.[53] The following year, the Sun Cities Ministerial Association took the lead in setting up a crisis counseling service, adult day care centers, and home health care services. The Webb Corporation donated space, and the program became a national model for the provision of such services.[54] Sun City residents did object in 1983 when the Webb Corporation sought to rezone a shopping center site for a combination nursing home and apartment facility. However, the county supported the Webb corporation over the residents.[55] Cortese likewise had a confrontation with the residents of Leisure World Laguna Hills when he wanted to add a life care facility in addition to independent living apartments. In this case, the residents prevailed, as discussed in chapter 4, although the average age of residents at Leisure World Laguna Hills in 1984 was seventy-six.[56]

In 1984, the first assisted living facility opened in Sun City West, and other types of facilities quickly followed, eventually including hospice care.[57] By 1992, Sun City, Sun City West, and adjacent towns had around fifteen "congregate and life care communities."[58] Since then, these facilities have continued to proliferate.

Residents of active adult communities have had mixed responses about the growing presence of all these health care facilities for the elderly. On the one hand, the presence of long-term health care facilities undercut the active adult image of the age-restricted communities. On the other hand, older residents appreciated the choice of facilities and the amount of social support available among their peers. Residents of independent and assisted living facilities in Sun City, Arizona, continued to have access to the recreation centers and other community facilities at a reduced fee on the theory that they would not use the amenities as much as other residents. That access helped to maintain their integration into the community. In 2005, Jane Freeman was living in a Sun City independent living complex where the average age was eighty-eight, and she was serving as the secretary for the Sun Cities Area Historical Society. She saw the Sun City lifestyle as conducive to living longer and the health care facilities as a reason to settle there.[59]

Another issue related to the declining mobility of the elderly was the availability of public transportation. While the Leisure World communities provided their own local bus service as part of their amenities fee, the Sun City communities did so only very sporadically and only when local business owners or the developer were willing to subsidize the operation. Given the housing recession of 1980, DEVCO president John Meeker was dealing with the problem of discontinuing bus service in Sun City and Sun City West.[60] As golf course communities, though, the elderly had an alternative means of transportation when they could no longer safely drive their cars due to deteriorating vision and slower physical coordination. That was the golf cart, which could be operated on the streets of these communities. Going slower than an automobile, golf carts were adequate transportation to the neighborhood shopping center or recreation center and less dangerous to operate within the community than a car.[61] Automobile drivers in these communities quickly learned to look out for the golf carts on the roads.

At Century Village and Leisure World, two communities with bus service, some building renovations occurred as the population aged. Both communities had some buildings with upper-floor apartments and no elevator access to them. Residents in some of those buildings later installed elevators or lifts. Another building renovation that reflected an aging population was when Century Village remodeled its clubhouses to accommodate wheelchairs. The addition of such classes as Learning to Live Alone reflected its aging population. However, within its gates, Century Village had no room for an assisted living facility or a nursing home. Residents in need of those arrangements have had to leave the community.[62] Nongated developments seem to have had more flexibility in integrating these facilities into their communities.

With the second-generation community of Sun City West plus the arrival of a second generation of homeowners in the original communities, a distinct subculture emerged. Studies showed that by the 1980s, most residents were participating in fitness programs and arts and crafts, but only a minority actually golfed regularly, even though their communities were designed as golf course communities. Instead, the aging population turned the golf cart into a favored mode of transportation on their community's streets. The aging population attracted a variety of elder care facilities and services that undercut the active adult image. With the passage of time, some of the earliest communities added historical societies to their list of cultural organizations, while new migrants kept the state clubs going. The price range of the housing expanded as developers tended to make each new neighborhood fancier and pricier than the last, while the older neighborhoods offered lower-priced resales.

The "Casserole Brigade"

The aging population of the active adult communities contributed to a gender imbalance that tended to increase the longer a community had been in existence. In 1983, journalist Frances FitzGerald drew attention to that imbalance with her description of five widows for every widower at Sun City Center. FitzGerald reports that some women were so eager for a heterosexual relationship that they would go to funerals of married women when they barely knew the deceased. Their purpose was "to check out the widower. If they're interested, they then go home and bake a casserole to take to the man. In some cases, remarriage occurs." Another "hunting ground" for the unattached women of Sun City Center was a St. Petersburg dance hall whose clientele was largely over fifty.[63] However, FitzGerald was not the first to use the casserole story. In 1981, Doris Byron, a reporter for the *Los Angeles Times*, did a profile of Leisure World Laguna Hills in which she wrote, "What other environment produces so many single women and so few single men—that the death of a wife triggers a rush of food-toting female visitors so predictable that they are known among Leisure World insiders as the 'casserole brigade.'"[64] Five years after Byron used the phrase in a *Los Angeles Times* article, Glenn B. Sanberg used it with reference to Sun City, Arizona, in an article in a local newspaper.[65]

The "casserole brigade" image has stood the test of time and become national. In 2005, when this researcher was interviewing John Bowker, president of the Sun City Center Historical Society in Florida, he joked that if he ever became a widower he would put on a lot of weight due to all the casseroles he expected to receive.[66] The following August, a reporter for the *Laguna Woods Globe* in what formerly was Leisure World Laguna Hills, California, used the "casserole brigade" phrase in a conversation with this author. Finally, the 2006 film about romance among the elderly in these communities in Florida, *The Boynton Beach Club*, repeatedly referred to elderly single women generously supplying an eligible widower with casseroles. The casserole brigade had become a standing joke referring to the extreme gender imbalance in these communities along with the image of numerous eager women pursuing the few men who were available. These communities, whether in Florida, California, Arizona, or New Jersey, shared a common subculture, and the casserole brigade became part of it.

The ratio of five widows to one widower that FitzGerald mentioned was fairly typical of age-segregated communities that had been in existence for a couple of decades. By the 1980s, the ratio of single women to single men at Sun City, Arizona, was six to one. Furthermore, those singles represented one-third of Sun City's population.[67] Leisure World Laguna Hills had a similar percentage of singles in 1981.[68] At Leisure Village West in New Jersey, the ratio was seven single women for each single man,[69] and in the older neighborhoods of Sun City, Arizona, the ratio could reach ten to one.[70] A journalist called Century Village near Palm Beach one "of the 'ten loneliest places in Florida.'"[71] The number of unattached women may not have been out of line nationally, given the tendency of women to live longer than men. However, communities that were concentrations of the elderly highlighted the "casserole brigade" situation.

The imbalance between unattached women and men in these communities was increasingly an issue, but it was one that developers tended to mask in their advertising. Most of the marketing in the early days of these communities and still in the twenty-first century targeted couples. For example, in the first years of Sun City, Arizona, Del Webb's advertising jingle contained the phrase, "Mr. Senior Citizen and Wife."[72] Ads tended to picture couples enjoying an active social life. However, one of the few early ads for Sun City that was aimed at the unattached elderly described the community as a place where they could find "new friendships, new companionships and new partners with whom to enjoy these best years of their lives."[73] The gender imbalance could make these communities a "happy hunting ground" for elderly single men. One early Sun City ad with this theme pictured a middle-age man on a patio by a picnic table with another couple and two women. It had the headline, " . . . and I Thought You Were a Bunch of Old Fogies."[74]

At Leisure World in California, a 1963 promotional film had a segment picturing the Leisure World communities as a place of romance, with two singles meeting at a weekly dance and the narrator claiming that weddings were numerous at Leisure World.[75] The *Leisure World News* also emphasized what weddings it could. For example, in the spring of 1965 two couples who had met outside Leisure World Laguna

Hills but were moving into the community took advantage of Leisure World's first clubhouse for their wedding receptions and received photos and write-ups in the developer-sponsored community newspaper, which was also sent to prospective residents.[76]

The reality was very different from the advertising and publicity. A sociologist who studied Sun City, California, remarked that residents had a greatly exaggerated perception of the number of widows and widowers remarrying in their community. Specifically in Sun City, California, out of around 5,500 residents, only ten marriages from the community occurred "within the county between December 30, 1970, and November 11, 1971," although the sociologist thought an unknown number of couples may have decided to live together without formally marrying.[77]

The gender imbalance did lend a certain character to the social life of singles in these communities. Although men were a minority in these communities, they occupied most leadership positions, in part because the women tended to defer to them. When the Arizona Sun City Home Owners Association came into being in 1963 to deal with civic issues such as zoning, nine of the ten members of the first board were men.[78] Women, however, had their own social groups. In 1965 at Leisure World Laguna Hills, seventy-one single women signed up for monthly meetings of the Ladies' Travel Group. That organization was formed in addition to a more general social group for single women.[79] One purpose of the latter group was to reach out to men by, as a group, inviting them to events such as treating them to a potluck dinner.[80] Groups for single women did play a very important role in these communities in providing peer support along with their more formal activities.

A significant problem was that much of the organized social life, like much of the marketing, was geared toward couples. At Sun City, Arizona, banquet tables were normally set for eight people, which meant that a single woman could find herself sitting next to an empty chair, an obviously awkward arrangement.[81] Social dancing was another couples-oriented activity. In 1979, a square dance group at Leisure World Laguna Hills typically had a dozen all-female squares. The women who took the men's parts were widows or divorcees or had ill or uninterested husbands. If a woman was taking the man's part, she wore slacks. The other women wore skirts.[82]

At Sun City, Arizona, the Sun Dial Dance Club, a general social dancing group, had a number of single women among its 1,100 members. The dance floor was ringed with tables, most of which couples used to relax and socialize. However, some tables were very prominently labeled as being for singles. To promote mixing, a standard feature was the "whistle dance." The emcee tried to get as many men as he could onto the dance floor to try to even out the gender ratio. The women formed an inner circle, faced outward, and sashayed around holding hands. The men formed an outer circle facing the women. When the whistle sounded, that was the signal for the women to grab partners. One observer compared it to "a game of musical chairs where there are many more players than chairs." Because there were more women than men, a number of women were left without male partners. They either left the dance floor or danced with other women. An observer commented that the single women "were determined to have a good time," that they enjoyed the mingling and dancing, and that they had a certain "survivor's quality" about them similar to what she had seen in a Sun City bereavement group.[83] The fact that this very large social dance group had an organized way of regularly accommodating more single women than men did say something about Sun City's reaching out to that group, although some unattached women may have resented the special attention.

When John Meeker looked back on his career in the retirement-community division of the Del Webb Corporation, assessing what the corporation did right and what it did wrong, one of the mistakes he mentioned was that the company should have included "more recreation facilities and activities for women."[84] He did not elaborate, but a male resident of Sun City in the mid-1980s suggested that the "recreation centers set up a special lounge for singles, and encourage informal socializing during special times of the day." That resident also thought bowling alleys could encourage "a mixed singles league" and "golf courses could arrange singles tournaments." Churches did have groups for singles, but he thought those groups needed "more creative planning" and more single men. Where they would come from, he did not say. His advice to women, which may have been hard in that highly competitive atmosphere for scarce males, was that they should relax and be themselves.[85]

A woman writer in 1982 decided that one should not blame the developers of the 1960s retirement communities for not entirely anticipating "the needs of those who would be left behind when their spouses died," because in 1930 the ratio of men sixty-five and older was roughly the same as women in that age group. However, "by 1980, the ratio was three women for every two men over 65."[86] Still another factor may have been the early expectation that as couples aged and a spouse died, the surviving spouse would move back to wherever she or he came from to be closer to children, but that did not always happen.

By the twenty-first century, developers were still aiming almost all their advertising at couples. Furthermore, some may have sensed that the modern women's movement had a limited impact on the generation they were trying to reach. A twenty-first-century resident in Florida's The Villages said the husbands "drag their wives down here for the golf. But the women miss their families. . . . That's the generation you've got here; the men make the decisions and the women follow them. . . . Ninety percent of the men love it here . . . But the women—that's another matter." On the other hand, that same resident of The Villages, who was a divorcee, praised what she called "an excellent support system for single women" in that Florida active adult community. The divorcee was one of the founders of a group called the Sociable Singles Club. The group attracted mostly women and featured activities that members could do comfortably without a partner of the opposite sex. As one of its founders explained, its purpose was not to help women meet men but "to provide a venue for single women to meet and make friends." Divorced after a twenty-seven-year marriage, that woman had a dim view of the quality of available men at The Villages and an appreciation for being free to make her own decisions. Another single woman said she felt safe in The Villages. She could go by herself to The Villages downtown square, enjoy the music, and watch the dancing, while in her home city of Boston, she was afraid to wander around by herself.[87]

Developers have done almost no advertising designed to attract elderly single women. One exception this researcher found was a 2008 flier promoting "Resort-Style Living" at Sun City Shadow Hills in Indio, California. A headline proclaimed, "25% of Del Webb Residents Are Single Women." It went on to note a trend toward more single-woman households, with divorced, widowed, and never married accounting for 47 percent of women nationally. The ad proclaimed, "This new wave of 'girl power' has found Del Webb's famed 'community within a community' lifestyle concept perfectly suited to how they desire to live. Their quest for a sense of security, companionship and thoughtfully-planned recreational facilities are addressed in every Del Webb community."[88]

It was realistic advertising, but using the word "girl" for women ages fifty-five and over this researcher found unfortunate.

Much better was a Sun City Shadow Hills electronic newsletter the following year that described a single woman's experience moving into the community. At fifty-eight, Dianne faced a career change and wanted to change her personal life. A friend encouraged her to look at Sun City Shadow Hills. She bought immediately. What she liked about the community was its numerous activities, sports, classes, excursions, and trips. For years, the newsletter said, "Sun City Shadow Hills has had a thriving singles club" featuring an "ongoing happy hour every Friday at the Clubhouse." Dianne summed up her life at Shadow Hills: "I have made so many friends and am having so much fun that I feel like a kid again." The video attached to this newsletter featured two women who moved to Shadow Hills from California beach communities. They praised the friends they had made and the facilities but were silent on the numbers of available men.[89]

Robson has found a more subtle way to appeal to the growing market of unattached, older women. In a sales brochure it listed dozens of existing groups in its individual communities. The three newest Robson active adult communities, Quail Creek near Green Valley in the Tucson area, Robson Ranch Arizona near Casa Grande, and Robson Ranch Texas near Denton all listed some sort of singles group. In addition, Robson chose to profile a single woman as a sample resident at Robson Ranch Arizona. The profile did not make an issue of the resident's unattached status. Instead, it described her introduction to Robson homes through a relative at Sun Lakes, her continuing job as a real estate agent, and her enthusiasm for the home she chose. The only clue to her single status was her plan to join Robson Ranch's singles group.[90] Webb took a similar approach to Robson when it included Singles of Sweetwater on a long list of activities and groups at Sweetwater near Jacksonville, Florida.[91]

For some elderly single women, the casserole-brigade situation probably contributed to sometimes vehement resentment of trophy wives or the presence in the community of much younger, unattached women who might compete for the scarce single men. In California in 1985, as described in chapter 5, residents in the Leisure Worlds and some other active adult communities lobbied the governor not only to legalize their ban against children under eighteen but also to ban adults under forty-five from permanently living in their communities. They failed. However, issues surrounding some residents' much younger partners living in their midst did not disappear.

Unlike the other Leisure Worlds, the one at Seal Beach instituted a policy requiring spouses under fifty-five to pay an extra twenty dollars per month association fee. At the same time, Leisure World Seal Beach denied anyone under fifty-five a vote in the cooperative and barred them from using the community's pool and golf course and from joining clubs. A fifty-three-year-old widow whose seventy-five-year-old husband died in 1994 had the previous year "filed a discrimination complaint" with California's Department of Employment and Housing. That department ruled in her favor. She then joined a few clubs and took up golf. Another woman at Leisure World Seal Beach, a forty-five-year-old teacher married to a sixty-six-year-old man, also started using the pool. The community was hardly inundated with much younger wives. Two wives were in their thirties, and only about thirteen others were under fifty-five. Yet the community animosity was there. A seventy-year-old female resident commented, "Who the heck would want to be in here if you're under 55 or especially in your 30s, anyway? . . . I guess it's O.K., just as long as they don't start having babies."[92]

However, Leisure World Seal Beach continued to ban adults under forty-five where it could. The Leisure World Seal Beach Web site in 2005 stated, "Co-occupants must be at least 45 years of age except if a spouse, medical or financial care provider."[93] In other words, Leisure World Seal Beach banned as permanent residents adult children, who may be divorced or unattached, if under forty-five and without some financial or medical caregiver role. It also banned live-in partners under age forty-five.

The Villages has a somewhat unusual definition of under-age children when it comes to which guests can use what swimming pools. At this age-restricted community of around 70,000 people in 2009, recreation centers fell into three classifications, with the medium-size centers having what were termed "family pools." Essentially, they were places that allowed visiting grandchildren to swim. However, that definition applied to anyone under the age of thirty. This researcher took that to mean that twenty-somethings could be as rowdy as teenagers.

Trophy wives do not appear to have been very numerous in any of these communities. In Sun City Center, Florida, the 1980 Census showed that of the 5,605 people living there and with fifty then the minimum age for one member of the household, only 33 wives were under forty-four years old.[94] Given their small numbers, the extreme animosity residents in these age-restricted communities directed at them says a lot about attitudes toward much younger spouses.

The law must, of course, be gender-neutral, although situations involving much younger husbands are considerably rarer. At Sun City, Arizona, a woman who was fifty-one in 1994 had moved there to care for her dying mother. That woman's husband was thirty-two. Even though a certain number of people who did not meet the zoning overlay age requirement could obtain temporary use permits and remain, the Maricopa County Board of Adjustment sided with the complaining neighbors and denied the couple the permit. Having succeeded in banning underage children, significantly younger adults became the next target group.

The Cemetery in Sun City, Arizona

While Frances FitzGerald deserves a lot of credit for giving national exposure to the casserole-brigade problem in these retirement communities, she actually was rather sloppy in her writing. For example, her 1983 article about Sun City Center consistently refers to the community as just "Sun City." She also erroneously perpetuated the myth about Del Webb not wanting a cemetery near Sun City, Arizona. She claimed that a speculator was threatening to turn some land that he owned near the community into a cemetery and that Webb was one of the retirement-community developers who wanted to keep graveyards, with their reminders of death, at a distance. As a result, FitzGerald wrote, Webb bought out the would-be cemetery developer at a price several times what the speculator had paid for it.[95] A quarter-century later, Marc Freedman repeated that erroneous story in his critique of retirement communities, *Prime Time*.[96] The community that FitzGerald actually visited for her article, Sun City Center, seems to have had an unwritten policy of no funeral homes or mortuaries until one opened there in 1996.[97] The actual story at Sun City, Arizona, was very different.

In a 1991 interview, Tom Austin, who was the original activities director at Sun City, Arizona, and who left in 1965 to head Sun City's first nursing home, recalled that originally "DEVCO did not want any cemeteries, mortuaries or hospitals to remind potential buyers they were mortal." He said when a DEVCO official "brought up the subject of cemeteries" at a meeting, "he was 'shushed' and told, albeit in jest, that we don't talk about those things here." The company executives initially thought "the presence of such institutions contradicted the active way of life they were marketing."[98] With the exception of Boswell Hospital, the company did not include those institutions in its marketing, but they were present.

The Webb Corporation owned a lot of land on the Sun City, Arizona, site, and developing a cemetery was one way of bringing in revenue. In 1962, the company approved the development of a cemetery that would front on one of the main Sun City roads in what became Phase 2 of Sun City.[99] Sunland Memorial Park opened in 1963.[100] The following year, the corporation built a mortuary, chapel, and administrative buildings, then leased them to Lundbergh Mortuary, which operated in the nearby communities of Youngtown and Glendale. Terms of the lease specified that DEVCO would receive "10 percent of the gross price of all funeral services held in either Youngtown or Sunland Chapel."[101]

In 1980, DEVCO was facing major expenses for infrastructure in Sun City West. To raise cash, its executives decided to sell a number of assets. One of these was the cemetery, on which the company realized a profit of $2,050,000.[102] The size of the cemetery was fifty acres; while it was in an area that was not developed until the 1970s, Sun City residents were well aware of its presence. It fronted a major street, Del Webb Boulevard. The company had begun to use land adjacent to the cemetery in 1965 for agricultural plots for residents who wanted to grow vegetable gardens but did not have that kind of space next to their homes.[103] In 2005, plans were to replace the agricultural plots with additional housing, even though the only access road to that housing would be through the cemetery—a constant reminder to future residents of their mortality along with a planning glitch.[104] Sun City was a community that had been totally planned and developed by one company, but the future held some unanticipated surprises, even under the best planning circumstances.

Race Relations in the Twenty-First Century

Still another criticism of retirement communities is that historically they have been for whites only. However, developers have sought to counter that image through advertising. By the twenty-first century with Webb now a brand of Detroit-based Pulte Homes, African Americans appear in a number of advertising photographs depicting life in various active adult communities. In writing about Celebration, a Disney-launched, intergenerational development near Orlando along the lines of the "new urbanism," Disney not only included people of color in its ads but also placed ads "in the local black press and in the wider mainstream media," with little result. Two writers who published a book on the town thought some of the continued reluctance of African Americans to move into Celebration might be Disney's racial stereotyping in its Disney World Jungle Cruise exhibit, the high price of the homes at Celebration, and architecture in the town center reminiscent of the plantation South.[105] However, far more obvious than plantation architecture in sending out a racist signal to African Americans was the name another developer gave his fifty-five-plus community near Orlando, The Plantation at Leesburg.[106] Also, the practice of referring to "resort-retirement" may conjure up images of the highly segregated resorts of the past, although that was not the intent of the companies placing those ads. Most companies in the active adult community business probably regard African Americans as a largely untapped market that they would very much like to exploit. It remains to be seen how successful they will be.

If The Villages is regarded as a cutting-edge community for active adults, its record with respect to attracting African American residents is not very encouraging. With close to 70,000 in residents in 2008, The Villages had only around 250 African Americans. One of those, an African American retiree in his sixties, said he chose The Villages because of the amenities and the services such as exterior maintenance. He saw relaxing and golfing at The Villages as his reward for climbing the corporate ladder and excelling "in a white man's world." Furthermore, he could afford the community.[107] Two hundred fifty is a large enough population to sustain an African American Club. At a BYOB event in The Villages in June 2009, that club featured an orthopedist as a speaker, and the club had a picnic scheduled for July.[108] The Villages was among the age-restricted communities featuring African Americans in its advertising. A Web site with revolving photos of activities showed an African American couple biking.[109]

For some northern migrants, moving into a Sunbelt retirement community has meant their first ongoing contacts with a large Spanish-speaking population. Sun City West's Spanish Club, organized in 1980, was not a club for Chicanos or Latinos. Instead, its purpose was to help members learn to speak and read Spanish and "to explore Spanish cultures throughout the world." That club was still going in 2005.[110] The Villages has produced a promotional video featuring the famous golfer Nancy Lopez, who happens to live in the community. While these retirement communities do have a number of ethnic clubs, beyond an interest in Spanish language and culture, Hispanics themselves originally did not appear to be very numerous in most of these communities. However, recently they have been major buyers of resale units at Century Village. Likewise, Asian buyers were relatively rare in the early days of Leisure World Laguna Hills, but by the twenty-first century that community had a Korean American Club. We may be seeing the beginnings of a trend toward more racial diversity, but these communities in general have a long way to go before their racial diversity mirrors that of the United States.

Youngtown Loses Its Age-Restricted Status

Another downside to age-restricted retirement communities that has an impact on children is that families with children in these communities may be forced to move. One common circumstance was where the grandparents took in a grandchild on a permanent basis. Another was when a salesperson eager to make a sale did not inform a buyer that the community was age-restricted and likely to enforce the zoning ordinance banning children as permanent residents. Still another problem was that these communities did attract some adults who moved in to avoid having to live around children. Those adults could exhibit considerable animosity toward children if they appeared to be living in the retirement community. The first age-restricted community, Youngtown, had a lot of trouble in this area and eventually lost its age-restricted status as a result.

As the first community to be age-restricted, Youngtown lacked the legal framework needed to make it work. Youngtown was advertised as age-restricted, something the developer could self-regulate on his own sales. The problem came with resales. The early deeds, while they did have some restrictions, did not legally ban children as permanent residents.[111] In 1975, the Youngtown city council (unlike many age-restricted communities, Youngtown was incorporated) added age restrictions to the town's bylaws.[112] The early residents of Sun City lacked those deed restrictions as well. However, just as in Sun City, where early residents had chased out the air conditioner repairman because he had underage children, and without a legal framework, those who felt strongly about the presence of children might resort to vigilante action. In Youngtown in 1976, the woman who headed a group called Save Youngtown for Retirees and a man were prosecuted for trespassing and assault. The pair had tried to run down some teenagers. They got six months probation.

With its age-restricted bylaw, the passage of a county senior overlay zoning ordinance and then the federal Fair Housing Act of 1988, Youngtown by the late 1980s did have a legal framework for enforcement when the issue surfaced again. Youngtown residents discovered several families with children and decided to force them to leave. One of the families was that of Efrin and Sylvia Gutierrez and their three children, two boys—one twelve and the other four months—and a ten-year-old girl.[113] Most Youngtown houses had been built for retirees and were small, but that also made them affordable. The family had moved into Youngtown in November 1989 after their "realtor told them the town's age zoning laws were not yet effective." The Gutierrez family put his sixty-one-year-old mother's name on the title, but what counted was occupancy, not ownership.[114] They chose the town because Efrin worked for a company in the community, Sylvia worked for Sun Health in the adjacent community of Sun City, and the parents were concerned about gang activity in their former hometown of Surprise. Furthermore, with a $29,000 price tag, they could afford the house.[115] Another family told to move was the Romeros. Efrin Gutierrez reportedly felt the town was picking on people with a Mexican background.[116] Consequently, he and six other families sent a complaint to the federal Department of Housing and Urban Development charging discrimination.[117] Efrin Gutierrez feared jail time at the hands of Youngtown officials and "complained that he [was] being treated like a criminal." However, the Gutierrez family and the others did not prevail. HUD, the federal Department of Housing and Urban Development, transferred their complaints to the Department of Justice, which dismissed them.[118]

One of the other families told to move out of Youngtown was that of Harold and Doris Brown, both in their thirties and with two teenage sons. The Browns argued that they bought their house in 1986 before the approval of the senior zoning overlay.[119] Due to the poor local housing market at the time, the Browns had difficulty selling. Doris Brown commented, "We heard rumors about age restrictions when we moved here, but we never thought they were serious about it." She recalled numerous times when the police were "called just because kids live here."

She talked about the "hatred" and the many "hurtful comments," including one at a Youngtown city council meeting equating children with the plague.[120] In fact, in 1990 Youngtown officials had told a total of thirty families to move, which were all the ones with underage children in the town at that time, and most did leave.[121] During the next four years, Youngtown evicted three hundred more people.[122]

The reality was that Youngtown had been inconsistent in its enforcement. In 1984, the Youngtown Civic Association began working for an ordinance to legally make the town age restricted.[123] The early 1990s crackdown may have been motivated by the requirement in the 1988 federal Fair Housing Act that 80 percent of the households have someone living there who was at least fifty-five. If Youngtown were to come in at less than 80 percent, it would lose its ability to bar children as permanent residents.

The case that eliminated Youngtown's age-restricted status occurred in 1998. A teenager, Chaz Cope, who was regarded by some people as having a behavior problem, was living with his grandparents because he had a stepfather who was physically abusive. Initially, the grandparents had paid a $300 filing fee, and Youngtown had given them permission to keep Chaz for three months. Town "officials also put a placard on the grandparents' front lawn" announcing that a juvenile was living there. When the grandparents requested an extension of their special permit for nine months so Chaz could live with them until graduating from high school, the city unanimously denied that permit.[124] Other Youngtown grandparents had gotten permission to permanently care for grandchildren, but in this case, Youngtown denied special permission.[125] The grandparents were threatened with a fine of $100 per day plus ten days in jail if they did not move or send the youngster to live elsewhere.[126]

The grandparents then appealed to Arizona's attorney general, who ruled that Youngtown's age-restricted districts were not properly created; therefore, Youngtown's age-restricted zoning was invalid.[127] Youngtown lacked the money to finance an appeal, but the ruling badly divided the town.[128] During the incident, the grandparents had their car vandalized. When Chaz played basketball in their driveway, neighbors charged that "he was violating anti-noise ordinances." According to writer Andrew Blechman, a member of the Youngtown city council "circulated a fabricated juvenile court record alleging that Chaz had been charged with possession of marijuana."[129] The councilman claimed that he wanted to counter the angelic way that Chaz was being portrayed in the press. The attorney general's ruling not only said that Chaz and other underage children could live in Youngtown, it also ordered the formerly age-restricted community to pay Chaz' grandparents $30,000. While small as restitution payments go, it seemed to Youngtown's seniors to be "a princely sum for a troublesome brat." Chaz and his grandparents soon left Youngtown, but writer Andrew Blechman tracked Chaz Cope down about ten years later. At that point, Chaz was a married man and active in Jehovah's Witnesses.[130]

The attorney general's ruling officially opened up Youngtown to families with children, even though most of the community remained in Sun City's unorganized school district. A local developer, Sivage Thomas, then began constructing hundreds of houses, mostly two-story ones, in the Agua Fria Ranch subdivision in Youngtown. Midway through this construction, Pulte Homes, now the owner of Del Webb, bought out Sivage Thomas. Thus, the parent company of Del Webb finally did complete a subdivision in the community adjacent to Sun City, but ironically, it was an intergenerational one.[131] The Agua Fria Ranch subdivision doubled Youngtown's population to 6,000.[132] Youngtown did pay fees to neighboring school districts for each child they took in from the community's unorganized school district, which was most of the town including the bulk of the new Agua Fria Ranch development.[133]

Enough families soon moved into Youngtown to elect a mayor in his forties and who rode around town on a Harley Davidson. The seniors objected to his plans for athletic facilities, including a skateboard park and playgrounds. Their attempts to dig up dirt on the mayor did produce the record of an arrest thirteen years earlier, but it was for parking in a handicapped spot.[134] Meanwhile, the town's changing demographics meant that the police got a sharp increase in domestic violence calls and a sharp drop in the number of seniors they discovered to have died in their homes.[135] In writer Andrew Blechman's view, which was shared by Youngtown's city manager, Mark Fooks, getting rid of its age-restricted status "has breathed new life" into the community.[136]

Sun City's Continuing Ban on Children

Although neighboring Sun City has never been in danger of losing its age-restricted status, the presence of an occasional child as a permanent resident continued to cause controversy in that community as well. In

1998, when an eighty-three-year-old grandmother allowed her daughter and seven-year-old grandchild to move in with her, the grandmother became a target of numerous prank telephone calls and received one letter that was so threatening that she contacted the county sheriff's department. When the grandmother applied to the County Board of Adjustment for a special permit to allow her granddaughter to continue living with her, the Sun City Homeowners Association chartered a bus to carry at least thirty people to the board's hearing to oppose the grandmother's request. The grandmother dropped her request for the special permit and decided to move out of Sun City, saying, "I'm not a fighter."[137]

The following year, a thirty-six-year-old woman who had "fled an abusive home" in 1996 with her young son and then given birth to a daughter in 1998 moved into a Sun City home owned by her mother. The young mother had applied for public assistance while she was trying to sort out whether she should apply for a job or get more education. She had paid a $100 application fee to the Board of Adjustment for a variance to remain in Sun City. However, approximately fifty of her neighbors were so upset about the situation that they signed a petition against the granting of the variance. The woman said she was helping her seventy-year-old mother with cooking, shopping, housework, and yard work. Nevertheless, the neighbors were adamant. One remarked, "Most people . . . come [to Sun City] to avoid . . . children and family."[138]

Still another Sun City case occurred in 2002 when a Sun City resident's twenty-one-year-old grandson was badly injured in a car accident. As a result, the Sun City resident took him, his parents, and his ten-year-old sister into their home. In this case, the county Board of Adjustment did grant the family a fourteen-month variance, but the Sun City Home Owners Association threatened to appeal that decision. Specifically, the neighbors objected to the vehicles and dogs around the family's home. Rather than fight, the family moved.[139] According to an official from HUD and an official from the Maricopa County Attorney's office, such complaints about the residence of children were common.[140]

Perhaps to counter the image that age-restricted communities hate children, a new Del Webb community, Lake Providence in Tennessee, announced as a sales promotion a "Grandparents Day with a Backyard Picnic." Prospective buyers were encouraged to bring their children and grandchildren to the event and introduce them to the Del Webb lifestyle.

This event included "a balloon artist and face painter for the kids, a DJ spinning tunes," refreshments, and, for current residents, "a 'Dessert Bake-Off' to see who is the best Dessert Chef in the neighborhood." Of course, those attending were encouraged to view the six elaborately decorated model homes and the clubhouse and sports complex under construction.[141]

By the twenty-first century, it became quite common for developers to designate a spot on their community plans as a "tot lot for visiting grandkids," probably because the majority of their buyers did have grandchildren. The Villages even did summer programming for visiting grandchildren. Camp Villages offered a variety of activities for youngsters ages five to fifteen, including magic shows, pizza making, and pool parties.[142]

Age Restriction and Property Values

Besides the family situations involving underage children that arose and tended to trigger animosity, sometimes extreme on the part of neighbors, another controversy regarding age restriction was whether or not it lowered property values by excluding some potential buyers. In 1993, 99 percent of Sun City's households had at least one occupant who was fifty-five or older.[143] Seven years later, Sun City's real estate market appeared to be stagnating. Some salespeople thought the market could be jump-started by lowering the minimum age for buyers, perhaps to forty. The community would still be able to keep its senior overlay zoning as long as a minimum of 80 percent of the households had at least one person fifty-five or older. The main problem for an older community where all the sales were resales and handled by a variety of agents was how to control the situation so the community did not sink below 80 percent. Even without officially making a temporary reduction in the minimum age for buyers, some agents were still selling to younger people.[144]

Sun City officials may have considered the idea of temporarily lowering the minimum age to purchase homes; at that time and in order to jump-start sales, the Webb Corporation dropped the minimum age to purchase homes in Sun City Grand to forty-five. Granted, it only allowed 10 percent of its buyers to be below the federally mandated fifty-five. Furthermore, those buyers had to agree to resell to people at least fifty-five.[145] Because Webb was the only seller in Sun City Grand at that time, it could control the situation, shutting down sales to those under fifty-five if the community was in danger of falling below the required 80 percent of homes occupied by someone fifty-five or older.

Congress, in providing for 20 percent of homes to be occupied by adults under fifty-five, vastly overestimated the number of significantly younger widows plus some family caregivers in these communities, so artificially lowering the age of buyers on a temporary basis was an option. Sun City West officials also considered a temporary lowering of the age restriction in 2002 but rejected the idea as impractical from a legal standpoint.[146] Then there was the situation of Youngtown, which lost its age-restricted status in 1998. Mark Fooks, the Youngtown city manager in 2005, predicted that age-restricted communities would become "dinosaurs." To illustrate his point, he produced lists of sale prices for homes in the new Agua Fria Ranch development in Youngtown. Within a couple of years, the sale prices of the homes had almost doubled, even though, as Fooks emphasized, the homes were virtually identical. He attributed the spike in prices to the word getting out that Youngtown was no longer age-restricted. However, another city employee disagreed. She had formerly worked for the recreation centers in Sun City and thought a niche market for the organized activity, age-restricted community would continue. As for the older homes in Youngtown, those also shot up in value. Writer Andrew Blechman has found that they increased "more than thirty percent practically overnight, and well over 200 percent in ten years."[147] However, it is important to remember that the Phoenix area was experiencing an overheated housing market in general during that period.

By late 2006 that overheated housing market began to take a nosedive, not just around Phoenix, but nationally. However, at that time the market for homes in age-restricted communities appeared to be holding up better than in intergenerational communities. Pulte, which by then owned Del Webb, built much of its housing in conventional communities. If its executives decided to take a particular piece of land and develop it as an age-restricted community, they did so because they thought that was the most profitable use of the parcel. In late 2006, Pulte had more than fifty Del Webb age-restricted communities scattered throughout the Sunbelt, and counting some in the Midwest and Northeast. To support a quality assortment of amenities in its Del Webb communities, Pulte was generally reluctant to go below a minimum of

750 housing units, and those Del Webb developments with the Sun City label were considerably larger.

Prior to acquiring the Del Webb Corporation in 2001, Pulte had bought DiVosta and Company, a builder of retirement-age-targeted but not specifically age-restricted communities in Florida. Pulte continued to develop these age-targeted communities under its DiVosta brand. However, by not advertising them as age-restricted to buyers "55 and better," Pulte could not exclude children as permanent residents of its DiVosta developments.[148] The homes in DiVosta communities tended to be more expensive than those in the Del Webb communities. While DiVosta communities were also amenity-rich, they featured model homes with optional individual pools. The decision of whether to age-restrict a community apparently also was related somewhat to the wealth of the projected buyer, with more expensive communities less likely to be age-restricted.

Congress in 1988 approached age-restricted communities as if the elderly had certain disabilities. Therefore, the Fair Housing Act of 1988 specified that age-restricted communities were to have "significant facilities and services specifically designed to meet the physical and social needs of older persons." However, those facilities and services could not be defined.[149] Frequently the buyers of homes in age-restricted communities did not want to think of themselves as potentially disabled and actually resisted such universal design features as a flush-threshold shower without a door and with a shower seat.[150] Consequently, Congress in the Housing for Older Persons Act of 1995 eliminated the "facilities and services" requirement.[151]

Leisure World Laguna Hills Incorporates and Becomes Laguna Woods

A number of the age-restricted communities were unincorporated when established and remained that way but not without internal controversy. This category encompassed The Villages, Florida, at around 70,000 population in 2009; Sun City, Arizona, at 46,000 people; Sun City West at 31,000; and the considerably smaller Sun City Center, Florida, and Sun City, California. At Sun City, Arizona, some early advocates for incorporation argued that with incorporation the town would be eligible for certain state and federal grants and would have more control over its zoning. Opponents said they had enough control through their homeowner association and other civic groups without running the risk of added expenses for municipal government. The Webb Corporation in the late 1970s hired an outside consultant who demonstrated that the community would be ahead financially if it incorporated, but the majority of the residents have consistently beaten back attempts to incorporate.[152]

One community that did finally incorporate was Leisure World Laguna Hills. What had driven the original layout of that community was the presence of El Toro Marine Naval Air Station nearby. To keep residences from being under the flight path, the center of the community was devoted to open-space uses such as the golf course. With the Marines leaving, some people outside of Leisure World wanted to convert the base into a commercial zone. Residents of Leisure World objected due to the noise. They decided they could better oppose civilian use of El Toro as an airport if they incorporated, which they proceeded to do. To meet the qualifications of an incorporated community in California, they had to be more than a gated residential development, so they annexed an adjacent shopping center and several long-term care facilities that were just outside their residential gates. The combined and incorporated territory took the name City of Laguna Woods.[153]

Leisure World Laguna Hills ran into conflict with Ross Cortese's heir Heidi Cortese over the use of the name Leisure World. Heidi Cortese obtained a court ruling allowing her to collect royalties for the use of the name. She apparently had her eye on the advertising revenue of the closed-circuit television station that operated at Leisure World Laguna Hills.[154] Rather than pay, the community chose to adopt the name of Laguna Woods Village. It could not just be Laguna Hills because the adjacent outside community already had that name.[155] Some other establishments changed their names as well rather than pay for the use of the name Leisure World. For example, real estate salespeople specializing in selling apartments at Leisure World Seal Beach—part of the community of Seal Beach because FHA would not finance an unincorporated development in the early 1960s—have modified their names.[156] They are calling themselves Leisure Properties, Leisure Living Resales, and Leisure Apartment Sales.[157]

Where Ross Cortese partnered with another developer, such as the IDI Group, use of the Leisure World brand name was not a problem.

IDI Group Companies have used Leisure World of Virginia and Leisure World of Maryland since 1980 for their high-rise, age-restricted, active adult developments; the Cortese company, RCC Inc., is a partner in those developments. The Leisure World brand name continues to be used by other Leisure World developments in other states, such as Leisure World in Mesa, Arizona.[158] Just as Del Webb made a brand out of his name, Ross Cortese initially attempted to make a brand out of his company's original name, Rossmoor, but that attempt fizzled. Rather belatedly, the Cortese family recognized that the public responded to Leisure World as the brand instead.

Psychological Advantages to Age Segregation

Much of the favorable assessment of age-restricted communities has related to the psychological advantages of age segregation. Some of these advantages were indicated through studies designed to measure the satisfaction of residents. A 1966 study of Leisure World residents showed that 75 percent were pleased with their choice of community, and less than 14 percent had considered leaving. A 1969 study comparing residents of age-restricted communities with those of age-integrated communities in Arizona found that the elderly in the age-restricted communities had "higher morale." Time and again, researchers have reported that the age-restricted communities offered "more opportunity for social contact" and less social isolation for the elderly than age-integrated or conventional communities.[159]

Concentrating the elderly helped to legitimize their leisure behavior.[160] While some commentators have said actual participation in leisure activities within these communities was not much for most individuals, a 1970 study found that 30 percent participated in recreational activities at least twenty hours per week and that 53 percent devoted at least ten hours per week toward them. Only 10 percent "were not regularly involved in any recreational activities."[161] There was insulation from those who might raise their eyebrows at seniors "who do not act their age." Social scientist Nancy Osgood is only one of many who have commented on age segregation as providing "a sanctuary and subculture with its own customs, gossip, and humor."[162] (The author of this book recalls seeing a group of seniors at Sun City Georgetown, Texas, taking advantage of an artificial stream that was part of the elaborate landscaping to have rubber duck races. They were enjoying themselves, knowing they could, within an age-restricted setting, have such childlike fun and not have to worry how they might appear to younger people.) As Ed Hemphill, coordinator of a 1982 study of Sun City's advantages and problems expressed it, retirement-community residents were "freer to make experiments and do things" they had not done before.[163]

Besides increasing the possibilities for interacting with their peers, these communities were a way of partially disengaging "with the current youth oriented culture, thereby creating their own subculture." Not only were the communities supportive psychologically in dealing with such issues as death, but they also concentrated the votes of the elderly, giving them more local political clout. In addition, the elderly tended to feel more secure in these communities. Finally, by concentrating the elderly in certain places, that concentration attracted the social and health care services that the elderly needed.[164]

While age-restricted communities were hardly the "fountain of youth," some have suggested that they may contribute to longevity in the elderly. The 1985 CEO of the Del Webb Corporation, Fred Kuentz, speculated that retirement communities might help their elderly residents live longer. While there was no statistical evidence to support that assertion, Dr. Michael Baker, formerly head of the Arizona Long Term Care Gerontology Center, did contend that the communities, by giving seniors "a new lease on life," might help to combat depression, contributing to their health.[165] The 2000 Census revealed that the median age in Sun City, Arizona, was seventy-five, making it the city with the oldest median age in Arizona. John Waldron, Del Webb's public affairs director, attributed the residents' longevity to their active lifestyles. Jane Freeman, who moved to Sun City in 1970 because of the recreational amenities and health care facilities and who was eighty-one in 2001, mentioned that there were "a lot of people in [the] same situation" and that sociability was very important to older people. In fact, the top four communities in Arizona with the oldest median ages were all age-restricted. Sun City West came in second with a median age of more than seventy-three years, Green Valley with more than seventy-two, and Sun Lakes with more than sixty-nine.[166] Out in California, Laguna Woods, formerly Leisure World Laguna Hills, claimed an average (not median) age in 2005 of 78.[167]

Sun City Grand

Perhaps the strongest affirmation of the value of these communities was that builders kept building new ones and buyers kept flocking to them. In 1994, as the Del Webb Corporation approached build-out at Sun City West, it made plans to cross Grand Avenue, which bordered Sun City West, and develop Sun City Grand. This community was within the city limits of the town of Surprise, so incorporation was not an issue. Originally, the Webb Corporation planned a commercial center at Sun City Grand; it then canceled those plans, perhaps because of ample commercial facilities at Sun City West. As for medical facilities, Del Webb Hospital was built in connection with Sun City West to serve what the developers originally thought would be a much larger community than Sun City West actually became.[168] Grand covered 4,000 acres with 9,500 homes, compared to 26,000 homes on 8,900 acres at Sun City and 17,500 homes on 7,100 acres at Sun City West.[169]

Grand took the concept of the amenity-rich retirement community to a new level for the Del Webb Corporation. When it opened in 1996, it already had in place a recreational complex that included an Olympic-size indoor pool, a large outdoor resort-style pool, high-quality golf courses, lighted tennis courts, and elaborate landscaping with manmade streams and ponds and many palm trees around thirty feet tall. Other amenities included a fitness center, walking paths,[170] and plenty of space for clubs and classes. By 2004, it had an arrangement with Arizona State University for the West Lifelong Learning Academy to meet the growing interest among seniors in adult education.[171] The model home park featured elaborately decorated homes and was lush with green grass and plants, even where the garage driveways would be. Some of the trends in these homes included home offices, spacious master suites, optional guest casitas, and a smaller third stall in the garage for golf cart storage. A person who visited Grand in the late 1990s commented on a sense of "excitement of future community and future festivities."[172] One of the models had a negative-edge pool, that is, it appeared to have no edge on one side as the water flowed over it into a catch basin below. To that visitor, the edgeless pool symbolized the seamless transition that Webb was making "between middle age and retirement."[173] The negative-edge pool also symbolized more affluence among retirees.

For less affluent retirees, the original Sun City with its much smaller, older homes was well supplied with resales. For those who wanted to spend even less, perhaps because they preferred the snowbird life-style to permanent relocation, in 1985 another developer opened the Happy Trails Resort for recreational vehicles near Sun City, Arizona.[174] Other developers who joined Webb in that area included major national home builder Lennar Homes, which had built retirement communities in Florida. It developed Ventana Lakes northwest of Sun City, where plans included 1,600 homes, pools, and other recreation facilities but no golf course. Continental Homes developed Arizona Traditions with 1,900 homes for retirees nearby.[175] Not as close but still in the area was a newer retirement community by Robson called Pebble Creek.

When Sun City Grand reached build-out in 2005 three years ahead of schedule, it had 17,000 residents. Webb was experimenting with a much smaller, gated community nearby called Corte Bella, projected at 1,700 seniors on completion. Just adding the population of the Del Webb communities in this area, which are contiguous or nearly so, they accommodated more than 95,000 people, most of whom were at least fifty-five years old. The Webb Corporation was not finished. On comple-tion of Grand, it went another ten miles down a main road from Grand to develop Sun City Festival. Staying in the area made sense because many of the buyers of homes in Grand and later Festival were moving up from the older communities.[176]

Webb did not just stay in the vicinity of its flagship community. An-other trend apparent by the 1980s was interest in developing retirement communities outside of the traditional retirement states of Florida, California, and Arizona. In 1988, the corporation opened Sun City Sum-merlin in Nevada, completing the community of 7,800 homes in 1999. Other Nevada Sun Cities included MacDonald Ranch, opened in 1996 with 2,500 projected homes, and Anthem, opened in 1998 with 9,100 projected homes. In 1994, the firm opened Sun City Hilton Head in South Carolina, with 8,500 homes planned. In Texas, Sun City George-town, known in 2009 as Sun City Texas, opened in 1996 with 9,500 homes projected. Del Webb kept building in more traditional retirement locations, too. The company opened the 2,500-home Sun City Tucson in 1987, completing it ten years later. In California, Sun City Palm Des-ert opened in 1992 with 4,800 homes projected, and Sun City Roseville opened in 1994 and was completed five years later with 3,100 homes. Del Webb's most daring expansion because it was in the Midwest was into Illinois with Sun City Huntley near Chicago, opening in 1998 with

5,100 projected homes.[177] That development was reaching build-out in 2006, with another Del Webb development in the area about to open. Part of the reasoning behind so many locations was that some retirees were attracted to the age-restricted, active adult lifestyle community, but they also wanted to stay relatively close to their former homes and their families.

By 2000, Del Webb was "the biggest company in its field." It led "a parade of copycat builders."[178] It had already developed a strategy of fielding a number of retirement communities in different parts of the country when, in 2001, Pulte Homes paid $1.73 billion for the company, primarily for the Del Webb brand name and its huge inventory of land.[179] Under Pulte, the number of age-restricted, active adult communities that its Del Webb brand was building exploded. By 2006, more than fifty Del Webb communities were marketing homes to those where one resident was at least "fifty-five or better."

Given the continuing development of age-restricted, active adult communities, the answer to Betty Friedan's question "Could a vital age be built . . . in a community walled off from the rest of the world?" was a resounding "Yes." Large communities of elderly people demonstrated their advantages for the residents. These ranged from sociability with one's peers to local political clout to acting as a magnet in attracting care facilities for the elderly. Age-restricted, active adult communities gave their residents the opportunity to develop their own subculture. Some of their problems have no easy solutions, such as the extreme gender imbalance between unattached men and women and the resulting "casserole brigade." Likewise, the extreme hostility of some residents toward underage children and the stories of some people forced to move out of these communities because they had children living with them were unfortunate. Also controversial was how some of these communities used their local political clout to vote down school bond issues. The flip side to that was that from the perspective of the elderly residents, they did have some local political clout. These communities accentuated the generational divide and helped to insulate the elderly from negative attitudes toward the aged that pervade the larger society. They developed a subculture that did provide the elderly with peer support. Finally, contrary to the "active adult" image their developers projected, with time these active adult communities tended to act as magnets attracting the services the elderly needed, if not right within the community itself, then just outside the gates. Most elderly Americans still rejected the idea of moving into an active adult, age-restricted community. However, a growing number, perhaps those more socially inclined and with the "energy" to move, are indeed deciding that they can best find "vital age" within them.

Assessment

Problems, Strengths, and Twenty-First-Century Trends

"Age segregation only reinforces negative stereotypes, leads to a willful forgetting of commonalities and encourages our less-charitable instincts," says writer Andrew Blechman.[1] Author of the 2008 book *Leisureville,* Blechman was highly critical of active adult, age-restricted communities for exacerbating generational divisions in American society.[2] In other words, while retirees were finding a sense of community in age-restricted settings, Blechman seemed to consider them selfishly "breaking their social contract" by ignoring their obligations to the younger generations.[3] As the most extreme examples of age segregation, these communities have spawned debate over a variety of their aspects going back to their inception. That debate continues. How has this debate evolved? What problems have their critics identified? What strengths have their defenders noted? Given the uniqueness of these communities to the United States, what does the international critique reveal about U.S. social and cultural values?

With respect to planning trends by the twenty-first century, "smart growth" and the "new urbanism" replaced the somewhat discredited "new town" concept of the 1960s and 1970s. Environmental concerns increased as well, especially those related to water quality. Demographically, those Americans "age 55 and better" became more numerous. So did the number of active adult communities. The first years of the century began on a high note of prosperity. Then, suddenly, in 2006, a major housing crisis emerged. By 2008, the country was in recession. How have these communities coped? At the end of the first decade of the century, what trends in these communities were in place?

Social Critics Assess Age-Restricted, Active Adult Communities

Critics of active adult, age-restricted communities have leveled a number of charges against them. Some of these critics are social scientists or other academics. Some are cultural commentators or popular writers. An occasional disgruntled resident of an age-restricted community has added to the debate. Among the issues they have emphasized have been the desirability of nearby intergenerational contact, the political implications of concentrating the elderly vote within a limited geographic area, the alleged ephemeral nature of the "active adult" lifestyle, the extreme homogeneity of these communities in terms of race and social class, not just age, and even the business ethics of their developers. As with many criticisms, what may be a negative to a critic outside these communities may be a positive from the perspective of a resident of an age-restricted community.

The urban philosopher Lewis Mumford was the first major critic. In the mid-1950s, the federal government was beginning to consider developing public housing projects that would be strictly for the elderly and would bar underage children as permanent residents. While Mumford acknowledged that the limited mobility and health problems of some elderly people meant that they had special housing requirements and that the elderly would like the companionship of their peers, he strongly favored mixing age groups in a community. That would preserve volunteer opportunities for the elderly to work with children, such as the carpenter willing to do little repair jobs for school-age children. It would also make available some small employment opportunities for the elderly, such as babysitting. The most segregation of the elderly Mumford would endorse was a grouping of up to a dozen apartment units for them within the larger community.[4] Given Mumford's reputation as a leading commentator on housing and city planning issues, his criticism of age-segregated housing for the elderly has been frequently cited.

The argument that the elderly will benefit from frequent and nearby contact with children has continued. For example, in 1999, Marc Freedman, head of Civic Ventures, "a nonprofit organization dedicated to expanding the contribution of older Americans in our society," published *Prime Time: How Baby Boomers Will Revolutionize Retirement and Transform America*.[5] His book promoted such programs as foster grandparents.[6] Furthermore, when he asserts that the vast majority of the elderly prefer to age in place, in part because of the intergenerational nature of their home communities, he does have a point. Also, more services were being developed to help the elderly age in place. As the 2005 director of MIT's AgeLab, "a think tank on aging," put it, "The die-with-a-golf-club-in-your-hand communities had better take notice."[7]

Among social scientists, Jerry Jacobs was a leading critic of isolating the elderly in age-restricted communities. In 1974, he published a book-length study of Sun City, California. In their forward to Jacobs' book, editors George and Luise Spindler wrote that these communities reflect "the nomadic and fragmented character of American social and particularly familial life," resulting in psychological and social problems for their residents.[8] According to Jacobs, "From the street the homes show no signs of life." The community was "designed to help overcome the shock one was likely to experience" upon retirement by substituting an active retirement lifestyle. However, Jacobs did not find much activity among the retirees. Geographically, that community was isolated, about thirty miles south of Riverside, California. It had no "major medical facilities of its own." Unincorporated, it lacked its own police and fire departments and had no mayor. A visit to the recreation center might show several card tables occupied in the men's club room and the same in the women's, only several people in each of the center's outdoor pools in spite of the desert heat, and a variety of posted announcements for clubs and special events, which were abundant in the town. However, out of the community's approximately six thousand residents, Jacobs estimated that only several hundred were "actively engaged in club activities."[9] Jacobs compared his Sun City subjects to residents of a low-income high-rise for the elderly. While the Sun City residents had more money, they spent more time worrying about eventually losing what they had. The result was, Jacobs concluded, that both groups "were just as unhappy."[10] The picture that Jerry Jacobs painted of the quality of life in these communities was bleak indeed.

Feminist Betty Friedan seconded Jacobs' charge that for most of their residents, the activities in active adult communities were quite empty. Friedan wrote that successful aging should involve work or a passionate commitment to a project or cause. In her landmark 1963 book, *The Feminine Mystique*, Friedan said women needed a sense of identity apart from being John's wife and Mary's mother. They needed to develop their own potential as individuals. For many women, that meant a career. About three decades later, when Friedan published *The Fountain of Age*, she applied the importance of work or a passionate interest to a sense of personal fulfillment among the elderly. As mentioned earlier, she had a low opinion of "active adult" communities, dubbing them "adult playpens." However, if a resident in one of these communities had a job or a project that was challenging or absorbing, that could justify living in them. She used her own mother, who ran the bridge games at Leisure World Laguna Hills, as an example. The job was mentally challenging because her mother had to do a lot of scheduling and frequently stepped in as the fourth in bridge games. Friedan concluded "that the ones who survived and continued to grow in Leisure World, finding vital age there, turned some activity of the adult playpen into a serious project, became seriously involved in the governance or some movement for change in the community itself; or in effect, they were lucky enough to die playing bridge."[11]

Yet most of the jobs at Leisure World available to the residents, such as being gate guards, were not mentally challenging. Friedan suspected that some people took those jobs not because they needed the money but because they needed the social stimulation or competitive challenge of the work. One of the problems with a work-oriented society is that much of a person's self-image is based on his or her occupation. Friedan persisted in advocating the work ethic even for retirees. Just keeping busy with an "active adult" lifestyle was not enough to replace the career or passionate commitment that she so valued. As another critic of these communities, Marc Freedman, commented, "Activity for activity's sake can be vapid, self-indulgent, and ultimately boring."[12]

Some gender differences may apply with respect to the "active adult" lifestyle. Women did not always retire from outside employment like their husbands did prior to moving to retirement communities. Historian John Findlay notes that the men were more attracted to the golf and myriad other activities, and their wives were more reluctant to leave behind their friends and relatives to migrate to Sun City. Findlay claimed that the men, having found a substitute for their work in their new active adult lifestyle, were happier than the women.[13]

On the other hand, Sun City residents Glenn Sanberg and Jane Freeman tended to agree with Jacobs and Friedan about the ephemeral nature of many of the activities. While they supported Findlay on the men being more enthusiastic about moving to Sun City, they thought that the women in general adjusted better. For example, some men dropped golf after a year or two in Sun City. Those who seemed the happiest were the ones involved in major projects, such as obtaining Sun City's first nursing home, helping a church get established, launching a volunteer charity, or getting involved in community governance.[14]

Still another common criticism of these communities was that they were not just homogeneous with regard to age but also with regard to other social characteristics. That was the main point in journalist Frances FitzGerald's portrait of Sun City Center, Florida, as it was in 1983. FitzGerald found no single subculture of aging because economic and racial circumstances divided the elderly in general so they did not speak with one voice.[15] Her goal was to describe the subculture of Sun City Center, which Del Webb had opened in 1962, sold about ten years later to another developer, and had around 8,500 elderly residents in 1983.[16] What struck her was the uniformity of the community, not just that all the residents were elderly and no young children were living there but that the residents all dressed casually, appeared well groomed, kept their houses tidy inside and out, and came from similar middle-class backgrounds, having been professionals, middle-management executives, or owners of small businesses. Most were Protestant, Republican, and "by temperament joiners."[17] She found the residents "childlike," in part because a number had collections of things like dolls but also because they were "so talkative, so pleasant, so eager to please." In addition, she associated the uniformity in age in the community with other places where age was uniform, like camp or school.[18] However, underneath all that pleasant uniformity were some people, perhaps many, who had problems with alcohol or were sick and feeble.[19]

Other authors were more explicit in their criticisms of uniformity in race and class. When Marc Freedman accused these communities of being anti-Semitic, he ignored the presence of synagogues and Jewish residents going back to their early days. He also ignored Century Village, where Jewish residents were definitely in the majority. He was on firmer ground when he accused them of being anti-black.[20] Using 2000 Census data, Andrew Blechman noted that the population of Sun City, Arizona, which then had a median age of seventy-five and most of whom were on fixed incomes, was only 0.5 percent black and "about 98.5 percent white."[21] At The Villages in 2008, out of around 68,000 people, 250 were black, and 97 percent were white.[22] A female resident Blechman met could not recall seeing any Asians there. She also told Blechman "that she didn't much care for" diversity. Instead, the woman said, "There are a lot of people just like us" living in The Villages, which was what she wanted.[23] Some developers like the Del Webb companies have tried reaching out to African Americans by including them in advertising photographs. For example, a 2008 sales brochure for Glenbrooke, a Del Webb community in Elk Grove, California, pictured around ten people socializing, of which two were African Americans.[24] So far, relatively few African Americans seem to be moving into active adult communities, although the 2010 Census results could well show otherwise.

Jack Tucker, a muckraker from the Sun City, Arizona, area who produced his own sarcastic and debunking history of Sun City on the occasion of its twenty-fifth anniversary, called attention to some fine gradations in social class in that area. Youngtown never had the quality infrastructure and recreational amenities of the contiguous community of Sun City, so Youngtown homes were generally cheaper. In Tucker's rather racist words, "Youngtowners can stare across 111th Avenue at Midas [Sun City], but like the Chicanos they can't touch."[25] Within Sun City, he noted the general social class gradations, with Phase 3 residents in the newest homes looking down on those in Phase 2, who looked down on those in the oldest homes in Phase 1, and those in the newer community of Sun City West looked down on all of the Sun City residents, regardless of in what phase their home was.[26] Sun City had many "doctors and dentists, who really live high on the retirement hog," but it also had a number of former residents of Hawaii who relocated to Sun City for the lower cost of living.[27] Tucker mentioned the elderly widows who had to work because inflation had eroded their income and those typically longtime residents who needed charity to hang onto their homes or cover nursing home bills.[28] While he noted that many residents found it easier to make friends in Sun City than in their former hometowns, he also asserted that Sun City had relatively high rates of alcoholism, prescription drug abuse, and death, including suicide.[29]

U.S. culture has a certain social stigma associated with being elderly. In this sense, a criticism of these communities is that they call attention to their residents' age. In fact, a few observers have thought of them as akin to nursing homes. Indeed, Ben Schleifer, who established the first age-restricted community, Youngtown, Arizona, in 1954, was trying to create a community that could serve as an alternative to the regimentation and loss of personal independence characteristic of nursing homes. In the minds of some outsiders, a stigma was associated with age segregation. They were "ghettoes for the elderly." Age-restricted communities were places where the rest of the population could get the elderly "out of [their] hair at all costs." An extremely harsh attitude likened age-restricted communities to Indian reservations and concentration camps. Old-age homes and naturally occurring retirement communities like St. Petersburg, Florida, were seen as places where the elderly just sat around. By promoting "active retirement" and stressing an amenity-rich community, Del Webb countered a dismal stereotype with an active, resort lifestyle image.[30]

Predictably, these communities got plenty of criticism from those who objected to their anti-tax policies, voting down of school bond issues, and refusal to incorporate. *Benson's View* was an editorial cartoon series in the *Arizona Republic*. It featured what one author has called numerous "scathing critiques of Sun City." One cartoon picturing deformed old people on a billboard was headlined, "Unincorporated, Untaxed, and Ungrateful." Another, referring to Sun City's repeated refusals to support school bond issues, depicted two Sun City residents engaged in a fox hunt, with two children as their prey. The general image was of relocating retirees coming into the area to colonize and exploit the natives.[31] While best known for rejecting school bond issues, Sun Citians also played a role in blocking freeway expansion and other regional projects. Because Sun City and other large retirement communities concentrated the votes of the elderly, nearby intergenerational communities resented their political clout.[32]

Then there was the conservative political image of "a callous leisure class, living in age-segregated retirement communities, inured to the needs of the rest of society" while jealously guarding and trying to expand their entitlements, such as Social Security payments.[33] Writer Andrew Blechman, as the father of a young child, was unhappy with seniors who "go 'tax shopping'" when considering a move to a retirement community.[34] He explicitly denounced the 1988 Fair Housing Act for legalizing age-restricted communities, thereby "endorsing discrimination against young families."[35] However, many of the residents of these communities may see Blechman's criticism as a reason to live in an active adult community. As elderly voters, these communities do give them political clout to act in their own self-interest, even if it is accentuating the generational divide. Blechman did concede that these communities gave their residents a sense of community, something often lacking when Americans on average move "12 times in a lifetime, so there is no 'home.'"[36]

Some social scientists talk about a social "contract across generations." By that they mean different age groups have expectations of and obligations toward each other.[37] Given the growing proportion of elderly, conflict across generations may be exacerbated. Organizers of Americans for Generational Equity (AGE), founded in 1984, have argued that the elderly, thanks to Social Security, Medicare, and other programs, were getting more than their share of resources at the expense of younger generations.[38] Some studies have shown that the aged in general, not just in active adult, age-restricted communities, are less supportive of public education than younger generations.[39] Ideally, the generations should cooperate in a reciprocal fashion. However, when large, age-restricted, active adult communities enable their residents to flex their political muscles in a selfish fashion, most typically by voting down school bond issues, it is not surprising that some members of the younger generations cry foul.

Finally, Tucker could not resist an attack on Sun City's founder, Del Webb. Specifically, he called attention to Webb's business dealings with mobsters such as Bugsy Siegel (Webb built Siegel's pioneering Flamingo casino and hotel on the Las Vegas Strip) and the Webb corporation's investments in Nevada casinos. He did give Webb credit for making "a tremendous and unique contribution to the well-being of senior Americana," as illustrated by the Sun City Pom Poms, "high stepping old gals [who did] not act their average age, which was 64."[40] The constant sarcasm with which he wrote about Sun City makes his lively but opinionated book rather grating in short order, and Tucker failed to be taken seriously.

Andrew Blechman's tendency to ridicule his subjects and go for the most bizarre examples he could find also tended to undercut his arguments about these communities widening the generational divide in American society. For example, he praised the developers of Sun City and The Villages for helping "a segment of older Americans to find community." These communities gave them a sense of security. Residents could leave "behind a culture that worships—and caters to—youth." Instead, "an older man with thinning hair, paunchy midsection, and bad knees can buy a woman a drink and not get heckled. A gray-haired woman succumbing to gravity's pull can dance the night away, swim at the pool, and be a cheerleader with pom-poms without feeling self-conscious or foolish." However, by ridiculing the residents before he gets to his main point, that "our federal government shouldn't be in the business of endorsing discrimination against young families," Blechman has squandered much of the sympathetic support he, as a young father, might have garnered.[41] The *New York Times* review of his book called *Leisureville* "an extended cheap shot even on its own terms."[42] While Blechman does point out that the typical intergenerational community does not do a very good job of providing "senior-friendly" facilities and services, avoiding people like Blechman who have a tendency to ridicule seniors may actually be another reason for some seniors to move into age-restricted communities.[43]

The Planners' Assessment: From "New Towns" to the "New Urbanism"

Sun City's opening in 1960 preceded the construction of "new towns" in the United States, although they existed at that time in England and northern Europe. There is no evidence that "new town" planning concepts such as surrounding the community with a greenbelt or including some low-income housing had a direct influence on the Webb Corporation. However, the company's executives did think of it as being more in the tradition of community building, not just construction. Furthermore, while some tentative planning was done in advance, they knew the company was operating in uncharted territory with Sun City. They would have to be flexible, see what worked, and not be wedded to initial plans. However, by the mid-1960s, "new towns" were becoming trendy in the United States, and the Webb Corporation adopted some of the language associated with them, such as "master-planned communities." According to historian John Findlay, around 1967 the Webb Corporation began comparing its larger projects with Britain's "new towns."[44] However, unlike the builders of the American "new towns," the developers of Sun City responded more to market research and their sense of what the public wanted as opposed to a preconceived plan. Most of the active adult, age-restricted communities became successes; most of the "new towns" in the United States either failed or moved away from their original concept.

By the 1990s, "new urbanism" and "smart growth" were getting a lot of attention in the planning field. Furthermore, they were discrediting certain aspects of the "new towns." Advocates of the "new urbanism" wanted more compact, pedestrian-friendly communities, which made them critical of the emphasis in "new towns" on open space and greenbelts. The "new urbanism" movement favored urban infill as opposed to the creation of new communities that were typically located a substantial distance from cities. Proponents of the "new urbanism" strongly promoted urban mass transit and pedestrian use and favored mixed-income neighborhoods and neotraditional architecture. These principles led to a critique based on planning principles of Sun City–type communities.

Andres Duany and Elizabeth Plater-Zyberk were the leading spokespersons for the "new urbanism." They noted that a growing percentage of seniors were "choosing to retire to a house in the suburbs, especially in the Sun Belt." However, once those retirees lost their driving licenses, they were stranded. In their view, the retirees' only choice at that point was to move to an institution where they would be "quarantined" with their peers. They dubbed the retirement community "just a way station" on the road to an isolated assisted living facility. It was their position that retirees would be better off settling in a neotraditional neighborhood that was part of a city, had urban mass transit, and featured a variety of mixed uses. They envisioned seniors walking to a bus stop, perhaps slowly, then waiting there to climb aboard a bus.[45]

What Duany and Plater-Zyberk did not take into account was that some elderly people have walking problems, would be uncomfortable standing for any length of time, could only negotiate the steps getting into a regular bus with difficulty if at all, and would find carrying heavy grocery bags on public transportation a problem. They ignored the frequent use of golf carts for intracommunity transportation. Seniors could often operate golf carts, which could get them to their neighborhood medical clinics or shopping centers and transport them and their grocery bags home quite easily. Furthermore, while Sun City, Arizona, in 2006 had no regular, public bus service, like some other places it did have special, curbside bus service (Dial-a-Ride) for people with special needs to arrange rides ahead of time.

Ignoring "smart growth" or the "new urbanism" may actually have some advantages for active adult, age-restricted communities. With the bulk of their residents retired, the communities do not need to be located near strong job markets. Also, by building farther out from the urban core, land is cheaper, which in turn should make housing in these communities more affordable. As for environmental concerns, air quality may be better than in more compact, urbanized areas.

As for assisted-living facilities, residents of active adult, age-restricted communities were hardly isolated from them. By 2005, Sun City and Sun City West had a variety of such facilities plus other "age in place" services such as Meals on Wheels. Jane Freeman, a resident of an independent-living, high-rise apartment building in Sun City, said the two communities had "become saturated" with those types of facilities.[46] That did not stop the author of a recent book for developers on building active adult retirement communities from declaring, "Adults in the market do not want to see uses that are associated with aging, debility, or death, so locations adjacent to a nursing home, cemetery, or medical institution are generally not desirable."[47] Actually, developers have found that a first-class hospital nearby is a selling point. Webb's building and promotion of Boswell Hospital around 1970 to kick off sales in Phase 2 of Sun City is a case in point. However, by promoting the "active adult" image, the developers typically have avoided calling attention to such facilities as cemeteries and assisted-living complexes, but to charge that they avoided locating near them was going too far. What seems to have happened is that these communities, once built, became magnets for such facilities.

There is some evidence that developers in the twenty-first century may be taking a more realistic attitude toward the presence of elder-care facilities. The Villages in Florida publishes a monthly magazine featuring activities in the community that it distributes free to prospective home buyers. A sample issue includes numerous ads for various medical facilities plus a full-page ad for the community's continuing care facility. That facility has a sales office in The Villages' downtown of Spanish Springs. As of May 2008, the continuing care facility was said to be "nearly 80% sold out."[48]

Advocates of "new urbanism" have been critical of gated communities. In the twenty-first century, not all active adult, age-restricted communities are gated, although a significant proportion are. A lot depends on the regional location of the community. In the Northeast, residents in gated communities with homeowner associations appear to value the gates for the perceived social status they confer. In the Sunbelt, with its reputation for keeping taxes low, residents perceive gated communities as having cost-effective services. In some parts of the country, gated communities fit into a trend toward privatization in general. Whether the gates actually deter crime or make neighborhoods safer is debatable. In defiance of the "new urbanism" position against them, gated communities have become increasingly popular in certain regions and not just for age-restricted, active adult communities. The number of people living behind gates in the United States increased "from four million in

1995 to roughly seventeen million (over six percent of the U.S. population) in 2001." They remain virtually absent in Minnesota, but "in some regions, one in ten people lives behind gates."[49] Going back to the 1960s, when a gated community of modest homes was something of a novelty, active adult, age-restricted communities played a major role in popularizing what continues to be a strong trend in community planning in certain regions.

The International Critique

Age-restricted, active adult communities are an American original that have attracted considerable foreign curiosity but almost no foreign imitation.[50] International interest goes back to the early 1960s. In 1963, a German film crew spent several weeks at Sun City, Arizona, documenting its residents' way of life.[51] The interest continued. The number of contractors from Germany, France, Australia, and elsewhere who came to Sun City, Arizona, to study its resort retirement lifestyle and "to find out why it had such great appeal" left an impression on the Webb marketing staff. A general conclusion of the foreign visitors was that the abundance of amenities "attracted interesting residents and provided the most important human need . . . in abundance—'Companionship.'" As a result, in 1974 Sun City promoters began calling it "the Standard of the World in Resort-Retirement Living."[52]

International visitors also made their way to Leisure World Laguna Hills. In 1978, a television crew from Paris visited all thirteen guarded gates and the five clubhouses then in existence in that community. The emphasis on security fascinated the crew.[53] The following year, the Andrus Gerontology Center at the University of Southern California put on a five-day seminar for fifteen West Germans. Included was a tour of Leisure World Laguna Hills along with a discussion of how it operated. While Germany proportionally had more people over sixty-five than the United States, the German visitors concluded that the German elderly were "more family oriented."[54]

Meanwhile, the Sun Cities in California and Arizona continued to receive international attention, along with Wynmoor Village in Florida, a condo development of 9,000 residents that began as a Leisure World before the developer of Century Village, H. Irwin Levy, became the manager and renamed it. In 1980, sixteen Japanese tourists chartered a bus to see Sun City, California, because they had heard so much about it in Japan.[55] Ten years later, another group of Japanese tourists visited Wynmoor Village in Coconut Creek, Florida. While the Japanese were impressed with Wynmoor's fitness center and other amenities, they decided that elderly Japanese would choose to live with their adult children rather than move into that type of community. A Wynmoor Village resident concluded that the Japanese were "far more family-oriented."[56] In the twenty-first century, the 2006 newsletter of the Sun Cities Area Historical Society has reported hosting a group of foreign professionals from various fields. What fascinated them was the importance of volunteers to Sun City, Arizona's operations. They were used to government performing many of the services that Sun City volunteers did, but the reaction of members of the historical society was how much more it would cost to run Sun City without the volunteers.

The Internet has facilitated international communication with the Sun Cities Area Historical Society. Riccardo Tonon, a student at the School for Architecture and Society in Milan, Italy, decided to do his master's thesis on the sociological implications and history of active adult retirement communities, including Sun City, Arizona. He did not visit, but through the Internet he ordered materials from the society. He reported that no such communities existed in Italy since Italians over fifty-five prefer to remain in their hometowns rather than relocate.[57] The general foreign reaction seems to be fascination but then a rather smug assertion that age-restricted retirement communities would not work in their countries because their citizens have a stronger sense of family values than Americans do.

On the other hand, the American age-restricted, active adult retirement communities have attracted a small number of residents from other countries. Some Canadians have adopted the American snowbird lifestyle, probably to escape the cold Canadian winters. As estimated in the 1988 monograph *Snowbirds in the Sunbelt: Older Canadians in Florida*, a quarter-million Canadians spent their winters in Florida, and others, especially from Canada's western provinces, headed for Arizona, California, Nevada, and Hawaii. However, they limited their stays to no longer than five months because they did not want to lose their benefits under the Canadian national health insurance system. Their pattern may be similar to northern Europeans heading for sunnier places in Spain, France, and elsewhere, with some European resort communities becoming destinations for elderly, seasonal migrants. Only about 20 percent of the Canadians in the 1988 study considered permanently relocating, even though some did own second homes in U.S. retirement communities,[58] while it appears that most of their U.S. counterparts became permanent residents of their active adult communities.

The Canadian trend has persisted into the twenty-first century. By 2007, so many French-speaking Canadians were migrating to Hollywood, Florida, that that city was publishing "two newspapers in French, with a Quebecois tilt" and a large Quebec bank had established three branches "complete with French-flashing ATMs" in the area.[59] In 2008, *Robson Living,* a promotional publication for the Robson active adult communities, profiled new resident Anna-Lisa Anderson, a Swedish immigrant who had just become a naturalized citizen of the United States, an event that was celebrated by no less than three Robson Ranch Texas groups to which Anderson belonged.[60]

The flip side of foreigners migrating to U.S. retirement communities is American citizens relocating to retirement destinations abroad. A lower cost of living in certain places combined with the glamour of living abroad, often as part of an expatriate community such as that in San Miguel de Allende, Mexico, may be attracting more Americans.[61] More retirees heading abroad may provide an incentive for developers in other countries to try active adult, age-restricted communities on the American model.

An American woman who married a Mexican national and who has lived in Mexico for four decades, Diane Gravell y Hernandez, says she initially thought the reason Mexicans have resisted retirement communities was that Mexicans depend much more on their extended family members than do "individualist" Americans. In other words, stronger family values on the part of Mexicans would work against acceptance of age-restricted retirement communities.[62] A few days later, she had a second thought and suggested that the reason age-restricted communities did not exist in Mexico was the relative poverty of the vast majority of Mexicans. Their children are, in a sense, their "social security" in their old age because they depend on them financially. However, the Mexican government does sponsor some senior centers where seniors can work on crafts, dance, and socialize.[63]

Then, a few weeks later, came her third thought. A Mexican friend had told her about a retirement community near Monterrey, Mexico, called El Legado, and she forwarded a link to that community's Web site.[64] The site, which had an English-language version, began, "Picture yourself living in a place where you live without the concerns regarding domestic help," so one knew right away that it was not in the United States. However, with the exception of references to a "chauffeur at your disposal" and "a team of professional service providers who. . . . are fully bilingual," the rest of the description sounded very much like American retirement communities. In fact, the Web site stated, "It is a [*sic*] very similar to some of the luxury facilities for those 50 years and older in the States, but at Mexican prices. . . . El Legado caters to those who want to retire in a safe, tranquil, active, and exclusive community." El Legado consisted of apartments in a five-story building. Specific activities included computer classes, yoga workshops, art, and films. The site's sponsoring organization, Solutions Abroad, offered to help those interested in other types of relocation to Mexico.[65] Among U.S. developers of age-restricted, active adult communities, Ross Cortese had thought about taking his concept abroad but never did.[66] As for Internet marketing, by the twenty-first century that was common among developers in the United States and abroad. If El Legado succeeds, more international development of these communities may follow.

For his 2008 book, *Leisureville,* Andrew Blechman noted that several foreign nationals attended a recent National Association of Home Builders conference on age-restricted housing in Phoenix. A Mexican developer was considering an age-restricted development in Baja, not for Mexicans but for American expatriates. In his view, Mexicans would not be interested because, traditionally and out of economic necessity, their practice was to live with their families. An Australian at the conference thought age-restricted communities were "growing in popularity" in his country, but there was still resistance to what he called the fake American "fantasyland in the middle of the desert." (One satisfied resident of The Villages, Florida, did call it "Disneyworld for Adults" but praised its wide range of activities and opportunities to develop "individual pursuits.")[67] Two Swiss bankers at the Phoenix conference said Europeans would want to be close to urban culture and their families, not isolated in an age-restricted community. Besides, building such a community in Europe would be prohibitive due to land costs, more restrictive land use policies, and higher building code standards.[68] Nevertheless, the success of active adult communities among American retirees continues to fascinate people from other parts of the world.

Meanwhile, the British have been promoting "Florida-style" retirement complexes for their own senior citizens. Birmingham, England, was doubling its "retirement villages" to eight. These were complexes of 200–300 flats with a gym and social, crafts, medical, and commercial facilities "in a village-type setting." Missing from the description were more elaborate active adult amenities such as a golf course, resort-style swimming pool, and tennis courts.[69] The British use the term "retirement village" to refer to what in the United States would be called assisted living or continuing care facilities; the Richmond Coventry retirement village features optional "24-hour nursing care."[70] Again, the U.S. "active adult" image of significantly larger communities sharing luxurious facilities through common ownership just was not present in England. It may also be that Americans are more willing to share luxurious facilities in order to afford them.

Del Webb in the Twenty-First Century

Going into the twenty-first century, Del Webb was still "widely considered the industry's brand leader [setting] the pace for others to follow—or at least to watch very carefully."[71] It was also the largest builder of active adult, age-restricted communities. In 2001, Pulte Homes Inc., one of the country's largest home builders, bought the Del Webb corporation and has continued to use the Del Webb brand name. At that time, the acquisition of the Del Webb corporation made Pulte the third largest home builder of residential units in the United States.[72] Pulte also acquired DiVosta, which has done age-targeted, as opposed to age-restricted, communities in Florida. While DiVosta communities do have some shared facilities, the generally wealthier residents are less reliant on them than in the Del Webb communities. That may be why DiVosta home owners are less concerned about the permanent residence of some underage children.

As the industry leader for active adult communities, it has been incumbent on Del Webb to engage in ongoing research to keep up with changing times and current trends. For example, in the 1960s, Del Webb's goal was to bring a country club lifestyle to those retirees who had not been able to afford to join country clubs in their home communities and could enjoy those amenities in Sun City. The Webb corporation subsequently dropped the country club theme. Instead, its emphasis shifted to a resort-like "lifestyle," while the phrase "active adult" continued to be used. By 2006, the company was aiming to keep its home prices below $500,000 (some were under $200,000), so it was not going after the very wealthy retirees. Other developers tended to follow the same theme.

The market for this type of community in the twenty-first century was more diverse than it was back in the 1960s. World War II veterans tended to retire at sixty-five, and retirees in the twenty-first century are more likely to retire younger, perhaps even in their early fifties. These retiring baby boomers are also less likely to stay retired and more likely to start working again. Furthermore, with the baby boomers, the number of retirees has increased. About 25 percent would like to relocate on retiring, but about a third of those would not be able to afford a Del Webb community. Health has played a role as well, but a number of people with disabilities do move to "active adult" communities. What was most important was that they have the will to move and also be interested in social interaction.

In the 1960s, Del Webb's vision was of communities around 10,000 acres with at least 26,000 small, two-bedroom ramblers. In the twenty-first century, those large parcels of land have become difficult to obtain. As for trends in amenities and lifestyle, the company has continued to do surveys to determine the preferences of potential buyers. An on-line survey in November 2006 was intended to gauge attitudes toward gated communities, distance from a major hospital, inclusion of assisted living facilities within the community, the driving of golf carts on the community's streets, and how much one would be willing to spend on association fees. The latter related to the size of the community because a certain number of households would be needed to keep the cost of maintaining elaborate recreational facilities affordable. This survey also was designed to get data on interest in a variety of sports and recreational activities, preferences for different types of music and some other cultural activities, travel habits (maintenance-free condos can appeal to those frequently absent), and even interest in a matchmaking service for singles.[73] Individual Webb communities such as La Cresta near Orlando, Florida, have done more limited surveys covering buyer preferences as to house type, cost, and level of association fees.[74] Pulte closed this development for a short time during the 2007–10 housing crisis, then reopened it with a new name, Del Webb Orlando.

In 2006, Pulte had fifty-four Del Webb, age-restricted communities that were open for sales of homes. That compared to five Del Webb communities selling new homes in 1990. Under Pulte, the philosophy seems to be that the more places the company was doing business, the wider its appeal would be. The company's marketing followed an assumption that a certain number of retirees would like to move to an active adult community, but they preferred to stay relatively close to home as opposed to relocating halfway across the country. For example, some Midwesterners wanted to experience the change of seasons. With Sun City Huntley approaching build-out in 2008, Del Webb was offering three other communities in the Greater Chicago area—Edgewater in Elgin, Grand Dominion in Mundelein, and Shorewood Glen in Shorewood. As an e-mail pitch put it, "Del Webb communities are popping up all over the nation as folks like you decide they want to stay close to home and close to family, friends and familiar surroundings after retirement."[75] By the 1990s, Cape Cod had emerged as a retirement area. Out of the ten towns in Massachusetts with the largest number of residents over age sixty-five, seven were on Cape Cod. Retirees were generating "one quarter of Cape Cod's income," with summer residents, tourists, and locals who were not retirees making up the rest.[76] By the twenty-first century, Webb was in that area as well.

While some of Webb's fifty-plus communities were in the Midwest and the Northeast, the company's strategy was to increase its presence in the traditional southern retiree areas. In 2006, the most successful Webb communities were in North Carolina, Arizona, and Texas and near Chicago. All had quality recreational center amenities, but not all had golf courses. Only the very largest ones had a commercial core. Grocery stores, for example, tend to locate where their market would consist of at least a couple of thousand dwelling units. On the other hand, a community of around 700 to 800 homes would be large enough to support Del Webb–type amenities. One of the smaller Del Webb communities, Rancho Diamante, near Hemet, California, in 2006 was projected at 586 homes along with a 25,000-square-foot clubhouse, outdoor and indoor pools, and bocce ball and tennis courts. The community would not be gated or have its own golf course.[77] Two years later, Rancho Diamante, which opened in August 2006, was renamed Solera Diamond Valley and had 1,125 homes projected.[78] The company only put the Sun City label on its communities that had at least 3,000 house lots. It used Solera to indicate a smaller, fancier, age-restricted community.

To locate a community in a given area, a number of things needed to come together. In 2005, this researcher received several postcard advertisements for a Del Webb development called Water's Edge in Hugo, a suburb north of St. Paul, Minnesota. A 2005 Parade of Homes catalog indicated that Water's Edge was a master-planned community with a clubhouse "featuring an outdoor swimming pool, exercise area . . . and meeting space" plus "10 miles of walking trails" and "80 acres of open space." The Del Webb designation was not mentioned, but the presence of a planned elementary school on the site was. The community was "association maintained."[79] There was demand for a Del Webb age-restricted, active adult community in the Twin Cities area, but the area lacked large parcels of land for sale, and what was available was expensive. Furthermore, the area was politically fragmented, meaning that permits need to be obtained from a variety of government agencies. Also, Minnesota goes beyond federal standards when it comes to protection of wetlands. While the author does not know the specific reasons for the misfire in Hugo, a more descriptive name for Water's Edge would be "Wetland City." The inclusion of an elementary school in a community with a lot of two-bedroom homes seemed strange to this researcher as well, but developers may be putting a school on their plan to quell fears that a bunch of "active adults" will vote down school bond issues. Instead, what the redirection of Water's Edge illustrates is that the amenity-rich, association-maintained community is a twenty-first-century planning trend that is being applied to some intergenerational communities, not just "active adult" communities.

With Del Webb holding back on developing an age-restricted, active adult community in Minnesota, another national home builder, K. Hovnanian, opened a small, age-restricted, active adult community in Maple Grove, northeast of Minneapolis, in 2007. While Del Webb was reluctant to go much below 800 homes to support its amenities, Four Seasons at Rush Creek was planned for 300 homes at build-out. Unfortunately for K. Hovnanian, Rush Creek's opening coincided with the housing recession. As of March 2009, Hovnanian had sold only twenty-two homes in that development. However, the community featured a fully appointed, 15,000-square-foot clubhouse. When this researcher toured that clubhouse, it had water in the indoor pool, exercise equipment in the fitness center, was completely decorated, and not one other person, not even a staff person, was in sight. The activities director doubled as the salesperson and was busy greeting prospective buyers in the community's three beautifully decorated model homes. The only regular activity appeared to be Tuesday night poker. It was the most inactive active adult community this researcher has encountered. Hovnanian, like Pulte, was building intergenerational communities in the area. Also, like Pulte with Del Webb, Hovnanian had built other active adult, age-restricted Four Seasons communities in California, Texas, New Jersey, and Pennsylvania. In terms of Four Seasons at Rush Creek as well as the company overall, Hovnanian was rather like a downsized Pulte Homes. The slogan on its sales brochure was "A New Generation of Active Adult Living."[80]

Much more important than physically planning these communities and building the homes was creating and marketing the "lifestyle." Del Webb did that in 1960 at the grand opening of Sun City. Not only did buyers see furnished model homes, but they saw people using equipment in the various craft rooms in the recreation center and playing golf on the adjacent golf course. The original Sun City came with an activities director whose job it was to introduce new residents to each other, find out their backgrounds and interests, and then organize various clubs, groups, and events. By the twenty-first century, the activities director had been renamed the lifestyle director. Even the small Rancho Diamante (Solera Diamond Valley) development had a full-time lifestyle director who, like the others, worked in close association with the marketing people.[81] One of the duties of the lifestyle directors was to explain the nature of the community to sales prospects along with getting clubs and activities going for the new residents.

To get an idea of how Del Webb was defining this lifestyle in 2005, this researcher attended a seminar arranged to promote the latest Sun City in the Phoenix area, Sun City Festival. One had to register in advance. Since the community was not yet built, Webb used its sales center and ballroom at Sun City Grand for the event. A live, loud rock band greeted a couple of hundred attendees as they entered. The slide presentation described Sun City Festival as an "active adult" community. It began with a brief history of Del Webb and the other three Sun Cities in the immediate area (the original Sun City, Sun City West, and Sun City Grand), then noted that needs have evolved to include health and personal enrichment, with Festival being "like living in a resort." Festival, located ten miles west of Grand, was being planned for 7,200 homes and was part of a larger master-planned community expected to eventually reach 100,000 people. The Webb community will feature a 31,000-square-foot "wellness and higher learning center." Besides the pools, spa, tot lot for grandchildren, fitness center, large restaurant, and golf courses, the developers had forged a partnership with Arizona State University for adult education classes and were stressing the "new" themes of "well-being" and "connectivity." Homes would range from 1,373 square feet to 2,849 square feet, would be priced from $190,000, and would carry $80 per month homeowner association fees. That compared favorably to $230 per month at K. Hovnanian's Four Seasons at Rush Creek with the smallest model at 1,204 square feet selling for a discounted price of $249,990 in March 2009. Unlike previous Webb communities, at Festival buyers would not have as many decorating choices, but granite countertops would be standard. This preview presentation relied on computer simulation to illustrate facilities that had not yet been built. It was one of about a dozen such "seminars" planned in December 2005 to launch the community.[82] Apparently, a number of those in the audience were already residents of nearby Sun Cities and were looking to possibly "trade up."

In marketing this resort-like "lifestyle," Webb was still relying on organizing events and printing community newsletters to entice buyers into its communities. Some of the events were reflective of recent trends in recreational and cultural activities. For example, the Webb communities of Riverwood and Sweetwater, both near Jacksonville, Florida, organized a "training camp" to prepare for Jacksonville's Senior Games. Held in those communities and free to participants were sessions on physical fitness, how to improve one's bridge game, tennis game, golf game, table tennis game, billiards game, and bocce ball game, a 5K race for walkers and runners (some new communities have indoor walking/jogging tracks), and a session explaining what the popular new sport of pickle ball was all about (a tamer version of tennis). The closing ceremony for Jacksonville's annual Senior Games in 2007 was scheduled for Sweetwater.[83]

In Arizona, Sun City Anthem at Merrill Ranch's grand opening in March 2007 featured live music, cooking and golfing demonstrations, games of bocce, pickle ball, and horseshoes, a classic car show, "Polynesian poolside entertainment," a wine tasting, and a free barbecue lunch. The grand opening also highlighted the growing interest in adult education with Arizona State University's Lifelong Learning Academy presenting workshops on NASA, Successful Aging, and Writing Your Family History.[84] Virtually missing in the recent descriptions of facilities and events programming for all retirement communities was the ubiquitous shuffleboard, much less popular in the twenty-first century than it was in the 1960s.

Given the "resort lifestyle" marketing theme, it may be surprising that "vacation specials" became something of a temporary rarity. Del Webb dropped them after Pulte acquired the company. On the other hand, the 1950s pioneer in Florida beachfront condos for the elderly, On Top of the World, subsequently decided to try a Del Webb–style community. It bought more than 11,000 acres of land inland near Ocala, Florida, designed a master plan with a commercial town center and single-family homes, and, as of 2007, was doing "vacation specials." On Top of the World Communities offered prospective buyers three days (two nights) in two-bedroom villas and use of golf carts. Guests could select from a variety of activities, including golf, tennis, fitness classes, swimming, visiting clubs and events, and touring Ocala and its countryside of horse farms. One unusual facility at that community was a radio-controlled field for flying model airplanes.[85]

Webb may have dropped its vacation specials due to concerns about freeloading by not very interested prospective buyers, but competition from other developers soon brought them back. Its La Cresta community near Orlando did offer buyers from out of state who purchased homes in 2007 a refund of up to $1,000 for their lodging and airfare expenses.[86] The continuing housing crisis brought the refund at La Cresta up to $1,500 in 2009.[87] Another Del Webb development in Florida, Riverwood in Ponte Vedra, offered purchasers up to $1,500 in reimbursement for airfare, two nights at a hotel, car rental, and meals.[88]

In addition to cash incentives, the 2007–10 housing downturn had Webb reinstating the former vacation specials, now called the "new Vacation Getaway package." For example, at Stone Creek near Ocala, Florida, one could spend three days and two nights "in a luxury villa, along with access to the one-of-a-kind amenities and activities available at [the clubhouse] and [on the] championship 18-hole golf course." The cost was $89 per night,[89] a difficult price to beat at a resort with fewer amenities, even if one did have to listen to a sales pitch. The most successful active adult community in Florida in recent years, The Villages, offered what it called a "Mini Vacation at The Villages" for as little as $100 per night.[90] That price was later reduced.

The ads, the events, and the facilities offered the outlines for a "resort lifestyle" for active adults, but as Del Webb said from the beginning, it was the people who would make the community. His company, along with other developers, did leave certain things out of the advertised scripts. For example, in promoting Sun City, Webb made no mention of its cemetery. However, once Webb built a first-class hospital in the community, it did use that as a marketing tool, but it did not call attention to the nursing home that preceded it.

Likewise, Webb staff rarely mentioned the tax savings that buyers transferring their residence from states with high income taxes to states with little or no state income taxes would have. However, the firm did tend to locate a lot of its communities in low-tax states. In published ads and written communications to prospective buyers, neither Pulte, the owner of Del Webb, nor other developers of active adult, age-restricted communities emphasized the tax advantages of communities located in low-tax states, although individual salespeople might use that argument with certain potential buyers. One exception was a 2007 brochure advertising the Webb community of Stone Creek, which mentioned a Florida property tax break for homeowners and stated, "Florida residents also enjoy no state income tax."[91] A second exception occurred in a 2008 e-mail advertisement for La Cresta that mentioned "the lack of income tax" as one of "Florida's biggest perks."[92] Given that lack of a state income tax can save a middle-class retiree from a state with high income taxes thousands of dollars, it is remarkable that retirement communities do not do significantly more to encourage "tax shopping" among potential migrants. On the other hand, they need to maintain good governmental relations to get the building permits they need to operate.

Coping with the Twenty-First-Century Housing Crisis

The first several years of the twenty-first century saw a roaring housing market that included age-restricted, active adult communities. In 1995, fifteen such communities opened. In 2004, construction began on a hundred such communities. They joined approximately 1,500 already established age-restricted developments.[93] At The Villages, Florida, the single most successful active adult, age-restricted community at the turn of the twenty-first century, the developer was putting up more than 5,000 houses per year at its peak expansion. In the month of January 2006 alone, Sumter County approved 529 new house permits for that development. By November 2006, the number of housing permits for The Villages had dropped by 86 percent, to 76.[94] By then, it was clear that the housing market was in a downturn.

In November 2006, a Pulte executive said the age-restricted, active adult developments his firm was building were holding up better than Pulte's more conventional housing developments. It was hard to predict at the end of 2006 that the housing crisis was just beginning. In October 2007, Moody's cut its rating of the bonds of both Lennar and Pulte to junk. Lennar was the largest home builder in the United States and had built the active adult community of Ventana Lakes, Arizona. Pulte was the third largest and had far more involvement with active adult community development than Lennar. Then, in November 2007, Standard and Poor's cut not only Lennar and Pulte to junk status but also D. R. Horton, the nation's second largest home builder, whose Cambridge Homes unit developed active adult communities. Both Pulte and Lennar were reducing the value of their landholdings and claimed a combined loss including other items of $2 billion.[95]

Most retired buyers need to first sell their current homes in order to buy houses in active adult communities. In December 2008, Pulte announced that it was discontinuing the payment of regular dividends effective the first quarter of 2009.[96] In October of that year, financial writer Andrew Rice reported that K. Hovnanian, which ranked sixth in number of sales, was low on cash and that the current developer of Sun City Center, WCI, "had issued a warning that it couldn't cover its debts."[97] By the end of 2008, the housing situation had worsened to the point that people were questioning whether some of the big companies would survive, including those developing active adult, age-restricted communities. These are construction companies that make their money building and selling homes, but buyers were very difficult to find in 2008.

These companies adopted various survival strategies. Pulte's Web site in December 2008 listed sixty-two age-restricted, active adult communities spread over nineteen states. They stretched across the Sunbelt and into the mid-Atlantic and New England states plus some midwestern states and Colorado. Most had inventory homes—those built on speculation—for sale. A few Del Webb communities were listed as "coming soon" (Carolina Ridge at Ingleside in Denver, North Carolina) or "Expected Opening Date Coming Soon!" (Del Webb Houston in Richmond, Texas) or "Expected Opening Date 2009/2010" (Willow Shores in Stockton, California).[98] The company listed Coastal Club by Del Webb in

Lewes, Delaware, as "on hold indefinitely" in March 2008 and confirmed that it was still "on hold indefinitely" in December 2008.[99] The pace of building had slowed considerably, but Pulte was still adding to the glut of unsold, new homes. The Villages also continued to build new homes during the housing crisis, but at a much slower pace than formerly.

To try to move their homes in the midst of this housing crisis, Pulte and other builders stressed a number of attractive financial incentives. The most common was to lower the prices of their homes. In 2008, On Top of the World in Ocala, Florida, advertised $25,000 off selected models.[100] In November 2007, that community had offered "Free Golf Course Home Sites."[101] In December 2008, The Villages, Florida, offered to eliminate the premiums on luxury home sites, a savings of up to $40,000 on the golf course sites and $130,000 on lakefront sites. In May 2008, its Web site listed discounts on more than a hundred inventory homes.[102] For example, a conventional, two-bedroom, two-bath, ranch home in The Villages was discounted $5,382 for a price of $146,771. At the other end of the sales spectrum, The Villages offered a four-bedroom, three-bath home with a garden tub and golf cart garage at $607,570, a savings of $104,890 off the original list price.[103] In August 2008, Robson had discounts ranging from $60,000 to $110,000 on models at its five Arizona active adult communities. It also offered a three-night vacation special, its Preferred Guest Program, to prospective buyers that included a round of golf and a dinner for a total of $49 if booked for August or September.[104] During the peak season of January to March 2009, the price was less than $59 per night.[105]

One Arizona real estate agent specializing in the active adult market said that in his fifteen years of experience, he had "never seen pricing lower. . . . anywhere from 20% to 40% off."[106] At Sonora by Del Webb in the Tucson area, inventory homes in 2007 appeared to be going for almost half-price.[107] Price cutting in 2007 was dramatic at the Del Webb community of Stone Creek, Florida, where a two-bedroom, two-bath home with 1,604 square feet was listed for $207,600 during the first half of 2007. In August 2007, Webb cut the price on that home to $189,300. A 2,419-square-foot model was listed in early 2007 at $304,100. The firm cut the price on that home by $44,500 to $260,600 in August 2007.[108] Furthermore, Stone Creek salespeople were telling buyers that they would not have to close at the reduced price for a year, and the company was offering to delay mortgage payments to give buyers up to two years to sell their current homes.[109] Woodbridge by Del Webb in Manteca,

California, was also advertising no mortgage payments for two years.[110] By 2008, Martin Feldstein, a Harvard economist, estimated that one-quarter of home mortgages in general in the United States exceeded the 2008 value of those homes. Florida, Arizona, California, and Nevada were the worst states in this regard, in part because of overbuilding.[111] They were also among the leading states for active adult, age-restricted communities.

As the housing crisis deepened in 2007, financial incentives and low pricing took precedence over promoting the active adult lifestyle. To get potential buyers into their model home parks, the Communities of Del Webb in Arizona offered a drawing for a $2,000 cash prize,[112] while Del Webb in California offered those bringing its promotional e-mail to a model home park $20 in gasoline. If they actually bought homes, they would receive $1,500 worth of gas.[113] One limited-time incentive to buyers at Del Webb's La Cresta, Florida, was the choice of one of several styles of in-ground swimming pools at no added charge.[114] Other subsequent 2007 purchase incentives at La Cresta included free closing costs and the canceling of association fees the first year.[115] If someone purchased at Sun City Peachtree in Georgia, the savings was two years of association fees, and at Lake Oconee, another Webb community in Georgia, three years of association fees were canceled.[116]

Adjustable-rate mortgages had contributed to the housing crisis and were getting a bad image. Therefore, Webb in 2007 offered California buyers thirty-year mortgages at a fixed interest rate of 5.99 percent.[117] Terms were even better for buyers at La Cresta near Orlando. There the annual percentage rate on a thirty-year, fixed-rate mortgage was 5.503 percent interest with 10 percent down.[118] La Cresta offered to delay mortgage payments for half a year, and Del Webb communities in South Carolina and California were willing to defer payments for the entire first year.[119] Webb's program of free options and other, in-kind incentives also continued. In 2007, Del Webb at Lake Oconee offered to throw in a free sunroom.[120]

The housing crisis worsened in 2008, and the financial incentives for buyers got even better. On the East Coast, price reductions at Del Webb's Celebrate in Virginia were announced of up to $100,000 on some homes and no extra charge for certain options.[121] On the West Coast, prices on some models at Sun City Shadow Hills in Indio, California, were reduced $35,000 to $45,000.[122] On the other hand, Pulte did announce a price increase for its homes in southeastern and central Florida effective 1

November 2008.[123] However, the housing crisis got even worse going into 2009.

Meanwhile, financing terms continued to get better. In February 2008, the Del Webb community of Sweetwater, Florida, offered a 4 percent interest rate along with price reductions up to $40,000 and no association dues the first year.[124] Typically, special financing required buyers to go through Pulte Mortgage LLC. By October 2008, Sweetwater had a "teaser" rate of 3.875 percent for the first year.[125] At the end of 2008, home sales in the community at Lake Oconee, Georgia, had thirty-year, fixed-rate mortgages at 5.25 percent.[126] By December 2008, Pulte Homes of Orlando had an even lower fixed rate on thirty-year mortgages—4.99 percent.[127] In fact, Del Webb of the Mid Atlantic salespeople claimed that they had "over 100 loan programs available," offering buyers almost tailor-made loans.[128]

Likewise, the incentive packages continued to get better. In February 2008, the Del Webb community at Lake Providence, Tennessee, offered buyers four choices: a free sunroom, an enhanced garage, a free golf cart worth up to $5,400, or a "backyard living package."[129] The latter included options such as a built-in barbecue, a water feature, "an elegant fire pit," a paving stone patio, and extra landscaping.[130] At the same time, Sun City Festival, Arizona, was offering an incentive package that included a golf cart valued at $4,500, free landscaping, free appliances, no first-year association fees, and discounts on lot prices.[131] In Georgia, Sun City Peachtree took a cue from The Villages and offered free golf the first year. Other incentives included "a free outdoor stone fireplace," no association dues for the first two years, and delayed mortgage payments for six months.[132] By January 2009, WCI's Sun City Center was offering buyers three years of free golf in that community.[133] Nevada Del Webb communities offered up to $10,000 worth of free landscaping.[134] Their "free appliance package" included a washer, dryer, and refrigerator.[135] Del Webb Charleston in 2008 had similar incentives, plus a free sunroom.[136] On the West Coast, Solera at Diamond Valley, California (formerly Rancho Diamante), offered five years of association dues with a purchase.[137] At Solera Kern Canyon, in fall 2008, the incentive was a free initial membership in a local country club, a perk that Del Webb valued at $12,000.[138] In spite of all the financial incentives, home sales slowed.

Incentive packages continued into 2009. In April, buyers of select new homes in Del Webb at Woodbridge, California, could receive a solar power package worth as much as $16,000.[139] Another attractive incentive package offered at Sun City Anthem at Merrill Ranch in the hard-hit state of Arizona was a free kitchen upgrade to better appliances, cabinets, crown molding, and granite countertops.[140] Since prospective buyers differed as to their wants, Sun City Hilton Head offered $10,000 to $22,500 in incentives that a buyer could apply to appliances, prepaid home owners association fees, or other options.[141] Finally, Del Webb announced another coping strategy—a cutback on inventory homes.[142] Also, the number of open communities on the Del Webb Web site had shrunk from sixty-two at the end of 2008 to forty-six in April 2009.[143] While price cuts and incentive packages did not disappear, they were no longer as spectacular as they had been.

A big reason for offering the delayed mortgage payments as an incentive was that buyers of homes in active adult communities usually had existing homes they preferred to sell before buying their retirement homes. However, with the slowdown in the real estate market, many potential buyers had difficulty selling their current homes. Staff at the Del Webb community of Celebrate, Virginia, tried to allay that fear in the fall of 2008 by listing recent buyers, their hometowns, and the length of time their former homes had been on the market. All but one of the nine buyers who were publicized had sold their former homes in twenty-two days or less, and most were from other places in Virginia or the mid-Atlantic area.[144]

The company occasionally sought to help its potential buyers by offering tips on staging existing homes for sale. In November 2007, Del Webb Charleston brought in Terry Haas, the staging expert featured on HGTV's *Designed to Sell*, to put on a class for its sales prospects.[145] At the Del Webb community in Roseville, California, a company called We Stage Sacramento put on an event and claimed that a "staged" home sold "two to three times faster than the unstaged competition."[146] Del Webb offered to help its prospects with referrals to real estate agents, market statistics on how fast homes were selling in their hometowns, and contingency programs tailored to their situations.[147] The main effect of delaying the start of mortgage payments was to give buyers who had not sold their existing homes some temporary relief from having to carry two mortgages. When new home sales in the Phoenix area increased 44 percent between March and April 2009 and sales of existing homes rose 70 percent from a year earlier, Webb was quick to publicize those statistics.[148] Many of these sales techniques, programs, and incentives were new to the company. In spite of all these efforts, this was the worst housing crisis Del Webb had experienced in its nearly fifty years of selling homes in active adult communities.

Nevertheless, Webb was still managing to function. Del Webb Stone Creek near Ocala, Florida, opened just before the housing bubble burst. In December 2008, it celebrated its three-year anniversary. In spite of the downturn in housing, Stone Creek developers had built and sold 550 homes. The community had established more than twenty clubs, and its golf course, restaurant, and clubhouse were all functioning. It ranked among the top ten Del Webb communities nationwide for sales. Furthermore, it was outperforming other retirement communities near Ocala.[149] Writer Andrew Blechman in July 2008 called active adult communities the housing industry's "sweet spot."[150] As of December 2008, active adult communities were struggling, and not all survived.

Although in a weakened position, Pulte, the parent company of Del Webb, still managed to acquire or merge with rival home builder Centex in a stock deal for $1.3 billion. When the housing boom peaked in 2005, Centex built 37,022 homes that year to Pulte's 45,630. In 2008, "both companies built less than half" those numbers while slashing prices. Centex lost nearly $2.7 billion, wiping out its profits for the four preceding years. Pulte's losses over the past two years wiped out its profits for the previous three years.[151] The merger, which was completed in August 2009,[152] made Pulte the nation's largest, if still struggling, home builder.

As short sales and skyrocketing mortgage foreclosures presented increased competition for home builders, Del Webb specifically addressed the temptation of some buyers to look for bargains among resales by touting its ten-year warranty.[153] In Florida, that included "five-year leak protection."[154] However, foreclosures, short sales, and extremely low-priced resales were serious competition. At Century Village in West Palm Beach in June 2009, a one-bedroom, one-bath unit with new tile and a new refrigerator was listed for $13,000. Another, priced at $15,000, came with ceramic tile, carpeting, and some furniture.[155] While these were the lowest-priced units this researcher found, they do illustrate the housing crisis in mid-2009.

It was even lower mortgage rates and government programs that stabilized the situation. Buyers who purchased their first homes between 1 January and 1 December 2009 (later extended) qualified for an $8,000 tax credit. Indirectly, that could help buyers in active adult communities sell their existing homes. Directly, it could help them if they had not been homeowners for three years, perhaps renting or living with others.

Also, the FHA mortgage program got better, allowing for larger loans and requiring down payments of only 3.5 percent. Furthermore, Webb assured its sales prospects, "You don't need to have perfect credit to qualify."[156] When "mortgage rates hit a 52-year low" on 26 March, Webb salespeople let prospects know with e-mails the next day.[157] California joined the federal government in offering buyers of new homes in that state a state tax credit of $10,000.[158] Del Webb normally did not call attention to the absence of state income taxes in some states where it had communities, but it departed from that practice when it reminded potential buyers that Florida had no state income tax, a situation that, combined with the $8,000 credit for first-time home buyers and Webb's willingness to temporarily absorb closing costs, made spring 2009 an ideal time to buy.[159] However, the recovery was weak. When in fall 2009 Congress extended the credit for first-time home buyers and added a $6,500 tax credit for existing home owners, The Villages jumped on the publicity bandwagon, emailing its own list of sales prospects.[160] This last program likely did the most to help age-restricted, active adult communities recover from the housing crisis.

Promoting the Active Adult Lifestyle during the Housing Crisis

While financial incentives and price cutting took precedence over promoting the active adult lifestyle when the housing crisis hit, developers did not forget it. They continued to construct elaborate clubhouses and other recreational amenities. The Villages, Florida, ran a full-page ad in *AARP: The Magazine* in fall 2007 with the slogan "Live a millionaire's lifestyle on your retirement budget . . . and play golf FREE for the rest of your life!"[161]

Meanwhile, Del Webb was inviting sales prospects for its active adult community in Tennessee to take a Dusty Boot Tour, hard hats provided, to view the progress on its $15 million clubhouse. The building included a lap pool, fitness center, indoor jogging track, ballroom, craft room, and lounge areas. Outside was a "resort-style pool and spa" and courts for tennis, bocce, pickle ball, and basketball. Meandering through the community would be extensive walking trails, and visiting grandchildren would have a tot lot.[162] At the same time, Sun City Mesquite in Nevada was celebrating the grand opening of its community recreation center with a professional golfer doing a putting clinic on an "18-hole Putting Course," plus other events.[163] On the East Coast that month,

Celebrate by Del Webb in Virginia featured demonstrations by legendary golfers Jack Nicklaus and Arnold Palmer.[164] The previous month, Sun City Anthem at Merrill Ranch in Florence, Arizona, had staged a health and wellness fair to bring in prospective buyers.

It was easier for these communities to promote the active adult lifestyle through recreational amenities than it was through cultural activities. However, where possible, active adult communities have sought to keep up with the trend toward lifelong learning and adult education for retirees. Going back to the nineteenth century, it was fairly common for women in new communities to form cultural study groups. In the twentieth century, many school districts offered adult education programs. Credit for singling out retirees for educational opportunities goes to the New School for Social Research, which began a formal Learning in Retirement program in 1962. Since then, hundreds of colleges and universities have developed various kinds of peer education programs for retirees. Reasons for the growth in popularity of these programs have been the growing acceptance of the idea that continuing to learn can help stem cognitive decline, and lifelong learning can ease the adjustment to ending work and provide volunteer opportunities.[165]

The major problem for retirement communities is that many are some distance from colleges or universities that have such programs. Nevertheless, if those opportunities are available, retirement communities will seize them. An example is Arizona State University's Lifelong Learning at Sun City Anthem in Florence, Arizona. As a sales promotion, Del Webb kicked off a preview of the fall semester 2008 course offerings with a College Football BBQ.[166] Previously, the Del Webb community of Riverwood near Jacksonville, Florida, staged a live art auction in conjunction with a local art gallery.[167] College towns are serious competitors of active adult communities for migrating retirees, due in part to the availability of cultural programming.

Given the relative isolation of some of these communities, the performing arts and cultural organizations have had problems. Century Village, located near numerous other condo communities in West Palm Beach, added frequent and affordable theatrical productions to its active adult lifestyle, but most communities lacked performing arts theaters, let alone the ability to book shows. The art museum in the Sun City and Sun City West area has closed. On the other hand, the Sun Cities Area Historical Society was busy celebrating the fiftieth anniversary of Sun City, Arizona, in 2010. Plans included renewed promotion of the first model home as a museum, publication of a commemorative booklet, *Reshaping Retirement in America*, and special programs throughout the year.[168]

Still another concern arising from the relative isolation of many active adult communities is the availability of nearby commercial facilities. Again, The Villages' success with its mini-downtowns of restaurants, boutique shops, and entertainment venues may have contributed to the trend among other developers of emphasizing nearby commercial facilities where they are available. Del Webb's two developments closest to The Villages, La Cresta and Stone Creek, both let prospective buyers know of nearby national retail outlets that were opening in spring 2008.[169] About that time, Del Webb Charleston was putting on a business fair at which more than thirty local businesses would distribute coupons, samples, and advice to sales prospects at the community's Welcome Center.[170] In Georgia, Sun City Peachtree staged a breakfast for sales prospects that featured information on a nearby mall.[171] The use of events to attract potential buyers went back to the 1960s at the original Sun City. What was new was the use of such themes as nearby commercial and cultural facilities.

With more developers of active adult communities in the twenty-first century, there is also more imitating of each other's advertising gimmicks. For example, ads depicting the constant round of activities of a hypothetical, and hyperactive, couple go back to Sun City, Arizona, in the 1960s, but some of the activities are different now. In January 2008, it was The Villages running such an ad in *The Villages Magazine*.[172] Many of the activities listed, such as tennis and auditioning for a play, were fairly typical of the 1960s. On the other hand, a Spanish class at The Villages Lifelong Learning College and a workout session at the wellness center were more representative of the twenty-first century. Andrew Blechman commented that it seemed like every time he turned around while researching The Villages, someone, a radio announcer or a tour guide, was using the greeting "It's a beautiful day in The Villages." Perhaps the most annoying example of one developer copying the marketing ploys of another was when the standard greeting on a Del Webb toll-free number was "It's a beautiful day at the Del Webb communities," no matter that a major snowstorm was hitting the Chicago-area ones on that particular day.[173]

Another way Del Webb may have been influenced by the success of The Villages was the company's greater sensitivity to snowbirds' concerns about how they would be accepted in their new, active adult communities. Promoters of The Villages like to bill it as "Florida's Friendliest Hometown." An ad in *The Villages Magazine* used the phrase and featured photographs of residents along with quotes about how they influenced others from back home to join them and even got reacquainted with people they had known there.[174]

Webb put together a seventy-six-question survey designed to let people find out if they were suited to an active adult community. The survey had people rate their feelings about moving to a new community and living in an age-restricted environment (Sample question: "It's too easy for my kids to ask us to baby sit") and asked respondents if they "worry about social cliques and snobbery in a new community." Webb even included a second copy so each spouse could fill it out individually. Respondents returned the survey to the Webb sales office and then received results in the mail. The survey had no questions that specifically targeted singles nor to try to find out who may be tax shopping among the states, but it did leave plenty of room for respondents to bring up those and other issues in addition to the specific survey questions.[175] It appeared to be a fairly sophisticated device that a salesperson could use to target good prospects and allay some anxieties that potential buyers may have had. While The Villages may have a lock on the phrase "Florida's Friendliest Hometown," Del Webb in fall 2008 was advertising its "Feel at Home" vacation getaways in Sun City Festival and Sun City Anthem, Arizona, for $39 per night.[176]

Social Trends in Twenty-First-Century Active Adult Communities

The desire to keep children out was the main reason for requiring that at least one resident of each unit be "age 55 or better." Looking at Sun City Center, Florida, journalist Frances FitzGerald in the 1980s mentioned residents who said that "they 'missed seeing children around,' which they meant quite literally. They wanted to see them, but from a distance. Few wanted them around all the time."[177] Twenty-some years later, a fifty-six-year-old woman who worked a computer job from her home explained that she decided to move into a Del Webb community in the Chicago area because she wanted a quieter neighborhood, one "without someone bouncing a basketball next door or racing down the street on an electric skateboard or a motorcycle."[178] In 2008, a grandmother from Sun City Texas (formerly called Sun City Georgetown) reported that a common saying in that age-restricted community with respect to visiting grandchildren was "We're glad to see the headlights, and the taillights are wonderful, too."[179] A critic of these age-restricted communities and a young father, Andrew Blechman, may find it unnatural that in The Villages to be sure visiting grandchildren do not become permanent residents, those grandchildren are "given visitors' passes that time out like visas";[180] but that certainly does not bother the growing number of residents of these age-restricted communities.

Besides the elderly wanting to maintain their independence, the developers accurately sensed a desire for homogeneity among their buyers. Their communities have been called "'lifestyle enclaves' where people get their identity from shared or similar leisure and consumption." By segregating themselves, the elderly insulated themselves against a society that devalued old age.[181] A buyer of a home in a Del Webb community in Elgin, Illinois, in 2005 explained, "'We'll be living among our peers, people who speak the same language and listen to our stories. . . . Del Webb appeals to friendlier people who want to be with other people.'"[182] Accompanying this preference for social homogeneity was a continuing tendency toward conservative politics but not without some major exceptions.

Campaign 2008 in Century Villages and The Villages

While most active adult communities tend to vote Republican and hold fairly conservative political views, there is also substantial support for Democrats. For example, the Century Village communities in southeast Florida tend to draw residents from fairly liberal northeastern states, with Interstate 95 being the connecting link. On the other hand, The Villages in central Florida is closer to Interstate 75, providing a migratory link to the more conservative Midwest. When Hillary Clinton campaigned for universal health care in Boca Raton's Century Village in September 2007, she was greeted with cheers.[183]

Not just party affiliation but age identification played a role during the 2008 campaign. A dramatic example was the Democratic primary in Florida. Elderly voters in Century Village and other age-restricted communities supported Hillary Clinton over the more youthful Barack Obama by overwhelming margins. In Century Village, Pembroke Pines, the vote was 3,657 for Clinton to 591 for Obama. At Century Village, Deerfield Beach, it was 1,393 for Clinton, 225 for Obama; and at Century

Village west of Boca Raton, the vote was 1,526 for Clinton, 134 for Obama. The president of the last community's Democratic Club called the primary results "a clash of generations." He also saw a desire "to restore the Clinton '90s" or "to recapture the past." Clinton's ten-to-one victory in retiree condo communities north of Miami helped her win Florida, but Florida's early primary date caused controversy and resulted in no delegates.[184]

On the other hand, The Villages has a history of strong support for Republicans. Not only was the community's developer, Gary Morse, a big contributor to the Florida Republican Party, but he also contributed early on to the gubernatorial campaign of Jeb Bush and the presidential campaign of Jeb's brother, George W. Bush. In fact, Jeb Bush was the first major politician to realize that Sumter County, where most of The Villages is located, was "a treasure trove of votes . . . and campaign cash." That county has twice as many Republicans as Democrats and a very high voter turnout as well. In 2004, a grateful George W. Bush became the first president to visit The Villages. Since then, that active adult community has been a campaign stop for a series of other leading politicians. In 2007, both Mitt Romney and Fred Thompson, then leading contenders for the Republican nomination, kicked off their Florida primary campaigns in The Villages.[185]

The Villages continued to play a role during the final phase of the 2008 presidential campaign. Republican vice presidential candidate Sarah Palin made her first Florida appearance in The Villages. George W. Bush had attracted a crowd of 20,000 during his campaign stop at The Villages in 2004, but Sarah Palin did even better, drawing some 25,000 to 30,000 people, with the Republican Party claiming the crowd was more than twice that size.[186]

The Obama campaign did not ignore The Villages, either. It sent in Caroline Kennedy, who drew more than a thousand people for her speech connecting Obama with her father's ability to inspire. An African American woman in the crowd, Adelaide Staton, remembered being denied service by a South Carolina restaurant in the 1960s and other examples of discrimination; she saw former President Kennedy as a force for change and Obama as carrying on his legacy.[187]

Florida has become an important state in presidential elections. It has also become a state where retirees have more than the usual political clout. In 2000, Florida had 5 percent more people over the age of sixty-four than the nation as a whole. That meant that it had a higher percentage of people dependent on Social Security and investment income than did the average state. It also meant less commitment to education and more commitment to law enforcement on the part of state and local governments.[188] On the other hand, urban historian Jon Teaford has called attention to nearly a hundred towns in Massachusetts that have welcomed smaller, age-restricted developments because they add to the tax base but do not burden the school system with additional students.[189] As for communities that are against children as residents, Teaford pointed out that some caught up in the desire to preserve open space with large-lot zoning and other environmental rules have as their goal simply excluding as many people in general as possible.[190] Probably more than any other state, Florida has demonstrated the impact of the elderly on politics.

Boomers and Active Adult, Age-Restricted Communities

Developers are starting to specifically target the baby boomer generation, which means swelling numbers in the "age 55 or better" category. In summer 2008, Del Webb at Somersett near Reno, Nevada, staged a sales event or party with a 1950s theme. Included was 1950s-style band music, a classic car show, and "diner-style refreshments."[191] Several months later, Sun Cities of Arizona were inviting sales prospects to a boomer event, Festival of the Wise, in Scottsdale. It featured music from the Beatles and other musicians from the 1960s and 1970s, a "Boomer women's fashion show," and a "muscle car rally."[192]

Meanwhile, gerontologists were noting that not only were people living longer, but the elderly were less plagued with disabilities.[193] That may be why The Villages built some two-story homes, and Del Webb's Fireside at Desert Ridge in north Phoenix was following suit.[194] Boomers were showing some resistance to universal design features to help people with mobility problems, such as wider hallways and showers without steps. However, a speaker at the recent National Association of Home Builders 50+ Housing Symposium advised other industry professionals not to "mention aging in place." Instead, he suggested telling sales prospects those features will "make life easier when their parents visit." This speaker contended that Boomers did not like being called seniors, active adults, or "fifty-five and better." His recommendation was to simply say that a development was "age-qualified," not "age-restricted." He also suggested emphasizing the lifestyle. When asked at what age they would "finally consider themselves old," the typical response was eighty-five. Actuaries predict many of them will die two years before that. Perhaps that is why the housing expert advised, "We're selling an *ageless* lifestyle."[195]

While some people think boomers will resist moving halfway across the country to an age-restricted, active adult community, the trend actually shows growing acceptance of this lifestyle. When the National Association of Home Builders staged its first conference on fifty-plus housing shortly after the beginning of the twenty-first century, only around thirty developers came.

Six years later, the conference drew eight hundred industry professionals. Del Webb, the leading builder of these communities, is regarded as the best researcher of trends in these communities. The company predicts 25 percent will want age-restricted housing. Other estimates range from 15 to 70 percent. Given the growing number of boomers, however, 15 percent still translates into 12 million boomers, or 4 percent of all Americans.[196] They should be able to afford a nice home in an amenity-rich community since many are either delaying their retirement or getting other jobs after officially retiring.[197] Job considerations, not just family ones, may be why some boomers are choosing to move into active adult communities closer to home. In 1995, a little over 20 percent of age-restricted communities were being built outside the Sunbelt. In 2005, 60 percent of those communities were in the north.[198] However, the largest ones still tended to be in Sunbelt states. While the housing crisis has affected the Sunbelt especially hard, active adult, age-restricted communities are still expanding.

In summary, the trend showing continual expansion and growing acceptance of active adult, age-restricted communities is probably the strongest answer to the critics of these developments. To understand why, it is important to look at the criticisms through the perspectives of the various critics and then through the perspectives of those who choose to live in active adult, age-restricted communities. Critics argue that age segregation is bad because the younger generations need the volunteer efforts and contributions of the elderly, such as in foster grandparent programs, and the elderly benefit from interaction with nearby children, grandchildren, and a wide range of people of different ages. However, residents of age-restricted communities may prefer not being so readily available for babysitting, having to pay extra taxes to support schools, and putting up with occasionally demeaning attitudes toward old people. A large, age-restricted community can give them political clout. As for the ephemeral nature of many of the activities in active adult communities, is it the influence of the work ethic carried over into retirement that one's retirement activities should be meaningful and positively self-defining? The advertising associated with these communities has given the elderly a positive image with which to identify.

With respect to the "new urbanism" advocates, perhaps their most significant criticism is the relative isolation of many of these communities, which may mean that some are rather light on access to cultural activities and fairly far from major commercial areas as well. On the other hand, "new urbanism" advocates should look more carefully at the widespread use of golf cart transportation within many of the active adult communities plus the fact that the older, larger communities do tend to attract a variety of elder care facilities and provide support groups as their residents age. Active adult, age-restricted communities have made major contributions toward such planning trends as golf course communities, gated communities, and common-interest communities rich with shared amenities.

International critics' reactions do a lot to underscore American values and the breadth of the middle class in the United States. These communities are largely unique to the United States because it has a substantial elderly middle class that can afford a "resort-like" lifestyle as long as the cost of the amenities is shared among hundreds, sometimes thousands, of households; and many Americans are willing to do that kind of sharing of amenities. Also, the United States was the birthplace of Disneyland; if some aspects, such as the mini-downtowns at The Villages with music being piped out of speakers attached to lamp posts is rather fake, for many in the United States it is also welcome entertainment. A migratory lifestyle is more welcome as well. These communities have been hit hard by the housing crisis that began in 2006, but they have continued to expand, if more slowly. The demographics of the boomer generation are with their future.

Conclusion

The Significance of Active Adult, Age-Restricted Communities

"The making of a new town, the search for a new utopia, is a great American tradition," observe Douglas Frantz and Catherine Collins at the start of their book on Celebration, the Disney Corporation's interpretation of the "new urbanism" near Orlando, Florida.[1] While Disney's planners designed Celebration to be a pedestrian-friendly, child-friendly place stressing health and wellness with an elaborate fitness center and an innovative public school, it did attract some retirees. However, it was never an age-restricted, active adult community. This study has focused specifically on the development and evolution of age-restricted, active adult communities, not naturally occurring retirement communities. It has also focused on communities of at least five hundred units, not individually age-restricted buildings or much smaller communities. Furthermore, except for noting the contributions of amenity-rich trailer courts for retirees to the concept of the active adult community, this study has not focused on trailer courts, RV parks, or manufactured home communities, all of which continue to be tremendously popular with retirees.

In analyzing the significance of age-restricted, active adult communities, this history has looked at both the plans of the developers and how their buyers influenced and modified those plans. The starting point was tracing the evolution of "wintering" in the south and noting how age-restricted, active adult communities emerged from that trend. In marketing their creations, retirement-community developers promoted the image of the elderly person as the "active adult" who had some income, in contrast to the impoverished and physically dependent image that most Americans around 1960 had of the elderly.[2] Early developers of active adult, age-restricted communities were not just selling homes. They were also selling a lifestyle or marketing a certain script. To some extent, the buyers of that lifestyle or script created a kind of subculture. At times the subculture took the developers by surprise. The early developers were creative in a city planning sense and deserve more recognition for their innovations, some of which have not been limited to retirement communities. Developers in general, along with the developers of retirement communities, kept track of their competition, kept track of changing trends, and evolved over time, thus blurring their early differences. Finally, as these communities continue to expand a half-century after the first one appeared, certain aspects of their story have come full circle.

First of all, these communities were pioneer "lifestyle" communities and perhaps the most successful among them as well. They are significant in promoting the active adult image for middle-class retirees, for the way their developers engaged in social engineering, and the way in which residents responded by developing their own subculture. Amenity-rich trailer courts restricted to retirees provided an important precedent for active adult communities. However, once the active adult, age-restricted communities appeared, this history has not focused on the trailer courts, RV parks, and manufactured home communities; still, they all continued to attract retirees who did not want to spend a lot of money on retirement homes, either because they did not have it or because they only expected to use it for several months out of the year. Del Webb, Ross Cortese, and their imitators generally built for the middle-class retiree, not the very wealthy one or the one on a small income. Furthermore, while a significant number of their buyers did follow the snowbird practice of becoming seasonal residents, the majority of the residents in the Sun Cities, Leisure Worlds, and The Villages were permanent ones. That contrasted with the trailer courts, which came close to being ghost towns when summer arrived in the Sunbelt.

Trailer parks have remained popular in the traditional retirement destinations. In the mid-1980s, trailer courts were attracting more migrating retirees than the Leisure Worlds and Sun Cities.[3] By 2000, half of the 1.2 million residents of trailer courts were senior citizens.[4] By the twenty-first century, the technology had evolved so that in addition to the traditional trailer court, the elderly were also flocking to RV parks and manufactured home communities. All of these were exceptionally popular in Florida. In fact, they probably had a lot to do with Florida having a million "snowbirds" by 2000. Historian Gary R. Mormino even claimed that thousands of "snowbirds" voted in both New York *and* Florida in 2000.[5]

Trying to sort out permanent residents from snowbirds can be difficult because many retain emotional ties and allegiances to their home states but transfer their legal residence to Florida or another low-tax state. For someone from a state where it seems like the winters are seven months long, living six months and one day in a state like Florida is not a hardship. The amount of the tax incentive to do this varies by the individual and the home state, but it would not be unusual for a middle-class couple from a state like Minnesota to save more than $10,000 per year in state income taxes by transferring their legal residence to a low-tax state like Texas or Florida. Jana and Brad Ristamaki, retired Minnesotans who bought a second home in Sun City, Texas, did calculate a savings of more than $10,000 but then decided not to change their legal residence to Texas because of their desire to make frequent trips back to Minnesota to see their grandchildren and Jana's mother, plus other travel.[6]

With respect to taxes, one should take into account whether states have estate taxes and how high sales taxes and property taxes are in different states. A 2006 study found that New York had the second highest tax burden and Florida was twelfth from the bottom. The tax burdens of Texas, Nevada, and Virginia were even less than those in Florida.[7] Iowa officials became so concerned about retirees fleeing to low-tax states that they decided in 2006 "to phase out taxes on Social Security benefits and eliminate state income taxes for singles age 65 and older making $24,000 or less and couples making $32,000."[8]

While one needs to consider the relative cost of housing, trailer courts and manufactured home communities are quite affordable in most locations. Their prevalence in Florida along with Florida's long history as a retirement destination has done a lot to keep Florida the leading mecca for retirees. While there is some evidence that retirees are looking at other Sunbelt states and retirement communities have sprung up in states like Illinois and Massachusetts, Florida in the 1990s attracted three times more retirees than Arizona, which had risen to the second most popular retirement destination.[9]

The early developers did not fully anticipate the degree to which some of their buyers, as they aged, would choose to remain in "active adult" communities. As a result, early developers did not anticipate the degree to which their communities would attract a variety of nursing homes, independent and assisted living complexes, continuing care institutions, and other special services for the elderly such as home health care agencies and Meals on Wheels. In fact, one reason developers may have emphasized the "active adult" image at the beginning was that they did not want the communities to be seen as an alternative to nursing homes. While Ben Schleifer deliberately did want to present an alternative to a nursing home and was very influential in building the first age-restricted community, at Youngtown, Arizona, he did not try to promote the amenity-rich "active adult" image and even stayed away from having someone function as an activities director because he thought that might appear to be too much regimentation. Schleifer had the oldest minimum age of any of these communities when he started Youngtown in 1954. It was sixty-five, soon to be lowered.

Residents of these communities had mixed attitudes toward the inclusion of such facilities as assisted living. However, even if local residents succeeded in blocking efforts to add these facilities later and if such facilities did not make it within the walls of the community, they sprang up right outside. The expression "Build it and they will come" rings true when a developer builds a large retirement community and the providers of special facilities for the elderly, with the passage of time, are drawn to that community like it is a magnet. The Villages, Florida, by advertising its continuing care facility in the magazine it sends to prospective residents, may be including a healthy dose of reality along with its emphasis on "free golf." In their history of Sun City's first twenty-five years, residents Jane Freeman and Glenn Sanberg mention the arrival of that community's first nursing home in 1965, list a number of other elder care facilities in or near the community, and note efforts to establish a hospice in 1978.[10] In his history of the first twenty-five years of Sun City West, Edson Allen devotes an entire chapter to "Human Services" and another to "Assisted Living and Extended Care."[11] A significant number of residents of these communities as they aged found the number and variety of these facilities, along with the support networks that they developed among their peers, to be invaluable.

Nevertheless, the "active adult" image the developers promoted persists since many prefer not to be reminded of the realities of aging. These communities do differ as to how the residents of these facilities are integrated into the social fabric. Granted, elder care facilities were somewhat unanticipated by the developers and the retirees themselves who typically assumed that when they ceased to be "active adults," they would move back to their state of origin to be closer to children or other relatives. While that scenario was the case for a lot of residents, many others chose to remain as they aged. The elder care institutions that those who remained supported gave these communities a dimension beyond that of their well-publicized "active adult" image.

These communities seem to have a genuine appeal from the perspective of social interaction. There is a continuing subculture of friendliness among the residents. Some of that subculture is based on fostering connections with other migrants from their states of origin and promoting former-state identity. Telephone directories that index people by their former states and the ongoing popularity of state clubs, even in the older communities, reflect that element. America was and still is a country of migrants, and these active adult communities definitely reflect that characteristic. Developers knew that once migrants arrived from a particular locality, they could act like a magnet to attract others from that place. In a sense, the residents and the developers joined together in emphasizing state identity or community. It became an ongoing part of their subculture, along with the "casserole brigade" joke about the gender imbalance and a tendency toward conservative politics, with some major exceptions. Del Webb and Ross Cortese definitely created a new kind of social community.

A large part of the appeal of the active adult, age-restricted communities was their homogeneity. They bar underage children as permanent residents and require that at least one resident of each housing unit be "age 55 or better," a significant experiment in social engineering; but if the similarities in house prices in the smaller communities and within neighborhoods in the larger communities is any indication, residents can expect to be surrounded by neighbors of their own social class, not just their own age group. Tourism historian Dona Brown has documented how tourists seek out resorts that cater to people like themselves. In her view, today's tourists are even more concerned with who their counterparts will be at a vacation destination than were the nineteenth-century patrons of the great resort hotels. Concerns today go beyond social class to "factors like age, profession, and 'lifestyle.'" Some vacationers buy property in certain tourist spots and eventually make those properties their retirement homes.[12] When Del Webb opened Sun City, the community was fairly isolated. One of his ways of attracting potential buyers was to feature local tourist attractions in his sales brochures. In 2008, Robson, which has some active adult communities in relatively isolated locations, featured such tourist attractions as a western theme park and Old Tucson Studios in its sales brochure.[13]

To emphasize the fine gradations in housing prices and amenities, four active adult communities on a recent National Association of Home Builders tour in the Phoenix area ranged from "affordable" Sundance, projected to have 1,000 homes at build-out, to the unusually posh Del Webb community of Corte Bella. A handout stated that the average Sundance resident had an income of $70,000. That community has no gates. Homes are relatively small, as were the recreation center and the two outdoor pools.[14] Two other active adult communities on this tour were progressively fancier. The fanciest was the Del Webb development of Corte Bella, which is gated, has more luxurious homes, and features higher-quality amenities. Within The Villages, house prices in June 2009 ranged from $65,000 for a manufactured home in the oldest neighborhood to more than $1 million in a neighborhood of premier homes; residents live in small neighborhoods or "villages" within which the prices and sizes of the homes are quite uniform. Planning ideas such as "new towns" and "new urbanism" may promote heterogeneity in housing within communities, but successful developers of active adult communities responded to a rather extreme desire for homogeneity on the part of their buyers. These are communities characterized by luxurious amenities made affordable because their ownership and use is shared among the residents. With so much shared public space, the homogeneity of the residents takes on added importance.

Besides creating a new kind of socially innovative community, the early developers deserve a lot more recognition than they have received for some of their physical planning innovations. While Del Webb was not the first to construct a golf course winding through a community to increase the number of lots backing onto it, he was probably the first to utilize that concept in a community of modestly priced homes. It was a concept that became increasingly popular in the decades that followed. When some residents complained that the courses were designed more to sell as many abutting lots as possible than to provide a quality golfing experience, the firm built a course capable of hosting national tournaments at Sun City West along with additional real estate–oriented courses.

Webb's initial leading competitor, Ross Cortese, pioneered the concept of the modern, walled, and guard-gated development, Rossmoor, in the Los Angeles area. A number of scholars attribute the guard-gated community to Cortese's Leisure Worlds, but they were built after Rossmoor. Like the golf course community, the guard-gated community became quite a trend in subsequent decades, especially in the Sunbelt. Both Cortese and Webb picked up on the idea of amenity-rich communities from the earlier retiree trailer parks in Florida; but again, the active adult community developers did a lot to popularize the concept of the common-interest development, in which the residents own the amenities in common and control access to them through a homeowners association. All of these innovations, while initially associated with retirement communities, came to be applied to many intergenerational communities as well. Webb and Cortese deserve much credit for their innovations, their willingness to take risks, and above all, their extensive advertising campaigns to promote new kinds of developments that historian Jon Teaford has termed "lifestyle communities."[15]

Developers and planners cannot predict everything for certain, as the developers of these communities were well aware. Early plans for Sun City Center, Florida, had school locations designated, which indicated that Del Webb was trying to hedge his bets in case an age-restricted community did not sell well enough to reach build-out. In this case, buyers supported the age-restricted concept, and the school sites disappeared from subsequent plans. However, developers in the twenty-first century still worry about the market for age-restricted communities. Hence, in some locations, including Sun City Festival, the developer will plan the bulk of the community to be age-restricted and designate a portion initially to be intergenerational. That leaves the developer with an "out" should the age-restricted market in the location dry up.

Still another approach, given the multiple divisions of Webb's parent company, Pulte Homes, was to develop a community assigning different sections to its different brands. An example is Ave Maria, Florida, where Pulte is dividing its land among three of its brands—Del Webb, which is age-restricted; DiVosta, which is age-targeted but not age-restricted; and Pulte Homes traditional, which is intergenerational.[16] Furthermore, in the case of both Ave Maria and Sun City Festival, Pulte purchased several thousand acres from corporations that own much more in those locations. Pulte's developments will fit into much larger master plans for those communities. Developers plan as best they can for their target markets, but they do not always get it exactly right.

And completely unanticipated things happened. Both the flagship communities of Webb and Cortese experienced situations neither developer anticipated from the start. What drove the physical layout of Leisure World Laguna Hills more than anything was the determination and clout of El Toro Marine Naval Air Station to protect its flight path through the center of that community. Hence, the military insisted on no housing under that flight path. It would be interesting to know if Ross Cortese had originally considered designing his twenty-seven-hole golf course to wind through the community. However, to please the Marines, that golf course was compacted into the middle, under the flight path, along with stables, bridle paths, a plant nursery, and other nonhousing aspects of the community. What Cortese did not anticipate when he went to court to get the Marine Corps to reimburse him for lost development opportunities was that the base would eventually close. At that point, Cortese had sold his development rights and could not do much about it. As for the residents of Leisure World Laguna Hills, they decided that they liked the open space and campaigned to keep it that way. Had the air base closed before Cortese arrived on the scene, the layout of Leisure World Laguna Hills, or Laguna Woods as it is known today, would probably have been very different.

Another plan that made sense in the 1960s but not more than forty years later was the Webb firm's decision to locate agricultural or garden plots adjacent to its cemetery for interested residents to use. With the recent decision to turn those agricultural plots into housing, the fact that the only access road to them is through the cemetery is unfortunate. Planning means projecting into the future, but no developer has a perfect crystal ball.

It may be the lack of a crystal ball or just changing times, but some things have tended to come full circle by the twenty-first century. Around 1971, Del Webb sold Sun City Center, Florida, and Sun City, California, to other developers. Three decades later, WCI was continuing to build in Sun City Center, and other developers were expanding Sun City, California. As for the Del Webb brand of Pulte Homes, it had returned to both areas to develop nearby communities. Solera Diamond Valley was Webb's age-restricted community in Hemet, California, about fifteen miles from Sun City, California. Wiregrass by Del Webb in the Tampa and Sun City Center vicinity, planned for about 2,300 homes, was tentatively scheduled for a fall 2008 opening.[17] However, Pulte never built any homes at Wiregrass. In December 2009, it sold its eight hundred acres there at a loss to another developer while opening another community in the Tampa Bay area, Del Webb Southshore Falls, which did have both single-family and town homes for sale in 2010.

Given the penchant for developers to keep an eye on their competitors, it is not surprising that with the passage of time, their distinctive approaches to building retirement communities would blur. Del Webb for decades avoided doing guard-gated communities or multistory condos, both characteristic of most of the Leisure World communities. However, in the twenty-first century, the Webb brand of Pulte was using guarded gates at Corte Bella near Sun City West. Near Jacksonville, its Sweetwater development included condominiums in four-story buildings with elevators, although these are still not as tall as some high-rises at several east-coast Leisure Worlds.

Meanwhile, Kenneth Colen, son of Florida high-rise condominium developer Sidney Colen, was marketing single-family homes in Ocala, Florida, similar to those at Sun City Grand. In 1965, Sidney Colen was quoted as saying, "Retirement isn't isolation or vegetation. I think a cross-section community is much better."[18] In 2007, an ad for Colen's On Top of the World Communities in Ocala, Florida, touted "55+ Active Adult Communities."[19] Colen was borrowing from the original Leisure World concept as well. The Indigo East neighborhood at On Top of the World in Ocala was gated.[20] Directly next to Colen's 2007 ad in the *AARP Bulletin* was a Del Webb ad featuring its Florida communities, including Stone Creek at Ocala. Webb had never been really strong in the Florida market but was trying to catch up. On Top of the World was an 11,088-acre community planned to eventually have 32,400 homes. Pulte purchased property within the Colen development for its Del Webb community of Stone Creek.[21] And with The Villages setting the pace in sales at the turn of the twenty-first century, some of its innovations, such as large and two-story homes, are being tried by Webb.

Other things never seem to completely go away. The interstate land scam situation has been much alleviated since the 1960s, thanks to significant legislation at both the federal and state levels. However, in 2007, a company called Florida Top Land was selling undeveloped land in Texas to buyers who were paying $15,000 to $20,000 for twenty-acre parcels. Florida Top Land was telling potential investors that Home Depot would be building an outlet in the nearby town of Dell City. Home

Depot denied the story. Furthermore, the land being sold had problems with drinking water and spotty electrical service. The nearest gas station was a hundred miles away. Yet the president of Florida Top Land insisted that in twenty years, people would "be building all over" that desert land.[22] Buyers still need to be vigilant.

In assessing the greatness of some of the leading individuals who were responsible for these communities, Del Webb stands out. He was a self-made success, a prominent sportsman as co-owner of the New York Yankees, and a visionary who encouraged his staff to do innovative, cutting-edge development. Today, not only does Pulte continue to use the Del Webb brand name, but occasional advertising materials feature Webb's photograph and a brief biography. However, in some ways, Del Webb comes up short. Webb got his start in community building with the construction of the Japanese relocation camp at Poston, south of Parker, Arizona. Later, he built the first casino on the Las Vegas Strip, but his client was the mobster Bugsy Siegel. Webb also got his firm involved for a time in the ownership of Nevada casinos. As for the very creative Ross Cortese, he was something of a recluse who lacked the financial resources of Del Webb. Both Sun City and The Villages have erected statues of their founders. In the case of The Villages, founder Harold Schwartz is remembered for his friendliness and relatively modest lifestyle in contrast to his son, Gary Morse, who, while choosing to live in The Villages, remains a very private person. H. Irwin Levy also deserves credit for adding to the "active adult" concept with frequent and affordable stage entertainment in his Century Village gated condo communities. These men deserve more attention than they have received as influential innovators in social and physical planning.

While not as significant as Webb and Cortese or even Harold Schwartz and H. Irwin Levy, two elderly widows who were intrigued with the idea of age-restricted communities and sold their ranchlands for them deserve special recognition. Both were personally interested in the developments that followed. Frances Greer donated her ranch house to the first age-restricted community, Youngtown, Arizona, to be used as a community center. She then decided to remain in Youngtown and built another home overlooking the Agua Fria riverbed. Likewise, Nellie Gail Moulton, after selling ranchland for Leisure World Laguna Hills, moved into one of Cortese's subsequent housing units. Furthermore, even though she was in her eighties, she got involved in that community's art association, joining other members as they packed bag lunches, then driving off to some scenic spot to spend the day painting outdoors. Both of these women chose to personally experience their ranchland transformed into age-restricted communities. As elderly widows, they literally got caught up in their buyers' visions.

While the housing crisis that began in 2006 may slow the growth of age-restricted, active adult communities, predictions are that they will continue to grow, although probably not as fast as formerly. The Villages, Florida, has 26,000 acres, enough for a projected population of 105,000, even if it does not reach that size by the predicted 2012. The ranks of retiring baby boomers are swelling. Writer Andrew Blechman has estimated that by 2012, 12 million Americans will live in active adult, age-restricted communities.[23]

To summarize the significance of age-restricted, active adult communities, they have changed the physical and social landscape of the United States. They deserve much more credit than they have received for such planning innovations as golf courses winding throughout communities, gated communities, and amenity-rich communities with homeowner associations maintaining extensive recreational facilities and clubhouses and giving the community's residents exclusive access to them. These are innovations that age-restricted communities have helped to popularize and that subsequently have been fairly extensively applied to intergenerational communities. However, probably the Sun Cities and Leisure Worlds are best remembered for their impact on the social landscape. When Youngtown opened in 1954 and Sun City in 1960, there were no laws that gave legal force to those communities' advertised age restrictions. That changed first at the local and state levels, then in 1988 at the federal level. Beyond the legal situation, the greatest significance of these communities was to change the stereotype of the elderly from impoverished adults in physical decline to an image of "active adults" who can afford a resort type of lifestyle. In the popular imagination, Grandma and Grandpa exchanged their rocking chairs for golf carts.

Notes

Preface

1. Therese Smith, national customer communications manager, Del Webb, to the author, received 12 January 2009.

Introduction: Ignoring the Obvious

1. Maureen West and Catherine Reagor, "Redefining Retirement," *Arizona Republic*, 17 March 2002, 1. Jerry Svendsen, public relations staff for Del Webb at Sun City, Arizona, from 1961 to 1982, gave me this clipping with his comments written in the margins. He further amplified these comments in an e-mail on 10 November 2009.

2. Among the authors who have produced books on the "new towns" and noted their failure to achieve much of a social class mix are Forsyth in *Reforming Suburbia* (4, 203–204) and Bloom in *Suburban Alchemy* (158–62).

3. Jon Teaford, "Reader's Questionnaire—Academic Manuscript," submitted to the University Press of Florida at the request of the press, 6 February 2009.

4. Steiner, *Politics of New Town Planning*, 221–22.

5. Forsyth, *Reforming Suburbia*, 19, 205–06. The "new towns" that included gated neighborhoods by the 1990s were Columbia, Maryland; The Woodlands, Texas; and Irvine Ranch, California.

6. Forsyth, *Reforming Suburbia*, 4–5.

7. Freeman and Sanberg, *Silver Anniversary Jubilee*, iii.

8. Boorstin, *Americans: The National Experience*, 49–112.

9. Teaford, *American Suburb*, 79.

10. Richard Pells, "Leaving Art out of History Is a Mistake," History News Network Web site, accessed 1 September 2007. The Pells item was based on a longer article in the *Chronicle of Higher Education*.

11. Suchman and Becker, *Developing Active Adult Retirement Communities*.

12. Hunt et al., *Retirement Communities*, 21–23.

13. Rothman, *Devil's Bargains*, 11.

14. Celebrate Virginia, e-mail to the author, 20 September 2007.

15. Robson Communities, "Preferred Guest Summer Getaway," ad received by the author on 1 July 2008.

Chapter 1. Democratizing Wintering in the South

1. Holland, "Interview with Thomas Edison," 35.

2. Abravanel with Miller, "Exploring the Area," 321.

3. Holland, "Interview with Thomas Edison," 35.

4. Colihan, "Spring Break."

5. Abravanel with Miller, "Exploring the Area," 321.

6. "Henry Flagler, Inventor of Modern Florida," 17.

7. Stephenson, *Visions of Eden*, 34–35.

8. Mormino, *Land of Sunshine*, 304.

9. Stronge, *Sunshine Economy*, 77.

10. Stephenson, *Visions of Eden*, 16.

11. Mormino, *Land of Sunshine*, 123.

12. Aron, *Working at Play*, 19.

13. Harwood, *Lives of Vizcaya*, xvii, 1–4.

14. Wing, "Live Outdoors in Florida," 38.

15. Glover, "Tampa's Beautiful 'Bay of Naples,'" 34–35.

16. Jakle, *The Tourist*, 58.

17. "Celebrities in Suniland," *Suniland* 3, no. 6 (March 1926): 30.

18. Aron, *Working at Play*, 49.

19. Martin and McCash, "From Millionaires to the Masses," 155–57.

20. Stronge, *Sunshine Economy*, 96.

21. "Biographical notes," George E. Merrick Papers, Historical Museum of Southern Florida, Miami (hereafter Merrick Papers).

22. Boorstin, *Americans: The Democratic Experience*, 278–80.

23. Stronge, *Sunshine Economy*, 100.

24. William B. Clark for N. W. Ayer and Son to George E. Merrick, 20 October 1926, box 1, fol. 1–3, Merrick Papers.

25. "Merrick's Realty Service," Fall 1936, box 1, fol. 1–14, Merrick Papers.

26. Eugene V. Lynch of George Merrick's Realty Service to Linder Advertising Agency, New York City, 3 February 1937; Emanuel Linder to Lynch, 23 January 1937; Linder to Lynch, 21 January 1937; Lynch to Linder, 12 January 1937; Lynch to Linder, 29 December 1936; Lynch to Linder, 4 November 1937, box 4, fol. 4–10, Merrick Papers.

27. F. Page Wilson to George Merrick, 30 April 1936, box 1, fol. 1–13; "Merrick's Realty Service," Fall 1936, pamphlet, box 1, fol. 1–14; Merrick Papers.

28. "George E. Merrick News Flashes," radio ad script, 26 June 1935, 2, box 5, fol. 5-4, Merrick Papers.

29. Historic Tampa/Hillsborough County Preservation Board, "The Cultural Resources of the Unincorporated Portions of Hillsborough County," in "Hillsborough County—Sun City (Pt. I)" folder, Hampton Dunn Collection, Special Collections, University of South Florida Library, Tampa (hereafter Dunn Collection).

30. John Bowker, Sun City Center historian, letter to the author, 28 October 2009.

31. Stronge, *Sunshine Economy*, 88–89.

32. Jakle, *The Tourist*, 58–59.

33. In Arsenault, *St. Petersburg and the Florida Dream*, 145–46.

34. Gjerde, "Middleness and the Middle West," 192–93.

35. Arsenault, *St. Petersburg and the Florida Dream*, 205.

36. D. Brown, *Inventing New England*, 174.

37. Ibid., 7.

38. Ibid., 176.

39. Arsenault, *St. Petersburg and the Florida Dream*, 186.

40. Stronge, *Sunshine Economy*, 89–91.

41. "For Those Who Never Want to Stop Learning," a brochure included in a packet of materials distributed at an opening seminar on Sun City Festival held at Sun City Grand, December 2005; in possession of the author.

42. Arsenault, *St. Petersburg and the Florida Dream*, 145–46; Aron, *Working at Play*, 114.

43. Irby, "Razing Gerontopolis," 3–4

44. Freedman, *Prime Time*, 33.

45. Margaret Warrington, "A Successful Experiment in Helping the Elderly," *Miami Herald*, 5 September 1965, 31, Florida Collection, Miami Dade Public Library, Miami (hereafter Florida Collection).

46. Retirement Research Welfare Association, Washington, D.C., list of retirement facilities in Florida, Florida Collection.

47. Jakle, *The Tourist*, 146.

48. Ibid., 160–62.

49. Arsenault, *St. Petersburg and the Florida Dream*, 189.

50. Jennifer Barrs, "Tin Can Tourists Trekked to Tampa by the Thousands," *Tampa Tribune*, 5 September 1994, in "Tin Can Tourists" folder, Dunn Collection.

51. Grismer, "How Much Does It Cost?" 46–47.

52. Leland Hawes, "Riverside Tourist Center Was Old-Timers' Hangout," *Tampa Tribune*, 26 October 1986, in "Hillsborough County—Tampa—Tampa Tourist Center" folder, Dunn Collection.

53. Mormino, *Land of Sunshine*, 264.

54. Hurley, *Diners, Bowling Alleys, and Trailer Parks*, 259–60.

55. S. Johnson, *Idle Haven*, 16–17.

56. Rockland, *Homes on Wheels*, 30.

57. Mormino, *Land of Sunshine*, 264.

58. Hurley, *Diners, Bowling Alleys, and Trailer Parks*, 259–61.

59. Ibid., 262–64.

60. Ibid., 262.

61. "Reminders from the Front Office" [1979], box 2, folder 11, Wilder's Park Collection, Special Collections, University of South Florida Library, St. Petersburg (hereafter Wilder's Park Collection).

62. James Schnur, archivist, University of South Florida, St. Petersburg, comments to the author, 4 November 2005.

63. D. Brown, *Inventing New England*, 7.

64. Rugh, *Are We There Yet?* 82.

65. Ibid., 167–68.

66. Ibid., 175–77.

67. Ibid., 162.

68. "Directory of Residents," December 1969, box 2, fol. 1; "Directory of Residents," 22 November 1978, box 2, fol. 11; Wilder's Park Collection.

69. Mesa, *General Plan*, 2002, sect. 7, p. 3.

70. Betty Thibert, seasonal resident of Park Place, comments to the author, 20 March 2005, Mesa, Ariz.

71. Friedan, *Fountain of Age*, 372.

72. Ibid.

73. Juanita Greene, "There Is Room and Pleasure in Miami Area for Aging," *Miami Herald*, 11 February 1959, Florida Collection.

74. Retirement Research Association, Washington, D.C., list of retirement facilities in Florida, 17 February 1966, Florida Collection.

75. "High Rises—A Way of Life," *Miami News*, 1 November 1968, 4C, Florida Collection.

76. Vesperi, *City of Green Benches*, 38.

77. Burt Garnett, "Retirement Hotels," *St. Petersburg Times*, 16 January 1972, 7F.

78. Stronge, *Sunshine Economy*, 203.

79. Ibid., 151.

80. Schnur, comments to the author, 4 November 2005.

81. Mormino, *Land of Sunshine*, 67.

82. Lee Butcher, "A Man on Top of the World," *St. Petersburg Times*, 12 September 1976, magazine section, 20.

83. Stronge, *Sunshine Economy*, 193.

84. Boyer, *Places Rated Retirement Guide*, 40.

85. "Having Condominium Is Just Like Owning Your Own Lot, Home," *Miami Herald*, 16 February 1964, 6-H.

86. Stronge, *Sunshine Economy*, 193.

87. Low, *Behind the Gates*, 176.

88. Ibid., 19.

89. Ibid., 177.

90. Ibid., 20.

91. Butcher, "A Man on Top of the World," 20.

92. Elizabeth Whitney, "Tenacious Builder," *St. Petersburg Times*, 20 June 1965, 1F.

93. "Condo Safety Dispute Settled," *St. Petersburg Times*, 6 June 1987.

94. Christina Hedrick, "Dissent Surfaces at Condo Complex," *St. Petersburg Times*, 1 July 2001.

95. Mormino, *Land of Sunshine*, 67.

96. Ibid., 132–34.

97. Ibid., 334.

98. Morrison, in *Retirement in the West* (56–58), describes a typical sales dinner. Tymon, in *America Is For Sale!* (81–82, 121), discusses these types of installment sales contracts. Another example of the books written for a popular audience appearing about this time to publicize the problem was Paulson's *The Great Land Hustle*.

99. Morrison, *Retirement in the West*, 56–58.

100. Mormino *Land of Sunshine*, 3.

101. Ibid., 53–56

102. Paulson, *Great Land Hustle*, 16–25.

103. Sheridan, "Rio Rico," 17. This article is also an excellent source for what the company was doing in Florida.

104. Ibid., 30.

105. Conboy, *Expose*.

106. Wolff, *Unreal Estate*, 266.

107. Conboy, *Expose*, 5.

108. Wolff, *Unreal Estate*, 132.

109. Ibid., 267.

110. Chet Jorgenson, commerce analyst, Minnesota Department of Commerce, telephone conversation with the author, 22 December 2005.

111. "New York Charges Pinellas Developer with Illegal Ads," *St. Petersburg Times*, 8 March 1969, 14B.

112. Paulson, *Great Land Hustle*, 168.

113. Stroud, *Promise of Paradise*, 62.

114. Sheridan, "Rio Rico," 19–21.

115. Ibid., 21.

116. Jorgenson, telephone conversation with the author, 7 October 2005.

117. Anonymous interview with the author, 4 February 2005.

118. Meeker, "Overview," Meeker Notebook, p. 17, Sun Cities Area Historical Society, Sun City, Ariz. (hereafter cited as SCAHS).

119. Meeker, "Sun City—A Look Back—1974," Meeker Notebook, SCAHS.

120. On Top of the World Communities Inc., "Company History," publicity pamphlet, 2005, in the author's possession.

121. "Survey Studies Oldsters' Housing Needs," *Miami Herald*, 14 September 1952, Florida Collection.

122. Ben Schneider, "Leisure City near Homestead," *Miami Daily News*, 20 March 1955, Florida Collection.

123. Hunt et al., *Retirement Communities*, 139–47.

124. Ford, "Part One," 40–45.

125. Ben Schleifer quoted in Sturgeon, "'It's a Paradise Town,'" 57.

126. Zarbin, "Man Who Started Them Talks," 7–8.

127. Candace S. Hughes, "Youngtown Paved Way with Restrictions on Age," *Daily News-Sun*, 12 November 1990, "Zoning—Age Restrictions" folder, vertical file, SCAHS.

128. Freedman, *Prime Time*, 34.

129. Zarbin, "Man Who Started Them Talks," 7–8.

130. Blechman, *Leisureville*, 29–30.

131. Ibid., 30.

132. "History of Youngtown," typescript, September 2002, Youngtown Historical Society.

133. Lucille Retheford, founder and president of Youngtown Historical Society and member of Youngtown City Council, interview with the author, 25 March 2005, in Sun City, Ariz.

134. Zarbin, "Man Who Started Them Talks," 7–8.

135. Sturgeon, "'It's a Paradise Town,'" 58.

136. Henry Fuller, "Retirement Cities Grown Together," *Arizona Republic*, 20 November 1960, "Sun City—History" folder, vertical file, SCAHS.

137. Sturgeon, "'It's a Paradise Town,'" 59.

138. Retheford, interview with the author, 6 December 2005, Youngtown, Ariz.

139. Sturgeon, "'It's a Paradise Town,'" 59–61.

140. Edwards et al., "What Home Means to Me," 10.

141. Glenn Fowler, "Price of Homes Up $1,500 in 1956," *New York Times*, 8 July 1956, 191.

142. Freedman, *Prime Time*, 34.

143. "History of Youngtown."

144. Sturgeon, "'It's a Paradise Town,'" 60.

145. Retheford, interview with the author, 6 December 2005.

146. "History of Youngtown."

147. Sturgeon, "'It's a Paradise Town,'" 61.

148. Ibid., 63.

149. Ibid., 61–62.

150. "History of Youngtown."

151. Tarbox, "Youngtown," 6–8. This 1957 article contains photographs of the Greer ranch house, which it identifies as the "Community Clubhouse."

152. "History of Youngtown."

153. Sturgeon, "'It's a Paradise Town,'" 62.

154. Ibid., 63.

155. "Chapter 1 reaches milestone," clipping, no newspaper identified, September 1980, vertical file, Youngtown Historical Society.

156. Retheford, interview with the author, 8 December 2005.

157. Retheford, interview with the author, 25 March 2005.

158. Blechman, *Leisureville*, 30.

159. Sheridan, "Rio Rico," 6.

Chapter 2. Del Webb's "Sun City" Concept

1. Del Webb quoted in "New Life in Retirement Communities," *Business Week*, 8 July 1972, "Demographics" folder, vertical file, SCAHS.

2. "'No Retiree He'—Del Webb Began Building When Paycheck Bounced," no source identified, 1962, "Webb, Del" folder, vertical file, SCAHS.

3. Finnerty, *Del Webb*, 2.

4. Freeman and Sanberg, *Silver Anniversary Jubilee*, 8.

5. Finnerty, *Del Webb*, 2.

6. Laurie Hurd-Moore, "New Biography Details Life of Sun Cities Developer," *Sun Cities Independent*, 11–17 December 1991, "Personalities Del E. Webb" folder, vertical file, SCAHS.

7. Finnerty, *Del Webb*, 4.

8. "Del Webb Revisits Fresno: 'My Mother Owned This Damned Land . . . ,'" *Fresno Bee*, 7 May 1972, "Webb, Del" folder, SCAHS.

9. Toni Ince, Webb's second wife, quoted in Finnerty, *Del Webb*, 4.

10. "Good Losers Get No Chapter in Winner Del Webb's Book," *Fresno Bee*, 8 March 1964, "Webb, Del" folder, SCAHS.

11. "Del Webb—His Rules Didn't Stifle Creativity," *Webb Spinner*, July 1974, 1, Sun City History File, SCAHS. The *Webb Spinner* was the in-house company publication.

12. Jerry Svendsen, interview with the author, 25 March 2005, Sun City, Ariz.

13. "Good Losers," SCAHS.

14. Finnerty, *Del Webb*, 43.

15. Freeman and Sanberg, *Silver Anniversary Jubilee*, 9.

16. Finnerty, *Del Webb*, 4.

17. Orien W. Fifer Jr., "Del Webb Equally Skilled in Carpentry and Baseball," *Arizona Republic*, 16 September 1961; reprint of a speech, 6 December 1987; "Webb, Delbert E." folder, vertical file, SCAHS.

18. Freeman and Sanberg, *Silver Anniversary Jubilee*, 9.

19. Charles Rayburn, "Builder Del E. Webb Recounts His Early Days in Phoenix," *Phoenix Gazette*, 13 April 1973, "Webb, Delbert Eugene" folder, vertical file, SCAHS.

20. Fifer, "Del Webb Equally Skilled in Carpentry and Baseball," SCAHS.

21. Robert Johnson, "Del E. Webb—The Man," typescript, 6 December 1987, "Webb, Delbert E." folder, SCAHS.

22. "Del E. Webb, on the Cover of *Time* Magazine August 3, 1962, with a shuffleboard court behind him in the artist's drawing, revealed nationally what and who he is," *Sun City Sun*, August 1962, "Webb, Delbert E." folder, SCAHS.

23. Allen, *Sun City West*, 3.

24. "About Del Webb," http://www.delwebb.com, accessed 4 October 2004.

25. Webb quoted in "Del E. Webb Dies: Builder of Sun City," *Arizona Republic*, 5 July 1974, "Webb, Del" folder, SCAHS.

26. "Webb Surrounded Himself with Visionaries," *Daily News-Sun,* 16 August 1999, "Webb, Delbert E." folder, SCAHS.

27. Ibid.

28. Finnerty, *Del Webb*, 8.

29. Ibid., 18.

30. Ibid., 24.

31. Ibid., 12.

32. Jane Freeman, conversation with the author, 9 December 2005.

33. Finnerty, *Del Webb*, 12.

34. Jane Freeman, conversation with the author, 9 December 2005; Sun City directories for 1970, 1971, 1989, and 1990. "2nd Wife Gets $1.5 Million in Del Webb Will," *Arizona Republic*, 13 July 1974, "Webb, Delbert E." folder, SCAHS.

35. Finnerty, *Del Webb*, 113.

36. "Phoenician Del Webb Weds L.A. Designer," *Arizona Republic*, 1 August 1961, "Webb, Delbert E." folder, SCAHS.

37. Finnerty, *Del Webb*, 113.

38. "Del E. Webb on the Cover of *Time* Magazine," SCAHS.

39. Carp, "On the Beam: The Del E. Webbs Are Everyday Folk," *Sun City News*, 29 June 1962, 6.

40. "2nd Wife Gets $1.5 Million in Del Webb Will," SCAHS.

41. William Overend, "Del Webb, One of the Biggest, Big-Time Contractors: 'I don't think anybody can stop progress,'" *Arizona Republic*, 14 January 1973, "Webb, Del" folder, SCAHS.

42. Finnerty, *Del Webb*, 12.

43. Advertising supplement, *St. Petersburg Times*, 31 December 1961, H.

44. "2nd Wife Gets $1.5 Million in Del Webb Will," SCAHS.

45. Jim Walsh, "Del E. Webb: They Treated Him Like a God, and Old Hands Still Call Him 'Mister,'" *Arizona Republic*, 9 January 1985, SC-5, "Webb, Delbert E." folder, SCAHS.

46. Bergsman, "Del E. Webb: The Life of the Showman Who Shaped the Southwest and Walked with Famous and Powerful Is Revealed in Rediscovered Photos from the Company Archives," *Phoenix Magazine*, August 1991, 86, "Webb, Delbert E." folder, SCAHS.

47. Henry Fuller, "Bayless Store Gave Del Webb His Start," *Arizona Republic*, January 1972, "Webb, Delbert Eugene" folder, SCAHS.

48. "Del Webb Revisits Fresno," SCAHS.

49. Ibid.

50. Finnerty, *Del Webb*, 41–42.

51. "Del Webb Revisits Fresno," SCAHS.

52. Jim Walsh, "FBI Probes Uncovered a Webb of Rich Trust," 8 September 1985, *Arizona Republic*, AA10, "Webb, Del" folder, SCAHS.

53. "About Del Webb," at http://www.delwebb.com, accessed on 4 October 2004.

54. R. Johnson, "Del E. Webb—The Man," SCAHS.

55. Freeman and Sanberg, *Silver Anniversary Jubilee*, 11.

56. The secretary was Maxine Newman. Steve Bersman, "Del Webb," *Phoenix Magazine*, August 1991, 88, "Webb, Delbert E. 1899–1974" folder, SCAHS.

57. "Editorial: In Memoriam," *Sun City Citizen* and *Youngtown Record*, 10 July 1974, "Webb, Del" folder, SCAHS.

58. Walsh, "FBI Probes Uncovered a Webb of Rich Trust," SCAHS. The *Arizona Republic* used the Freedom of Information Act to gain access to the FBI's file on Del Webb.

59. Jackson, *Crabgrass Frontier,* 234–35.

60. Ibid., 237.

61. Sturgeon, "'It's a Paradise Town,'" 75–76; Finnerty, *Del Webb,* 69–70; Pillsbury, "Consuming Retirement," 63.

62. Del Webb Corporation public affairs department, "Fact Sheet—The Del Webb Corporation," 1989, "Del Webb Corp." folder, vertical file, SCAHS.

63. P. Atwood Williams, "City Builder," *Daily News-Sun,* 12 January 1990, "Sun City—History" folder, SCAHS.

64. Freeman and Sanberg, *Silver Anniversary Jubilee,* 17.

65. Williams, "City Builder," SCAHS.

66. Bernice Jones, "Top Webb Aide Creates New Cities," *Arizona Republic,* 18 August 1963, "Webb Corp." folder, SCAHS.

67. Allen, *Sun City West,* 10.

68. Freedman, *Prime Time,* 34.

69. Sturgeon, "'It's a Paradise Town,'" 76–77.

70. Bret McKeand, "Sun City: 40 Years of Success!" *Sun City 40th Anniversary,* 2000, "Sun City—History" folder, SCAHS.

71. Blechman, *Leisureville,* 32.

72. Sturgeon, "'It's a Paradise Town,'" 77–79.

73. Freeman and Sanberg, *Silver Anniversary Jubilee,* 19.

74. Cumming and Henry, *Growing Old,* v–vii, 14–22, 212–13, 219.

75. Freedman, *Prime Time,* 36.

76. Freeman and Sanberg, *Silver Anniversary Jubilee,* 20.

77. Sturgeon, "'It's a Paradise Town,'" 80.

78. Freedman, *Prime Time,* 34–35.

79. T. E. Breen and Lou Silverstein, "Recommendations for Retirement Living," 16 March 1959, "DEVCO" folder, vertical file, SCAHS.

80. Ibid., 1.

81. Ibid., 1–2.

82. Ibid., 2.

83. Ibid., 4.

84. Ibid., 3–4.

85. Freeman and Sanberg, *Silver Anniversary Jubilee,* 19.

86. Freedman, *Prime Time,* 35–36.

87. "When Webb Launched Sun City in 1959, It Was Multi-Million Dollar Researched 'Risk,'" *Webb Spinner,* January 1970, 2, SCAHS.

88. Pillsbury, "Consuming Retirement," 64.

89. Finnerty, *Del Webb,* 84.

90. Sturgeon, "'It's a Paradise Town,'" 84.

91. "When Webb Launched Sun City in 1959," SCAHS.

92. Finnerty, *Del Webb,* 85.

93. Sturgeon, "'It's a Paradise Town,'" 116.

94. Meeker, "Sun City—A Look Back—1959," 1, Meeker Notebook, SCAHS.

95. Ibid., 2.

96. Ibid., 6.

97. Ibid., 2–3.

98. Ibid., 4.

99. Freeman and Sanberg, *Silver Anniversary Jubilee,* 30.

100. This home is partially preserved as a museum and is the headquarters of the Sun Cities Area Historical Society.

101. Thomas W. Ennis, "1959 Median Home Priced at $10,990," *New York Times,* 12 July 1959, accessed through ProQuest Newsstand.

102. Cory et al., *Golf Course Development in Residential Communities,* 3.

103. Adams and Rooney, "Evolution of American Golf Facilities," 420, 437–38.

104. Findlay, *Magic Lands,* 203.

105. Meeker, "Sun City—A Look Back," 5, SCAHS.

106. Pillsbury, "Consuming Retirement," 87–88.

107. Freedman, *Prime Time,* 62.

108. Ad mock-up, "The fairways wind all around," *Phoenix Republic,* 1 May 1960, SCAHS.

109. "The Philosophy of Retirement," *Del Webb's Sun City: Active Living for America's Senior Citizens,* first sales brochure, ca. 1960, vertical file, SCAHS.

110. Ibid.

111. Freedman, *Prime Time,* 64.

112. Freeman and Sanberg, *Silver Anniversary Jubilee,* 36.

113. Finnerty, *Del Webb,* 202.

114. Meeker, "Sun City—A Look Back—1959," 5, Meeker Notebook, SCAHS.

115. Findlay, *Magic Lands,* 203.

116. "Rock Lawns Very Popular," *Webb Spinner,* January 1970, 9, in Meeker, Meeker Notebook, SCAHS.

117. Freeman and Sanberg, *Silver Anniversary Jubilee,* 23.

118. Meeker, "Sun City—A Look Back—1959," 5, Meeker Notebook, SCAHS.

119. Pillsbury, "Consuming Retirement," 86.

120. "Del Webb's Sun City, Arizona General Plan" [1963?], Meeker Notebook, vol. 2, SCAHS.

121. Jacobson quoted in Freeman and Sanberg, *Silver Anniversary Jubilee,* 23.

122. Findlay, *Magic Lands,* 161.

123. "Name the Active Arizona Retirement Community," advertising scrapbook, SCAHS.

124. Meeker, "Sun City—A Look Back—1959," 5, Meeker Notebook, SCAHS; Freeman and Sanberg, *Silver Anniversary Jubilee,* 28.

125. Svendsen, interview with the author, 25 March 2005.

126. Meeker, "Overview," 23, Meeker Notebook, SCAHS.

127. Ibid., 24.

128. Svendsen, interview with the author, 25 March 2005.

129. "Good Losers Get No Chapter in Winner Del Webb's Book," *Fresno Bee,* 8 March 1964, "Webb, Del" folder, SCAHS.

130. Sturgeon, "'It's a Paradise Town,'" 90.

131. "McCall's Gives Del Webb's Sun City National Recognition for Its New Way-of-Life," ad published 1 July 1960, SCAHS.

132. Mock-up for the ad "America's senior citizens are on the move . . . to Del Webb's Sun City," SCAHS.

133. Findlay, *Magic Lands*, 176.

134. Mock-up for ad no. 6B, "'Was she glad to get rid of me!'" SCAHS.

135. Pillsbury, "Consuming Retirement," 70.

136. "A Big Double Serving of Entertainment," *Phoenix Republic*, 13 March 1960, SCAHS.

137. Mock-up for the ad "Spend a Cool Sunday Afternoon in the Refrigerated Air-Conditioned Comfort of Del Webb's Sun City," 12 June 1960, SCAHS.

138. "You Never Saw Such Fine Homes," ad, *Phoenix Republic*, 29 May 1960, SCAHS.

139. Mock-up for the ad "Co-operative Apartments," 26 June 1960, SCAHS.

140. "Sun City Potential Placed at 150,000 By Webb Chief," *Youngtown News* and *Sun City Sun*, 26 January 1961, SCAHS.

141. Freeman and Sanberg, *Silver Anniversary Jubilee,* 31–32.

142. Robert Garland, "Wake Up and Live in Sun City," quoted in full in Freeman and Sanberg, *Silver Anniversary Jubilee,* 243.

143. Meeker, "1961," 14, Meeker Notebook, SCAHS.

144. Pillsbury, "Consuming Retirement," 74.

145. Finnerty, *Del Webb*, 90–92.

146. "Recently Discovered Webb Diaries Debunk Opening Weekend Myth," *Sun Cities Area Historical Society Newsletter*, Summer 2009, unnumbered page.

147. Finnerty, *Del Webb*, 90–92.

148. Sturgeon, "'It's a Paradise Town,'" 89.

149. McKeand, "Sun City: 40 years of Success!" 14–15, SCAHS.

150. Sturgeon, "'It's a Paradise Town,'" 132–33. The letter was in the possession of the wife of Les Parry, the staff member who gave the early residents their house keys when they moved into Sun City.

151. "Del E. Webb: The All American Legend," *Arizona Highways*, June 1974, 35.

152. Freeman and Sanberg, *Silver Anniversary Jubilee*, 48.

153. Connie Cone Sexton, "Promises of 1960 Fulfilled in Sun City," *Arizona Republic*, 13 February 2000, "Sun City—History" folder, SCAHS.

154. In Freeman and Sanberg, *Silver Anniversary Jubilee,* 35.

155. Sturgeon, "'It's a Paradise Town,'" 87.

156. Freeman quoted in Sexton, "Promises of 1960," SCAHS.

157. Findlay, *Magic Lands,* 176.

158. Meeker, "1960," 8, Meeker Notebook, SCAHS.

159. Ibid., 10.

160. Ibid., 4.

161. Ibid., 11–12.

162. Ibid., 12.

163. John Bowker, president of Sun City Center Historical Society, interview with the author, 5 November 2005, Sun City Center, Fla.

164. Meeker, "Sun City—A Look Back—1962," 22, Meeker Notebook, SCAHS.

165. Bowker, interview with the author, 5 November 2005.

166. Meeker, "Sun City—A Look Back—1962," 22, Meeker Notebook, SCAHS.

167. Finnerty, *Del Webb*, 119. The developer who made the observation was Roy Drachman.

168. Meeker, "Sun City—A Look Back—1962," 23, Meeker Notebook, SCAHS.

169. "Construction Booming: Sun City Building Permits Near $5 Million as Home Sales Soar," *Sun City News*, 13 July 1962, 1.

170. Meeker, "Sun City—A Look Back—1962," 24, Meeker Notebook, SCAHS.

171. Freedman, *Prime Time*, 40.

172. Finnerty, *Del Webb*, 168.

173. Allen, *Sun City West*, 4.

Chapter 3. Ross Cortese's "Leisure World" Concept

1. Harry Johnson, head of FHA cooperative housing division in the early 1960s, quoted in Doris A. Byron, "Rossmoor's Last Gamble Pays Off," *Los Angeles Times*, SC-14, "Cortese, Ross—Clippings, 1981" folder, Historical Society of Laguna Woods (hereafter HSLW).

2. Zimmerman, "Ross Cortese," 25.

3. Harrison Fletcher and Andre Mouchard, "Ross Cortese Leisure World Builder, 74, Dies after Surgery," *Orange County Register*, 31 October 1991, A1.

4. Myra Neben, "Founding Father of Leisure World Dies," *Orange County Register*, 31 October 1991, SC-14, "Cortese, Ross—Obituary" folder, HSLW.

5. Strevey, *Fulfilling Retirement Dreams*, 3.

6. Byron, "Rossmoor's Last Gamble," HSLW.

7. "Ross Cortese: A Pioneer and a Gentleman," *Vitality*, Summer 1994, SC-14, "Ross Cortese—Commemorative Plaque" folder, HSLW.

8. Strevey, *Fulfilling Retirement Dreams*, 3.

9. Comments of Jim Dean to Tracy Strevey, SC-21, "F. R. Dream—Ross Cortese Contribution towards Gerontology Research" folder, HSLW.

10. "Reflecting the Happy-Go-Living Spirit, 'We Have Conquered the Challenge of Building,'" pamphlet, HSLW.

11. Zimmerman, "Ross Cortese," 25.

12. Byron, "Rossmoor's Last Gamble," HSLW.

13. Strevey, "I Remember Ross Cortese," 32.

14. Fletcher and Mouchard, "Ross Cortese Leisure World Builder."

15. Cheryl Walker, "Leisure World Pioneer Speaks: Engineer Worked Closely with Leisure World Developer," *Orange County Register*, 8 July 2004.

16. Fletcher and Mouchard, "Ross Cortese Leisure World Builder."

17. Zimmerman, "Ross Cortese," 25.

18. Nelson, "Early Days of Nursing in Leisure World," 51.

19. Ross W. Cortese, "It's a Great World," n.d., SC-14, "Great World" folder, HSLW.

The item begins, "Though our current speed of construction. . . ." For years Cortese wrote a column called "It's a Great World" for *Leisure World News*.

20. "History and Nature of Rossmoor" [after 1982], typescript, SC-21, F. R. Dream . . ." folder, HSLW.

21. "Ross W. Cortese, 57, Chairman of the Board. . . ." [1973], press release, SC 14, "Cortese, Ross—Profile" folder, HSLW.

22. "Cortese: The Man and the Idea," *Laguna Hills News-Post*, 23 June 1971, SC-14, folder 5, HSLW.

23. "Biography for Alona Marlowe," Internet Movie Database, http://imdb.com/name/nm0549255/bio, accessed 22 October 2007.

24. "Alona Cortese, 97, Co-Developer of Leisure World," *Los Angeles Times*, Orange County Sunday edition, 23 April 2006, B15, unfiled, HSLW. See also "Biography for Alona Marlowe."

25. Andre Mouchard, "Shunned Daughter Sues for Leisure World Riches," *Orange County Register*, 30 July 1993, A1; Ricky Young, "Daughter Ruled out of Fortune," *Orange County Register*, 12 September 1993, B1.

26. "Alona Cortese, 97, Co-Developer of Leisure World," HSLW.

27. Ibid.

28. Ibid.

29. Ibid.

30. Marilyn Robertson, transcript of interview with Ross Cortese, 20 December 1972, SC-14, "Cortese, Ross—Oral History" folder, HSLW.

31. Tom Barratt, vice president, Leisure World Historical Society, Seal Beach, interview with the author, 25 August 2006, Seal Beach, Calif.

32. "Ross Cortese: A Pioneer and a Gentleman," *Vitality*, Summer 1994, SC-14, "Ross Cortese—Commemorative Plaque" folder, HSLW.

33. Don Case, "News Release," SC-14, "Cortese, Ross—Profile" folder, HSLW.

34. Ibid.

35. "History of the Cortese Crest," SC-14, "Cortese, Ross—Crest" folder, HSLW.

36. Eve Lash, "Hoag 552 Club Makes a Splash with 'Free Willy' Fund-Raiser," *Orange County Register*, 12 August 1993, accessed through ProQuest Newsstand on 13 November 2009.

37. "R. W. Cortese Honored," *Leisure World News*, 17 March 1965, 18, HSLW.

38. "Del E. Webb, on the Cover of *Time* Magazine," SCAHS.

39. "Ross William Cortese," memorial service pamphlet, Clubhouse Three plaque dedication, SC-14, HSLW.

40. Heidi Cortese to Claire Still, Leisure World Laguna Hills resident, 23 July 1992, SC-14, "Cortese, Ross—Memorial Golf Tournament" folder, HSLW.

41. Myra Neben, "Teeing off for Seniors," 13 August 1992, SC-14, "Cortese, Ross—Memorial Golf Tournament" folder, HSLW.

42. Barratt, interview with the author, 25 August 2006. See also Cheryl Walker, "Name Change Now Official," *Orange County Register*, 16 March 2006, 1.

43. Neben, "Founding Father of Leisure World Dies," HSLW.

44. Robertson, transcript of interview with Ross Cortese, 6, HSLW.

45. Fletcher and Mouchard, "Ross Cortese Leisure World Builder."

46. Robertson, transcript of interview with Ross Cortese, 6, HSLW.

47. Brad Altman, "Millionaire Ross Cortese Says His Goals Are Fulfilled," *Orange County Register*, 13 May 1981, B4, SC-14, "Cortese, Ross—Clippings, 1981" folder, HSLW.

48. Ibid.

49. Candace Talmadge, "Leisure World Developer Set to Dissolve," *The Register*, 14 April 1981, C8, SC-14, "Cortese, Ross—Clippings, 1981" folder, HSLW.

50. "History and Nature of Rossmoor," HSLW.

51. Fletcher and Mouchard, "Ross Cortese Leisure World Builder."

52. Neben, "Founding Father of Leisure World Dies," HSLW. Cortese died on 29 October 1991.

53. Low, *Behind the Gates*, 14.

54. Fishman, *Bourgeois Utopias*, 94.

55. "Rossmoor, California," *Wikipedia*, accessed 22 October 2007.

56. Zimmerman, "No Oblivion for Rossmoor," 20.

57. Strevey, *Fulfilling Retirement Dreams*, 4.

58. Low, *Behind the Gates*, 111–12.

59. "Gated Community Planned in Blaine," *Duluth News Tribune,* 15 June 2006.

60. Blakely and Snyder, *Fortress America*, 5.

61. Pillsbury, "Consuming Retirement," 132.

62. Blakely and Snyder, *Fortress America,* 6.

63. Low, *Behind the Gates*, 11.

64. Ibid., 122.

65. Ibid., 11.

66. Ibid., 119.

67. Suchman and Becker, *Developing Active Adult Retirement Communities*, 75.

68. Low, *Behind the Gates*, 173, 231.

69. Ibid., 217.

70. Barker, *California Retirement Communities*, 84.

71. Suchman and Becker, *Developing Active Adult Retirement Communities*, 75.

72. Low, *Behind the Gates*, 23. The sociologists who did the study were Blakely and Snyder.

73. Ibid., 70–71.

74. Ibid., 12. Low cites the number of homes at 21,000, but that is an error.

75. Jim Radcliffe, "Focus: In Depth/Leisure World Hits Big 4-0," *Orange County Register,* 9 September 2004, A3, accessed through ProQuest Newsstand on 7 November 2009.

76. The author had that experience in August 2006. It seemed like anybody could enter.

77. In Low, *Behind the Gates*, 232.

78. Ibid., 229.

79. Suchman and Becker, *Developing Active Adult Retirement Communities*, 76.

80. Blakely and Snyder, *Fortress America,* 4.

81. Freedman, *Prime Time*, 72.

82. Low, *Behind the Gates*, 14.

83. Baxandall and Ewen, *Picture Windows*, 252.

84. Barker, *California Retirement Communities*, 43.

85. Comments of Jim Dean to Tracy Strevey, "F. R. Dream . . ." folder, HSLW.

86. Marjorie F. Jones, Leisure World Laguna Hills resident, "Ross W. Cortese" typescript, 1, "Ross Cortese—Bio" folder, HSLW.

87. Comments of Jim Dean to Tracy Strevey, HSLW.

88. Strevey, *Fulfilling Retirement Dreams*, 5.

89. Byron, "Rossmoor's Last Gamble," HSLW.

90. Zimmerman, "Ross Cortese," 23.

91. Ibid.

92. Ken Walker, president, and Tom Barratt, vice president, Leisure World Historical Society, Seal Beach, interview with the author, 25 August 2006, Leisure World Seal Beach.

93. Zimmerman, "Ross Cortese," 23.

94. "Seal Beach Leisure World 1962–1987: The First 25 Great Years." Collector Edition, July 1987, 6–8, Leisure World Historical Society, Seal Beach.

95. "Cortese: The Man and the Idea," *Laguna Hills News-Post*, 23 June 1971, SC-14, folder 5, HSLW.

96. Zimmerman, "Ross Cortese," 25.

97. Strevey, *Fulfilling Retirement Dreams*, 5–6.

98. "Important Dates in the Development of Leisure World," Leisure World Historical Society, Seal Beach.

99. Michael Sumichrast and Lew Sichelman, "Seal Beach Leisure World: Some Government Programs Do Work," *Los Angeles Herald Examiner*, 16 February 1979, C1.

100. Byron, "Rossmoor's Last Gamble," HSLW.

101. Zimmerman, "Ross Cortese," 26.

102. Zimmerman, "No Oblivion for Rossmoor," 21.

103. Sargent Jr., *Planned Communities in Greater Phoenix*, Table II.

104. Walker and Barratt, interview with the author, 25 August 2006.

105. Tom Barratt, e-mail to the author, 15 December 2009.

106. M. Jones, "Ross W. Cortese," 1, "Ross Cortese—Bio" folder, HSLW.

107. Barratt, interview with the author, 25 August 2006.

108. "Let George Do It," resale pamphlet of real estate agent George D. Reisch, SC-15 "Rossmoor—Misc. pamphlets, etc." folder, HSLW.

109. The author is indebted to Ken Walker for a tour on 25 August 2006 of his two-bedroom unit, bought by his parents in 1962 for $11,000, enlarged off the front, and in 2006 worth about $200,000.

110. "Rossmoor Leisure World: A New Way of Life," 1961, 6, 16–17, 20, 22–29, brochure, Leisure World Historical Society, Seal Beach.

111. Zimmerman, "Ross Cortese," 26.

112. Byron, "Rossmoor's Last Gamble," HSLW.

113. Zimmerman, "Ross Cortese," 26.

114. Meeker, "Sun City—A Look Back—1962," Meeker Notebook, 24, SCAHS.

115. "Buyers from 38 States at Leisure World," *Rossmoor Leisure World News*, September/October 1962, 1, Leisure World Historical Society, Seal Beach.

116. "Rossmoor Corporation" [1963], brochure, SC-15, HSLW.

117. "Former Sun City Manager Buys at Rossmoor Leisure World," *Rossmoor Leisure World News*, September/October 1962 4, Leisure World Historical Society, Seal Beach.

118. "Organizations, Clubs, Classes Thus Far at Rossmoor Leisure World," *Rossmoor Leisure World News*, September/October 1962, 2.

119. Bill Griffin, recreation coordinator, "Recreational Activities," *Rossmoor Leisure World News*, September/October 1962, 2.

120. Bill Griffin, "Recreational Activities," *Rossmoor Leisure World News*, March 1963, 2.

121. "World of Wonder," *RLW News*, Summer 1963, 8, Leisure World Historical Society, Seal Beach.

122. "Security Office Aids Residents," *Rossmoor Leisure World News*, March 1963, 5.

123. "Marks of Progress: Construction Booms at Leisure World," *Rossmoor Leisure World News*, March 1963, 5.

124. "Seal Beach Leisure World 1962–1987," 8, Leisure World Historical Society, Seal Beach.

125. "Leisure Word [sic]," flier, ca. 1963, Leisure World Historical Society, Seal Beach.

126. Douglas Doubleday, "And Some Other Thoughts on Retirement," *St. Petersburg Times*, 10 January 1965, 1F.

127. "FHA Proposes Conference," *Seal Beach Leisure World News*, 23 September 1965, 1, Leisure World Historical Society, Seal Beach.

128. Price Waterhouse report for the Golden Rain Foundation, "Leisure World is a composite of individual cooperatives," ca. 1964–1965, "Seal Beach Leisure World" folder, vertical file, HSLW.

129. USC Report No. 5 on Rossmoor Leisure World, Seal Beach, 23 April 1965, typescript, "Seal Beach Leisure World" folder, HSLW.

130. "What Makes Ross W. Cortese the World's Largest Home Builder?" reprint from *Practical Builder*, May 1966, SC-14, "Cortese, Ross—World's Largest Home Builder" folder, HSLW.

131. Diana Griego Erwin, "A Dreamer Who Built an Empire," *Sun-Sentinel*, 8 May 1989, accessed through Newsbank on 26 June 2009.

132. Byron, "Rossmoor's Last Gamble," HSLW.

133. "What Makes Ross W. Cortese the World's Largest Home Builder?" HSLW.

134. Al Ceresa, president of Rossmoor, and Paul Zimmerman, "Forgotten Facts about Leisure World/Laguna Hills," typescript, 1–2, HSLW.

135. "Ross W. Cortese—Narrative," typescript, 48, HSLW.

136. Zimmerman, "Ross Cortese," 28.

137. Zimmerman, "No Oblivion for Rossmoor," 21.

138. Mabie, "Laguna Hills Art Association," 131, 133.

139. "Ross W. Cortese—Narrative," 48, HSLW.

140. Strevey, *Fulfilling Retirement Dreams,* 142.

141. Ibid., 142.

142. Ceresa, "Some Facts about Leisure World," 36–38.

143. Zimmerman, "Ross Cortese," 28.

144. Strevey, *Fulfilling Retirement Dreams,* 143.

145. "Gala Opening Set in New Leisure World Center," *Leisure World News,* 17 March 1965, 1, HSLW.

146. "Ross W. Cortese—Narrative," 58, HSLW.

147. Lewis, "Bringing Green Space to Leisure World," 33–35.

148. "A Wonderful 'New Way of Life' . . . Where Freedom Is the Magic Key!" undated flier, SC-14, "Cortese, Ross—Clippings—undated" folder, HSLW.

149. Barker, *California Retirement Communities,* 46.

150. Heslip, "Towers Rise in Leisure World," 22–23.

151. Barratt, interview with the author, 25 August 2006.

152. Diana Griego Erwin, "Where Leisure Suits Residents of Various Leisure World Enclaves Simply Love Where They Live," *Sun-Sentinel,* 8 May 1989, accessed through Newsbank on 25 June 2009.

153. "For you *active, interesting people over 52,*" ad in *Independent* and *Press Telegram,* 21 February 1964, SC-15, "Rossmoor—Very early sales promotion" folder, HSLW.

154. "Rossmoor Leisure World—Laguna Hills," May 1966, n.p., SC-15, "Rossmoor—Very early sales promotion" folder, HSLW.

155. In Erwin, "Where Leisure Suits Residents."

Chapter 4. Creating Community: The Developers' Script

1. Del E. Webb Development Co. (DEVCO), a subsidiary of Del E. Webb Corporation, "Del Webb's Sun City: Active Living for America's Senior Citizens," 1960, SCAHS.

2. Meeker, "Overview," 23, Meeker Notebook, SCAHS.

3. Ibid., 3.

4. "Sun City's Pioneers," *Sun Citizen,* 2 January 1964, "Sun City (History)" folder, vertical file, SCAHS.

5. "Recap of 1969, 1975 & 1979 surveys," "Demographics" folder, vertical file, SCAHS.

6. Hunt et al., *Retirement Communities,* 251.

7. Freeman and Sanberg, *Silver Anniversary Jubilee,* 48.

8. Boorstin, *Americans: The National Experience.* In Part II Boorstin discusses transiency and in Part III, dealing with the "booster spirit," he mentions new cities with no history.

9. "Social Issues: New Life in Retirement Communities," *Business Week,* 8 July 1972, 70.

10. Cited in Mormino, *Land of Sunshine,* 125.

11. Bob Krauss, "Hawaii Ruled out as 'Sun City' Site," *Honolulu Advertiser,* 2 December 1964, "Webb Corporation" folder, vertical file, SCAHS.

12. Freeman and Sanberg, *Silver Anniversary Jubilee,* 35.

13. Findlay, *Magic Lands*, 197.

14. Ibid,, 194.

15. Sturgeon, "'It's a Paradise Town,'" 92–95.

16. "The Leisure World News," *Leisure World News*, Laguna Hills edition, 17 March 1965, 4, HSLW.

17. Ernest B. and Florence B. Price, future residents, "Dear Mr. Smith," *Leisure World News*, 3 June 1965, 4.

18. Svendsen, interview with the author, 25 March 2005.

19. Sturgeon, "'It's a Paradise Town,'" 125.

20. Ibid., 128.

21. Meeker, "Sun City—A Look Back—1966," 38, Meeker Notebook, SCAHS.

22. Freeman and Sanberg, *Silver Anniversary Jubilee*, 180.

23. Meeker, "Sun City—A Look Back—1966," 38, Meeker Notebook, SCAHS.

24. "Prices Attend Lunch Meeting," *Leisure World News*, 17 March 1965, 5.

25. "Calendar of Coming Events," *Leisure World News*, 25 March 1965, 6.

26. "New Activities," *Leisure World News*, 13 May 1965, 15.

27. Meeker, "Sun City—A Look Back—1977," 94, Meeker Notebook, SCAHS.

28. Hunt et al., *Retirement Communities*, 27.

29. Strevey, *Fulfilling Retirement Dreams*, 246.

30. "Clubhouse Calendars" and "State Clubs," *Laguna Woods Globe*, 17 August 2006, 8, 20.

31. Sturgeon, "'It's a Paradise Town,'" 135, 137.

32. "Vacations Last a Lifetime," advertising scrapbook, SCAHS.

33. Welch, "Retirement Communities in Maricopa County," 2.

34. "Clubhouse Calendars," "DAR Compiles, Donates 'Rosie's Daughters' Book," "Briefly," *Laguna Woods Globe*, 17 August 2006, 8, 13, 15.

35. Freedman, *Prime Time*, 66.

36. Horowitz, *Betty Friedan*, 20.

37. "Jewish Services Postponed Here," *Leisure World News*, 29 July 1965, 8.

38. Judy Hille, "2 pct. of Sun City Homes Have 3 or More Residents," vertical file, SCAHS.

39. Mormino, *Land of Sunshine*, 139–40.

40. Meeker, "Overview," 16, Meeker Notebook, SCAHS.

41. Judy Hille, "Poll Shows Growth as Biggest Problem," *Arizona Republic*, 20 July 1980, "Demographics" folder, SCAHS.

42. Welch, *Retirement Communities in Maricopa County*, 61.

43. Mormino, *Land of Sunshine,* 309.

44. Jacobs, *Fun City*, 46.

45. Ibid., 49.

46. Svendsen, interview with the author, 25 March 2005.

47. Freedman, *Prime Time*, 65.

48. Svendsen, e-mail to the author, 10 November 2009.

49. Sturgeon, "'It's a Paradise Town,'" 118.

50. Jacobs, *Fun City*, 50.

51. Tucker, *Sun City*, 7.

52. Welch, *Retirement Communities in Maricopa County*, 182.

53. "Sun City, Arizona 1960 Occupations," "S.C. Pioneers" folder, vertical file, SCAHS.

54. Hunt et al., *Retirement Communities*, 27.

55. Pillsbury, "Consuming Retirement," 79.

56. Sturgeon, "'It's a Paradise Town,'" 137.

57. Ibid., 140.

58. Freeman and Sanberg, *Silver Anniversary Jubilee*, 77.

59. Pillsbury, "Consuming Retirement," 81–84.

60. Del E. Webb Corporation's "Anyone who can retire" 1963 brochure was sent to the author because the Sun Cities Area Historical Society does not collect material on Sun Cities other than Sun City and Sun City West in Arizona. The brochure was included with material on Sun City, California.

61. R. H. Johnson to John Meeker, 21 December 1976, Meeker Notebook, SCAHS.

62. Starr, *California*, 238.

63. Hunt et al., *Retirement Communities*, 32.

64. C. Robert Moon, vice president, New Horizons Inc., exclusive sales corporation for Rossmoor Leisure World, to "Future Resident of Leisure World," ca. 1965, SC-15, "Rossmoor Misc. Correspondence" folder, HSLW.

65. R. Price, "How Leisure World Leadership Evolved," 44.

66. "From Model Home . . . to Museum," *Sun Cities Area Historical Society Newsletter*, Fall/Winter 2009, 6.

67. Meeker, "Sun City—A Look Back—1962," Meeker Notebook, SCAHS.

68. "Rock Lawns Very Popular," *Webb Spinner*, January 1970, 9, in Meeker Notebook, SCAHS.

69. Sturgeon, "'It's a Paradise Town,'" 104.

70. Both the Sun Cities Area Historical Society and the Sun City Center Historical Society have original Kentworth model homes as their headquarters; each has an Arizona or a Florida room.

71. Freeman and Sanberg, *Silver Anniversary Jubilee*, 69–71.

72. Meeker, "1960," 8, Meeker Notebook, SCAHS.

73. Don De Benedictis, sales manager, to "Friend," 23 May 1968, SC-15, "Rossmoor Misc. Correspondence" folder, HSLW.

74. Hunt et al., *Retirement Communities*, 32.

75. Findlay, *Magic Lands*, 202.

76. Ceresa, "Some Facts about Leisure World," 42.

77. Findlay, *Magic Lands*, 183.

78. Freeman and Sanberg, *Silver Anniversary Jubilee*, 69–71.

79. Meeker, "Overview," 13, Meeker Notebook, SCAHS.

80. Ibid., 12–13.

81. Bruce Ellison, "Former Webb President John Meeker Dies at Age 73," *Daily News-Sun*, 8 February 2000, "John Meeker" folder, vertical file, SCAHS.

82. Bruce Ellison, "Meeker Remembered for Responsiveness, Vision," *Daily News-Sun*, 12–13 February 2000, "John Meeker" folder, SCAHS.

83. "John Meeker Named Streets, Designed Homes," reprint of August 1963 article in *News-Sun*, 24 January 1980, "DEVCO" folder, SCAHS.

84. "Experimental Model Homes," *Sun Cities Area Historical Society Newsletter*, Winter 2008, 5.

85. Freeman and Sanberg, *Silver Anniversary Jubilee*, 72–74.

86. Findlay, *Magic Lands*, 191.

87. Pillsbury, "Consuming Retirement," 124.

88. Freeman and Sanberg, *Silver Anniversary Jubilee*, 69.

89. Hunt et al., *Retirement Communities*, 69.

90. Meeker, "Overview," 24, Meeker Notebook, SCAHS.

91. Boyer, *Places Rated Retirement Guide*, 59.

92. Pillsbury, "Consuming Retirement," 127–28.

93. Meeker, "Sun City—A Look Back—1964," Meeker Notebook, SCAHS.

94. J. Oswald Zounky, "From Ashton," January 1965, "Demographics" folder, SCAHS.

95. Meeker, "Sun City—A Look Back—1973," Meeker Notebook, SCAHS.

96. Patricia Barnes, "Sun City, AZ, U.S.A." *Arizona Highways*, June 1974, 30.

97. Meeker, "Sun City—A Look Back—1979," 106, Meeker Notebook, SCAHS.

98. Hunt et al., *Retirement Communities*, 62.

99. "Laguna Hills North Pennysave," advertising flier, 1968, and "$1.5 Million Sales in Day Recorded at Leisure World," 30 March 1969, K3, SC-15, "Rossmoor Building" folder, HSLW.

100. Freeman and Sanberg, *Silver Anniversary Jubilee*, 231.

101. Meeker, "Overview," 3, Meeker Notebook, SCAHS.

102. Ibid., 24.

103. Meeker, "Sun City—A Look Back—1965," Meeker Notebook, 32, SCAHS.

104. Meeker, "Overview," 24, Meeker Notebook, SCAHS.

105. "John Meeker Named Streets, Designed Homes," SCAHS.

106. Gail Reid, "Caddy to Kingpin," *Arizona Republic*, 9 April 1980, "DEVCO" folder, SCAHS.

107. "John Meeker Named Streets, Designed Homes," SCAHS.

108. Svendsen, interview with the author, 25 March 2005.

109. "Mr. John W. Meeker," short c.v., "DEVCO" folder, SCAHS.

110. Tim Clark, "Sun City's Man of All Seasons," *News-Sun*, 31 December 1977, "DEVCO" folder, SCAHS.

111. "John Meeker Named Streets, Designed Homes," SCAHS.

112. Zarbin, "Man Who Started Them Talks," 12.

113. Meeker, "Overview," 5, Meeker Notebook, SCAHS.

114. Svendsen, interview with the author, 25 March 2005.

115. Meeker, "Overview," 5, Meeker Notebook, SCAHS.

116. Ibid., 7.

117. Freeman and Sanberg, *Silver Anniversary Jubilee*, 232.

118. Meeker, "Overview," 6, 8, Meeker Notebook, SCAHS.

119. "Meeker's Departure," 14 September 1981, source unidentified, "Meeker" folder, vertical file, SCAHS.

120. Meeker, "Overview," 6, Meeker Notebook, SCAHS.

121. Ibid., 8, 10.

122. Ibid., 9.

123. Freeman and Sanberg, *Silver Anniversary Jubilee*, 232.

124. Meeker, "Overview," 6–7, Meeker Notebook, SCAHS.

125. Ibid., 10.

126. Meeker, "Sun City—A Look Back—1975," 82, Meeker Notebook, SCAHS.

127. Meeker, "Sun City—A Look Back—1977," 97, Meeker Notebook, SCAHS.

128. Meeker, "Sun City—A Look Back—1978," 99, Meeker Notebook, SCAHS.

129. Meeker, "Sun City—A Look Back—1981," 118, Meeker Notebook, SCAHS.

130. Julie Riddle, "John W. Meeker Jr. Dies," *Sun Cities Independent*, 16–22 February 2000, "John Meeker" folder, SCAHS.

131. Robert Price, "Memo from Your Administrator," *Leisure World News*, 22 July 1965, 5.

132. "Ross W. Cortese," typescript, page labeled "1972," SC-14, "Ross Cortese" folder, HSLW.

133. Cheryl Walker, "General Managers Speak," *Orange County Register*, 1 June 2006, 1, accessed through ProQuest Newsstand on 7 November 2009.

134. Blechman, *Leisureville*, 130, 134–36.

135. Ibid., 138.

136. "What Makes Ross W. Cortese the World's Largest Home Builder?" HSLW.

137. "Rossmoor Leisure World Laguna Hills," sales brochure, June 1967, SC-15, "Rossmoor—Very Early Sales Promotion" folder, HSLW.

138. Hunt et al., *Retirement Communities*, 35.

139. Strevey, *Fulfilling Retirement Dreams*, 23.

140. Hunt et al., *Retirement Communities*, 53.

141. Ibid., 38.

142. "Ross W. Cortese," typescript, 37, HSLW.

143. Ross W. Cortese, "It's a Great World," *Leisure World News*, 14 January 1971, SC-14, "Great World" folder, HSLW.

144. Hunt et al., *Retirement Communities*, 43.

145. Friedan, *Fountain of Age*, 369.

146. Ibid., 372–73.

147. Hunt et al., *Retirement Communities*, 38.

148. Kenneth J. Garcia, "Leisure World Growing Older: Generation Gap at Seniors' Mecca," *San Francisco Chronicle*, 15 February 1993, A1.

149. Freeman and Sanberg, *Silver Anniversary Jubilee*, 160.

150. Hunt et al., *Retirement Communities*, 38.

151. Bill Bryant, Leisure World golfing consultant, "Golf Is a Science, a Study," *Leisure World News*, 1 April 1965, 14–15.

152. Pillsbury, "Consuming Retirement," 90–91. The couple was Mr. and Mrs. Ira

Murphy. They are pictured with their sign in Freeman and Sanberg, *Silver Anniversary Jubilee,* 39.

153. Freeman and Sanberg, *Silver Anniversary Jubilee,* 38. The authors do concede that the bathroom story may be "apocryphal."

154. P. Atwood Fenner, "Search Underway for Oldest Golf Car and Unusual Custom Models," *Sun Cities Area Historical Society Newsletter,* Winter 2009, 1, 4.

155. Hunt et al., *Retirement Communities,* 30.

156. McCally, "Sun City Center," 37; Bowker, interview with the author, 5 November 2005.

157. Bowker, letter to the author, 28 October 2009.

158. Sturgeon, "'It's a Paradise Town,'" 153.

159. Vashti McKenzie, "Peoria Schools Victim of Sun City," *Arizona Republic,* 24 February 1969, "Taxes—School" folder, vertical file, SCAHS.

160. Blechman, *Leisureville,* 133.

161. McKenzie, "Peoria Schools Victim of Sun City," SCAHS.

162. Meeker, "Sun City—A Look Back—1974," Meeker Notebook, SCAHS.

163. Strevey, *Fulfilling Retirement Dreams,* 90–93.

164. Paul Zimmerman, "And to the Southeast—Laguna Hills," *Los Angeles Herald Examiner,* 16 February 1979, C1.

165. Barker, *California Retirement Communities,* 95–96.

166. Freedman, *Prime Time,* 15.

167. Meeker, "1964," 30, Meeker Notebook.

168. Freeman and Sanberg, *Silver Anniversary Jubilee,* 225.

169. Hunt et al., *Retirement Communities,* 249.

170. Welch, "Retirement Communities in Maricopa County," 91.

171. Meeker, "Overview," 29, Meeker Notebook, SCAHS.

172. Blechman, *Leisureville,* 142.

173. Ibid., 135.

174. Ibid., 133.

175. Ibid., 139.

176. Meeker, "Overview," 14, Meeker Notebook, SCAHS.

177. Meeker, "Sun City—A Look Back—1976," 90, Meeker Notebook.

178. Geno Lawrenzi, "Union Club Still Fights for Workers," *Sun City Independent,* 10 March 2004, "Union Club" folder, vertical file, SCAHS.

179. Meeker as quoted in Sturgeon, "'It's a Paradise Town,'" 105–06.

180. Meeker, "Overview," 29, Meeker Notebook, SCAHS.

181. Ibid.

182. Freeman and Sanberg, *Silver Anniversary Jubilee,* 48.

Chapter 5. Proliferation and Standardization

1. Statement of Stanley R. Hauseman, president, Florida West Coast Condominium Federation, before the Subcommittee on Civil and Constitutional Rights of the House of Representatives Committee on the Judiciary on H.R. 1158, Fair Housing

Amendments Act of 1987, *Hearings* (Washington, D.C.: Government Printing Office, 1987), 611.

2. John Guzzon, "Those Were the Days," *Daily News-Sun,* 3 March 2002, vertical file, SCAHS.

3. Sheridan, "Rio Rico," 2.

4. "Tucson Green Valley / Sponsored by Dartmouth College, Developed and Constructed by Maxon Construction," mimeograph, 1961, Arizona Archives, Arizona State University, Tempe.

5. Meeker, "1963," 27, Meeker Notebook, SCAHS.

6. Morrison, *Retirement in the West,* 80.

7. Meeker, "1963," 27–28, Meeker Notebook, SCAHS.

8. Meeker, "1961," 17, Meeker Notebook, SCAHS.

9. Welch, "Retirement Communities in Maricopa County," 59.

10. The author thanks Betty Thibert for arranging a visit to this home.

11. Biggar et al., "Sunbelt Update," 31, 34.

12. Frank Premack, "What the Developers Call Progress Could Create Another Los Angeles," *Minneapolis Tribune,* 27 February 1973, "Sun City General" folder, vertical file, SCAHS.

13. Morrison, *Retirement in the West,* 76.

14. Meeker, "Sun City—A Look Back—1971," 62, Meeker Notebook, SCAHS.

15. Meeker, "Sun City—A Look Back—1976," 89, Meeker Notebook, SCAHS.

16. Catherine Reagor, "Retirement's Midlife Crisis," *Arizona Republic,* 6 February 2000, "Del E. Webb Corporation" folder, SCAHS.

17. Meeker, "Sun City—A Look Back—1971," 62, Meeker Notebook, SCAHS.

18. Sargent Jr., *Planned Communities in Greater Phoenix,* 86.

19. Welch, "Retirement Communities in Maricopa County," 105.

20. Suchman and Becker, *Developing Active Adult Retirement Communities,* 166.

21. Welch, "Retirement Communities in Maricopa County," 55.

22. Suchman and Becker, *Developing Active Adult Retirement Communities,* 165–68.

23. "Tucson Green Valley / Sponsored by Dartmouth College," 31, Arizona Archives, Arizona State University, Tempe.

24. Biggar et al., "Sunbelt Update," 34.

25. "World Headquarters for Active Retirees," ad for Ridgewood Mountain Village, *St. Petersburg Times,* 31 December 1961.

26. Mark Levy, president of the Recreation Management Company for Century Villages, telephone interview with the author, 4 June 2009. Mark Levy is H. Irwin Levy's son.

27. Ibid.

28. Phil C. Lange, ed., "An Historical View of Sun City Center," in "Hillsborough—S.C.C." folder, Dunn Collection.

29. H. Irwin Levy, telephone interview with the author, 12 June 2009.

30. Mark Levy, telephone interview with the author, 4 June 2009.

31. H. Irwin Levy, telephone interview with the author, 12 June 2009.

32. Ibid.

33. Stronge, *Sunshine Economy*, 196.

34. Mark Levy, telephone interview with the author, 4 June 2009.

35. H. Irwin Levy, telephone interview with the author, 12 June 2009.

36. Mike Wilson, "Century Village Success Spawns Imitators around County and South Florida," *Miami Herald*, 1 July 1984, accessed through Newsbank on 26 June 2009.

37. In Christopher Boyd, "20 Years Young Retirement Living Revisited," *Miami Herald*, 15 January 1989, accessed through Newsbank on 26 June 2009.

38. Mormino, *Land of Sunshine*, 132–34.

39. Mark Levy, telephone interview with the author, 4 June 2009.

40. "Century Village, Florida," at City Data, http://www.city-data.com, accessed on 24 July 2008.

41. Mark Levy, telephone interview with the author, 4 June 2009.

42. Mormino, *Land of Sunshine*, 132–34.

43. H. Irwin Levy, telephone interview with the author, 12 June 2009.

44. Ibid.

45. Charles Passy, "Becoming Your Own Impresario," *Palm Beach Post*, 14 March 1993, accessed through Newsbank on 26 June 2009.

46. H. Irwin Levy, telephone interview with the author, 12 June 2009.

47. Julia Lawlor, "Snowbirds Flock Together: Northerners in Florida Huddle with Folks from Home," *New York Times*, 11 March 2007, L5, accessed through ProQuest Newsstand on 27 November 2007.

48. On Top of the World Communities Inc., "Company History," sales brochure, 1 June 2005.

49. Ibid.

50. Blechman in E. Brown, "Are Retirees Breaking Their Social Contract?"

51. Jim Tunstall, "Paradise in a Bubble," *Tampa Tribune*, 25 July 2005, 1.

52. "HearAtLast to Open First U.S. Hearing-Aid Clinic," PR Newswire Association LLC, 5 November 2007, accessed through ProQuest Newsstand on 27 November 2009.

53. Blechman, *Leisureville*, 39.

54. Mormino, *Land of Sunshine*, 138–39.

55. "Careers in The Villages," http://www.careersinthevillages.com, accessed 27 November 2007.

56. In E. Brown, "Are Retirees Breaking Their Social Contract?"

57. Blechman, *Leisureville*, 40–43.

58. Ibid., 42–43.

59. In E. Brown, "Are Retirees Breaking Their Social Contract?"

60. Blechman, *Leisureville*, 43–49.

61. Ibid., 53–57.

62. Ibid., 53–56.

63. Ibid., 39–40, 44–46, 61.

64. Ibid., 162–63.

65. Ibid., 44.

66. Ibid., 109–110.

67. Fogelsong, *Married to the Mouse*, 151.

68. Ibid., 199.

69. Blechman, *Leisureville*, 57.

70. In "'It's Disney World for Adults,'" reprint of the "Florida Home" section of the *Palm Beach Post*, 29 September 2007, in a June 2009 sales packet at The Villages.

71. Blechman, *Leisureville*, 144, 156–58.

72. Rothman, *Devil's Bargains*, 11.

73. Blechman, *Leisureville*, 224.

74. Patricia Steele, "School Board Member Suggests Moving One Meeting per Month to The Villages," *The Villages Daily Sun,* online edition, 26 November 2007.

75. Blechman, *Leisureville,* 224.

76. "Will You Outlive Your Nest Egg?" ad, *The Villages Magazine,* January 2008, 83.

77. Conboy, *Expose*, 196.

78. Elizabeth Whitney, "Its Ideas Are Slow to Grow," *St. Petersburg Times,* 3 October 1971, 1H.

79. "Parker Finds Satisfaction in Sun City Home Sales," *News-Sun*, 13 December 1984, "DEVCO" folder, SCAHS.

80. Meeker, "1960," 12, Meeker Notebook, SCAHS.

81. Meeker, "Overview," 4, Meeker Notebook, SCAHS.

82. Bowker, interview with the author, 5 November 2005.

83. Meeker, "Sun City—A Look Back—1970," 56, Meeker Notebook, SCAHS.

84. Meeker, "Sun City—A Look Back—1962," 22, Meeker Notebook, SCAHS.

85. "Del Webb Sells 10,000 Acres in Hillsborough," *St. Petersburg Times,* 19 July 1970, 3B.

86. Elizabeth Whitney, "Sun City . . . Three Years Later," *St. Petersburg Times,* 10 January 1965, 1F.

87. "Del Webb Revisits Fresno: 'My Mother Owned This Damned Land . . . ,'" *Fresno Bee,* 7 May 1972, A24.

88. Meeker, "Sun City—A Look Back—1962," 22, Meeker Notebook, SCAHS.

89. "Sunasco out to Buy Development," 13 August 1968, City and Town File, Miami Public Library.

90. "Lehigh Acres Project Aims at Retirees," 19 December 1970, *Miami Herald*, Florida Collection.

91. Lange, "An Historical View of Sun City Center," Dunn Collection.

92. Mormino, *Land of Sunshine,* 132.

93. McCally, "Sun City Center," 33.

94. Ibid., 37.

95. Ibid., 33.

96. Lange, "An Historical View of Sun City Center," Dunn Collection.

97. Bowker, interview with the author, 5 November 2005.

98. Meeker, "1960," 12, Meeker Notebook, SCAHS.

99. Meeker, "Sun City—A Look Back—1967," Meeker Notebook, SCAHS.

100. Meeker, "Overview," 4, Meeker Notebook, SCAHS.

101. Jacobs, *Fun City*, 45.

102. Archives Committee, *Sun City*, 82.

103. Ibid., 33.

104. Meeker, "Overview," 4, Meeker Notebook, SCAHS.

105. Archives Committee, *Sun City*, 80.

106. Ibid., 96.

107. Ibid., 123.

108. Ibid., 124.

109. Meeker, "Sun City—A Look Back—1961," 17, Meeker Notebook, SCAHS.

110. Pillsbury, "Consuming Retirement."

111. "Around Leisure Worlds," *Leisure World News*, 17 March 1965, 17.

112. Barker, *California Retirement Communities*, 91–94.

113. Findlay, *Magic Lands*, 168.

114. "Trust Agreement between Suburban Trust Company and Maryland Mutual No. One, Inc.," 9 March 1966, 19–21, 23, HSLW.

115. Hunt et al., *Retirement Communities*, 253.

116. "History and Nature of Rossmoor," "F. R. Dream . . ." folder, HSLW.

117. Ibid.

118. Tom Toolen, "Changing the Nature of Retiree Homes," *New York Times*, 16 January 1994, A13.

119. "Cortese: The Man and the Idea," *Laguna Hills News-Post*, 23 June 1971, box 14, fol. 5, Special Collections, HSLW.

120. "History and Nature of Rossmoor," HSLW.

121. Meeker, "Sun City—A Look Back—1962," 24, Meeker Notebook, SCAHS.

122. Sargent Jr., *Planned Communities*, 72–73.

123. Meeker, "Sun City—A Look Back—1971," 62, Meeker Notebook, SCAHS.

124. Meeker, "Sun City—A Look Back—1973," 75, Meeker Notebook, SCAHS.

125. "History and Nature of Rossmoor," HSLW.

126. Sargent, *Metro Arizona*, 120.

127. "America's Most Famous Adult Lifestyle . . . from $17,900," ad, *Fort Lauderdale News and Sun-Sentinel*, 11 May 1974, SC-15, "Rossmoor Sales outside Leisure World" folder, HSLW.

128. "History and Nature of Rossmoor," HSLW.

129. H. Irwin Levy, letter to the author, 3 November 2009.

130. Mark Levy, telephone interview, 4 June 2009.

131. H. Irwin Levy, interview with the author, 12 June 2009.

132. Mark Levy, telephone interview, 4 June 2009.

133. "Wynmoor Residents Fear Rules May Hurt Sales," *Sun-Sentinel*, 23 April 2009, accessed through Newsbank on 26 June 2009.

134. "History and Nature of Rossmoor," HSLW.

135. H. Irwin Levy, letter to the author, 30 November 2009.

136. Heintz, *Retirement Communities*, 16–19.

137. Ibid., 26.

138. Donald Janson, "Retirement Towns Flourish in Jersey's Fields," *New York*

Times, 5 March 1984, A1, accessed through ProQuest Newsstand on 27 November 2007.

139. Ibid.

140. Hunt et al., *Retirement Communities*, 112–15.

141. Ibid., 114–17.

142. Ibid., 112–36.

143. Ibid., 136.

144. "Growing 'Grey Brigade' Is Swiftly Getting in Line to Purchase New Housing," *San Diego Union*, 8 December 1985, F14.

145. M. Baker, "Arizona's Retirement Communities," 16.

146. Mike Garrett, "Tuffs Finds Niche at Devco," *News-Sun*, 18 February 1985, "DEVCO" folder, SCAHS.

147. Tuffs in Findlay, *Magic Lands*, 346.

148. Meeker, "Overview," 22, Meeker Notebook, SCAHS.

149. Allen, *Sun City West*, 18–20.

150. Ibid., 119.

151. Meeker, "Overview," 22, Meeker Notebook, SCAHS.

152. "Poll Shows Growth as Biggest Problem," *Arizona Republic*, 20 July 1980, "Demographics" folder, SCAHS.

153. Allen, *Sun City West*, 59–61.

154. Bruce Ellison, "Sun City West Nears Final New-Home Sale," *Daily News-Sun*, 8 April 1998, "Real Estate" folder, vertical file, SCAHS.

155. Friedan, *Fountain of Age*, 59.

156. Vesperi, *City of Green Benches*, 14.

157. Suchman and Becker, *Developing Active Adult Retirement Communities*, 134.

158. Svendsen, interview with the author, 25 March 2005.

159. Farrell, *Family*, 136.

160. Ken Plonski and Martha Moyer, "Baby Boomers Planning Early Retirements," Del Webb's Sun City West press release, 1987, "DEVCO" folder, SCAHS.

161. Gordon, "Work and Patterns of Retirement," 48.

162. Graebner, *History of Retirement*, 16.

163. Hughes, "Youngtown Paved Way," SCAHS. Hughes cites Calvin Brice, Youngtown's attorney, and a late-1950s episode of *The Garry Moore Show*.

164. Welch, "Retirement Communities in Maricopa County," 61.

165. James A. Peterson, "The Early History of the Gerontology Center at the University of Southern California and Its Relationship to Leisure World: Research and Service," typescript, n.d., HSLW.

166. FitzGerald, *Cities on a Hill*, 242; John Findlay quoted in Scott Bontz, "Historian Chronicles Life in the 'Magic Kingdom'—Sun City," *Daily News-Sun*, 27 October 1986, "Sun City—History" folder, SCAHS.

167. Statement of Stanley R. Hauseman, 610.

168. Welch, "Retirement Communities in Maricopa County," 68–69.

169. Meeker, "1960," 10, Meeker Notebook, SCAHS.

170. Barker, *California Retirement Communities*, 46.

171. Archives Committee, Sun City, 113.

172. Jacobs, *Older Persons*, 70–71.

173. Archives Committee, Sun City, 190.

174. Ibid., 222.

175. Gillian Silver, "Senior Overlay Tough to Bend," *Sun Cities Independent*, 29 May–4 June 1985, "Senior Overlay" folder, vertical file, SCAHS.

176. Deborah Bolten, "Seniors Fight for Exemption from Age Law," *The Register*, 20 March 1984, HSLW.

177. Myrtle Ring, "Legal loophole," *Leisure World News*, 26 May 1983, HSLW.

178. Nancy Harding, "Anti-Legislation Letters Inundate Governor's Desk," *Leisure World News*, 6 September 1984, HSLW.

179. George Deukmejian to "Friend," 15 October 1984, HSLW.

180. Hearings before the Subcommittee on Civil and Constitutional Rights of the Committee on the Judiciary, House of Representatives, 22, 29 April and 6, 7, 13, and 14 May 1987 (Washington, D.C.: U.S. Government Printing Office, 1987), 609–18.

181. Suchman and Becker, *Developing Active Adult Retirement Communities*, 141–61.

Chapter 6. An Active Adult Subculture: The Residents' Script

1. Friedan, *Fountain of Age*, 367, 369–70.

2. In Osgood, *Senior Settlers*, 3.

3. "Survey Reflects Profile of Residents," *Arizona Republic*, 16 March 1983, "Demographics" folder, SCAHS.

4. In "Demographers Eye Sun Cities," *Daily News-Sun*, 1 December 1989, "Demographics" folder, SCAHS.

5. Mike Garrett, "65 Percent of SCW Warms to Summer, Poll Reveals," *Daily News-Sun*, 4 February 1992, "Demographics" folder, SCAHS.

6. Allen, *Sun City West*, 263.

7. Ibid., 52–55.

8. Ibid., 27.

9. "'Refer-A-Friend' Adds Sales," *News-Sun*, 28 March 1986, "DEVCO" folder, SCAHS.

10. Edson Allen, "Message from the President," *Sun Cities Area Historical Society Newsletter*, Summer 2007, 2.

11. "Retired Business, Journalism Teachers Join Staff," *Sun Cities Area Historical Society Newsletter*, Fall 2008, 2.

12. Walker and Barratt, interview with the author, 25 August 2006.

13. FitzGerald, *Cities on a Hill*, 235.

14. Allen, *Sun City West*, 27–28.

15. "Parker Finds Satisfaction in SC Home Sales," *News-Sun*, 13 December 1984, "DEVCO" folder, SCAHS.

16. E-mail from the Sun City Festival sales staff to the author in January 2006 said homes could only be purchased as primary or secondary residences.

17. "'Empty-nesters' Are Moving Up," *Arizona Republic*, 27 May 1987, "Demographics" folder, SCAHS.

18. "In Search of Yesterday," *Sun Cities Area Historical Society Newsletter*, Summer 2006, 3; Diana Shaughnessy, *Sun Cities Independent*, 30 April 2003, "SCW—Real Estate" folder, vertical file, SCAHS.

19. David Savageau, relocation counselor and author of *Retirement Places Rated*, quoted in "Is a Retirement Community for You?" *Parade Magazine*, 29 September 1991, "Retirement" folder, vertical file, SCAHS.

20. Allen, *Sun City West*, 269–71.

21. Meeker, "Sun City—A Look Back—1974," 77, Meeker Notebook, SCAHS.

22. Findlay, *Magic Lands*, 191.

23. Allen, *Sun City West*, 34.

24. Freeman and Sanberg, *Silver Anniversary Jubilee*, v.

25. Katy O'Grady, "Del Webb Book Details Sun City's 42-Year History," *Daily News-Sun*, 26 August 2002, "Del E. Webb" folder, SCAHS.

26. Phyllis Gillespie, "Sun City Ages Well in 30 Years," *Arizona Republic*, 14 January 1990, "Sun City—History" folder, SCAHS.

27. Archives Committee, Sun City.

28. Bowker, interview with the author, 5 November 2005.

29. Strevey, *Fulfilling Retirement Dreams*.

30. Allen, *Sun City West*, 105.

31. Freeman and Sanberg, *Silver Anniversary Jubilee*, 120.

32. Meeker, "Sun City—A Look Back—1978," 100, Meeker Notebook, SCAHS.

33. Meeker, "Sun City—A Look Back—1981," 116, Meeker Notebook, SCAHS.

34. Chris Rasmussen, "Countdown to an Election," source unidentified, 1998, "Dysart School District" folder, vertical file, SCAHS.

35. Lori Baker, "Dysart Vote Doesn't End Split," *Arizona Republic*, 13 March 1998, "Dysart School District" folder, SCAHS.

36. P. Solomon Banda, "Tax Group Pickets Del Webb," *Daily News-Sun*, 22 January 1997, "Dysart School District" folder, SCAHS.

37. David R. Beck, "Donors Save Dysart Sports," *Daily News-Sun*, 16 September 1997, "Taxes (School)" folder, vertical file, SCAHS.

38. L. Baker, "Dysart Vote Doesn't End Split," SCAHS.

39. Steve Benson, *Benson's View* cartoon, *Arizona Republic*, 6 November 1997, "Dysart School District" folder, SCAHS.

40. L. Baker, "Dysart Vote Doesn't End Split," SCAHS.

41. Bruce Ellison, "Sun Citians Shoulder More School Costs," *Daily News-Sun*, 16 February 2001, "Taxes" folder, vertical file, SCAHS.

42. Suchman and Becker, *Developing Active Adult Retirement Communities*, 26.

43. John Handley, "Let It Snow . . . ; Over 55 Developments Move Closer to Home," *Chicago Tribune*, 31 July 2005, 1.

44. Carolyn Jung, "New Growth May Alter Creek's Political Base," *Sun-Sentinel*, 14 November 1986, accessed through Newsbank on 26 June 2009.

45. Josh Hafenback, Michael Turnbell, and Ryan McNeill, "Condo Villages' Retirees

Retain Democratic Clout," *South Florida Sun-Sentinel*, 10 February 2008, accessed through Newsbank on 26 June 2009.

46. Irv Rikon, "Century Village Then and Now," accessed 20 April 2009 at http://www.centuryvillagewpb.org/cvthennow.htm.

47. Welch, *Retirement Communities in Maricopa County*, 108.

48. Freeman and Sanberg, *Silver Anniversary Jubilee*, 121.

49. Dorothy A. Bernhardt, "History of Lake Towers" and "History of Freedom Plaza," "Hillsborough—S.C.C." folder, Dunn Collection.

50. Meeker, "Sun City—A Look Back—1974," 77, Meeker Notebook, SCAHS.

51. Archives Committee, *Sun City*, 185.

52. Meeker, "Sun City—A Look Back—1978," 98, Meeker Notebook, SCAHS.

53. Meeker, "Sun City—A Look Back—1980," 111, Meeker Notebook, SCAHS.

54. Allen, *Sun City West*, 221–26.

55. Freeman and Sanberg, *Silver Anniversary Jubilee*, 228.

56. Deborah Bolten, "Average LW Resident Now 76 Years Old," *The Register*, 20 November 1984, HSLW.

57. Allen, *Sun City West*, 229–33.

58. Welch, *Retirement Communities in Maricopa County*, 109.

59. Jane Freeman, interview with the author, 24 March 2005, Sun City, Ariz.

60. Meeker, "Sun City—A Look Back—1980," Meeker Notebook, 111, SCAHS.

61. Pillsbury, "Consuming Retirement," 11.

62. Angie Francalancia, "Century Village: The Second Generation—Younger Retirees Are Changing the Face of West Palm Beach's 29-Year-Old Retirement Community," *Palm Beach Post*, 2 March 1997, accessed through Newsbank on 26 June 2009.

63. FitzGerald, *Cities on a Hill*, 237. This book contains a reprint of the 1983 article.

64. Doris A. Byron, "Test of Time: Communities for Elderly Come of Age," *Los Angeles Times*, 19 May 1981, HSLW.

65. Glenn B. Sanberg, "For Singles, Life in the Sun Cities Can Be Disappointing," *Daily News-Sun*, 20 November 1986, "Demographics" folder, SCAHS.

66. Bowker, interview with the author, 5 November 2005.

67. Sanberg, "For Singles," SCAHS.

68. Hunt et al., *Retirement Communities*, 26.

69. Ibid., 116.

70. Welch, "Retirement Communities in Maricopa County," 62.

71. Mormino, *Land of Sunshine*, 143.

72. Findlay, *Magic Lands*, 196.

73. Pillsbury, "Consuming Retirement," 104.

74. Mock-up for ad 1B, "And I Thought You Were a Bunch of Old Fogies," SCAHS.

75. *Rossmoor Leisure World with Harry Babbitt*, 27-minute promotional videotape of 1963 film, in the possession of Kenneth Walker, president, Leisure World Historical Society, Seal Beach.

76. "Cass Hahns Mark First Laguna Hills Wedding," *Leisure World News*, 22 April 1965, 13; "Wedding Bells Ring Out for Leisure World Resident," *Leisure World News*, 27 May 1965, 12.

77. Jacobs, *Fun City*, 45, 50.

78. Freeman and Sanberg, *Silver Anniversary Jubilee*, 123.

79. "Ladies' Travel Group," *Leisure World News*, 27 May 1965, 2; "Single Women Launch Name Contest," *Leisure World News*, 27 May 1963, 8.

80. "Single Ladies to Treat Men to Potluck Dinner," *Leisure World News*, 26 August 1965, 20.

81. Sanberg, "For Singles," SCAHS.

82. Orman Day, "Hi! I'm a Boy!: Women Take Men's Parts in Square Dance," *Orange County Register*, 28 October 1979, SC-15, "Rossmoor Publicity" folder, HSLW.

83. Pillsbury, "Consuming Retirement," 15–19.

84. Meeker, "Overview," Meeker Notebook, 29, SCAHS.

85. Sanberg, "For Singles," SCAHS.

86. Althia Hardt, a local freelance writer, "Single in Sun City," *Arizona*, 14 November 1982, "Demographics" folder, SCAHS.

87. Blechman, *Leisureville*, 169–70.

88. "Sun City Shadow Hills, Indio, CA," sales brochure, received by the author 7 May 2008.

89. "Singles Delight in Del Webb's Welcoming Lifestyle," accessed 5 June 2009 at http://delwebbresponse.com.

90. "Loving Life at Robson Ranch Arizona" and "Activity Calendar," sales brochure, *Robson Living*, Summer/Fall 2008, 20, 29–30.

91. Tara M. Jinks, Sweetwater sales associate, e-mail to the author, 3 December 2008.

92. Deborah Belgum, "Younger Set Scores One," *Orange County Register*, 12 April 1995, "Seal Beach L.W." folder, vertical file, HSLW.

93. "Frequently Asked Questions about Leisure World," accessed 17 August 2005 at http://www.lwsb.com/faq.htm.

94. McCally, "Sun City Center," 40.

95. FitzGerald, *Cities on a Hill*, 244.

96. Freedman, *Prime Time*, 61.

97. Daniel Ruth, "Bay View: Sooner or Later We All Get There," *Tampa Tribune*, 5 April 1996, in "Hillsborough County—S.C.C." folder, Dunn Collection.

98. Tom Austin, taped interview, 1991, SCAHS.

99. Meeker, "Sun City—A Look Back—1962," 19, Meeker Notebook, SCAHS.

100. Meeker, "1963," 27, Meeker Notebook, SCAHS.

101. Meeker, "Sun City—A Look Back—1964," 29, Meeker Notebook, SCAHS.

102. Meeker, "Sun City—A Look Back—1980," 112, Meeker Notebook, SCAHS.

103. Meeker, "Sun City—A Look Back—1965," 32, Meeker Notebook, SCAHS.

104. Jane Freeman, interview with the author, 24 March 2005, Sun City, Ariz.

105. Frantz and Collins, *Celebration, U.S.A.*, 217–19.

106. "Award-Winning, Gated Active Adult Community 30 Minutes from Orlando," ad in *AARP, The Magazine*, May/June 2005, 89.

107. Blechman, *Leisureville*, 210.

108. "African-American Club to Meet Wednesday," *Daily Sun*, 22 June 2009, D4.

109. *"The Villages Vmail—January 2009—Come Visit,"* accessed 9 January 2009.

110. "Bienvenidos," pamphlet promoting the Spanish Club, Sun City West Visitors Center, December 2005.

111. Harriette A. Reckner, "Harassment not the Answer," *Youngtown Record*, 28 January 1976, vertical file, Youngtown Historical Society.

112. Blechman, *Leisureville*, 71.

113. Candace S. Hughes, "Youngtown Works to Move Family of Five," 17 July 1990, vertical file, Youngtown Historical Society.

114. "Too Young for Youngtown," 27 June 1990, vertical file, Youngtown Historical Society.

115. Hughes, "Youngtown Works to Move Family," Youngtown Historical Society.

116. "Too Young for Youngtown," Youngtown Historical Society.

117. "Youngtown Delays Action in Age-Violation Charge," *Daily News-Sun*, 26 July 1990, vertical file, Youngtown Historical Society.

118. Candace S. Hughes, "Age Tempers Adults-Only Convictions," *Daily News-Sun*, 17 November 1990, "Zoning—Age Restrictions" folder, SCAHS.

119. Candace S. Hughes, "Man Pleads Innocent in Age Case," *Daily News-Sun*, 10 July 1990, A3, vertical file, Youngtown Historical Society.

120. Hughes, "Age Tempers Adults-Only Convictions," SCAHS.

121. Peg Keith, "Youngtown Defends Attack Against Age-Restriction Law," *Sun Cities Independent*, 14 August 1990, vertical file, Youngtown Historical Society.

122. Blechman, *Leisureville*, 66.

123. Hughes, "Age Tempers Adults-Only Convictions," SCAHS.

124. Blechman, *Leisureville*, 67.

125. Retheford, interview with the author, 5 December 2005, Youngtown, Ariz.

126. Bruce Ellison, "AG Examines Town's Senior-Zoning Law," 13 January 1997, vertical file, Youngtown Historical Society.

127. John Skolich, "Youngtown Lost Overlay in 1998," newspaper and date unidentified, vertical file, "Age restrictions" folder, SCAHS.

128. Retheford, interview with the author, 5 December 2005.

129. Blechman, *Leisureville*, 67.

130. Ibid., 71–73.

131. Retheford, interview with the author, 5 December 2005.

132. Blechman, *Leisureville*, 77.

133. Retheford, interview with the author, 5 December 2005.

134. Blechman, *Leisureville*, 74–76.

135. Ibid., 78.

136. Ibid., 140.

137. David Miller, "HOA Kept Busy with Age Protest," *Daily News-Sun*, 8–9 August 1998; Miller, "Age Request Withdrawn," *Daily News-Sun*, 11 August 1998; "Zoning—Age Restrictions" folder, SCAHS.

138. Ruthann Hogue, "Neighbors Petition for Kids' Removal," *Daily News-Sun*, 14 April 1999, "Age Restrictions" folder, SCAHS.

139. Michael Maresh, "Family Honors Promise to Move from Sun City," *Daily News-Sun,* 14 August 2002, "Age Restrictions" folder, SCAHS.

140. John Sokolich, "Age Overlay Complaints Common in State," *Daily News-Sun,* 13–14 April 2002, "Senior Overlay" folder, SCAHS.

141. Lake Providence, e-mail to the author, 5 September 2007.

142. "Camp Villages Begins June 15," *The Villages Magazine,* June 2009, 97.

143. Lori Baker, "It's Official: Sun City for Seniors," *Arizona Republic/Phoenix Gazette,* 14 July 1993, "Age Restrictions" folder, SCAHS.

144. Mike Russo, "Is Sun City's Luster Fading?" *Sun Cities Independent,* 12–18 September 2001, "Age Restrictions" folder, SCAHS.

145. Jeanne Winograd, "'Pulte' Sun Cities Will Remain under Webb Management," *Daily News-Sun,* 11 September 2001, "Del Webb Corp." folder, SCAHS.

146. SCW Age Restriction to Remain Intact," *Sun Cities Independent,* 2 October 2002, "Age Restrictions" folder, SCAHS.

147. Blechman, *Leisureville,* 74.

148. Suchman and Becker, *Developing Active Adult Retirement Communities,* 257.

149. Ibid., 142–43.

150. Ibid., 114.

151. Ibid., 143.

152. Sturgeon, "'It's a Paradise Town,'" 155.

153. Bob Ring, president, Historical Society of Laguna Woods, e-mail to the author, 8 November 2009.

154. Cheryl Walker, "Name Change Now Official," *Orange County Register,* 16 March 2006, accessed through ProQuest Newsstand on 7 November 2009.

155. Bob Ring, president of the Historical Society of Laguna Woods, interview with the author, 23 August 2006, Laguna Woods, Calif.

156. Barratt, interview with the author, 25 August 2006.

157. Ads in *Seal Beach Leisure World Golden Rain News,* 24 August 2006, 28–30.

158. Suchman and Becker, *Developing Active Adult Retirement Communities,* 191–92.

159. Hunt et al., *Retirement Communities,* 2.

160. Bultena and Wood, "Leisure Orientation," 3.

161. Ibid., 8.

162. Osgood, *Senior Settlers,* 5.

163. Ed Hemphill quoted in Cheryl Sweet, "Study Notes SC Advantages, Problems," *Daily News-Sun,* 9 November 1983, "Demographics" folder, SCAHS.

164. Hancock, *Housing the Elderly,* xxxi, introduction to Stephen M. Golant, "In Defense of Age-Segregated Housing."

165. Jim Walsh, "Does the Lifestyle Lengthen Life?" *Arizona Republic,* 9 January 1985, SC-16, "Demographics" folder, SCAHS.

166. Jodie Lau, "Sun City Wins Honors, Sun City West, 2nd," *Daily News-Sun,* 29 May 2001, "Demographics" folder, SCAHS.

167. "Fulfilling Retirement Dreams Since Sept. 10, 1964," Leisure World Laguna Woods—Active Adult Resort Living—California Style, accessed 17 August 2005 at http://www.lwlagunawoods.com/article.cfm?id=150.

168. Chuck Roach, general manager, Del Webb Corporation, remarks to the Long Range Planning Workshop, April 1994, vertical file, SCAHS.

169. Patrick O'Grady, "NW Valley Flourishes as Haven for Retirees," *Sun Cities Independent,* 26 June–2 July 1996, 3, "Retirement" folder, SCAHS.

170. Catherine Reagor, "Developments to Keep State Retiree Mecca," *Arizona Republic,* 25 June 1999, "Retirement" folder, SCAHS.

171. Sun City Grand, e-mail to the author, 3 May 2004.

172. Pillsbury, "Consuming Retirement," 135.

173. Ibid., 136.

174. P. O'Grady, "NW Valley Flourishes," SCAHS.

175. Ibid.

176. Jane Freeman, interview with the author, 24 March 2005, Sun City Grand.

177. Reagor, "Retirement's Midlife Crisis," SCAHS.

178. Ibid.

179. David Madrid, "Buckeye Set to Welcome Sun City Development," *Arizona Republic*, 3 August 2002, "Pulte Homes, Inc." folder, vertical file, SCAHS.

Chapter 7. Assessment: Problems, Strengths, and Twenty-First-Century Trends

1. Andrew D. Blechman, "'Leisurevilles' Are Just a Form of Age Segregation," *Deseret News* (Salt Lake City), 13 July 2008, G5, accessed through ProQuest Newsstand on 23 December 2008.

2. Blechman, *Leisureville*, 137, 225.

3. In E. Brown, "Are Retirees Breaking Their Social Contract?"

4. Mumford, "For Older People."

5. Freedman, *Prime Time*, 293.

6. Ibid., 109–11.

7. Basler, "Declaration of Independents," 14.

8. George Spindler and Louise Spindler, forward to Jacobs, *Fun City*, vi.

9. Jacobs, *Fun City*, 1–5, 57.

10. Jacobs, *Older Persons*, 85.

11. Friedan, *Fountain of Age,* 371–72.

12. Freedman, *Prime Time*, 69.

13. Findlay, *Magic Lands*, 196–97.

14. Freeman and Sanberg, *Silver Anniversary Jubilee*, 48.

15. FitzGerald, *Cities on a Hill*, 211–12.

16. Ibid., 204.

17. Ibid., 217–18, 225, 231.

18. Ibid., 226.

19. Ibid., 227.

20. Freedman, *Prime Time*, 67–69.

21. Blechman, *Leisureville*, 132.

22. Ibid., 210.

23. Ibid., 6.

24. "October 18th, 2008. The party is about to unfold," sales brochure, received by the author 11 October 2008.

25. Tucker, *Sun City*, 10.

26. Ibid., 97.

27. Ibid., 294–95.

28. Ibid., 13, 48.

29. Ibid., 54–55, 296.

30. Pillsbury, "Consuming Retirement," 108.

31. Ibid., 130–31.

32. Welch, "Retirement Communities in Maricopa County," 89.

33. Freedman, *Prime Time*, 13–14. Freedman quotes Pete Peterson, Nixon's secretary of commerce, who published a book called *Grey Dawn* in 1999 in which he claimed that the aged would sink the world due to their entitlements while not contributing to society.

34. Blechman, *Leisureville*, 225.

35. Ibid., 221.

36. In E. Brown, "Are Retirees Breaking Their Social Contract?"

37. Bengston, "Is the 'Contract across Generations' Changing?" 3.

38. Ibid., 12.

39. Vinovskis, "An Historical Perspective on Support for Schooling," 53, 57.

40. Tucker, *Sun City*, 378–79.

41. Blechman, *Leisureville*, 218–21.

42. "In These Places, Old Age Becomes a Team Sport," *New York Times*, 22 May 2008.

43. Blechman, *Leisureville*, 227.

44. Findlay, *Magic Lands*, 192.

45. Duany, Plater-Zyberk, and Speck, *Suburban Nation*, 122–24.

46. Jane Freeman, interview with the author, 23 March 2005, Sun City, Ariz.

47. Suchman and Becker, *Developing Active Adult Retirement Communities*, 62.

48. "You Snooze . . . You Lose!" ad, *The Villages Magazine*, May 2008, 117.

49. Ross, "Duct-Tape Nation," 113, 114–17.

50. Welch, "Retirement Communities in Maricopa County," 13.

51. Meeker, "1963," Meeker Notebook, SCAHS.

52. Meeker, "1974," 78, Meeker Notebook, SCAHS.

53. Ross Cortese, "Great World" column, 25 May 1978, SC-14, "Great World" folder, HSLW.

54. Don Watt, "During Gerontology Seminar: Germans Tour Leisure World," *The Register*, 4 October 1979, B7.

55. Archives Committee, *Sun City*, 137.

56. Ronald Dawkins, "Japanese Visitors Have Yen for Condos," *Miami Herald*, 28 June 1990, accessed through Newsbank on 26 June 2009.

57. "SCAHS, International!" *Sun Cities Area Historical Society Newsletter*, Summer 2006, 3.

58. Longino and Marshall, "North American Research on Seasonal Migration," 229–33.

59. Julie Lawlor, "Snowbirds Flock Together."

60. "Robson Ranch Texas Has a New United States Citizen," *Robson Living*, sales brochure, Summer/Fall 2008, 20.

61. Financial reporter Jonathan Pond expressed that view in a National Educational Television broadcast, "Great Retirement," 8 December 2006.

62. Diane Gravell y Hernandez, e-mail to the author, 25 January 2007.

63. Diane Gravell y Hernandez, e-mail to the author, 30 January 2007.

64. Diane Gravell y Hernandez, e-mail to the author, 28 February 2007.

65. The Web page for El Legado was accessed on 15 March 2007 at http://www.solutionsabroad.com.

66. Barratt, interview with the author, 25 August 2006.

67. Unclewillie 46 quoted in E. Brown, "Are Retirees Breaking Their Social Contract?"

68. Blechman, *Leisureville*, 183, 185–86.

69. Jane Tyler, "Demand Sees Four More OAP Villages," *Birmingham Mail*, 3 July 2008, 19, accessed through ProQuest Newsstand on 23 December 2008.

70. Karen Hambridge, "We're Staying Together Thanks to Special Village," *Coventry Evening Telegraph*, 14 December 2006, 40, accessed through ProQuest Newsstand on 23 December 2008.

71. Suchman and Becker, *Developing Active Adult Retirement Communities*.

72. "Pulte Homes," *Wikipedia*, http://en.wikipedia.org/wiki/Pulte_Homes, accessed 11 July 2008.

73. Del Webb potential buyer preference survey, e-mail to the author, 21 November 2006.

74. "La Cresta at Ridgewood Lakes Feedback Survey," http://www.zoomerang.com/recipient.survey, accessed 19 April 2007.

75. "Del Webb—Active-Adult Living in the Midwest," e-mail from Del Webb Illinois to the author, 1 July 2008.

76. D. Brown, *Inventing New England*, 212.

77. "Solera at Rancho Diamante by Del Webb," flier, 2006.

78. "Del Webb" Web site, http://www.delwebb.com, accessed on 11 December 2008.

79. *Parade of Homes*, Greater Twin Cities area, Minnesota, 12 February–20 March 2005, 113–14.

80. "K. Hovnanian's Four Seasons: An Active Adult Community," sales brochure, and enclosed community plan for Four Seasons at Rush Creek, no date, in possession of the author.

81. Solera at Rancho Diamante, e-mail to the author, 21 February 2007.

82. Sun City Festival seminar, Sun City Grand, 9 December 2005.

83. "2007 Jacksonville Senior Games Training Camp," brochure, received by the author in September 2007.

84. Sun City Anthem at Merrill Ranch, e-mail to the author, 22 March 2007.

85. "Find Your Place in the World," On Top of the World vacation special brochure, 2005; "More Choices, Best Value! Homes from the $190s–$3000's," ad, *AARP, The Magazine*, May/June 2007.

86. La Cresta e-mail to the author, 5 April 2007.

87. "Del Webb Orlando: Legendary Lifestyle. Magical Location," ad, *AARP, The Magazine*, January/February 2009, 15.

88. Riverwood, e-mail to the author, 30 July 2007.

89. "Sample the Del Webb Lifestyle on a Vacation Getaway!" *Del Webb Stone Creek: Sharing the Best Life*, November 2007, n.p.

90. "Come Visit," The Villages newsletter, accessed 24 July 2008.

91. Pulte Homes Corporation, "Stone Creek Community Information," sales brochure, 2007, 3.

92. La Cresta, e-mail to the author, 22 April 2008.

93. Blechman, *Leisureville*, 223.

94. Christine Giordano, "Construction in The Villages on the Rise Again," *Ocala Star-Banner*, 27 March 2007, accessed through ProQuest Newsstand on 27 November 2007.

95. Brian Louis, Bloomberg News, "S & P Cuts Home Builders' Ratings to Junk." *International Herald Tribune*, 5 November 2007, Finance, 15, accessed via Lexis Nexis on 5 December 2008.

96. "Pulte Homes Declares Regular Quarterly Dividend, Announces Discontinuation of Future Dividends," *Lab Business Week* via NewsRx.com, 14 December 2008, accessed on 5 December 2008.

97. Andrew Rice, "Master Builder Over," *Conde Nast Portfolio*, October 2008, 177–78.

98. Del Webb company, at http://www.delwebb.com, accessed on 11 December 2008.

99. Julie Thompson, Pulte, e-mail to the author, 31 March 2008; Del Webb Mid-Atlantic, e-mail to the author, 6 December 2008.

100. "Numbers Don't Lie," ad, *AARP, The Magazine*, September/October 2008, n.p.

101. "Free Golf Course Home Sites Available Now!" ad, *AARP Bulletin*, November 2007, 33.

102. "Picture This View from Your New Home!" The Villages Vmail accessed 11 December 2008.

103. "The Villages: Home and Villa Savings," http://www.thevillages.com, accessed on 14 May 2008.

104. "The Robson Summer Savings Event!" postcard ad, received by the author 18 August 2008.

105. "Escape to Beautiful Sunny Arizona This Winter!" postcard ad, received 29 December 2008.

106. Todd Stengel, Windermere Real Estate, to the author, 6 October 2008.

107. Sonora, e-mail to the author, "Del Webb Monster Sale," 12 October 2007.

108. The first price list was dated 2007. The second price list said, "Effective 8/20/07, Stone Creek Price List"; in possession of the author.

109. Deborah Balogh-Sumey, sales associate, Del Webb Stone Creek, e-mail to the author, 25 August 2007.

110. Pulte Homes and Del Webb, e-mail to the author, 16 September 2007.

111. Kevin G. Hall, "Economist Sees Worse Times for Housing Market," *Duluth News Tribune,* 23 November 2008, A9.

112. "Del Webb—Arizona—Win a Gift Card for the Holidays," e-mail to the author, 21 November 2007.

113. "Del Webb—Woodbridge—We're Buying Your Gas," e-mail to the author, 21 November 2007.

114. La Cresta, e-mail to the author, 10 August 2007.

115. "Del Webb—Nevada invites you to Unwrap the Savings," Del Webb Communities, e-mail to the author, 26 November 2007; and "Del Webb Monster Sale," Stone Creek, e-mail to the author, 12 October 2007.

116. Sun City Peachtree, e-mail to the author, 12 October 2007; "Monstrous Savings! Del Webb at Lake Oconee," postcard, received by the author 15 October 2007.

117. "Del Webb—Woodbridge—A Big Chill of a Deal," Woodbridge, e-mail to the author, 5 December 2007.

118. Pulte Homes Orlando, e-mail to the author, 16 November 2007.

119. La Cresta, e-mail to the author, 13 December 2007; Britt Freeman, Pulte, e-mail to the author, 6 December 2007; Del Webb postcards for Lincoln Hills and other California communities, received by the author on 16 and 19 October 2007.

120. Del Webb Lake Oconee, e-mail to the author, 21 December 2007.

121. Celebrate Virginia, e-mail to the author, 14 October 2008.

122. Del Webb brand of Pulte, e-mail to the author, 13 November 2008.

123. Pulte Homes Orlando, e-mail to the author, 29 October 2008.

124. Sweetwater, e-mail to the author, 21 February 2008.

125. Sweetwater, e-mail to the author, 10 October 2008.

126. Del Webb Lake Oconee, e-mail to the author, 3 December 2008.

127. Pulte Homes of Orlando, e-mail to the author, 17 December 2008.

128. Del Webb company, e-mail to the author, 9 December 2008.

129. Lake Providence, e-mail to the author, 21 February 2008.

130. Lake Providence, e-mail to the author, 13 February. 2008.

131. Sun City Festival, e-mail to the author, 20 February 2008.

132. *SunCityPeachtree@rsvp.delwebb.com* Sun City Peachtree, e-mail to the author, 22 February 2008.

133. WCI Communities Inc., e-mail to the author, 6 January 2009.

134. Del Webb Nevada, e-mail to the author, 21 April 2008.

135. "Incredible active adult living. Dazzling incentives!," postcard, received by the author 23 June 2008.

136. Del Webb Charleston, e-mail to the author, 22 February 2008.

137. "Aloha!" postcard, received 19 July 2008.

138. Del Webb brand of Pulte, e-mail to the author, 18 October 2008.

139. Woodbridge, e-mail to the author, 15 April 2009.

140. Sun City Anthem, e-mail to the author, 16 April 2009.

141. Del Webb Pulte, e-mail to the author, 28 May 2009.

142. Scott Denning, sales associate, Sun City Anthem at Merrill Ranch by Del Webb, e-mail to the author, 3 April 2009.

143. Del Webb Web site, accessed 20 April 2009.

144. Celebrate Virginia, e-mail to the author, 1 October 2008.

145. Del Webb Charleston, e-mail to the author, 6 November 2007.

146. James Bentley, sales associate, Del Webb's The Club at Roseville, e-mail to the author, 16 September 2008.

147. Del Webb at Lake Oconee, e-mail to the author, 24 January 2008.

148. Del Webb of Phoenix, e-mail to the author, 2 July 2009.

149. "Del Webb Stone Creek: Sharing the Best Life," advertising brochure, December 2008.

150. Andrew D. Blechman, "'Leisurevilles' Are Just a Form of Age Segregation," *Deseret News* (Salt Lake City), 13 July 2008, G5.

151. "Pulte Homes Agrees to Buy Centex in $1.3 Deal," 8 April 2009, accessed at Money Central online, 15 April 2009.

152. Del Webb Pulte, e-mail to the author, 18 August 2009.

153. Del Webb Pulte, e-mail to the author, 9 May 2009.

154. Del Webb of Central Florida, e-mail to the author, 19 May 2009.

155. Ad for Century Village Real Estate Inc., *UCO Reporter,* June 2009, 16.

156. Del Webb Communities of the Mid-Atlantic, e-mail to the author, 19 March 2009.

157. Del Webb Communities, e-mail to the author, 27 March 2009.

158. Del Webb Communities, e-mail to the author, 20 March 2009.

159. Del Webb of Central Florida, e-mail to the author, 23 April 2009.

160. "The Villages," e-mail to the author, 18 November 2009.

161. "The Villages, Florida," ad, *AARP: The Magazine*, September/October 2007, 117.

162. Lake Providence, e-mail to the author, 5 December 2007.

163. "Community Recreation Center Grand Opening," postcard, received by the author in November 2007.

164. Celebrate Virginia, e-mail to the author, 12 November 2007.

165. Arthur L. Peterson, national expert on education for seniors, presentation, University of Minnesota, Duluth, 6 September 2008.

166. Sun City Anthem team, e-mail to the author, 18 September 2008.

167. Riverwood at Nocatee, e-mail to the author, 5 November 2007.

168. "Events in 2010 Observe Sun City's Golden Celebration!" *Sun Cities Area Historical Society*, Fall/Winter 2009, 13.

169. La Cresta, e-mail to the author, 15 April 2008; "Del Webb Stone Creek: Sharing the Best Life," sales brochure, May 2008.

170. Del Webb Charleston team, e-mail to the author, 6 May 2008.

171. Sun City Peachtree sales team, e-mail to the author, 28 April 2008.

172. "A Week in the Life-Style," ad, *The Villages Magazine,* January 2008, 89–90.

173. The author got that greeting from a live person after dialing 1-888-224-2246 on 18 December 2008.

174. "Why Do They Call The Villages *Florida's Friendliest Hometown*," ad, *The Villages Magazine*, January 2008, 16.

175. "Where Will You Live Your Dreams?" Del Webb survey received by the author on 12 December 2008.

176. "Your Sun City—Arizona Team," e-mail to the author, 6 September 2008.

177. FitzGerald quoted in Farrell, *Family*, 160.

178. Handley, "Let It Snow," 1.

179. Jana Ristamaki, comment to the author, 3 August 2008.

180. E. Brown, "Are Retirees Breaking Their Social Contract?"

181. Blaikie, "Imagined Landscapes," 168.

182. Handley, "Let It Snow," 1.

183. Beth Reinhard and Marc Caputo, "Fla. Retirement Center Is a GOP Bastion," *Sunday Gazette-Mail*, Charleston, W. Va., 23 September 2007, 10A, accessed through ProQuest Newsstand on 27 November 2007.

184. "Condo Villages' Retirees Retain Democratic Clout," *South Florida Sun-Sentinel*, 10 February 2008, accessed through Newsbank on 26 June 2009.

185. Reinhard and Caputo, "Fla. Retirement Center."

186. Beth Reinhard, "Sarah Palin Excites Huge Florida Crowd," *McClatchly-Tribune News Service*, 22 September 2008, accessed through ProQuest Newsstand on 23 December 2008.

187. Anthony Violanti, "Caroline Kennedy Praises Obama in Villages," *Ocala Star-Banner*, 30 October 2008.

188. Stronge, *Sunshine Economy*, 238–40.

189. Teaford, *American Suburb*, 75.

190. Ibid., 221–22.

191. "Where the Poker Run Ends, Our Party Begins," postcard ad for Del Webb at Somersett, received by the author on 25 July 2008.

192. Sun Cities of Arizona, e-mail to the author, 26 November 2008.

193. Frank Greve, "Growing Older Gets Easier: Fewer Seniors Are Disabled," *Duluth News Tribune*, 17 December 2007, A1, A5.

194. Fireside at Desert Ridge sales team, e-mail to the author, 25 November 2008.

195. Blechman, *Leisureville*, 180, 189, 194–95. Blechman identifies this speaker only as Bill.

196. Ibid., 187, 191.

197. "Trends: What's Happening to Your Money," *Parade*, 13 April 2008, 16.

198. Blechman, *Leisureville*, 192.

Conclusion: The Significance of Active Adult, Age-Restricted Communities

1. Frantz and Collins, *Celebration, U.S.A.*, 11.

2. Achenbaum, *Old Age in the New Land*, 163.

3. M. Baker, "Arizona's Retirement Communities," 15.

4. Mormino, *Land of Sunshine*, 144.

5. Ibid., 144.

6. Jana and Brad Ristamaki, letter to the author, 6 November 2009.

7. Tara Siegel Bernard, "Before Switching States, Check the Tax Climate," *Minneapolis Star Tribune,* 14 May 2006, D6.

8. "Hawkeye Hustle," *AARP Bulletin,* July/August 2006, 4.

9. Mormino, *Land of Sunshine,* 147.

10. Freeman and Sanberg, *Silver Anniversary Jubilee,* 136–37, 160–61.

11. Allen, *Sun City West,* 213–34.

12. D. Brown, *Inventing New England,* 210–11.

13. "Check Out This Area Attraction," *Robson Living,* sales brochure, Summer/Fall 2008, 6, 18.

14. Blechman, *Leisureville,* 182–83.

15. Teaford, *American Suburb,* 79.

16. Pulte Homes of Southwest Florida, e-mail to the author, 26 September 2007.

17. Larry Manne, Pulte, e-mail to the author, 15 February 2007.

18. Elizabeth Whitney, "Tenacious Builder," *St. Petersburg Times,* 20 June 1965, 1F.

19. "It's Your Life. It's Your Dream Home. On Top of the World Communities," ad, *AARP Bulletin,* July/August 2007, 38.

20. On Top of the World, "Indigo East at Circle Square Ranch—Find Your Place in the World," sales brochure, 2005, n.p.

21. Pulte Homes Corporation, "Stone Creek Community Information," sales brochure, 2007, 3.

22. Alicia A. Caldwell, "'It's a Desert? What We Bought Is Desert?'" *Duluth News Tribune,* 6 May 2007, A13.

23. E. Brown, "Are Retirees Breaking Their Social Contract?"

Bibliography

Abbott, Carl. *The Metropolitan Frontier: Cities in the Modern American West.* Tucson: University of Arizona Press, 1993.

Abravanel, Lesley, with Laura Lee Miller. "Exploring the Area: Touring the Estates." In *Frommer's Florida 2006*, 321. Hoboken, N.J.: Wiley, 2006.

Achenbaum, W. Andrew. *Old Age in the New Land: The American Experience since 1790.* Baltimore: Johns Hopkins University Press, 1978.

———. *Older Americans, Vital Communities: A Bold Vision for Societal Aging.* Baltimore: Johns Hopkins University Press, 2005.

———. *Shades of Gray: Old Age, American Values, and Federal Policies since 1920.* Boston: Little, Brown, 1983.

Adams, Robert L. A., and John F. Rooney Jr. "Condo Canyon: An Examination of Emerging Golf Landscapes in America." *North American Culture* 1 (1984): 65–75.

———. "Evolution of American Golf Facilities." *Geographical Review* 75, no. 4 (October 1985): 420–38.

Allen, Edson, ed. *Sun City West Silver Celebration: The First Twenty-Five Years.* Sun City, Ariz.: Sun Cities Area Historical Society, 2003.

Archives Committee, Eve Hoover, chairman. *Sun City: The First Thirty Years.* Sun City, Calif.: Sun City Civic Association, 1992.

Arizona Archives. Arizona State University, Tempe.

Aron, Cindy. *Working at Play: A History of Vacations in the United States.* New York: Oxford University Press, 1999.

Arsenault, Raymond. *St. Petersburg and the Florida Dream, 1888–1950.* Gainesville: University Press of Florida, 1996.

Baker, Evan W. "Leisure World's Life-Saving Communities." *Leisure World History* 1, no. 2 (Fall 1980): 48–61.

Baker, Michael. "Arizona's Retirement Communities and the Changing Needs of an Aging Population." *Arizona Review* 32 (1984): 14–22.

Barker, Michael B. *California Retirement Communities.* Berkeley, Calif.: Center for Real Estate and Urban Economics, 1966.

Basler, Barbara. "Declaration of Independents: Home Is Where You Want to Live Forever: Here's How." *AARP Bulletin*, December 2005, 14–15.

Baxandall, Rosalyn, and Elizabeth Ewen. *Picture Windows: How the Suburbs Happened.* New York: Basic Books, 2000.

Bellah, Robert N., Richard Madsen, William Sullivan, Ann Swidler, and Seten M. Tipton. *Habits of the Heart: Individualism and Commitment in American Life.* Berkeley: University of California Press, 1985.

Bengston, Vern L. "Is the 'Contract Across Generations' Changing? Effects of Population Aging on Obligations and Expectations across Age Groups." In *The Changing Contract Across Generations,* edited by Vern L. Bengston and W. Andrew Achenbaum, 3–23. New York: Aldine de Gruyter, 1993.

Bengston, Vern L., and W. Andrew Achenbaum, eds. *The Changing Contract Across Generations.* New York: Aldine de Gruyter, 1993.

Biggar, Jeanne C., Cynthia B. Flynn, Charles F. Longino Jr., and Robert F. Wiseman. "Sunbelt Update: Older Americans Head South." In *Housing the Elderly,* edited by Judith Ann Hancock, 31–34. New Brunswick, N.J.: Center for Urban Policy Research, 1987.

Blaikie, Andrew. "Imagined Landscapes of Age and Identity." In *Ageing and Place: Perspectives, Policy, Practice,* edited by Gavin J. Andrews and David R. Phillips, 164–75. London: Routledge, 2005.

Blakely, Edward J., and Mary Gail Snyder. *Fortress America: Gated Communities in the United States.* Washington, D.C.: Brookings Institute Press, 1997.

Blechman, Andrew D. *Leisureville: Adventures in America's Retirement Utopias.* New York: Atlantic Monthly Press, 2008. Reprinted in paperback as *Leisureville: Adventures in a World Without Children.* New York: Grove Press, 2008.

Bloom, Nicholas Dagen. *Merchant of Illusion: James Rouse, America's Salesman of the Businessman's Utopia.* Columbus: Ohio State University Press, 2004.

———. *Suburban Alchemy: 1960s New Towns and the Transformation of the American Dream.* Columbus: Ohio State University Press, 2001.

Boorstin, Daniel. *The Americans: The Democratic Experience.* New York: Vintage, 1974.

———. *The Americans: The National Experience.* New York: Random House, 1965.

Boyer, Richard. *Places Rated Retirement Guide: Your Guide to Finding the Best Places to Live in America.* Rand, McNally, 1983.

Brown, Dona. *Inventing New England: Regional Tourism in the Nineteenth Century.* Washington, D.C.: Smithsonian Institution Press, 1995.

Brown, Elizabeth N. "Are Retirees Breaking Their Social Contract? An Interview with Andrew D. Blechman." *AARP Bulletin Today,* 27 May 2008.

Buhler-Wilkerson, Karen. *No Place Like Home: A History of Nursing and Home Care in the United States.* Baltimore: Johns Hopkins University Press, 2001.

Bultena, Gordon, and Vivian Wood. "Leisure Orientation and Recreational Activities of Retirement Community Residents." *Journal of Leisure Research* 2 (1970): 3–14.

Burgess, Ernest W., ed. *Retirement Villages.* Ann Arbor: Division of Gerontology, University of Michigan, 1961.

Chapman, Kathryn. *The Lives of Vizcaya: Annals of a Great House.* Miami: Banyan Books, 1985.

Ceresa, Al. "Some Facts About Leisure World." *Leisure World History* 3 (Winter 1982): 130–40.

Cocks, Catherine. *Doing the Town: The Rise of Urban Tourism in the United States, 1850–1915.* Berkeley: University of California Press, 2001.

Colihan, Jane. "Spring Break: Wildlife, Shells, and Thomas Edison's Laboratory." *American Heritage,* February/March 2006, 25–26.

Conboy, Vince. *Expose: Florida's Billion Dollar Land Fraud.* Naples, Fla.: Vince Conboy, 1972.

Cory, Gregory L., Ronald M. Garl, Laurence A. Hirsh, David L. Leininger, David A. Mulvihill, William B. Renner Jr., James J. Scavo, Anita M. Welch, and Stephen A. Winter. *Golf Course Development in Residential Communities.* Washington, D.C.: Urban Land Institute, 2001.

Costa, Dora L. *The Evolution of Retirement: An American Economic History, 1880–1990.* Chicago: University of Chicago Press, 1998.

Cumming, Elaine, and William E. Henry. *Growing Old: The Process of Disengagement.* New York: Basic Books, 1961.

Dickinson, Peter A. *Sunbelt Retirement: The Complete State-by-State Guide to Retiring in the South and West of the United States.* Washington, D.C.: AARP and Scott Foresman, 1986.

Duany, Andres, Elizabeth Plater-Zyberk, and Jeff Speck. *Suburban Nation: The Rise of Sprawl and the Decline of the American Dream.* New York: Farrar, Straus, Giroux, 2000.

Dunn, Hampton, Collection. Special Collections. University of South Florida Library, Tampa.

Edwards, John, Isabel Allende, Bob Dole, Maya Lin, and Steven Spielberg. "What Home Means to Me." *Life,* 17 November 2006, 10.

Ericksson, Sandra H. "Will the Development of Golf Follow Any Particular Trend in the Remainder of This Decade?" *Golf Course Management,* 1983.

Farrell, Betty G. *Family: The Making of an Idea, an Institution, and a Controversy in American Culture.* Boulder, Colo.: Westview Press, 1999.

Findlay, John M. *Magic Lands: Western Cityscapes and American Culture After 1940.* Berkeley: University of California Press, 1992.

Finnerty, Margaret. *Del Webb: A Man, A Company.* Flagstaff, Ariz.: Heritage, 1991.

Fishman, Robert. *Bourgeois Utopias: The Rise and Fall of Suburbia.* New York: Basic Books, 1987.

FitzGerald, Frances. *Cities on a Hill: A Journey through Contemporary American Cultures.* New York: Simon and Schuster, 1986.

Fletcher, Harrison, and Andre Mouchard. "Ross Cortese Leisure World Builder, 74, Dies after Surgery." *Orange County Register,* 31 October 1991, A1.

Florida Collection. Miami Dade Public Library, Miami.

Fogelsong, Richard E. *Married to the Mouse: Walt Disney World and Orlando.* New Haven: Yale University Press, 2001.

Ford, Norman D. "Part One: Cities of Tomorrow." *Harvest Years,* April 1968, 38–45.

Forsyth, Ann. *Reforming Suburbia: The Planned Communities of Irvine, Columbia, and The Woodlands*. Berkeley: University of California Press, 2005.

Frantz, Douglas, and Catherine Collins. *Celebration, U.S.A.: Living in Disney's Brave New Town*. New York: Henry Holt, 1999.

Freedman, Marc. *Prime Time: How Baby Boomers Will Revolutionize Retirement and Transform America*. New York: Public Affairs, 1999.

Freeman, Jane, and Glenn Sanberg. *Silver Anniversary Jubilee: A History of Sun City, Arizona*. Sun City, Ariz.: Sun City Historical Society, 1984.

Friedan, Betty. *The Fountain of Age*. New York: Simon and Schuster, 1993.

Galatas, Roger, with Jim Barlow. *The Woodlands: The Inside Story of Creating a Better Hometown*. Washington, D.C.: Urban Land Institute, 2004.

Gjerde, Jon. "Middleness and the Middle West." In *The Identity of the American Midwest: Essays on Regional History*, edited by Andrew R. L. Cayton and Susan E. Gray, 180–95. Bloomington: Indiana University Press, 2001.

Glover, F. H. "Tampa's Beautiful 'Bay of Naples.'" *Suniland* 1, no. 1: 34–35.

Gordon, Margaret S. "Work and Patterns of Retirement." In *Aging and Leisure: A Research Perspective into the Meaningful Use of Time*, edited by Robert W. Kleemeier, 15–53. New York: Oxford University Press, 1961.

Graebner, William. *A History of Retirement: The Meaning and Function of an American Institution, 1885–1978*. New Haven: Yale University Press, 1980.

Grismer, Karl H. "How Much Does It Cost to Winter in Florida?" *Suniland* 1, no. 3 (December 1924): 46–47.

Hancock, Judith Ann, ed. *Housing the Elderly*. New Brunswick, N.J.: Center for Urban Policy Research, 1987.

Harwood, Kathryn Chapman. *The Lives of Vizcaya: Annals of a Great House*. Miami: Banyan Books, 1985.

Havighurst, Robert J. "The Nature and Values of Meaningful Free-Time Activity." In *Aging and Leisure: A Research Perspective into the Meaningful Use of Time*, edited by Robert W. Kleemeier, 309–44. New York: Oxford University Press, 1961.

Heintz, Katherine McMillan. *Retirement Communities for Adults Only*. New Brunswick, N.J.: Center for Urban Policy Research, Rutgers University, 1976.

"Henry Flagler, Inventor of Modern Florida." In *Flagler's Florida*. Palm Beach: Henry Morrison Flagler Museum, 2008.

Heslip, Malcolm. "The Towers Rise in Leisure World." *Leisure World History* 1, no. 2 (Fall 1980): 20–29.

Historical Society of Laguna Woods. Special Collections. Laguna Woods, Calif.

Holland, George. "Interview with Thomas Edison, 'Florida Has Added Five Years to My Life.'" *Suniland* 3, no. 6 (March 1926): 35.

Hooyman, Nancy R., and H. Asuman Kiyak. *Social Gerontology: A Multidisciplinary Perspective*. 4th edition. Boston: Allyn and Bacon, 1996.

Horowitz, Daniel. *Betty Friedan and the Making of the Feminine Mystique*. Amherst: University of Massachusetts Press, 1998.

Hunt, Michael E., Allen G. Feldt, Robert W. Marans, Leon A. Pastalan, and Kathleen L.

Vakalo. *Retirement Communities: An American Original*. New York: Haworth Press, 1984.

Hurley, Andrew. *Diners, Bowling Alleys, and Trailer Parks: Chasing the American Dream in the Postwar Consumer Culture*. New York: Basic Books, 2002.

Irby, Lee. "Razing Gerontopolis: Green Benches, Trailer Trash, and Old People in St. Petersburg, Florida, 1910–1970." Master's thesis, University of South Florida, 1999.

Jackson, Kenneth T. *Crabgrass Frontier: The Suburbanization of the United States*. New York: Oxford University Press, 1985.

Jacobs, Jerry. *Fun City: An Ethnographic Study of a Retirement Community*. New York: Holt, Rinehart, and Winston, 1974.

———. *Older Persons and Retirement Communities: Case Studies in Social Gerontology*. Springfield, Ill.: Charles C. Thomas, 1975.

Jakle, John A. *The Tourist: Travel in Twentieth-Century North America*. Lincoln: University of Nebraska Press, 1985.

Johnson, Sheila K. *Idle Haven: Community Building among the Working Class Retired*. Berkeley: University of California Press, 1970.

Jones, Marjorie F. "I Remember the Old Days." *Leisure World History* 1, no. 1 (Spring 1980): 32–42.

Le Goix, Renaud. "Gated Communities: Sprawl and Social Segregation in Southern California." In *Gated Communities,* edited by Rowland Atkinson and Sarah Blandy, 131–51. London: Routledge, 2006.

Leisure World Laguna Hills Records. Historical Society of Laguna Woods, Laguna Woods, Calif.

Leisure World Seal Beach Records. Historical Society of Leisure World, Seal Beach, Calif.

Lewis, Thelma B. "Bringing Green Space to Leisure World." *Leisure World History* 2, no. 1 (Spring 1981): 30–36.

Logan, Michael. *Desert Cities: The Environmental History of Phoenix and Tucson*. Pittsburgh: University of Pittsburgh Press, 2006.

Longino, Charles F. Jr., and Victor Marshall. "North American Research on Seasonal Migration." *Ageing and Society* 10 (1990): 229–35.

Low, Setha. *Behind the Gates: Life, Security, and the Pursuit of Happiness in Fortress America*. New York: Routledge, 2003.

Mabie, Ethel. "The Laguna Hills Art Association." *Leisure World History* 3 (Winter 1982): 130–40.

Mahoney, Sarah. "Great Places to Live." *AARP, the Magazine,* September/October 2007, 60–67.

Martin, C. Brenden, and June Hall McCash. "From Millionaires to the Masses: Tourism at Jekyll Island, Georgia." In *Southern Journeys: Tourism, History, and Culture in the Modern South,* edited by Richard D. Starnes. Tuscaloosa: University of Alabama Press, 2003.

McCally, David. "Sun City Center: Something New Under the Sun for Retirees." *Tampa Bay History* 14, no. 1 (1992): 31–43.

McGirr, Lisa. *Suburban Warriors: The Origins of the New American Right*. Princeton: Princeton University Press, 2001.

Meeker, John W. *Meeker Notebook*. Typescript. Sun Cities Area Historical Society. Sun City, Ariz.

Mergen, Bernard. *Recreational Vehicles and Travel: A Resource Guide*. Westport, Conn.: Greenwood Press, 1985.

Merrick, George E. Papers. Historical Museum of Southern Florida. Miami.

Merritt, Rob. "Leisure World's Television." *Leisure World History* 1, no. 2 (Fall 1980): 30–39.

Mesa, City of. *General Plan*. 2002. Government Documents. Arizona State University, Tempe.

Mormino, Gary R. *Land of Sunshine, State of Dreams: A Social History of Modern Florida*. Gainesville: University Press of Florida, 2005.

Morrison, Marie. *Retirement in the West: How and Where to Enjoy the Best Years of Your Life*. San Francisco: Chronicle Books, 1976.

Mumford, Lewis. "For Older People—Not Segregation *But* Integration." In *Housing the Elderly*, edited by Judith Ann Hancock, 44–45. New Brunswick: State University of New Jersey Press, 1987. Originally published in *Architectural Record*, May 1956.

Neben, Myra. "The People Speak." *Leisure World History* 3, no. 1 (Winter 1982): 94–102.

———. "We Love to Learn." *Leisure World History* 2, no. 2 (Fall 1981): 35–42.

Nelson, F. Margaret. "Early Days of Nursing in Leisure World." *Leisure World History* 2, no. 1 (Spring 1981): 50–59.

Olson, Laura Katz. *The Not So Golden Years: Caring Labor, the Frail-Elderly, and the Long-Term Care Establishment*. Lanham, Md.: Rowman and Littlefield, 2003.

Osgood, Nancy J. *Senior Settlers: Social Integration in Retirement Communities*. New York: Praeger, 1982.

Paine, Doris. "The Sun City Story." *Phoenix Magazine*, July 1978.

Paulson, Morton G. *The Great Land Hustle*. Chicago: Henry Regnery, 1972.

Pew, Thomas W. "Peddling the Great West." *Saturday Review* 4 (September 1971): 48–51.

Pillsbury, Elizabeth Joy. "Consuming Retirement: The Creation of the Recreational Retirement Community, Del Webb's Sun City, 1960–Present." A.B. honors in history thesis, Kenyon College, Ohio, April 1998.

Pollak, Patricia Baron, and Alice Nudelman Gorman. *Community-Based Housing for the Elderly*. Washington, D.C.: American Planning Association, 1989.

Price, Robert. "How Leisure World Leadership Evolved." *Leisure World History* 1, no. 1 (Spring 1980): 43–61.

———. "Recollections of Early Days." *Leisure World History* 3, no. 1 (Winter 1982): 55–64.

Quadagno, Jill, et al. "Research on Cohorts and Generations." In *The Changing Contract Across Generations*, edited by Vern L. Bengston and W. Andrew Achenbaum, 263–72. New York: Aldine de Gruyter, 1993.

Rockland, Michael Aaron. *Homes on Wheels*. New Brunswick, N.J.: Rutgers University Press, 1980.

Ross, Andrew. "Duct-Tape Nation: Land Use, the Fear Factor, and the New Unilateralism." In *Sprawl and Suburbia: A Harvard Design Magazine Reader*, 110–21. Minneapolis: University of Minnesota Press, 2005.

Rothman, Hal K. *Devil's Bargains: Tourism in the Twentieth-Century American West.* Lawrence: University Press of Kansas, 1998.

Rugh, Susan Sessions. *Are We There Yet? The Golden Age of American Family Vacations.* Lawrence: University Press of Kansas, 2008.

Sargent, Charles, ed. *Metro Arizona.* Scottsdale: Biffington Books, 1988.

Sargent, Charles S., Jr. *Planned Communities in Greater Phoenix: Origins, Functions and Control.* Tempe: Arizona State University Press, 1973.

Seidelman, Florence. *Boynton Beach Club.* DVD. Directed by Eric Morgan. Sony Pictures, 2006.

Sheridan, Thomas E. *Arizona . . . A History.* Tucson: University of Arizona Press, 1995.

———. "Rio Rico and the Great Arizona Land Rush." *Journal of the Southwest* 48 (Spring 2006): 1–36.

Simpson, Ida Harper, Kurt W. Back, and John C. McKinney. "Continuity of Work and Retirement Activities, and Self-Evaluation." In *Social Aspects of Aging*, edited by Ida Harper Simpson and John C. McKinney, 106–19. Durham, N.C.: Duke University Press, 1966.

Smith, Kathryn. "The Selling of Leisure World." *Leisure World History* 2, no. 2 (Fall 1980): 48–54.

Starr, Kevin. *California: A History.* New York: Modern Library, Random House, 2005.

Steiner, Frederick. *The Politics of New Town Planning: The Newfields, Ohio Story.* Athens: Ohio University Press, 1981.

Stephenson, R. Bruce. *Visions of Eden: Environmentalism, Urban Planning, and City Building in St. Petersburg, Florida, 1900–1995.* Columbus: Ohio State University Press, 1997.

Streib, Gordon, and Clement J. Schneider. *Retirement in American Society: Impact and Process.* Ithaca, N.Y.: Cornell University Press, 1971.

Strevey, Tracy E., ed. *Fulfilling Retirement Dreams: The First Twenty-Five Years of Leisure World, Laguna Hills.* Santa Ana: Leisure World Historical Society of Laguna Hills, California, 1989.

———. "I Remember Ross Cortese." *Leisure World History* 3, no. 1 (Winter 1982): 26–34.

Stronge, William B. *The Sunshine Economy: An Economic History of Florida since the Civil War.* Gainesville: University Press of Florida, 2008.

Stroud, Hubert B. *The Promise of Paradise: Recreational and Retirement Communities in the United States since 1950.* Baltimore: Johns Hopkins University Press, 1995.

Sturgeon, Melanie I. "'It's a Paradise Town': The Marketing and Development of Sun City, Arizona." Master's thesis, Arizona State University, August 1992.

Suchman, Diane, and William E. Becker. *Developing Active Adult Retirement Communities.* Washington, D.C.: Urban Land Institute, 2001.

Sun Cities Area Historical Society (SCAHS). Vertical file. Sun City, Ariz.

Tarbox, Tom. "Youngtown, Arizona, U.S.A." *Arizona Highways*, January 1957, 6–9.

Teaford, Jon C. *The American Suburb: The Basics*. New York: Routledge, 2007.

Tucker, Jack M. *Sun City: 60-Plus and Hanging Tough*. Phoenix: Quail Run Books, 1985.

Tymon, Dorothy. *America Is for Sale!* Rockville Centre, N.Y.: Farnsworth, 1973.

Vesperi, Maria D. *City of Green Benches: Growing Old in a New Downtown*. Ithaca, N.Y.: Cornell University Press, 1985.

Vinovskis, Maris A. "An Historical Perspective on Support for Schooling by Different Age Cohorts." In *The Changing Contract Across Generations*, edited by Vern L. Bengston and W. Andrew Achenbaum, 53–57. New York: Aldine de Gruyter, 1993.

———. "Social Contexts of the Generational Contract." In *The Changing Contract across Generations*, edited by Vern L. Bengston and W. Andrew Achenbaum, 43–65. New York: Aldine de Gruyter, 1993.

Welch, Charlotte Anne. "Retirement Communities in Maricopa County: From Segregated Towns to Integrated Neighborhoods." Master's thesis in environmental planning, Arizona State University, May 1992.

Wilder's Park Collection. Special Collections. University of South Florida, St. Petersburg.

Wing, Frank S. "Live Outdoors in Florida and Live a Hundred Years." *Suniland* 1, no. 1 (1924): 38.

Winnikoff, Albert. *The Land Game or How to Make a Fortune in Real Estate*. New York: Lyle Stuart, 1970.

Wolff, Anthony. *Unreal Estate*. San Francisco: Sierra Club, 1973.

Youngtown Historical Society. Vertical file. Youngtown, Ariz.

Zarbin, Earl. "The Man Who Started Them Talks." *Arizona Days and Ways*, 26 January 1964, 6–11.

Zimmerman, Paul. "No Oblivion for Rossmoor." *Leisure World History* 3, no. 1 (Winter 1982): 18–25.

———. "Ross Cortese—The Man Who Made Retirement Fun." *Leisure World History* 1, no. 1 (Spring 1980): 20–31.

———. "Security: Leisure World's Strongest Magnet." *Leisure World History* 1, no. 2 (Fall 1980): 10–19.

———. "Why the Marine Corps Paid Off Rossmoor." *Leisure World History* 3, no. 1 (Winter 1982): 72–76.

Index

Judith Ann Trolander is a professor of history at the University of Minnesota Duluth. She is the author of *Settlement Houses and the Great Depression* (Wayne State University Press, 1975) and *Professionalism and Social Change: From the Settlement House Movement to Neighborhood Centers, 1886 to the Present* (Columbia University Press, 1987).